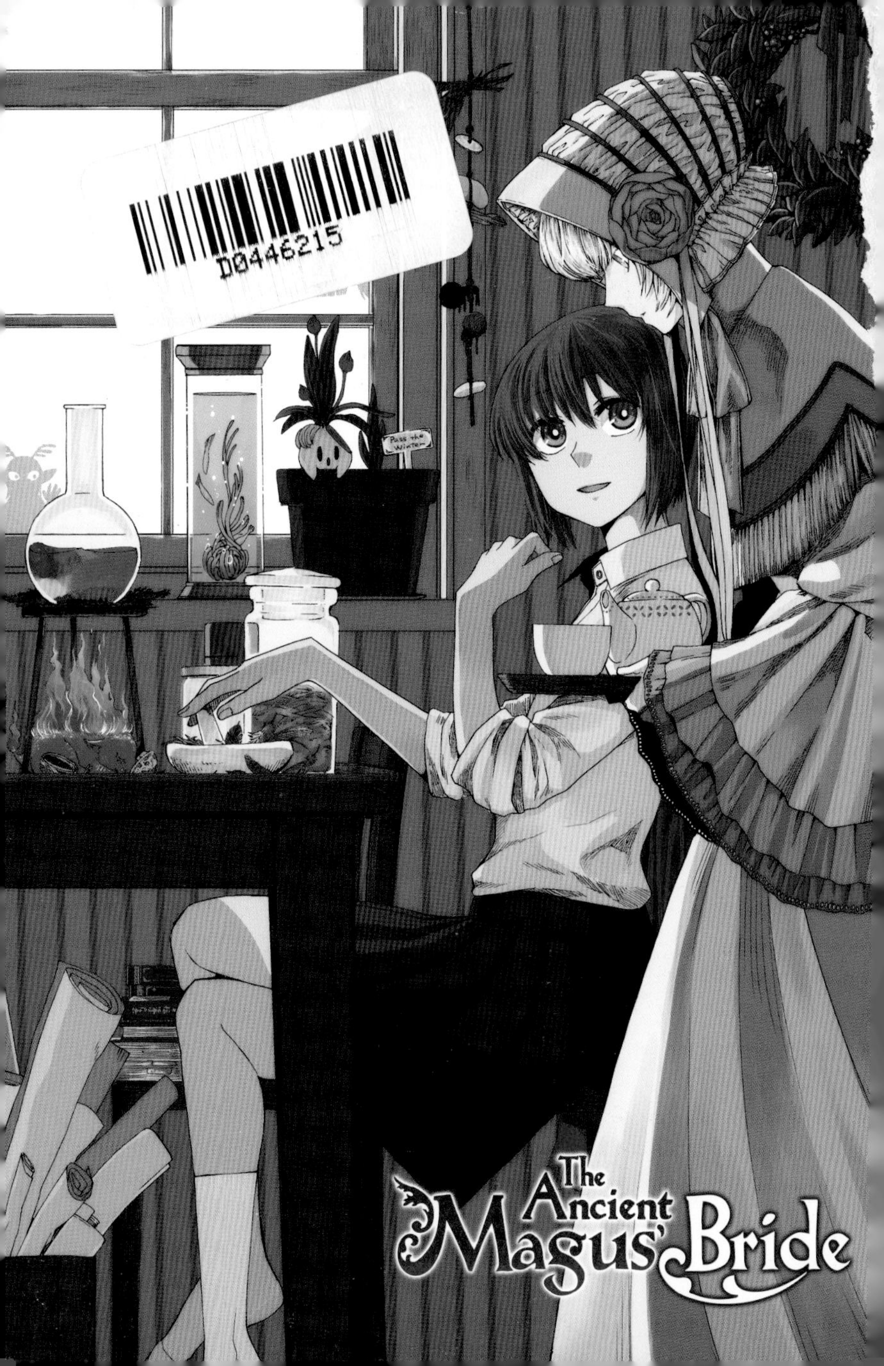
Pass the Winter
The Ancient Magus' Bride

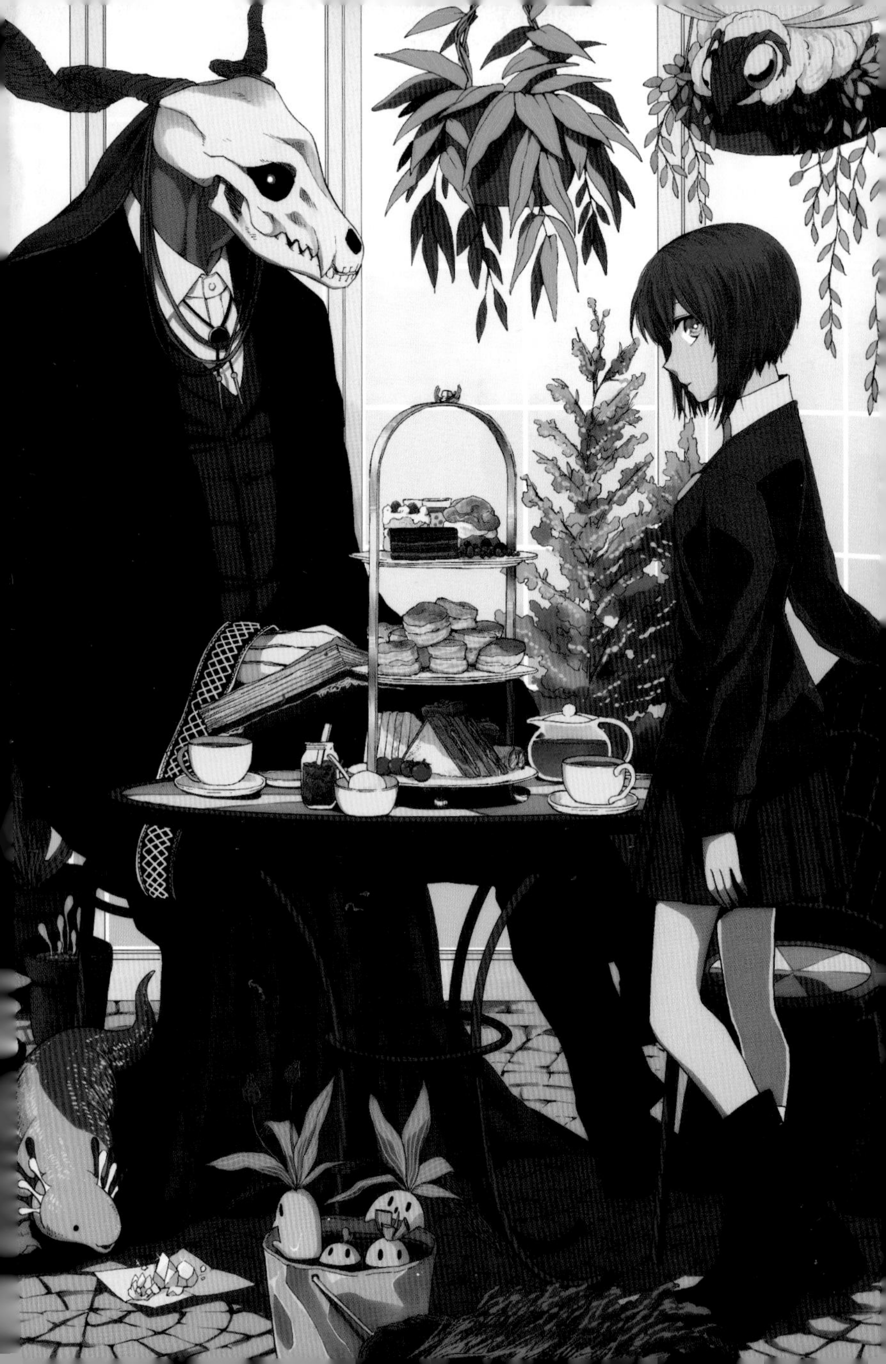

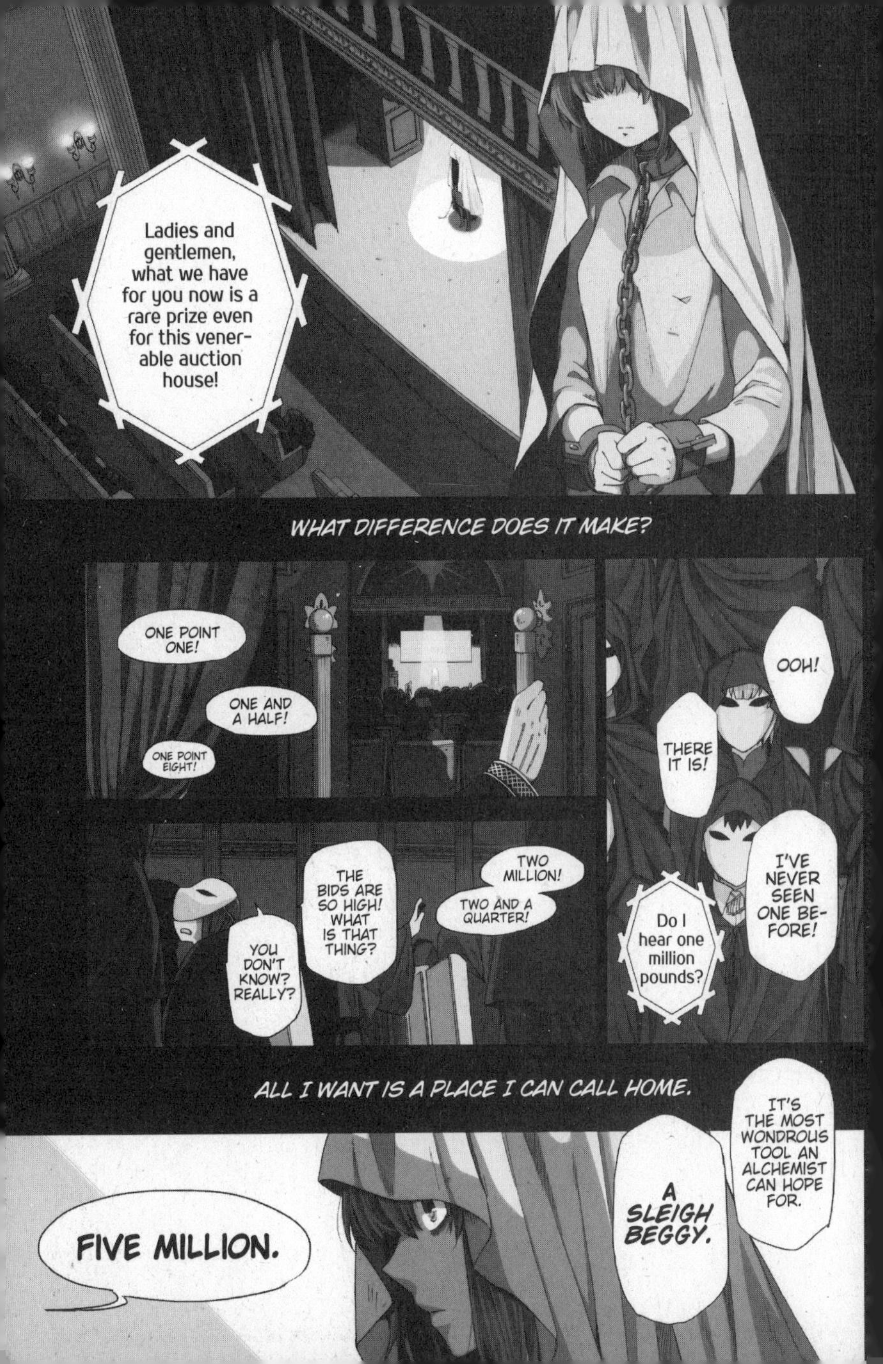
Ladies and gentlemen, what we have for you now is a rare prize even for this venerable auction house!
WHAT DIFFERENCE DOES IT MAKE?
OOH!
THERE IT IS!
I'VE NEVER SEEN ONE BEFORE!
Do I hear one million pounds?
ONE POINT ONE!
ONE AND A HALF!
ONE POINT EIGHT!
TWO MILLION!
TWO AND A QUARTER!
THE BIDS ARE SO HIGH! WHAT IS THAT THING?
YOU DON'T KNOW? REALLY?
ALL I WANT IS A PLACE I CAN CALL HOME.
IT'S THE MOST WONDROUS TOOL AN ALCHEMIST CAN HOPE FOR.
A SLEIGH BEGGY.
FIVE MILLION.

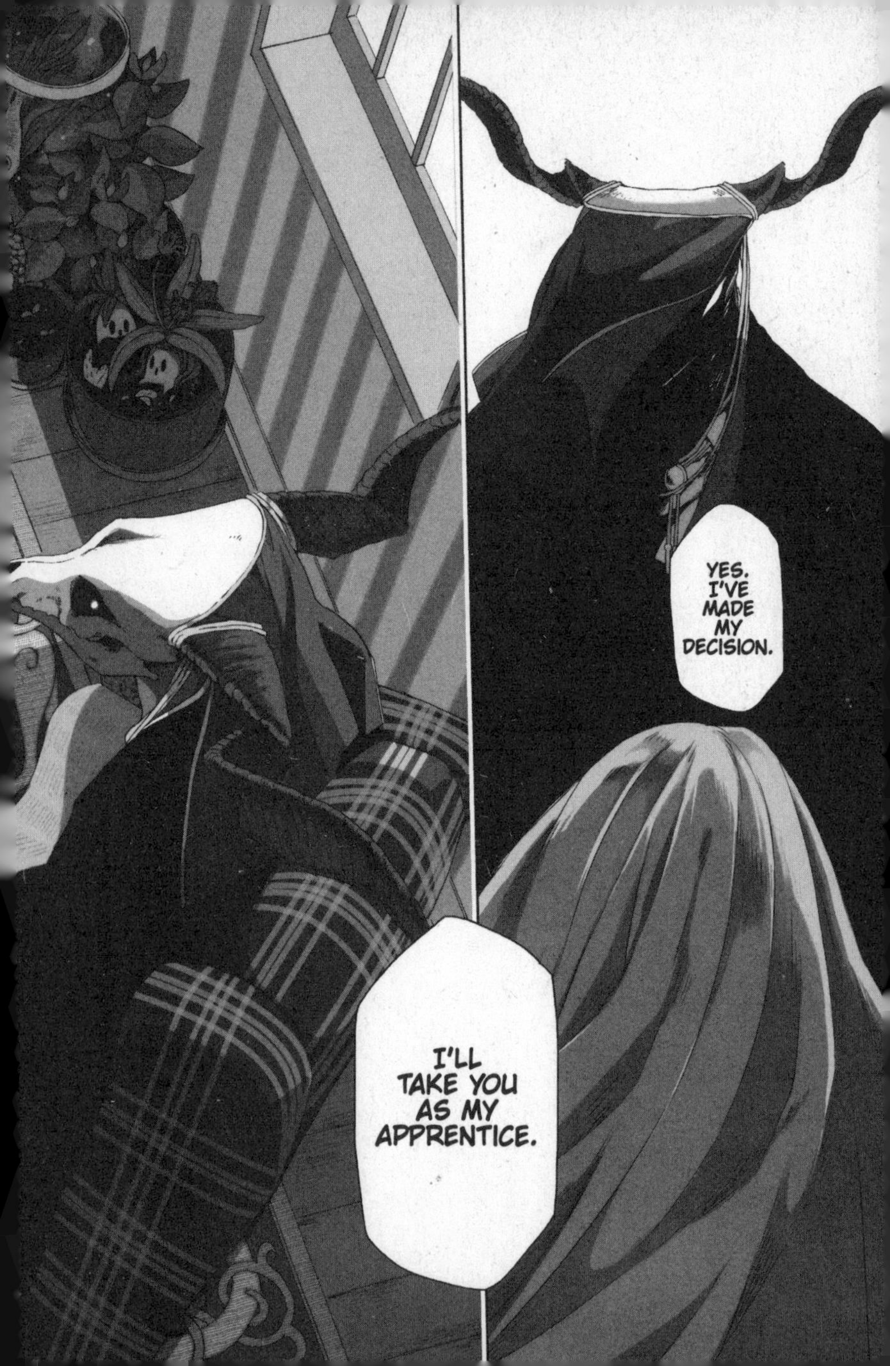
YES. I'VE MADE MY DECISION.
I'LL TAKE YOU AS MY APPRENTICE.

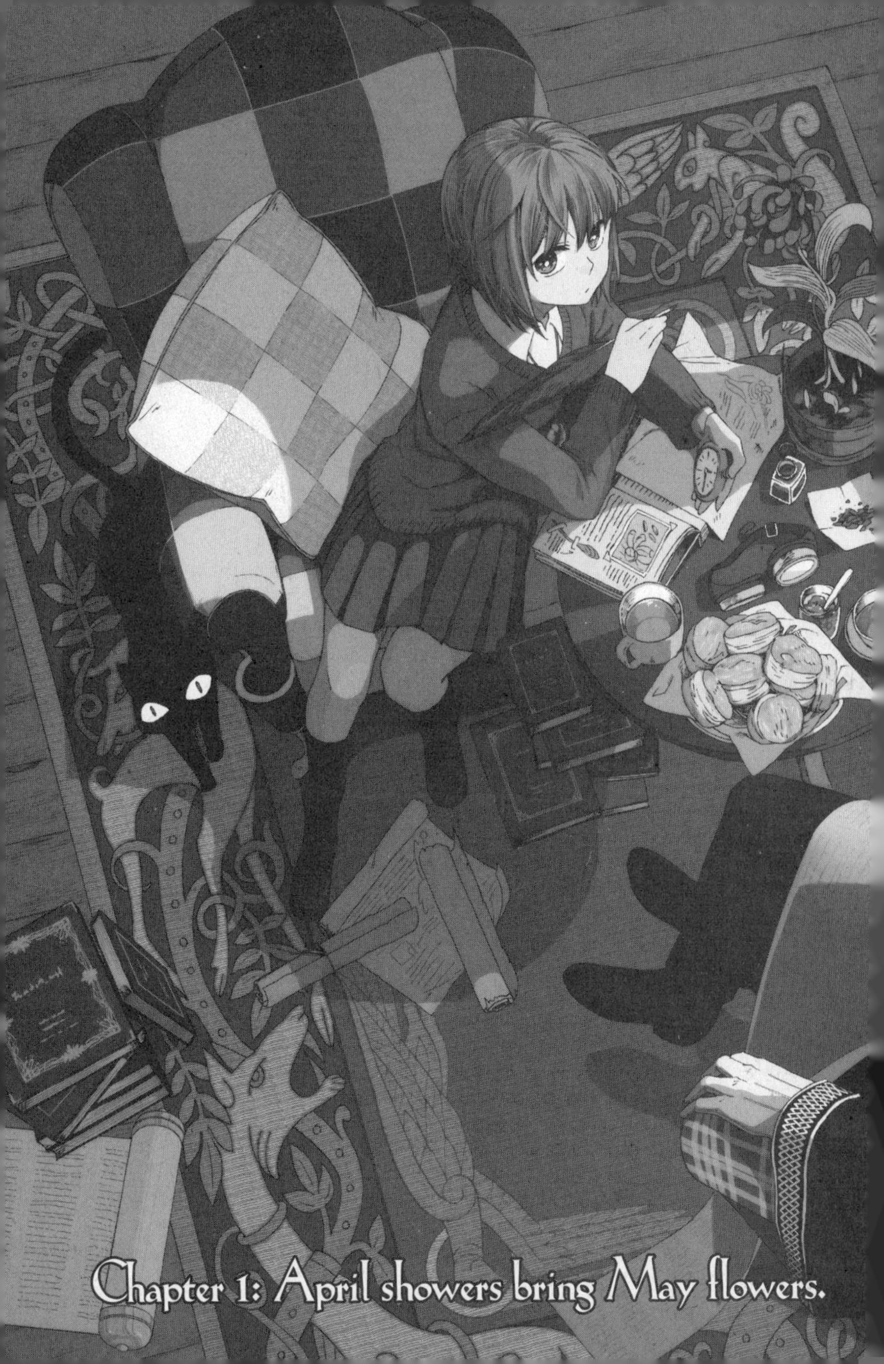

Chapter 1: April showers bring May flowers.

The Ancient Magus' Bride

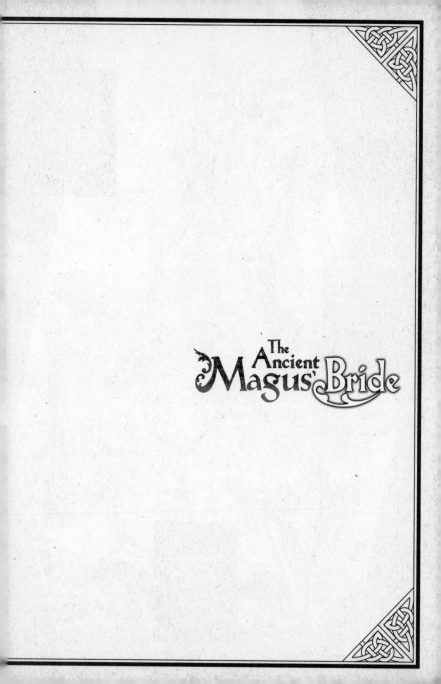

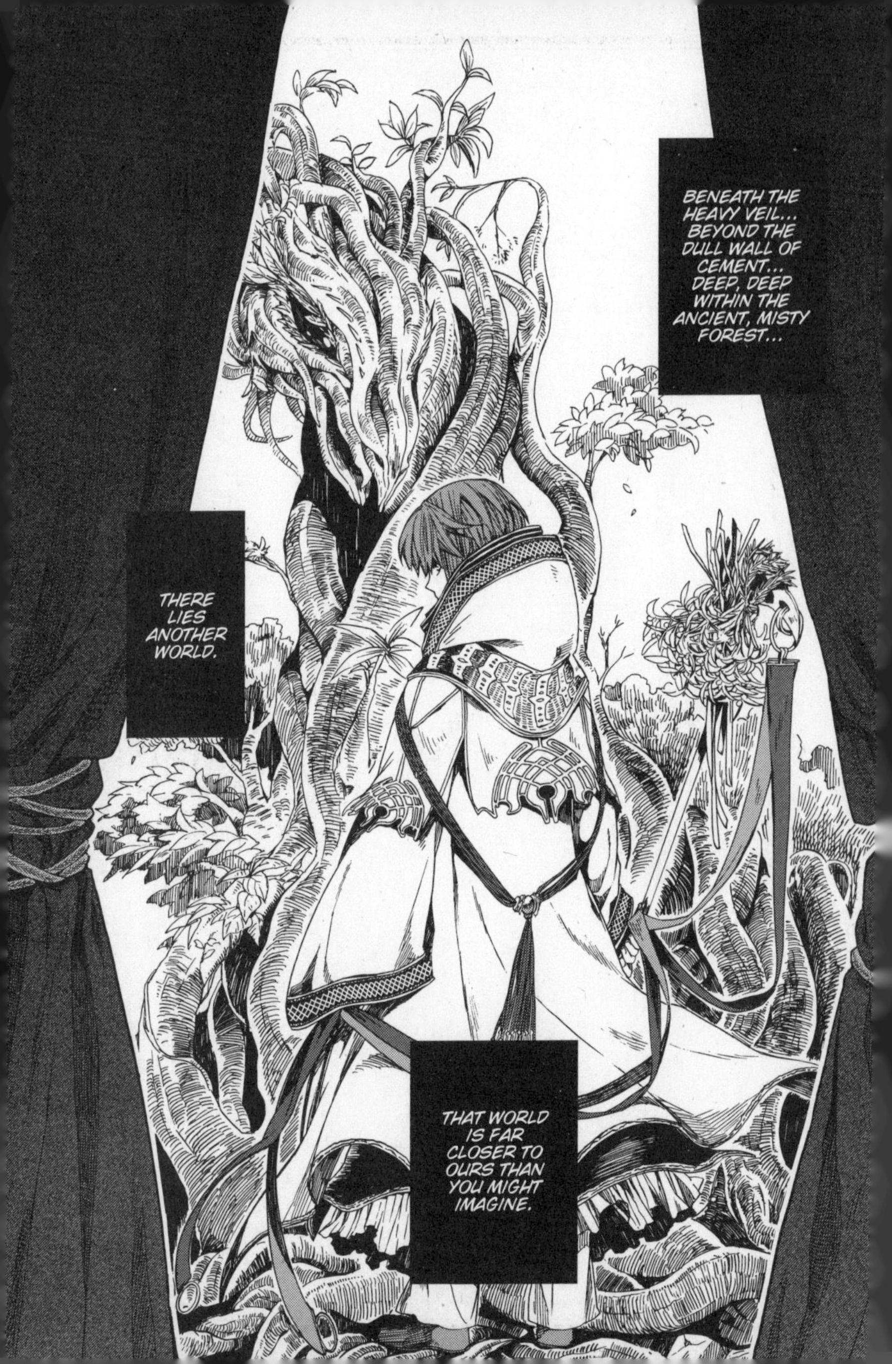
BENEATH THE HEAVY VEIL... BEYOND THE DULL WALL OF CEMENT... DEEP, DEEP WITHIN THE ANCIENT, MISTY FOREST...
THERE LIES ANOTHER WORLD.
THAT WORLD IS FAR CLOSER TO OURS THAN YOU MIGHT IMAGINE.

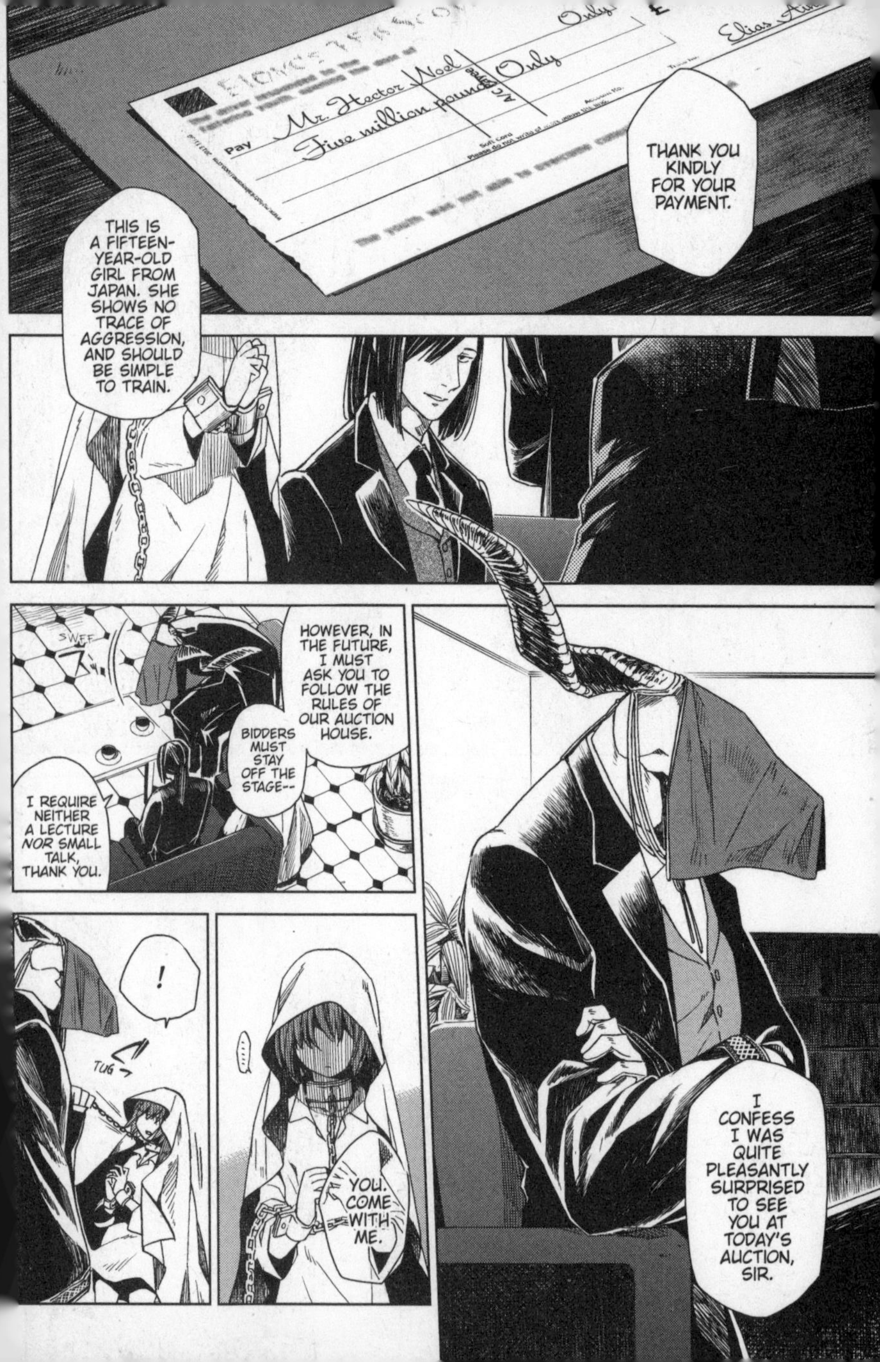

Pay
Mr. Hector Noel
Five million pounds
Only
A/C Payee
Only
THANK YOU KINDLY FOR YOUR PAYMENT.
THIS IS A FIFTEEN-YEAR-OLD GIRL FROM JAPAN. SHE SHOWS NO TRACE OF AGGRESSION, AND SHOULD BE SIMPLE TO TRAIN.
I CONFESS I WAS QUITE PLEASANTLY SURPRISED TO SEE YOU AT TODAY'S AUCTION, SIR.
HOWEVER, IN THE FUTURE, I MUST ASK YOU TO FOLLOW THE RULES OF OUR AUCTION HOUSE.
SWFF
BIDDERS MUST STAY OFF THE STAGE--
I REQUIRE NEITHER A LECTURE NOR SMALL TALK, THANK YOU.
....
YOU. COME WITH ME.
!
TUG

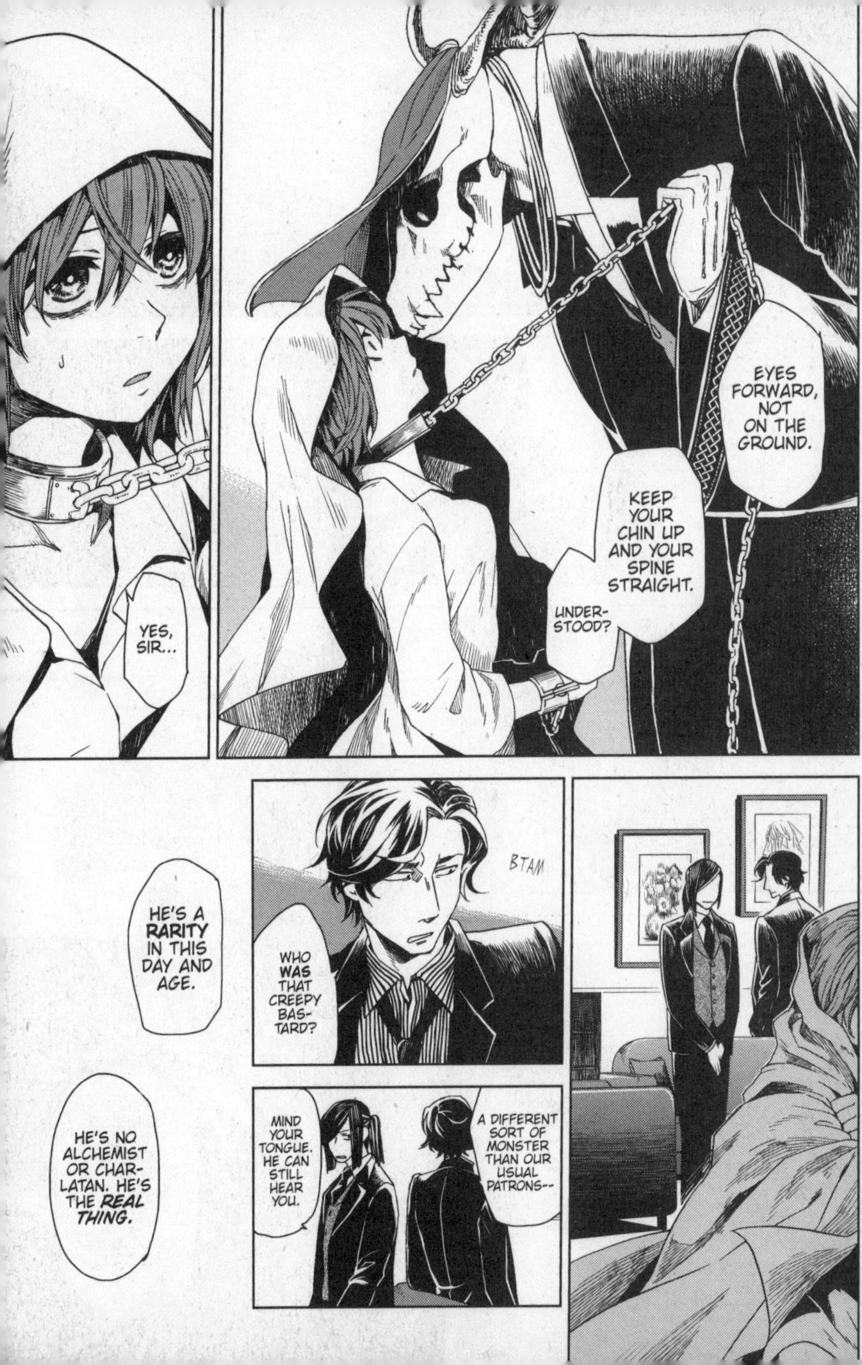
EYES FORWARD, NOT ON THE GROUND.
KEEP YOUR CHIN UP AND YOUR SPINE STRAIGHT.
UNDER-STOOD?
YES, SIR...
BTAM
WHO **WAS** THAT CREEPY BAS-TARD?
HE'S A **RARITY** IN THIS DAY AND AGE.
A DIFFERENT SORT OF MONSTER THAN OUR USUAL PATRONS--
MIND YOUR TONGUE. HE CAN STILL HEAR YOU.
HE'S NO ALCHEMIST OR CHAR-LATAN. HE'S THE ***REAL THING.***

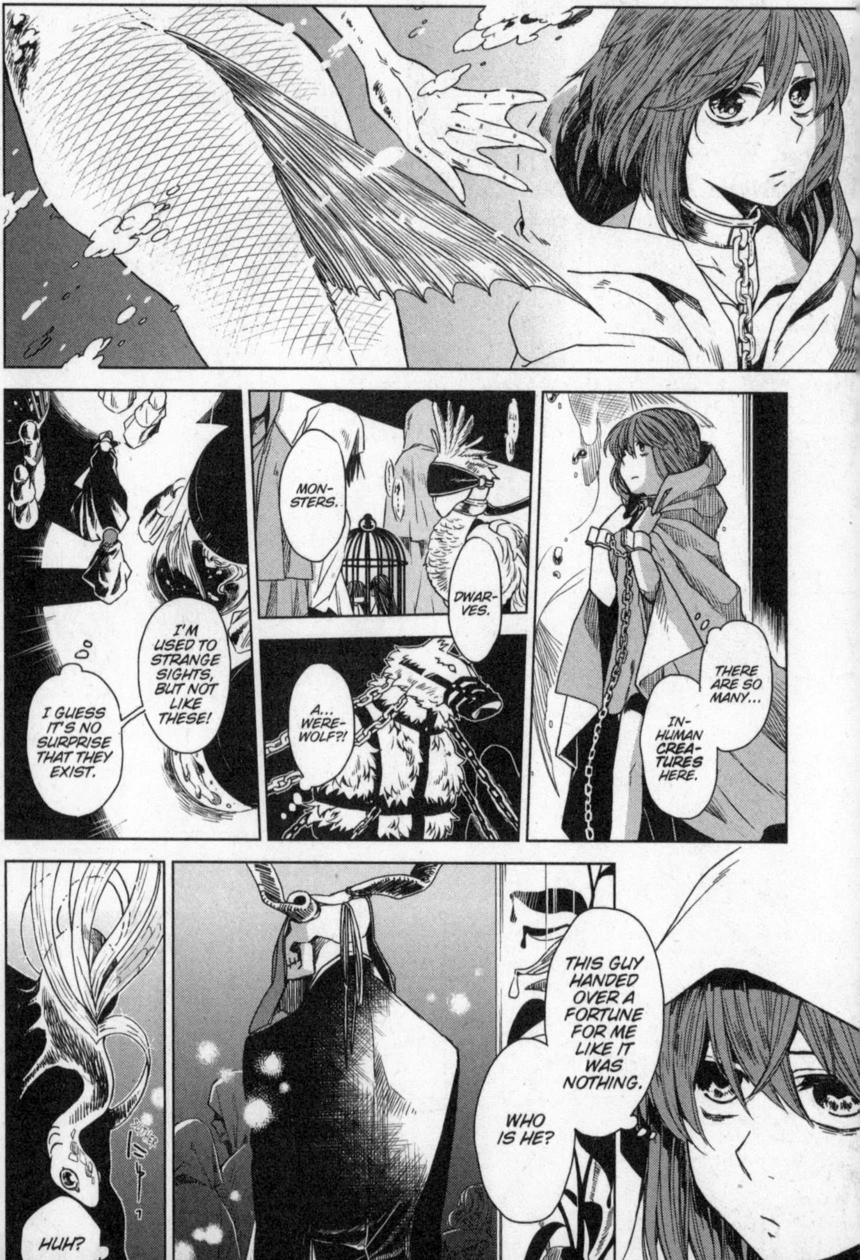

THERE ARE SO MANY...
IN-HUMAN CREATURES HERE.
MONSTERS.
DWARVES.
A... WEREWOLF?!
I'M USED TO STRANGE SIGHTS, BUT NOT LIKE THESE!
I GUESS IT'S NO SURPRISE THAT THEY EXIST.
THIS GUY HANDED OVER A FORTUNE FOR ME LIKE IT WAS NOTHING.
WHO IS HE?
SHIVER
HUH?

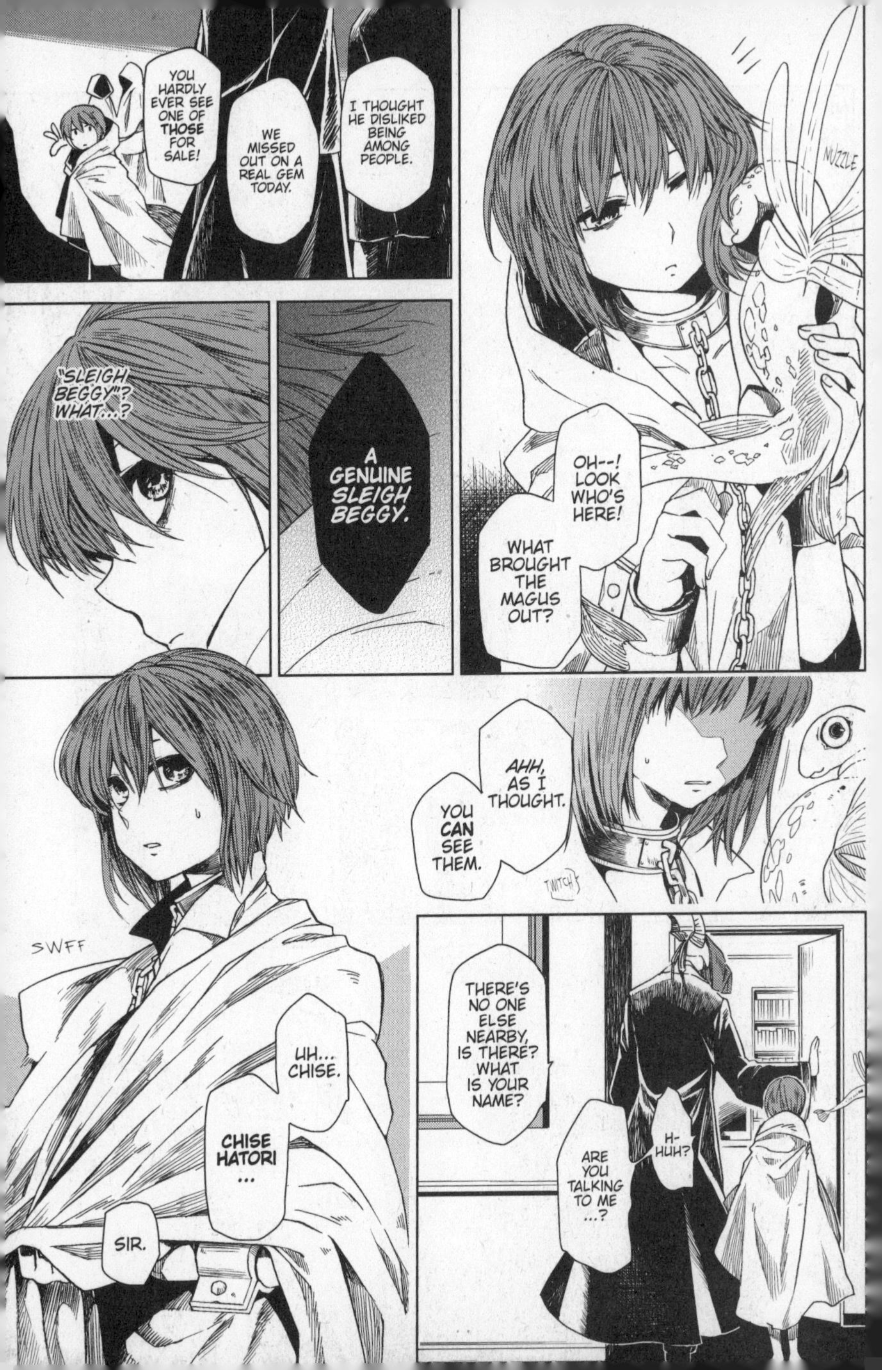
NUZZLE
OH--! LOOK WHO'S HERE!
WHAT BROUGHT THE MAGUS OUT?
I THOUGHT HE DISLIKED BEING AMONG PEOPLE.
WE MISSED OUT ON A REAL GEM TODAY.
YOU HARDLY EVER SEE ONE OF THOSE FOR SALE!
A GENUINE SLEIGH BEGGY.
"SLEIGH BEGGY"? WHAT...?
AHH, AS I THOUGHT.
YOU CAN SEE THEM.
TWITCH
THERE'S NO ONE ELSE NEARBY, IS THERE? WHAT IS YOUR NAME?
H-HUH?
ARE YOU TALKING TO ME ...?
SWFF
UH... CHISE.
CHISE HATORI ...
SIR.

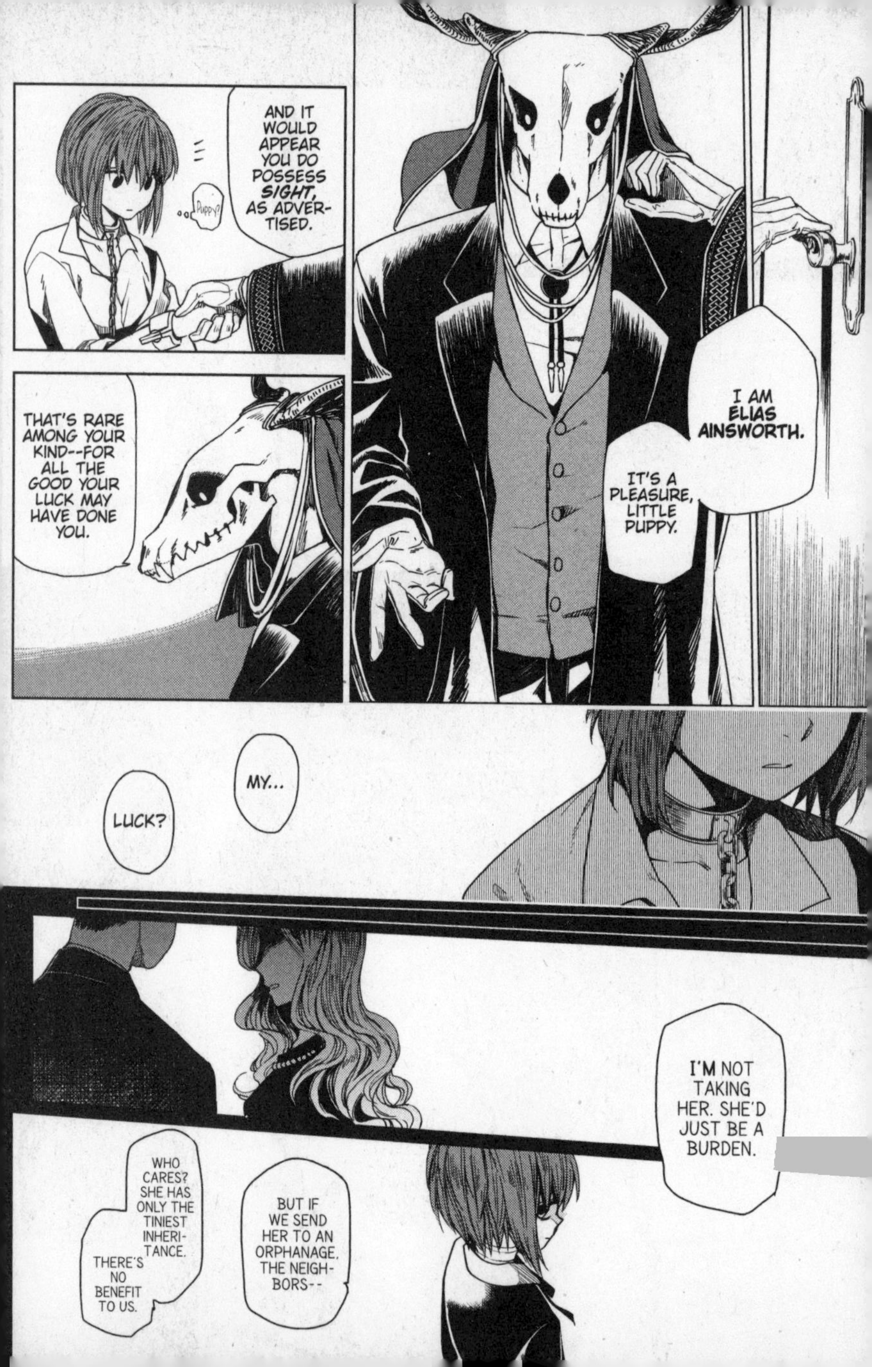
I AM ELIAS AINSWORTH.
IT'S A PLEASURE, LITTLE PUPPY.
AND IT WOULD APPEAR YOU DO POSSESS SIGHT, AS ADVERTISED.
Puppy?
THAT'S RARE AMONG YOUR KIND--FOR ALL THE GOOD YOUR LUCK MAY HAVE DONE YOU.
MY...
LUCK?
I'M NOT TAKING HER. SHE'D JUST BE A BURDEN.
BUT IF WE SEND HER TO AN ORPHANAGE, THE NEIGHBORS--
WHO CARES? SHE HAS ONLY THE TINIEST INHERITANCE.
THERE'S NO BENEFIT TO US.

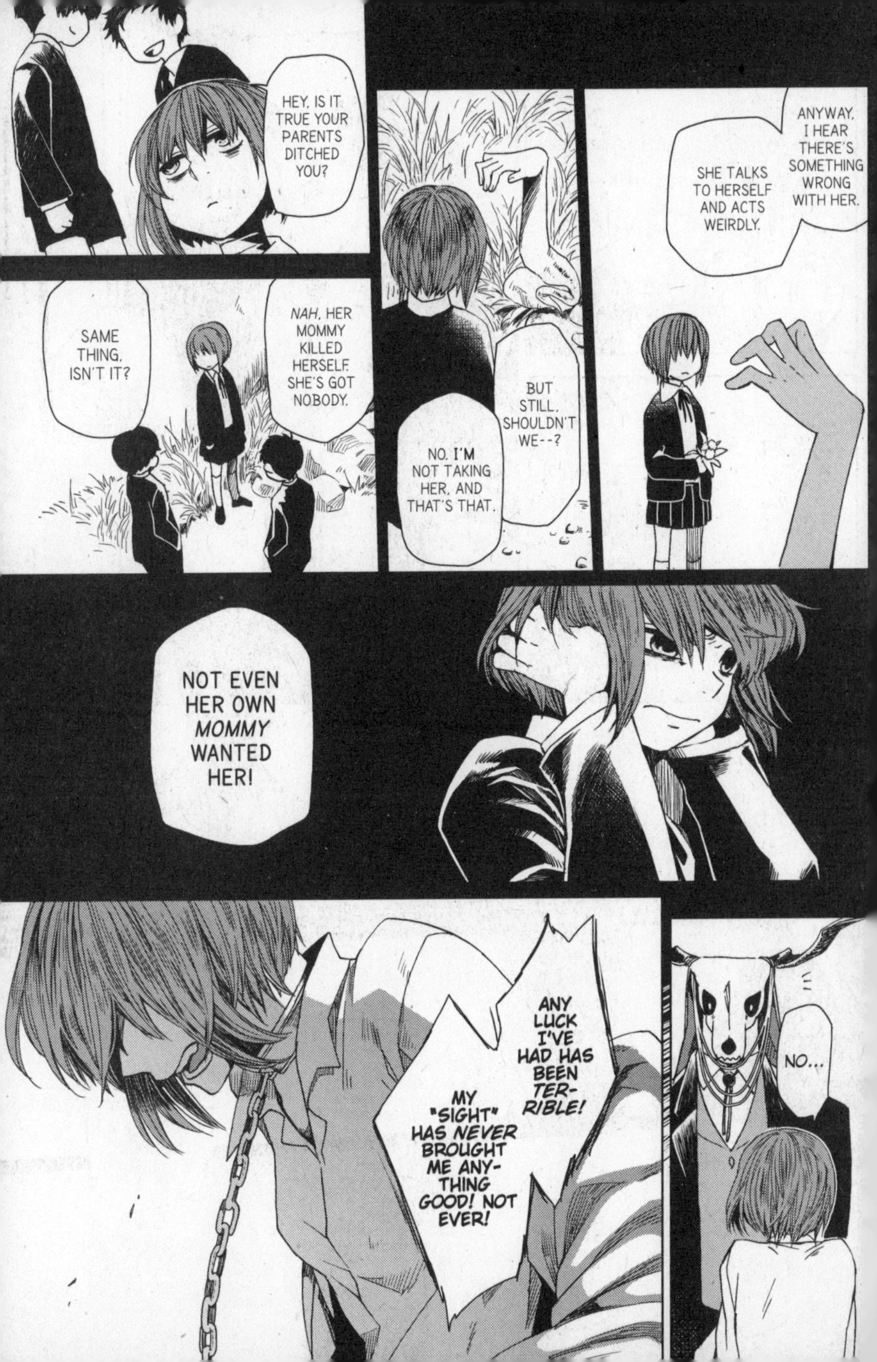
ANYWAY, I HEAR THERE'S SOMETHING WRONG WITH HER.
SHE TALKS TO HERSELF AND ACTS WEIRDLY.
BUT STILL, SHOULDN'T WE--?
NO. I'M NOT TAKING HER, AND THAT'S THAT.
HEY, IS IT TRUE YOUR PARENTS DITCHED YOU?
NAH, HER MOMMY KILLED HERSELF. SHE'S GOT NOBODY.
SAME THING, ISN'T IT?
NOT EVEN HER OWN *MOMMY* WANTED HER!
NO...
ANY LUCK I'VE HAD HAS BEEN TER-RIBLE!
MY "SIGHT" HAS *NEVER* BROUGHT ME ANY-THING GOOD! NOT EVER!

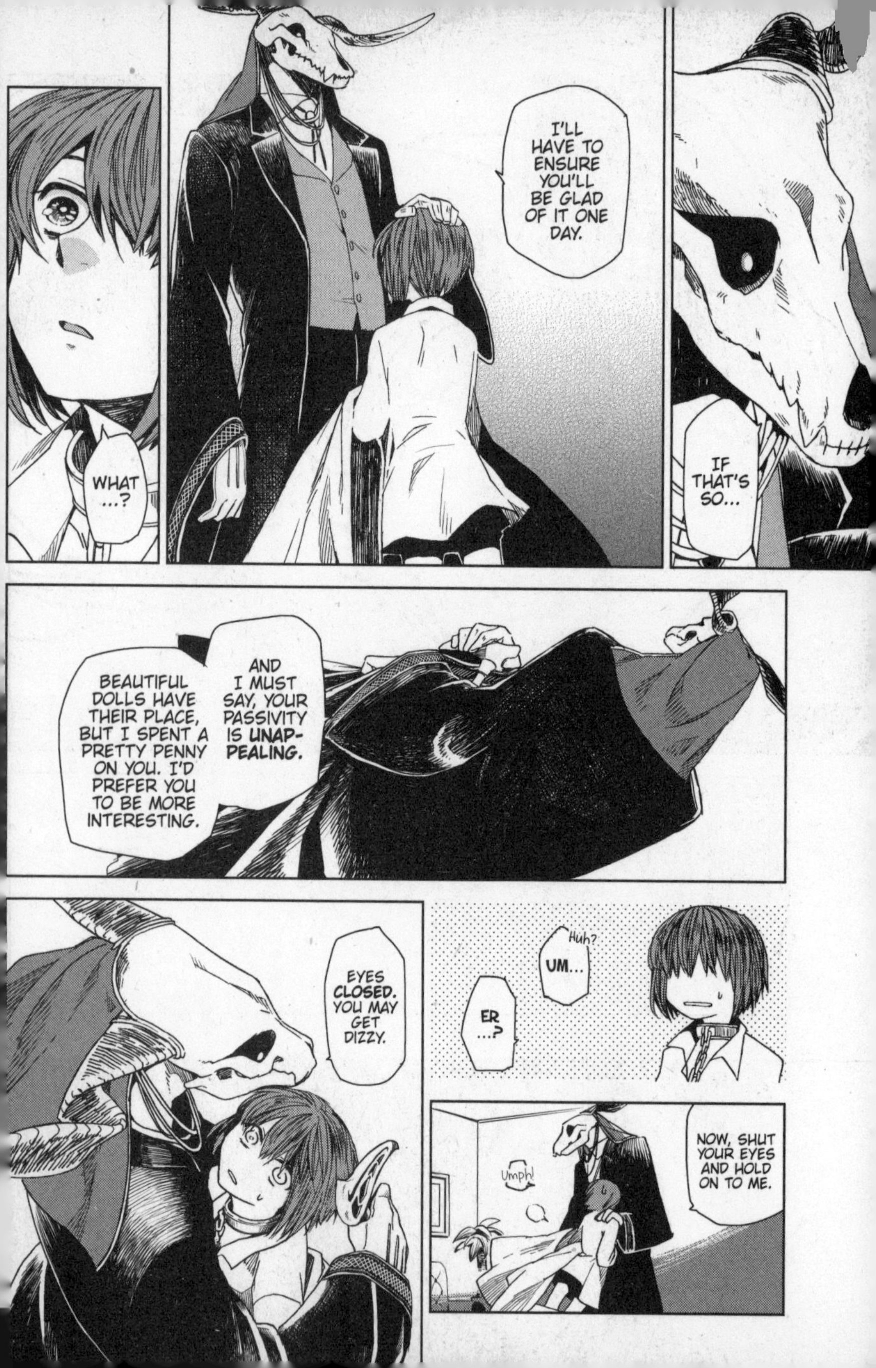
IF THAT'S SO...
I'LL HAVE TO ENSURE YOU'LL BE GLAD OF IT ONE DAY.
WHAT ...?
AND I MUST SAY, YOUR PASSIVITY IS UNAPPEALING.
BEAUTIFUL DOLLS HAVE THEIR PLACE, BUT I SPENT A PRETTY PENNY ON YOU. I'D PREFER YOU TO BE MORE INTERESTING.
Huh?
UM...
ER ...?
NOW, SHUT YOUR EYES AND HOLD ON TO ME.
Umph!
EYES CLOSED. YOU MAY GET DIZZY.

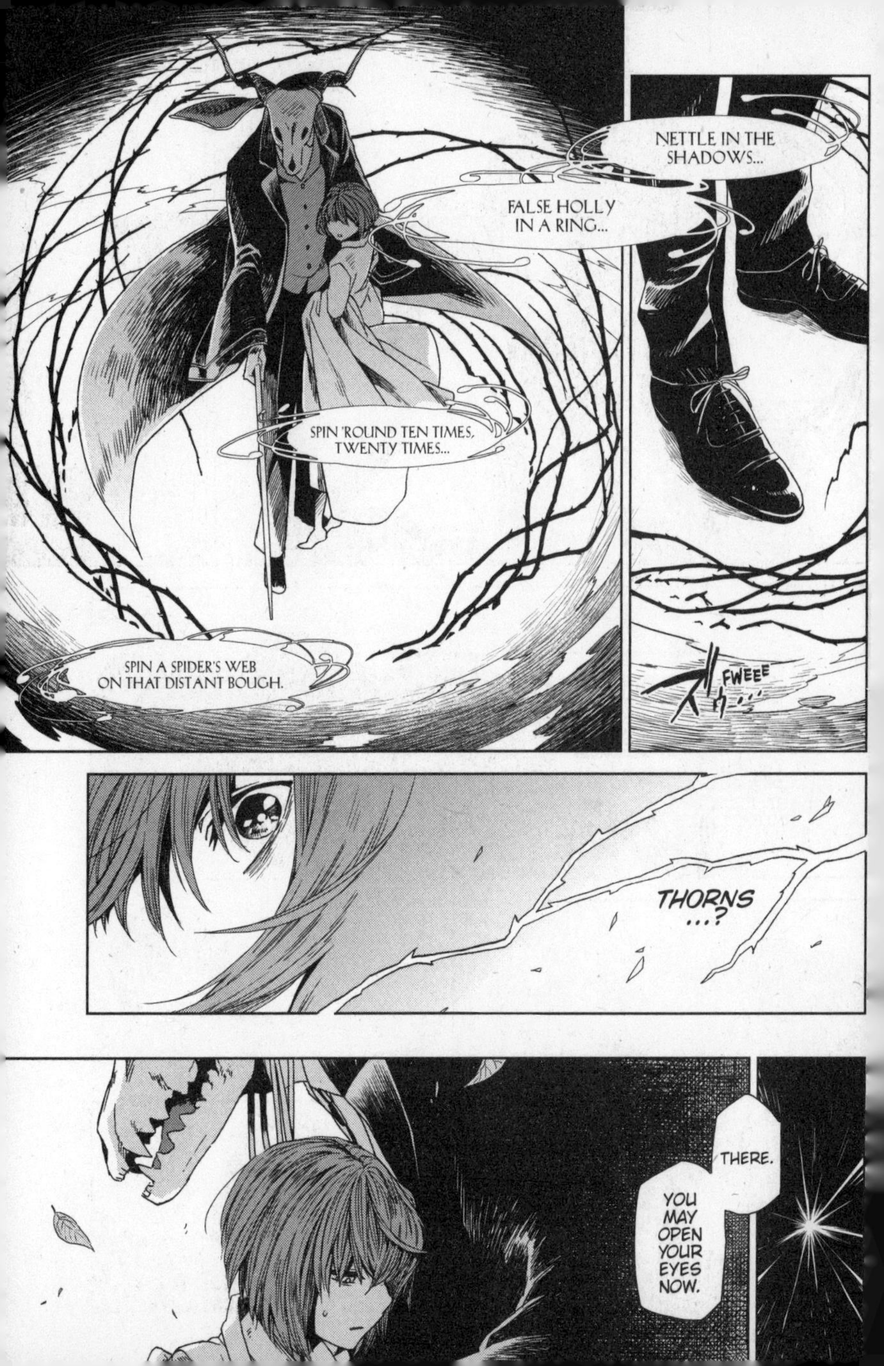
NETTLE IN THE SHADOWS...
FWEEE
FALSE HOLLY IN A RING...
SPIN 'ROUND TEN TIMES, TWENTY TIMES...
SPIN A SPIDER'S WEB ON THAT DISTANT BOUGH.
THORNS ...?
THERE.
YOU MAY OPEN YOUR EYES NOW.

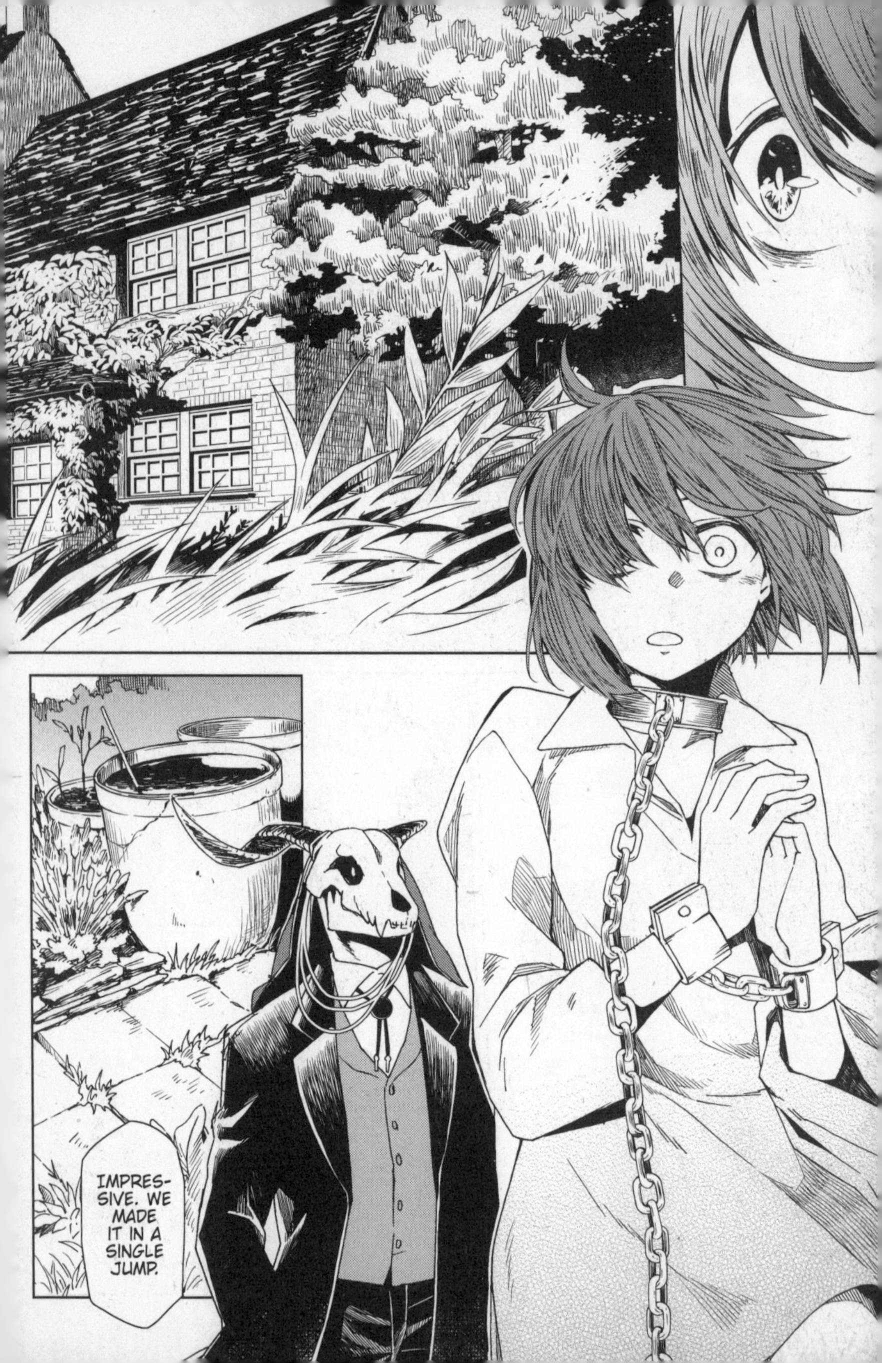
IMPRES-SIVE. WE MADE IT IN A SINGLE JUMP.

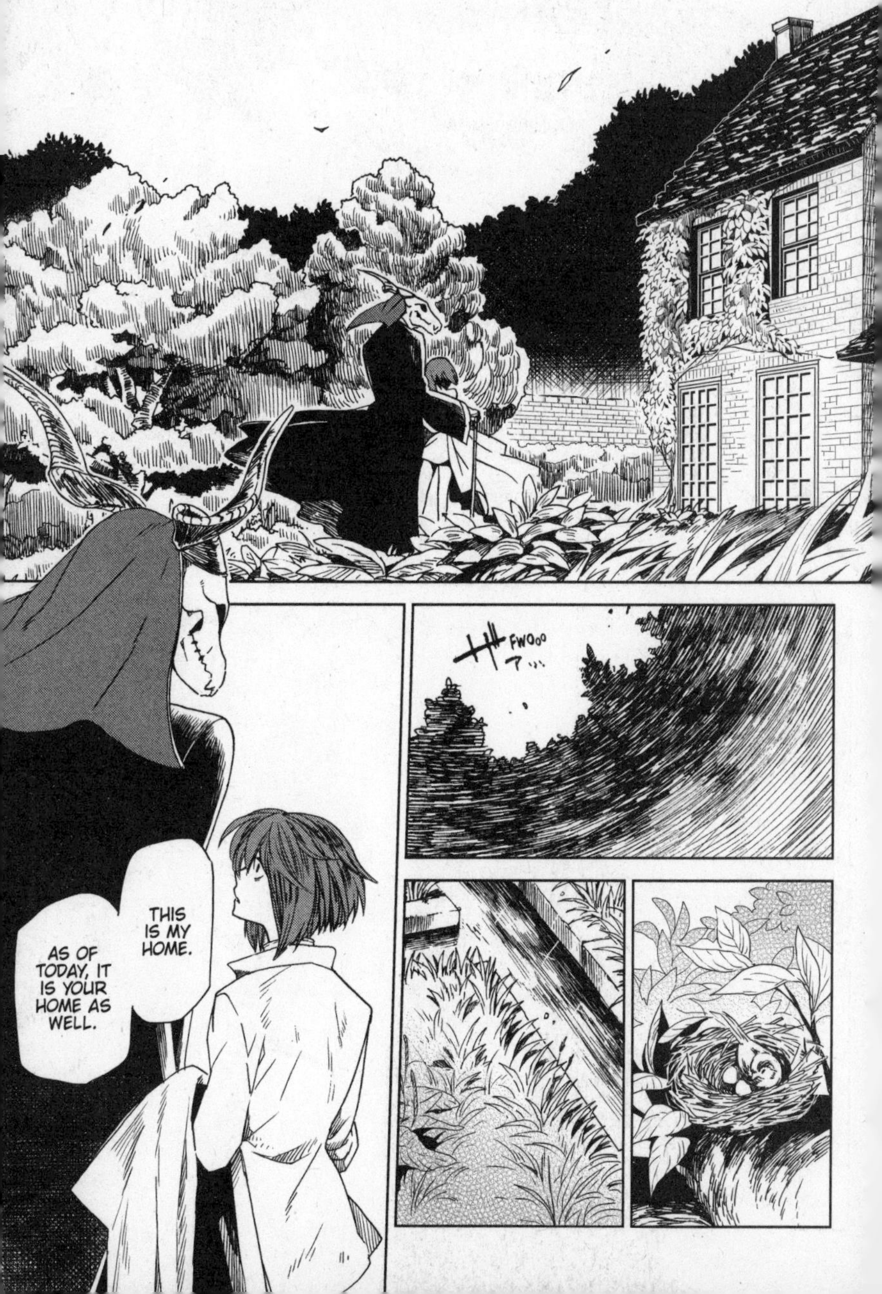
FWOOO
THIS IS MY HOME.
AS OF TODAY, IT IS YOUR HOME AS WELL.

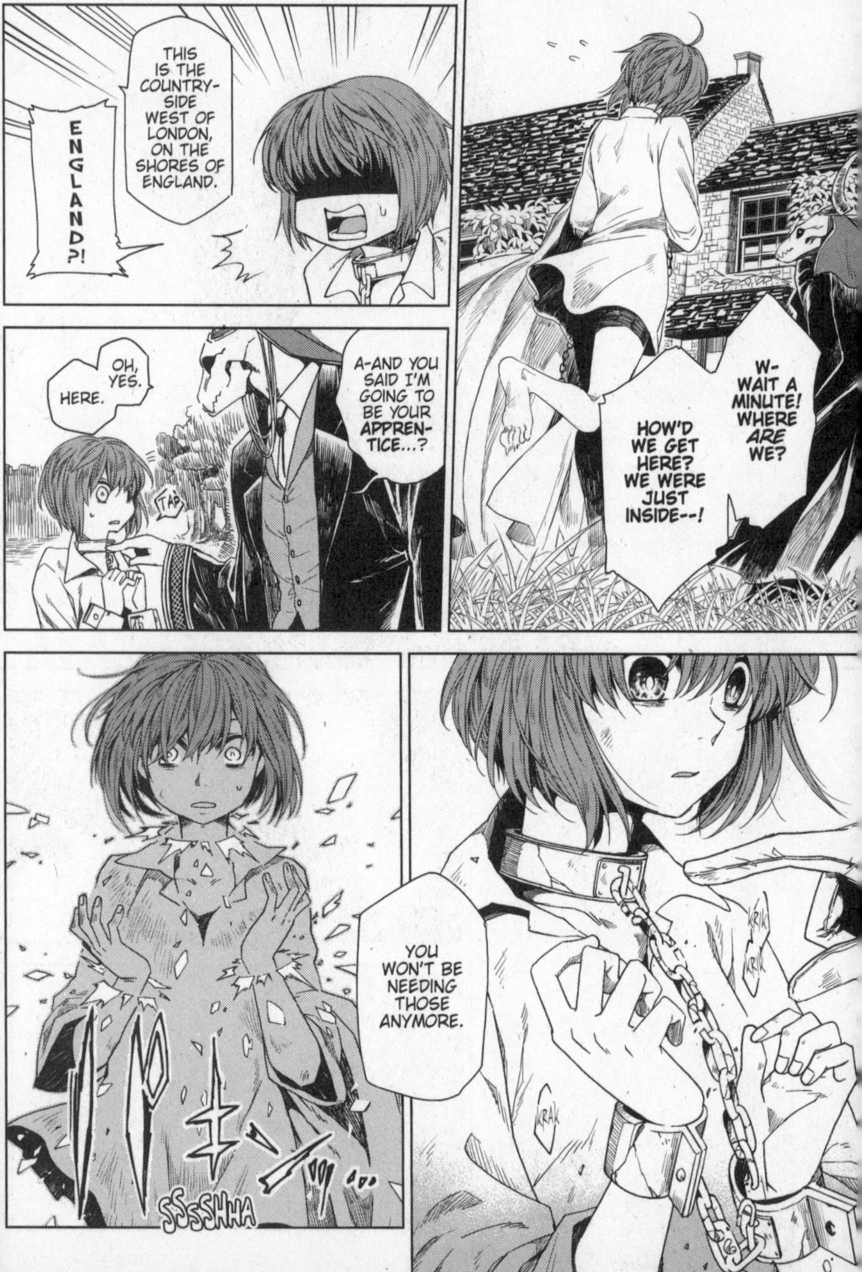
W-WAIT A MINUTE! WHERE ARE WE?
HOW'D WE GET HERE? WE WERE JUST INSIDE--!
THIS IS THE COUNTRY-SIDE WEST OF LONDON, ON THE SHORES OF ENGLAND.
ENGLAND?!
A-AND YOU SAID I'M GOING TO BE YOUR APPREN-TICE...?
OH, YES. HERE.
TAP
YOU WON'T BE NEEDING THOSE ANYMORE.
KRIK
KRIK
KRAK
SSSSHHA

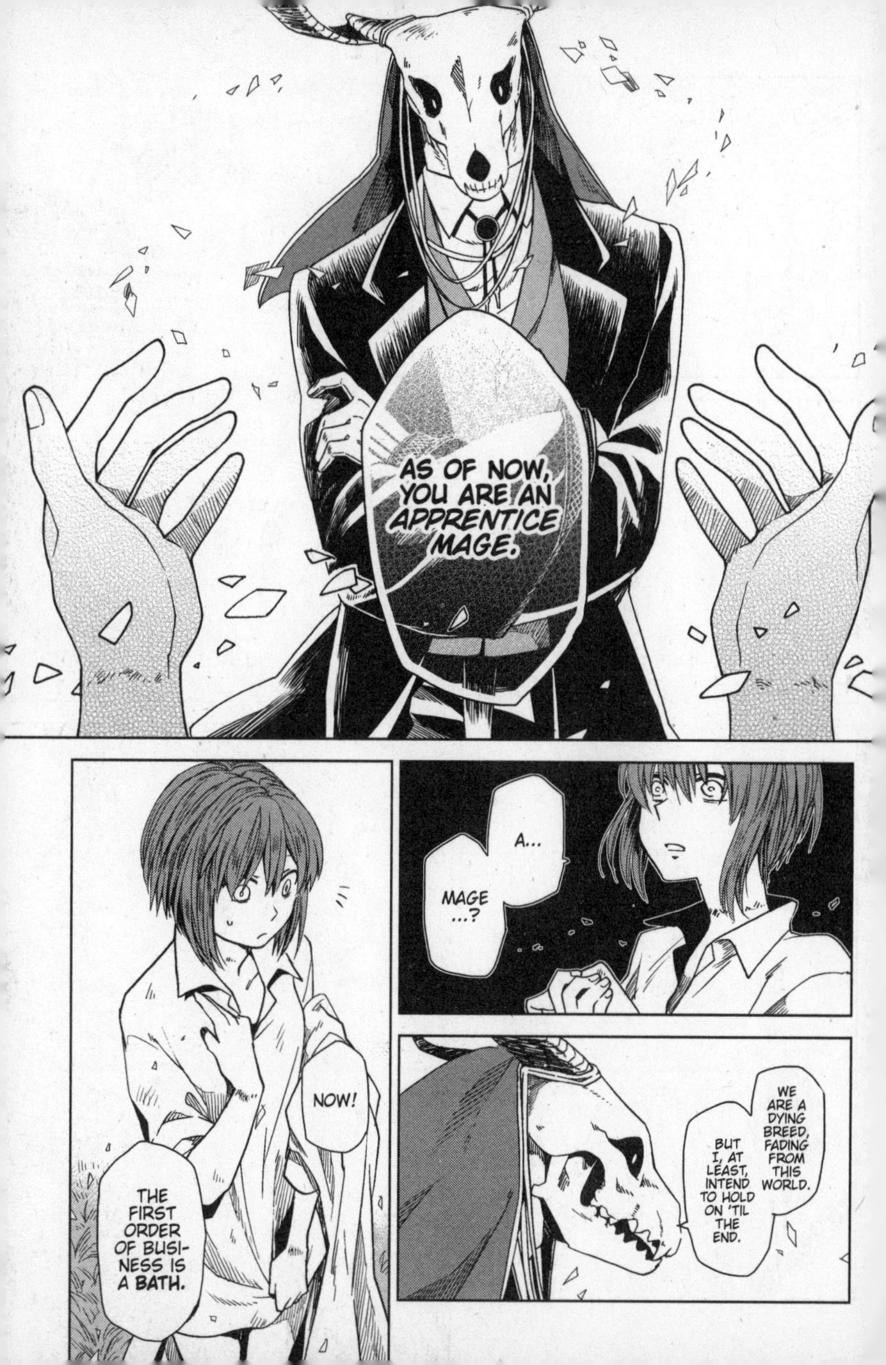
AS OF NOW, YOU ARE AN APPRENTICE MAGE.
A...
MAGE ...?
WE ARE A DYING BREED, FADING FROM THIS WORLD.
BUT I, AT LEAST, INTEND TO HOLD ON 'TIL THE END.
NOW!
THE FIRST ORDER OF BUSI-NESS IS A BATH.

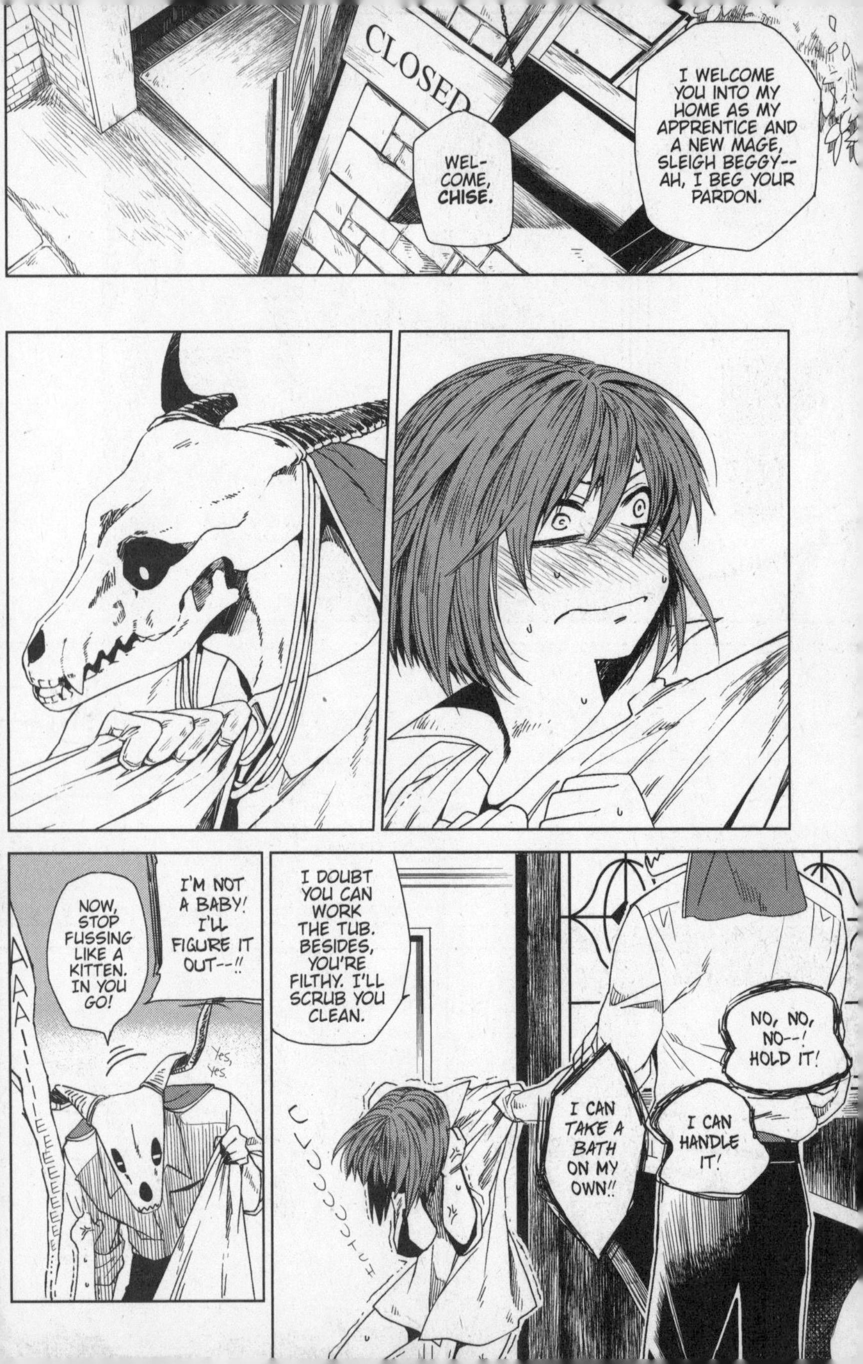
I WELCOME YOU INTO MY HOME AS MY APPRENTICE AND A NEW MAGE, SLEIGH BEGGY--AH, I BEG YOUR PARDON.
WEL-COME, CHISE.
CLOSED
NO, NO, NO--! HOLD IT!
I CAN HANDLE IT!
I CAN TAKE A BATH ON MY OWN!!
I DOUBT YOU CAN WORK THE TUB. BESIDES, YOU'RE FILTHY. I'LL SCRUB YOU CLEAN.
I'M NOT A BABY! I'LL FIGURE IT OUT--!!
NOW, STOP FUSSING LIKE A KITTEN. IN YOU GO!
Yes, yes.

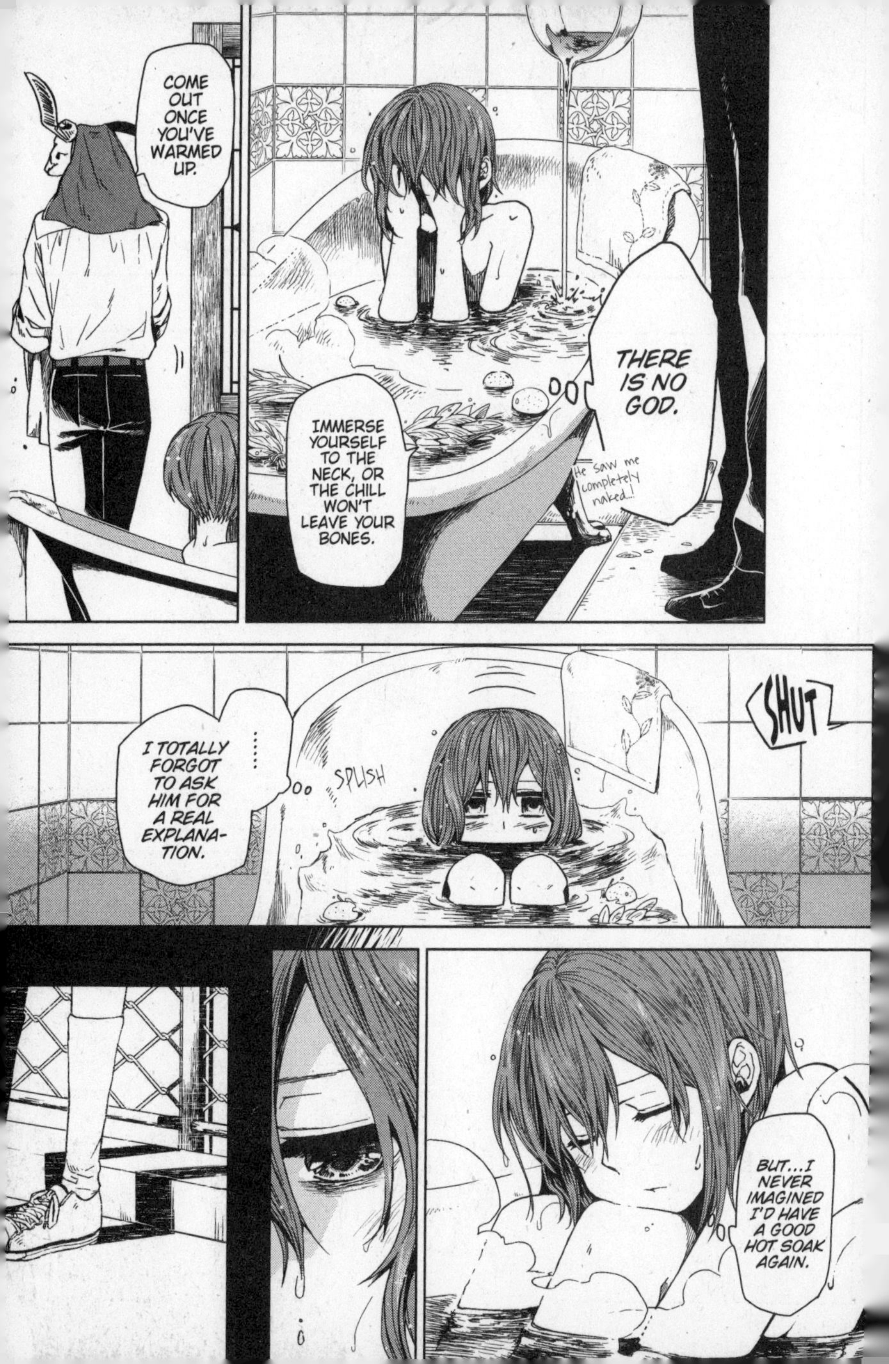
THERE IS NO GOD.
He saw me completely naked..!
IMMERSE YOURSELF TO THE NECK, OR THE CHILL WON'T LEAVE YOUR BONES.
COME OUT ONCE YOU'VE WARMED UP.
SHUT
......
SPLISH
I TOTALLY FORGOT TO ASK HIM FOR A REAL EXPLANATION.
BUT...I NEVER IMAGINED I'D HAVE A GOOD HOT SOAK AGAIN.

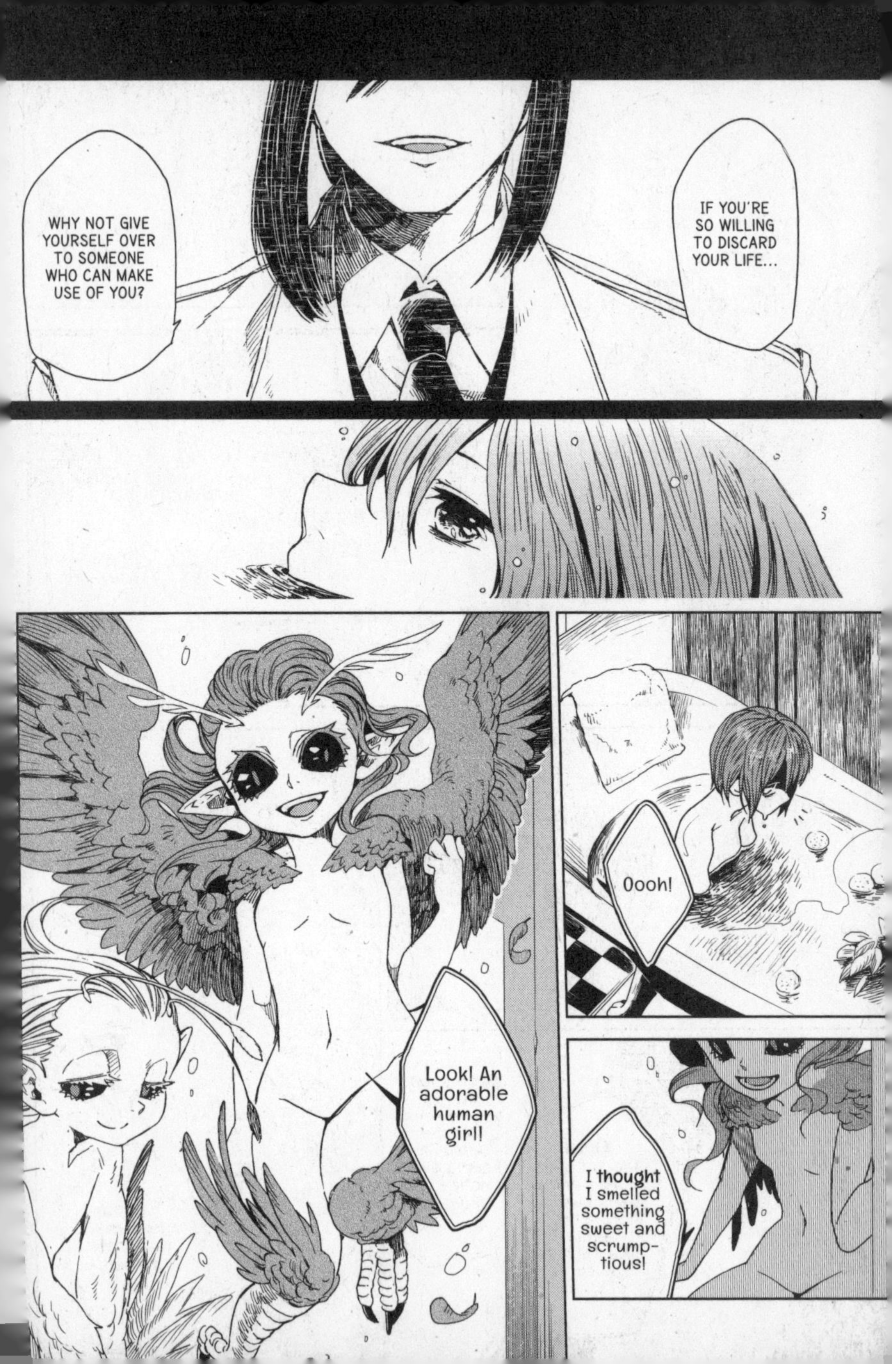
IF YOU'RE SO WILLING TO DISCARD YOUR LIFE...
WHY NOT GIVE YOURSELF OVER TO SOMEONE WHO CAN MAKE USE OF YOU?
Oooh!
I thought I smelled something sweet and scrump-tious!
Look! An adorable human girl!

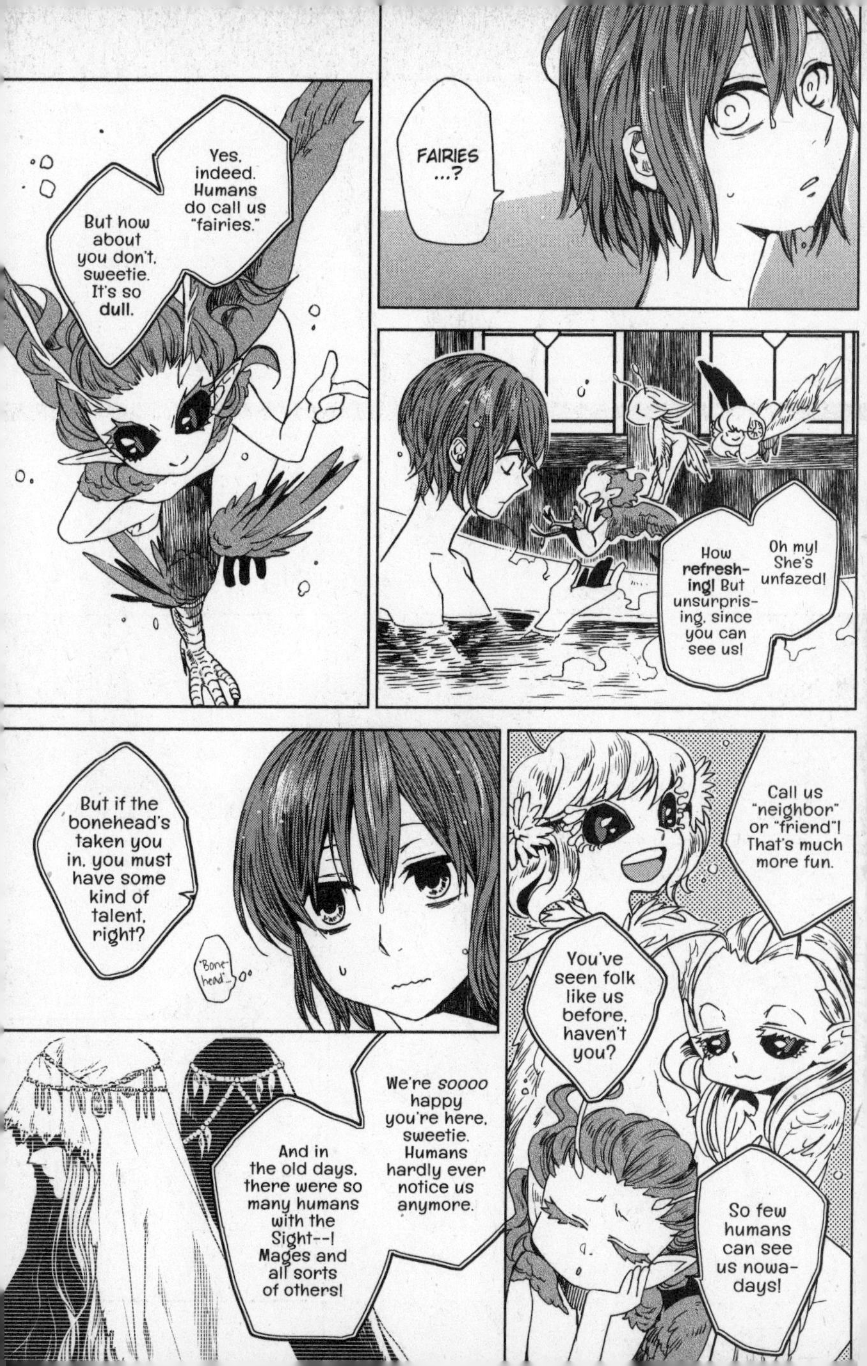
FAIRIES ...?
Oh my! She's unfazed!
How **refreshing!** But unsurprising, since you can see us!
Yes, indeed. Humans do call us "fairies."
But how about you don't, sweetie. It's so **dull.**
Call us "neighbor" or "friend"! That's much more fun.
You've seen folk like us before, haven't you?
So few humans can see us nowadays!
But if the bonehead's taken you in, you must have some kind of talent, right?
"Bonehead"...
We're *soooo* happy you're here, sweetie. Humans hardly ever notice us anymore.
And in the old days, there were so many humans with the Sight--! Mages and all sorts of others!

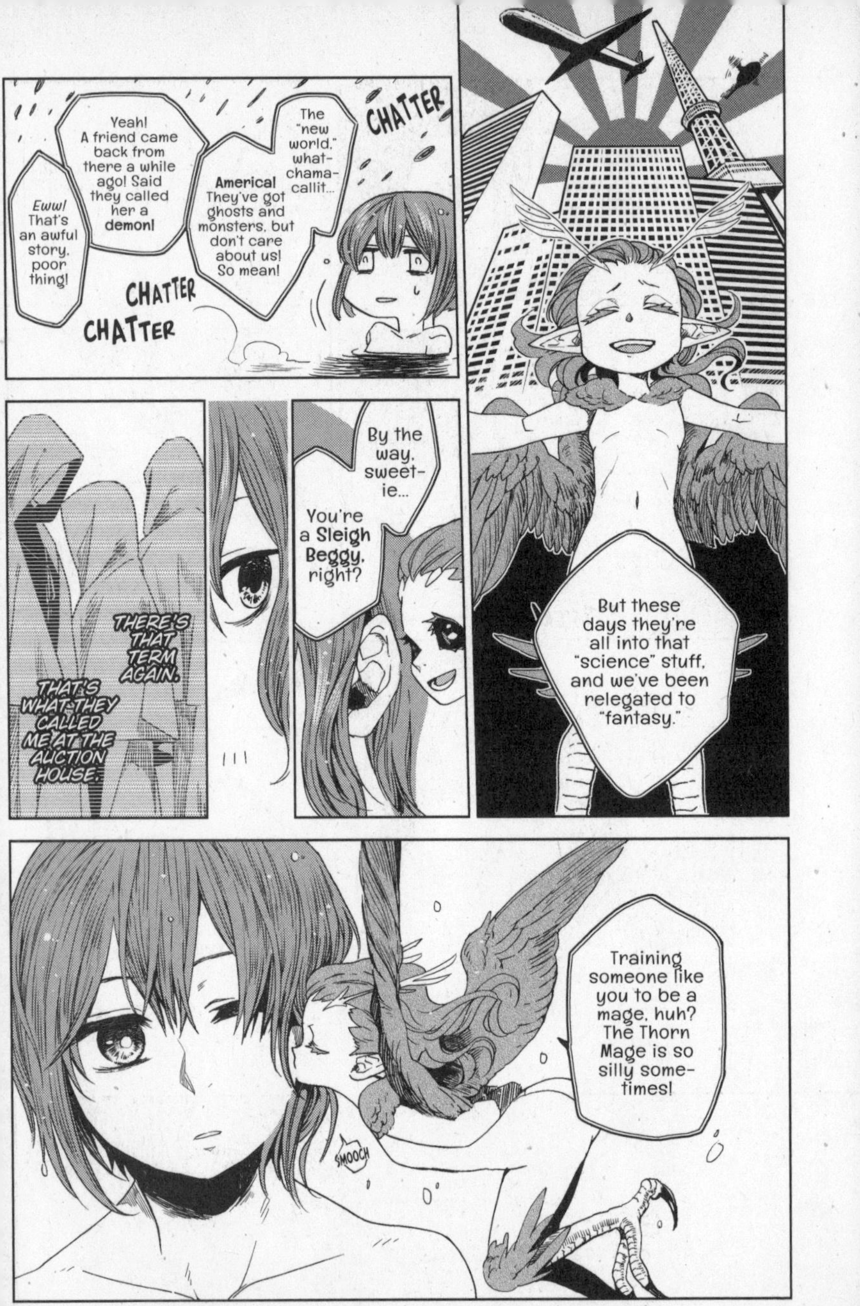
But these days they're all into that "science" stuff, and we've been relegated to "fantasy."
CHATTER
The "new world," whatchamacallit... **America!** They've got ghosts and monsters, but don't care about us! So mean!
Yeah! A friend came back from there a while ago! Said they called her a **demon!**
Eww! That's an awful story, poor thing!
CHATTER
CHATTER
By the way, sweetie...
You're a **Sleigh Beggy**, right?
THERE'S THAT TERM AGAIN.
THAT'S WHAT THEY CALLED ME AT THE AUCTION HOUSE.
Training someone like you to be a mage, huh? The Thorn Mage is so silly sometimes!
SMOOCH

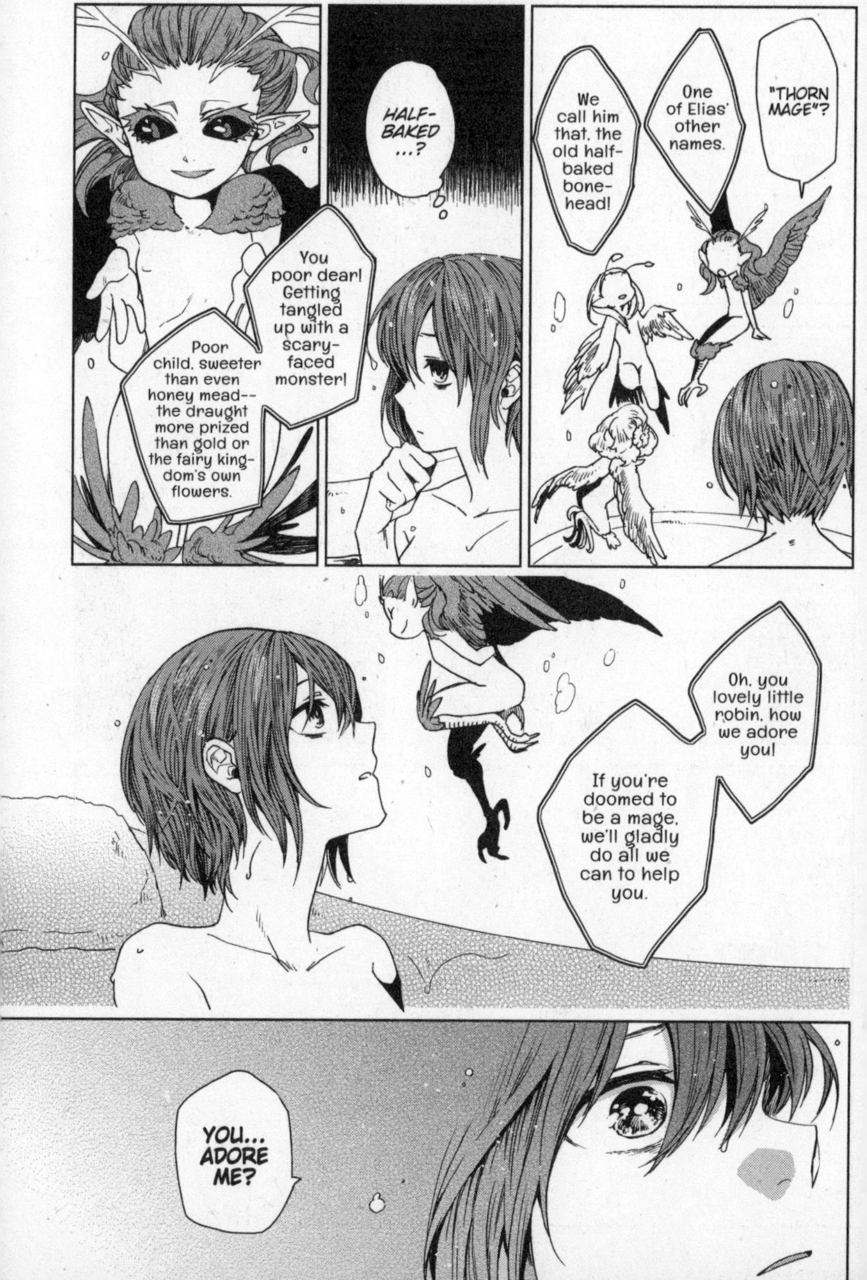
"THORN MAGE"?
One of Elias' other names.
We call him that, the old half-baked bonehead!
HALF-BAKED...?
You poor dear! Getting tangled up with a scary-faced monster!
Poor child, sweeter than even honey mead--the draught more prized than gold or the fairy kingdom's own flowers.
Oh, you lovely little robin, how we adore you!
If you're doomed to be a mage, we'll gladly do all we can to help you.
YOU... ADORE ME?

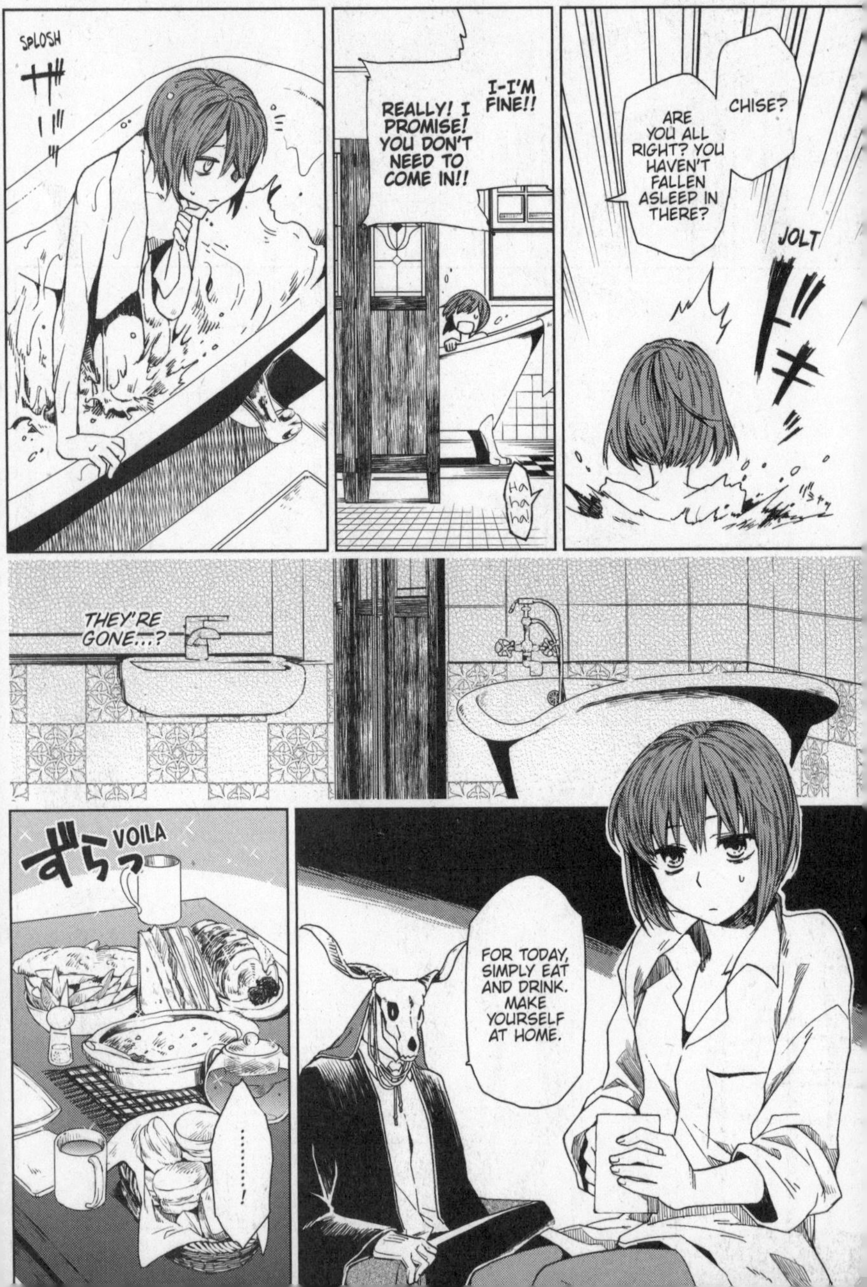
CHISE?
ARE YOU ALL RIGHT? YOU HAVEN'T FALLEN ASLEEP IN THERE?
JOLT
ドキ
I-I'M FINE!!
REALLY! I PROMISE! YOU DON'T NEED TO COME IN!!
Ha ha ha!
SPLOSH
THEY'RE GONE...?
FOR TODAY, SIMPLY EAT AND DRINK. MAKE YOURSELF AT HOME.
ずらっ
VOILA
......!

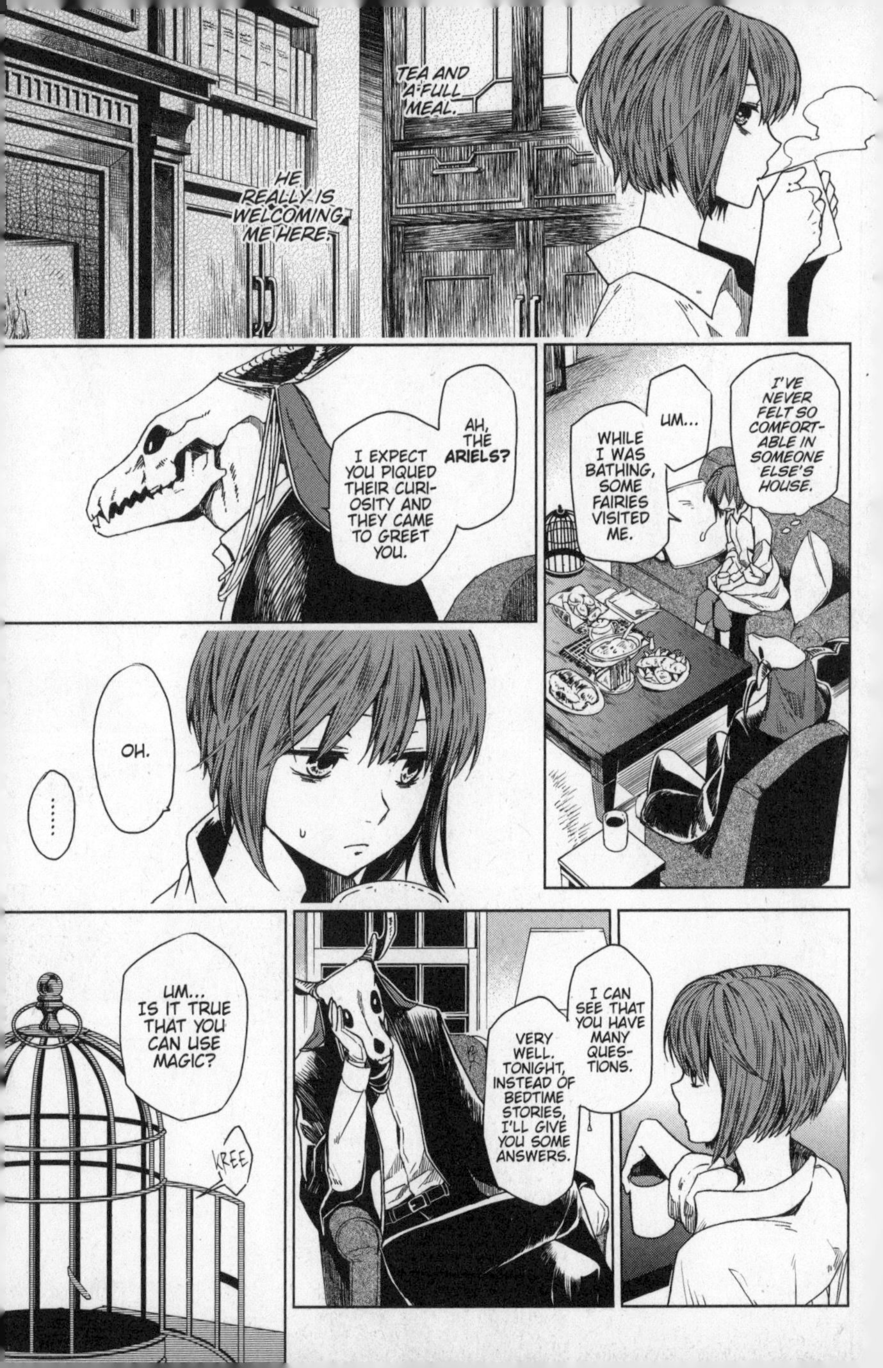
TEA AND A FULL MEAL.
HE REALLY IS WELCOMING ME HERE.
I'VE NEVER FELT SO COMFORT-ABLE IN SOMEONE ELSE'S HOUSE.
UM...
WHILE I WAS BATHING, SOME FAIRIES VISITED ME.
AH, THE ARIELS?
I EXPECT YOU PIQUED THEIR CURI-OSITY AND THEY CAME TO GREET YOU.
OH.
......
I CAN SEE THAT YOU HAVE MANY QUES-TIONS.
VERY WELL. TONIGHT, INSTEAD OF BEDTIME STORIES, I'LL GIVE YOU SOME ANSWERS.
UM... IS IT TRUE THAT YOU CAN USE MAGIC?
KREE

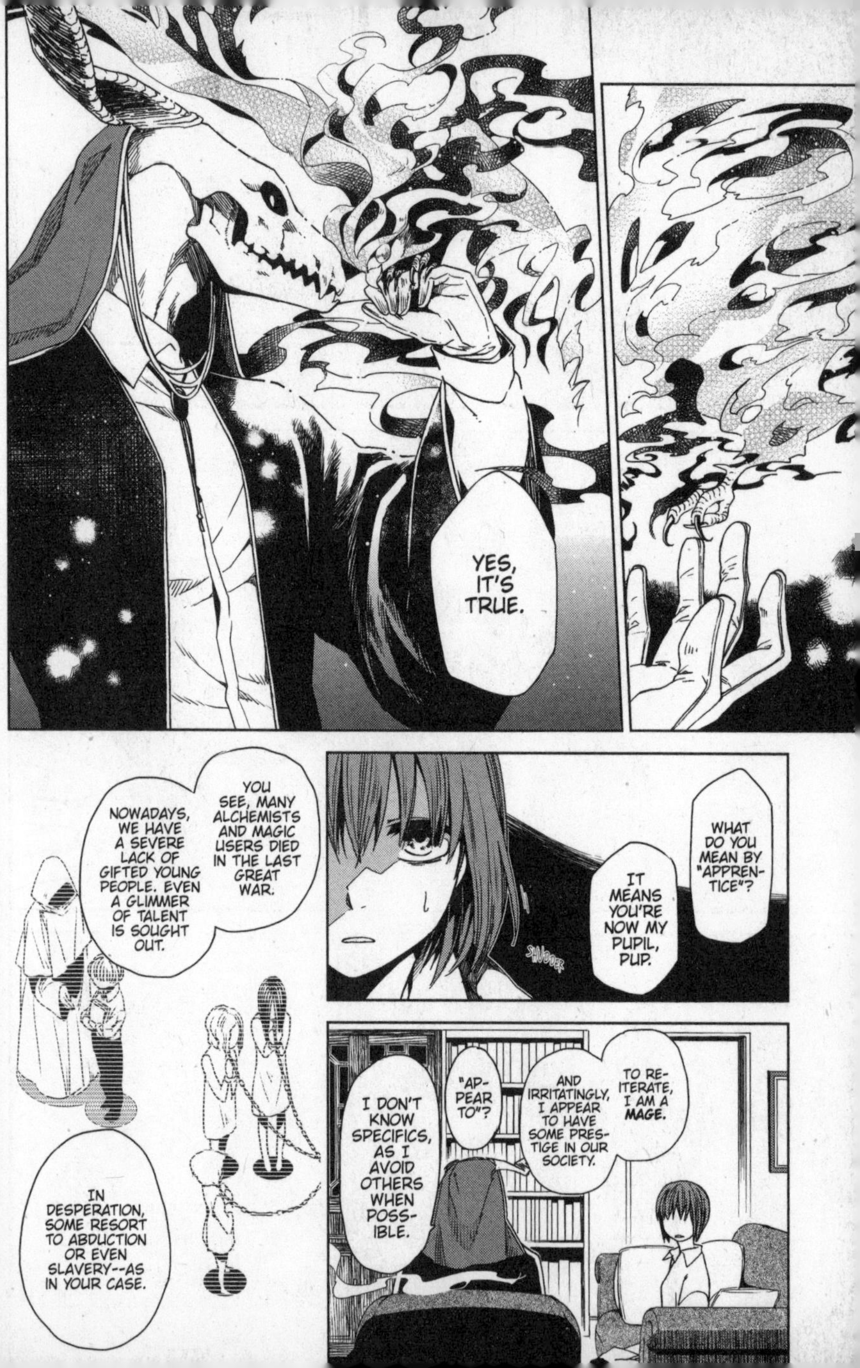
YES, IT'S TRUE.
WHAT DO YOU MEAN BY "APPRENTICE"?
IT MEANS YOU'RE NOW MY PUPIL, PUP.
SHUDDER
TO REITERATE, I AM A **MAGE**.
AND IRRITATINGLY, I APPEAR TO HAVE SOME PRESTIGE IN OUR SOCIETY.
"APPEAR TO"?
I DON'T KNOW SPECIFICS, AS I AVOID OTHERS WHEN POSSIBLE.
YOU SEE, MANY ALCHEMISTS AND MAGIC USERS DIED IN THE LAST GREAT WAR.
NOWADAYS, WE HAVE A SEVERE LACK OF GIFTED YOUNG PEOPLE. EVEN A GLIMMER OF TALENT IS SOUGHT OUT.
IN DESPERATION, SOME RESORT TO ABDUCTION OR EVEN SLAVERY--AS IN YOUR CASE.

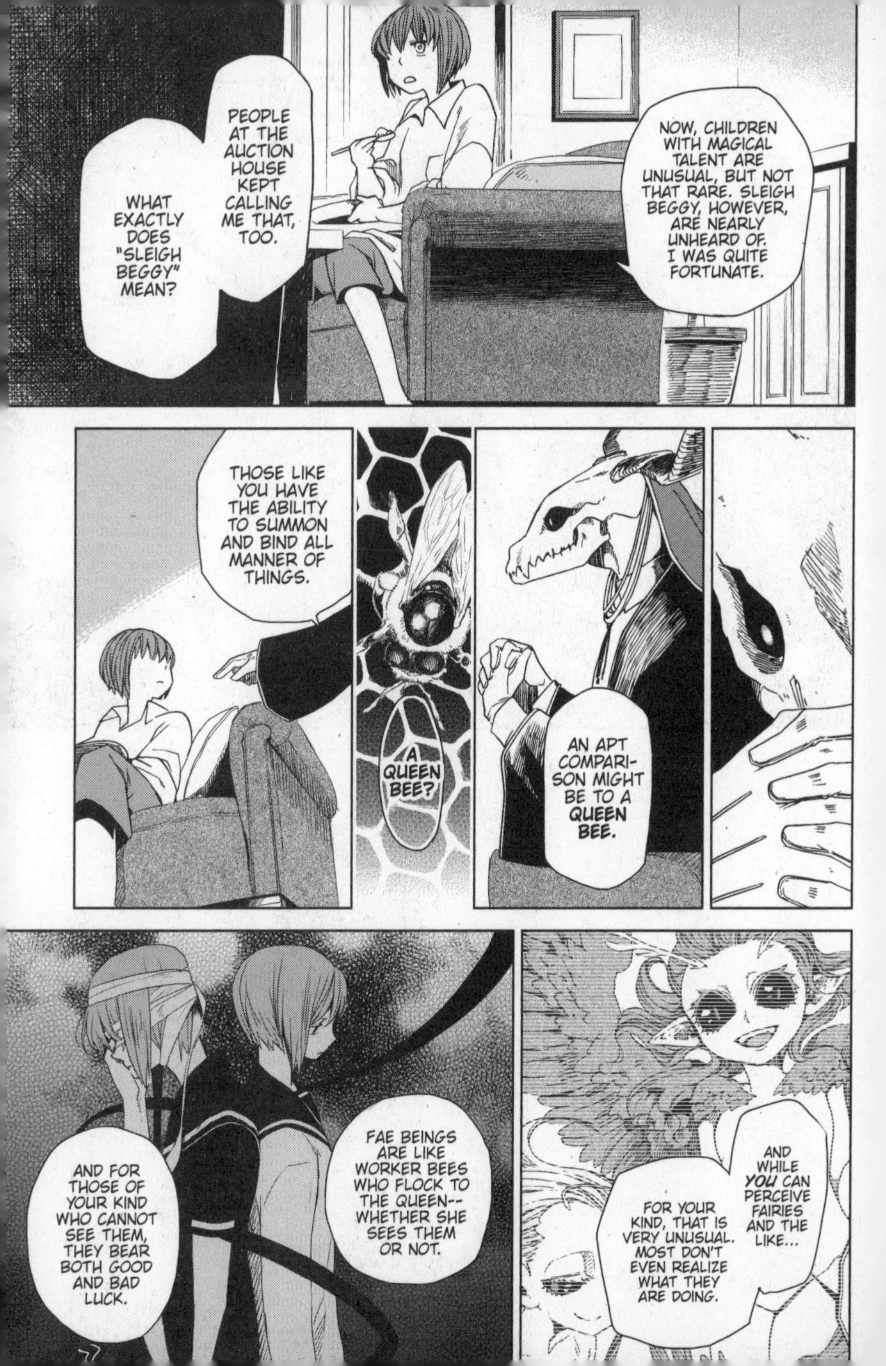
NOW, CHILDREN WITH MAGICAL TALENT ARE UNUSUAL, BUT NOT THAT RARE. SLEIGH BEGGY, HOWEVER, ARE NEARLY UNHEARD OF. I WAS QUITE FORTUNATE.
PEOPLE AT THE AUCTION HOUSE KEPT CALLING ME THAT, TOO.
WHAT EXACTLY DOES "SLEIGH BEGGY" MEAN?
AN APT COMPARISON MIGHT BE TO A QUEEN BEE.
A QUEEN BEE?
THOSE LIKE YOU HAVE THE ABILITY TO SUMMON AND BIND ALL MANNER OF THINGS.
AND WHILE YOU CAN PERCEIVE FAIRIES AND THE LIKE...
FOR YOUR KIND, THAT IS VERY UNUSUAL. MOST DON'T EVEN REALIZE WHAT THEY ARE DOING.
FAE BEINGS ARE LIKE WORKER BEES WHO FLOCK TO THE QUEEN--WHETHER SHE SEES THEM OR NOT.
AND FOR THOSE OF YOUR KIND WHO CANNOT SEE THEM, THEY BEAR BOTH GOOD AND BAD LUCK.

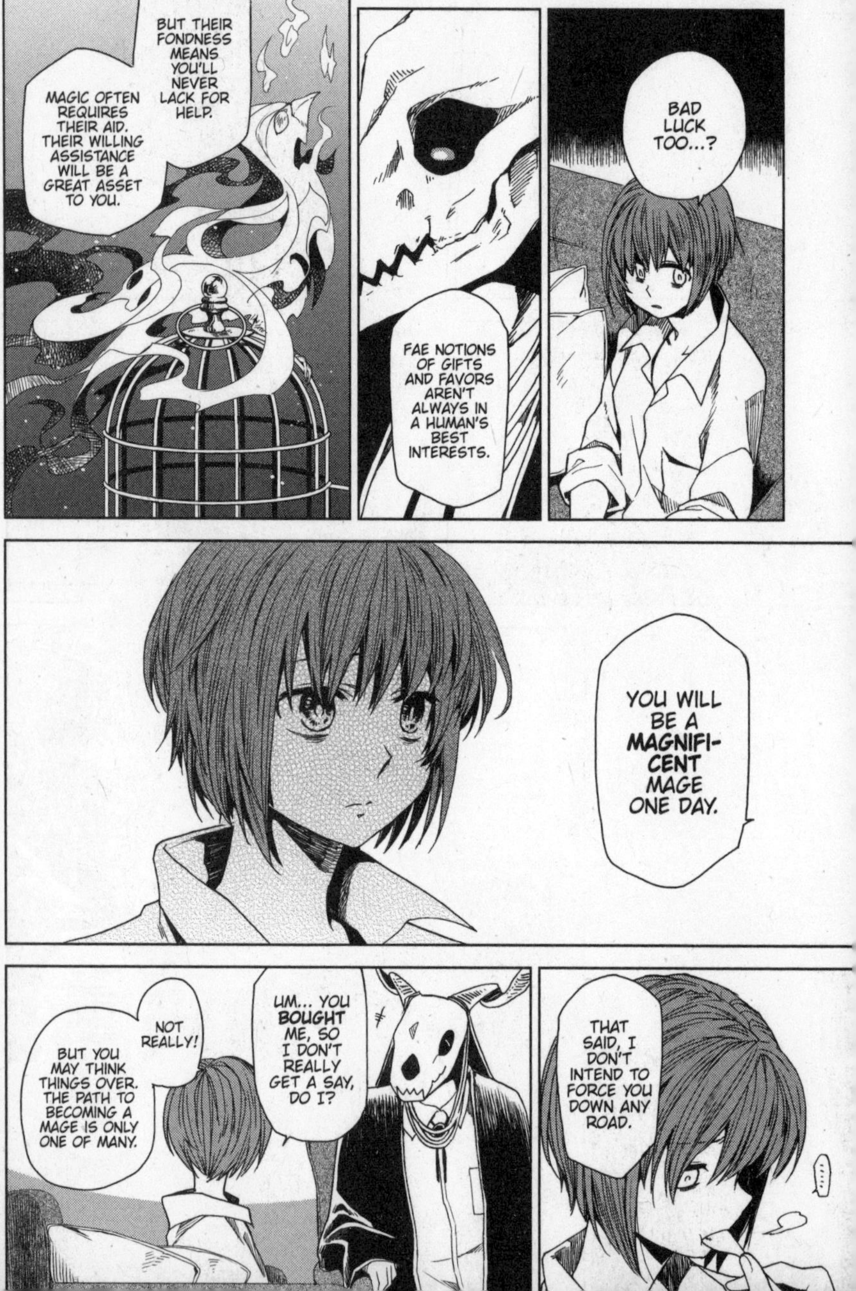
BAD LUCK TOO...?
FAE NOTIONS OF GIFTS AND FAVORS AREN'T ALWAYS IN A HUMAN'S BEST INTERESTS.
BUT THEIR FONDNESS MEANS YOU'LL NEVER LACK FOR HELP.
MAGIC OFTEN REQUIRES THEIR AID. THEIR WILLING ASSISTANCE WILL BE A GREAT ASSET TO YOU.
YOU WILL BE A **MAGNIFICENT** MAGE ONE DAY.
THAT SAID, I DON'T INTEND TO FORCE YOU DOWN ANY ROAD.
.....
UM... YOU **BOUGHT** ME, SO I DON'T REALLY GET A SAY, DO I?
NOT REALLY!
BUT YOU MAY THINK THINGS OVER. THE PATH TO BECOMING A MAGE IS ONLY ONE OF MANY.

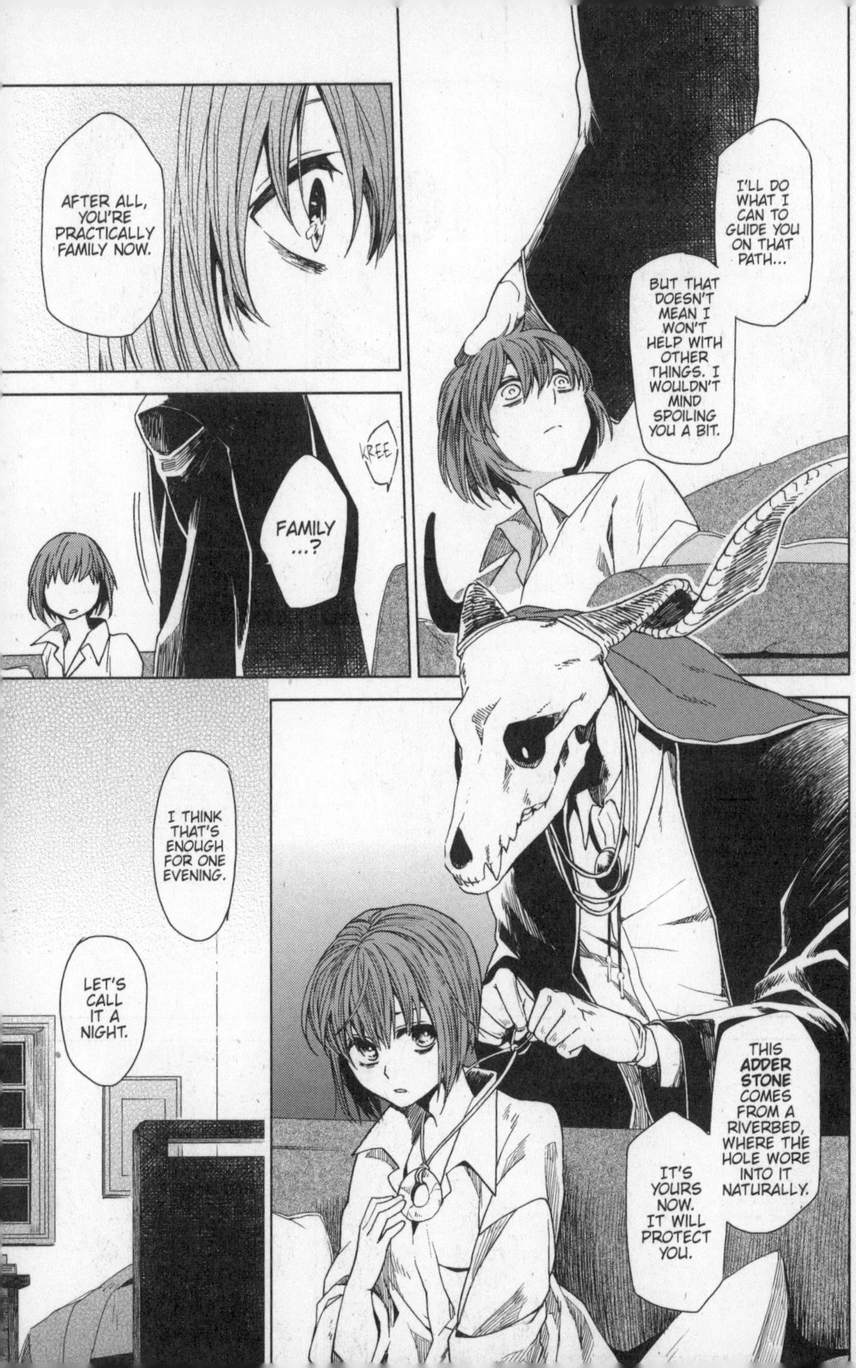
I'LL DO WHAT I CAN TO GUIDE YOU ON THAT PATH...
BUT THAT DOESN'T MEAN I WON'T HELP WITH OTHER THINGS. I WOULDN'T MIND SPOILING YOU A BIT.
AFTER ALL, YOU'RE PRACTICALLY FAMILY NOW.
KREE
FAMILY ...?
THIS ADDER STONE COMES FROM A RIVERBED, WHERE THE HOLE WORE INTO IT NATURALLY.
IT'S YOURS NOW. IT WILL PROTECT YOU.
I THINK THAT'S ENOUGH FOR ONE EVENING.
LET'S CALL IT A NIGHT.

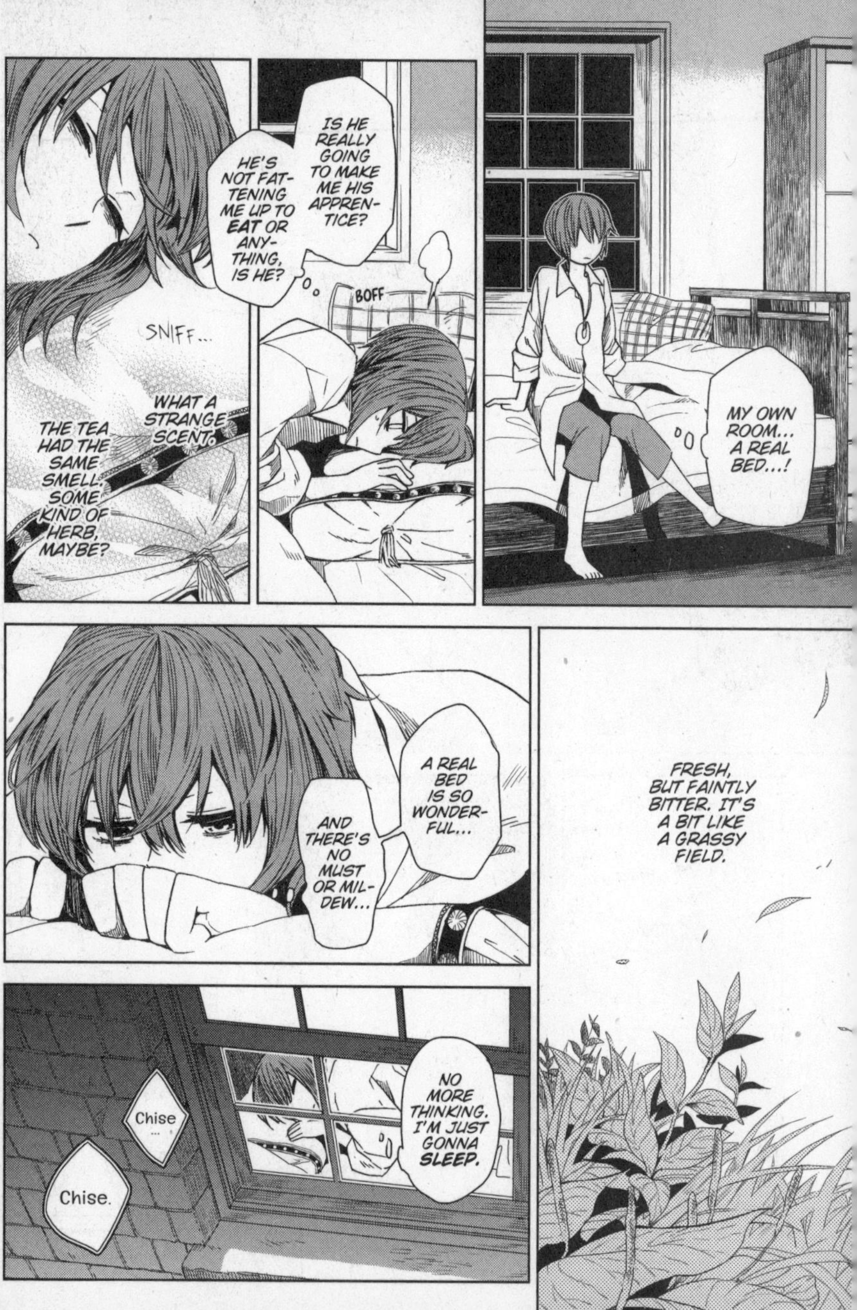
MY OWN ROOM... A REAL BED...!
IS HE REALLY GOING TO MAKE ME HIS APPRENTICE?
HE'S NOT FATTENING ME UP TO EAT OR ANYTHING, IS HE?
BOFF
SNIFF...
WHAT A STRANGE SCENT.
THE TEA HAD THE SAME SMELL. SOME KIND OF HERB, MAYBE?
FRESH, BUT FAINTLY BITTER. IT'S A BIT LIKE A GRASSY FIELD.
A REAL BED IS SO WONDERFUL...
AND THERE'S NO MUST OR MILDEW...
NO MORE THINKING. I'M JUST GONNA SLEEP.
Chise...
Chise.

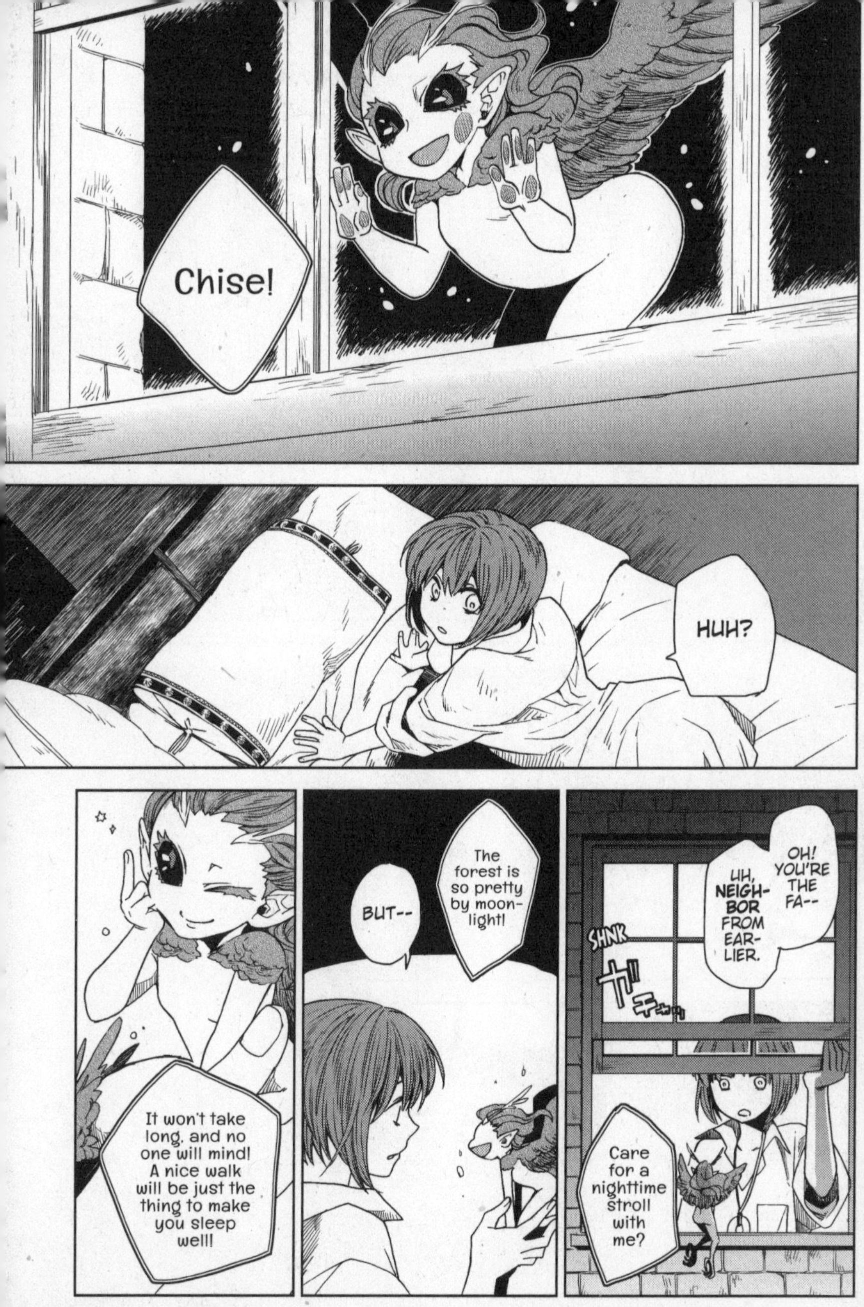
Chise!
HUH?
OH! YOU'RE THE FA--
UH, NEIGHBOR FROM EARLIER.
SHNK
Care for a nighttime stroll with me?
The forest is so pretty by moonlight!
BUT--
It won't take long, and no one will mind! A nice walk will be just the thing to make you sleep well!

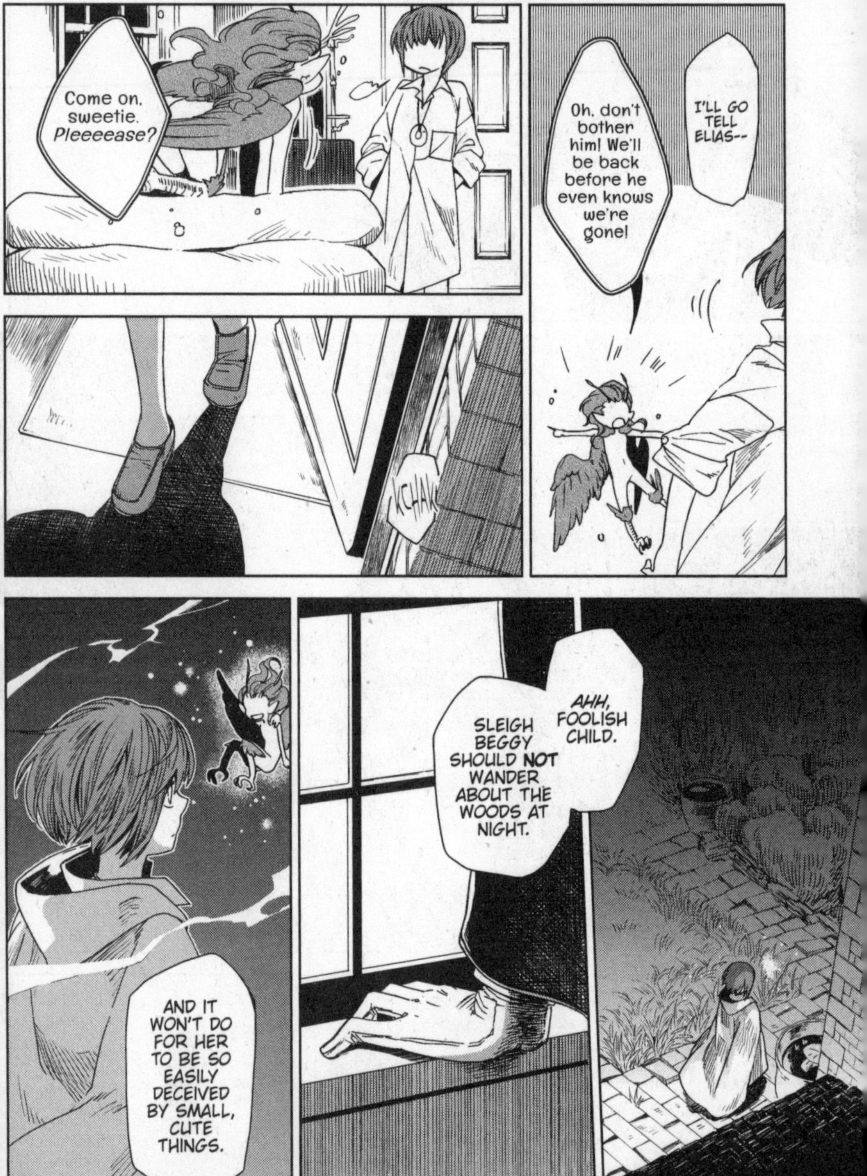
I'LL GO TELL ELIAS--
Oh, don't bother him! We'll be back before he even knows we're gone!
Come on, sweetie. *Pleeeease?*
KCHAK
AHH, FOOLISH CHILD.
SLEIGH BEGGY SHOULD **NOT** WANDER ABOUT THE WOODS AT NIGHT.
AND IT WON'T DO FOR HER TO BE SO EASILY DECEIVED BY SMALL, CUTE THINGS.

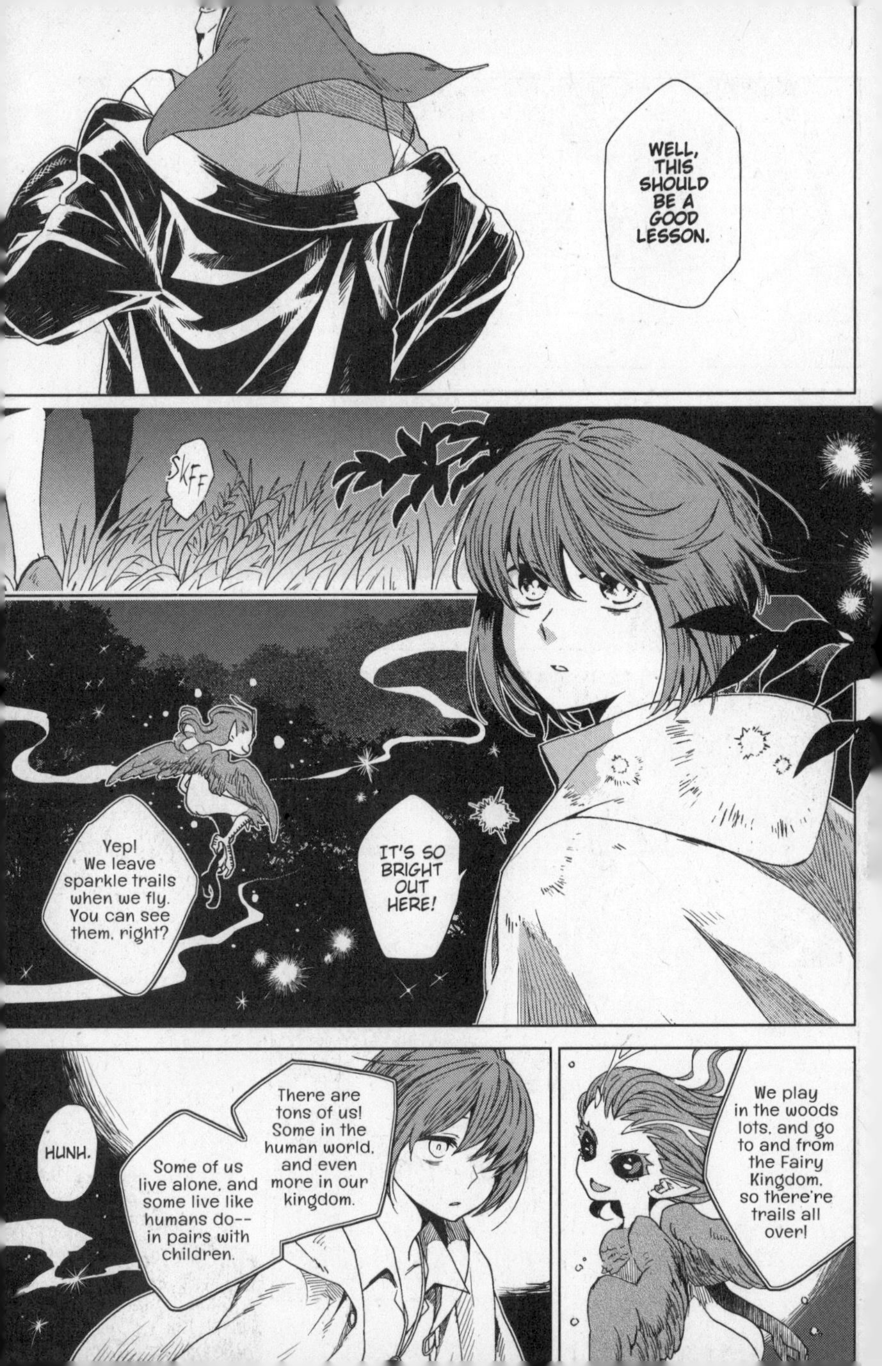
WELL, THIS SHOULD BE A GOOD LESSON.
SKFF
IT'S SO BRIGHT OUT HERE!
Yep! We leave sparkle trails when we fly. You can see them, right?
We play in the woods lots, and go to and from the Fairy Kingdom, so there're trails all over!
There are tons of us! Some in the human world, and even more in our kingdom.
Some of us live alone, and some live like humans do-- in pairs with children.
HUNH.

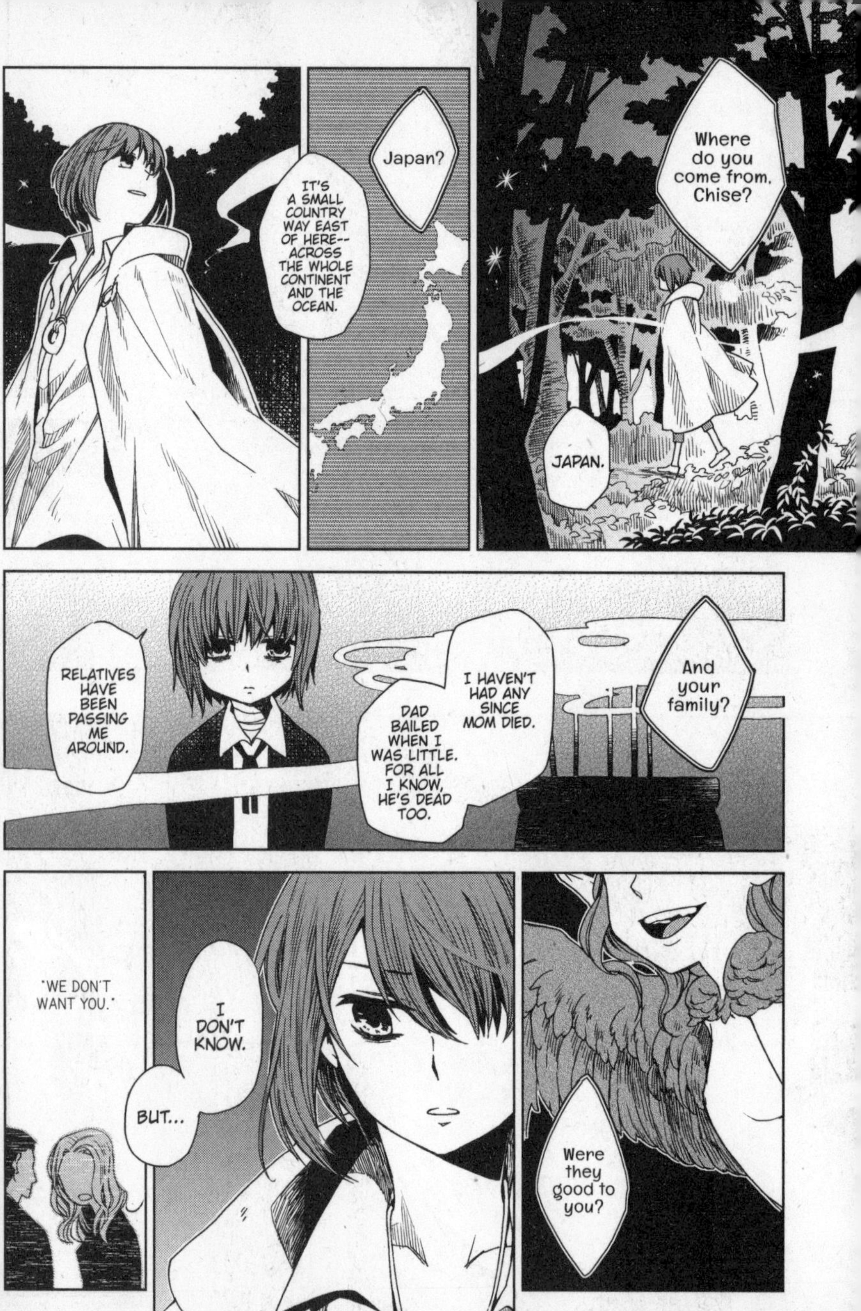
Where do you come from, Chise?
JAPAN.
Japan?
IT'S A SMALL COUNTRY WAY EAST OF HERE--ACROSS THE WHOLE CONTINENT AND THE OCEAN.
And your family?
I HAVEN'T HAD ANY SINCE MOM DIED.
DAD BAILED WHEN I WAS LITTLE. FOR ALL I KNOW, HE'S DEAD TOO.
RELATIVES HAVE BEEN PASSING ME AROUND.
Were they good to you?
I DON'T KNOW.
BUT...
"WE DON'T WANT YOU."

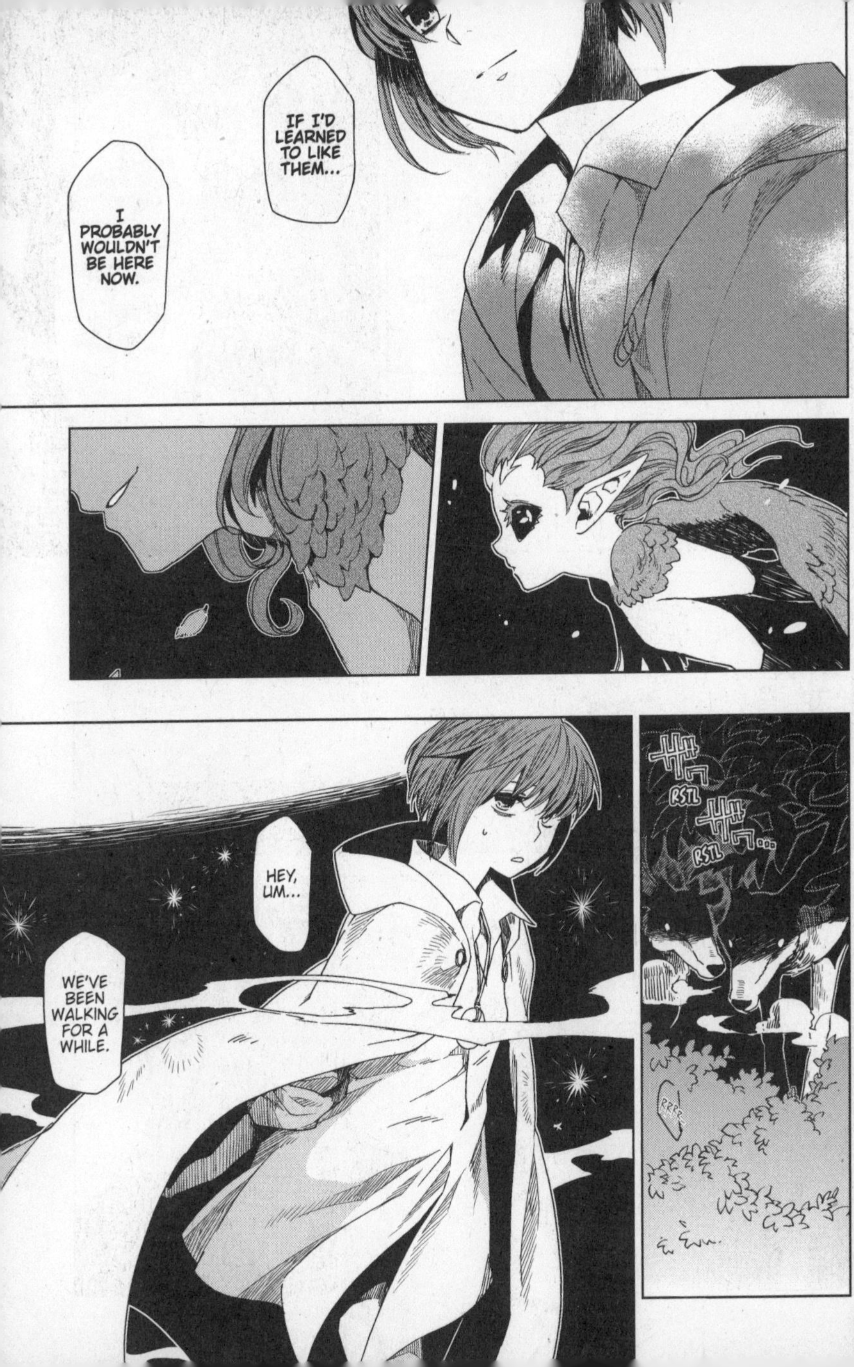
IF I'D LEARNED TO LIKE THEM...
I PROBABLY WOULDN'T BE HERE NOW.
RSTL
RSTL...
RRRR...
HEY, UM...
WE'VE BEEN WALKING FOR A WHILE.

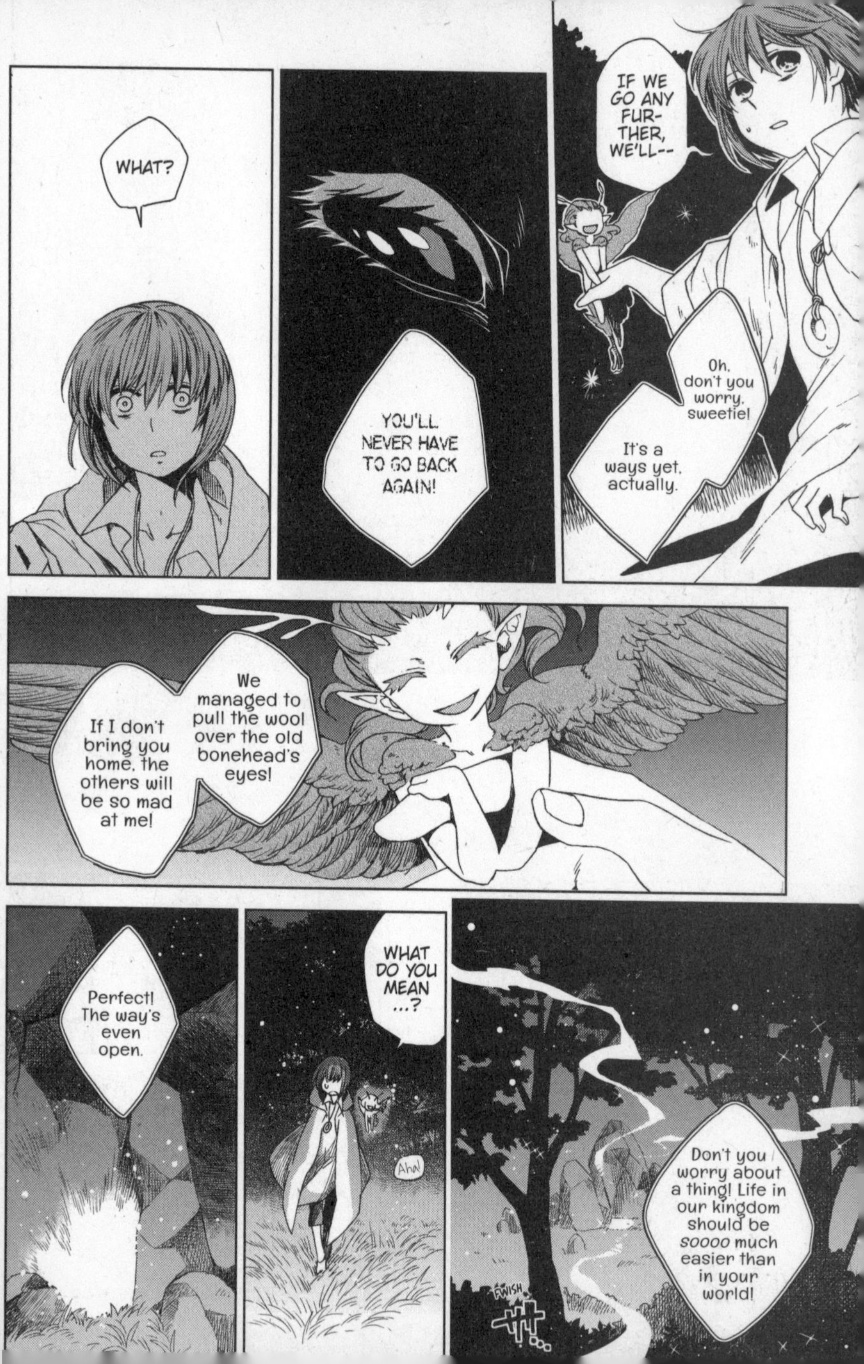
IF WE GO ANY FURTHER, WE'LL--
Oh, don't you worry, sweetie!
It's a ways yet, actually.
YOU'LL NEVER HAVE TO GO BACK AGAIN!
WHAT?
We managed to pull the wool over the old bonehead's eyes!
If I don't bring you home, the others will be so mad at me!
Don't you worry about a thing! Life in our kingdom should be *soooo* much easier than in your world!
FWISH
WHAT DO YOU MEAN ...?
Aha!
Perfect! The way's even open.

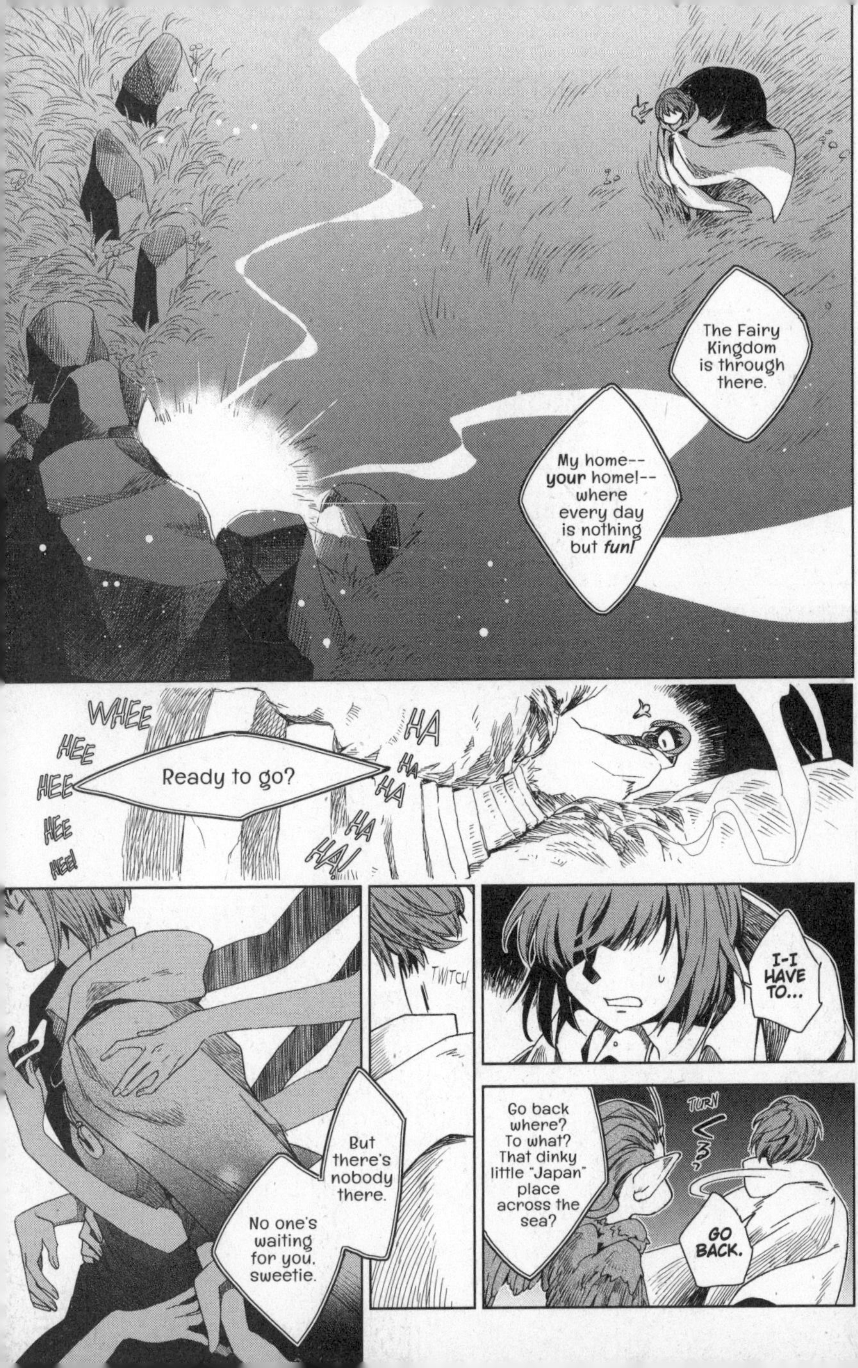
The Fairy Kingdom is through there.
My home-- **your** home!-- where every day is nothing but ***fun!***
HA HA HA HA HA!
Ready to go?
WHEE HEE HEE HEE HEE!
I-I HAVE TO...
TURN
GO BACK.
Go back where? To what? That dinky little "Japan" place across the sea?
TWITCH
But there's nobody there.
No one's waiting for you, sweetie.

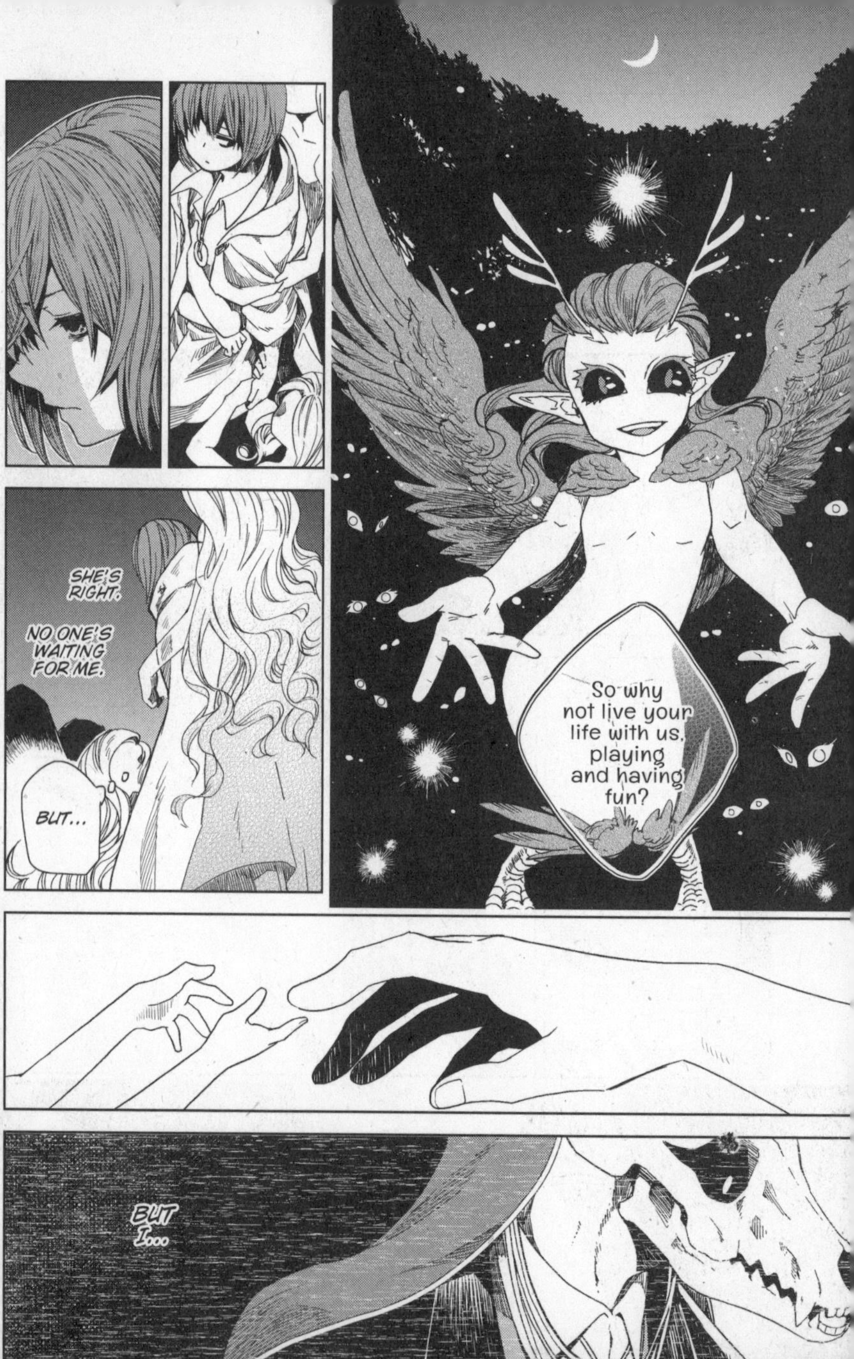
So why not live your life with us, playing and having fun?
SHE'S RIGHT.
NO ONE'S WAITING FOR ME.
BUT...
BUT I...

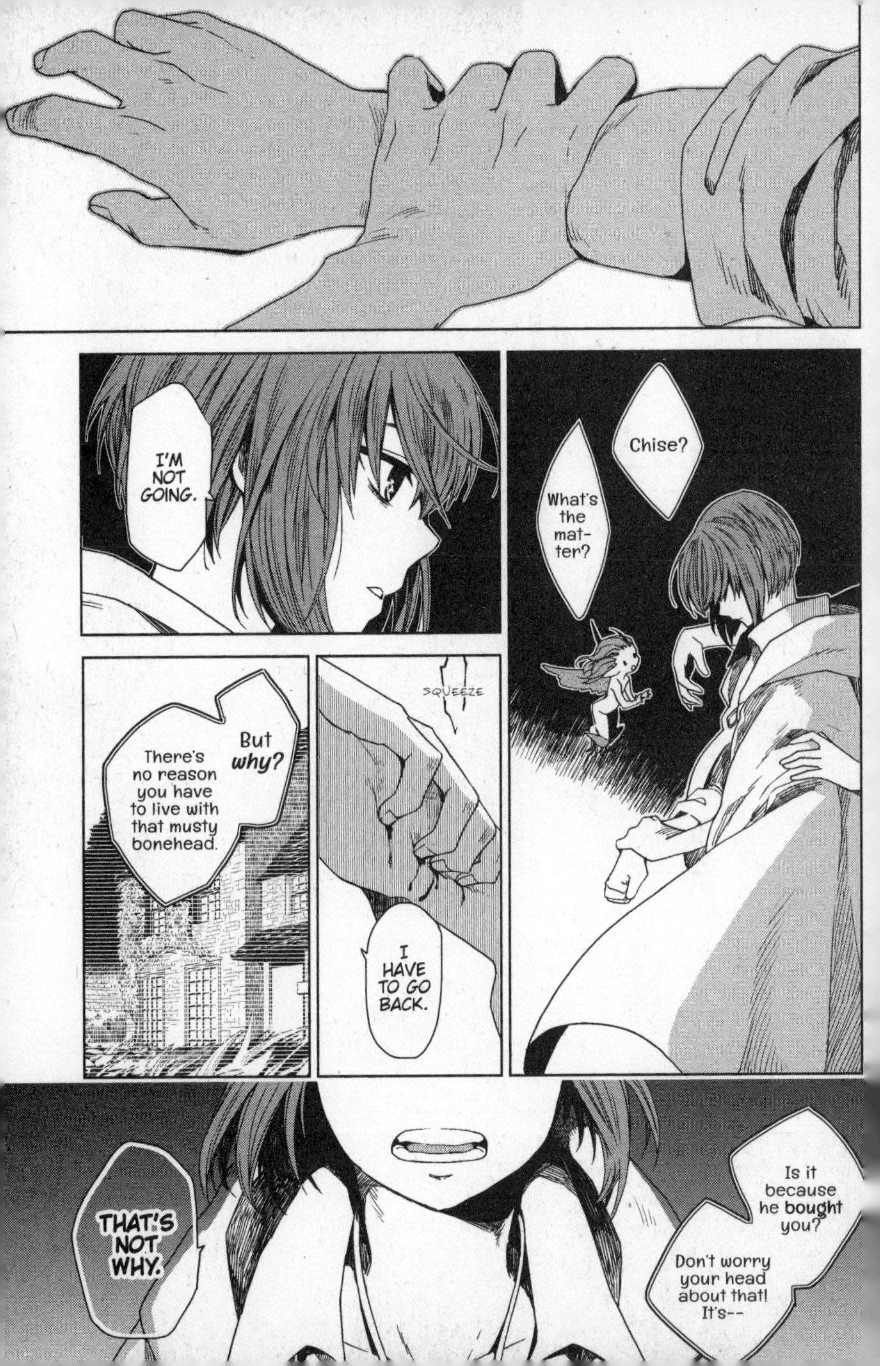
Chise?
What's the matter?
I'M NOT GOING.
SQUEEZE
I HAVE TO GO BACK.
But why?
There's no reason you have to live with that musty bonehead.
Is it because he bought you?
Don't worry your head about that! It's--
THAT'S NOT WHY.

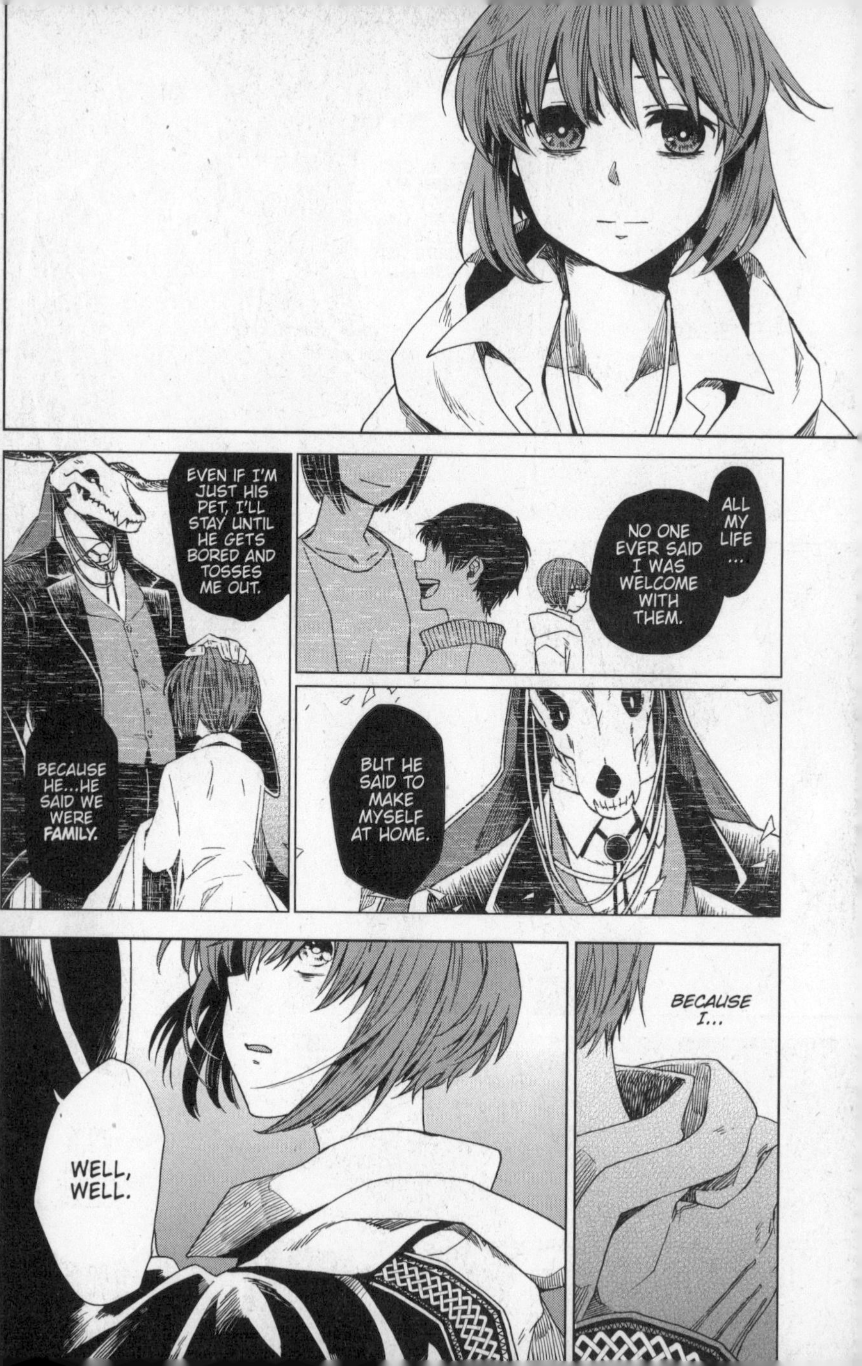
ALL MY LIFE...
NO ONE EVER SAID I WAS WELCOME WITH THEM.
BUT HE SAID TO MAKE MYSELF AT HOME.
EVEN IF I'M JUST HIS PET, I'LL STAY UNTIL HE GETS BORED AND TOSSES ME OUT.
BECAUSE HE...HE SAID WE WERE **FAMILY.**
BECAUSE I...
WELL, WELL.

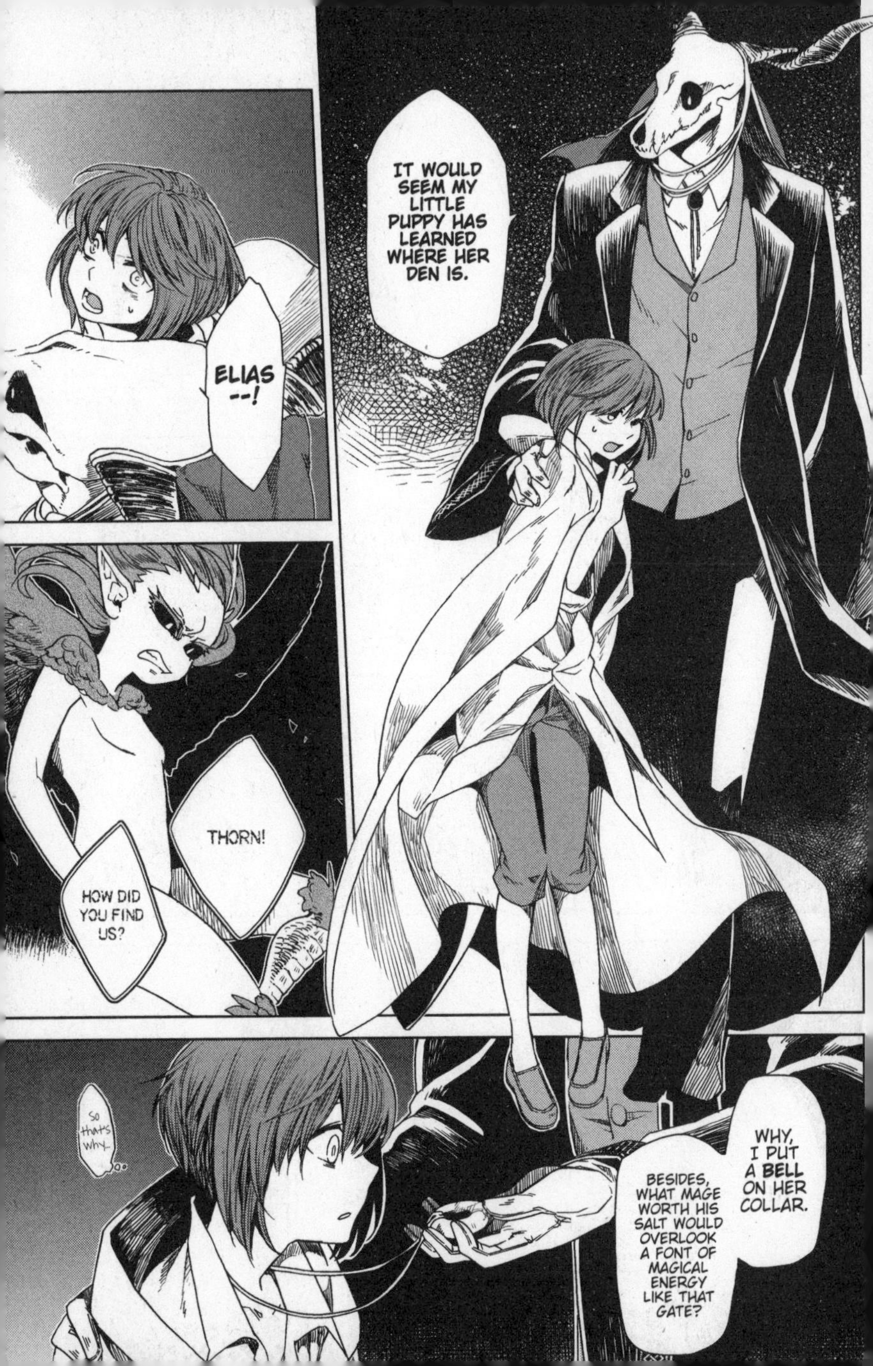
IT WOULD SEEM MY LITTLE PUPPY HAS LEARNED WHERE HER DEN IS.
ELIAS --!
THORN!
HOW DID YOU FIND US?
WHY, I PUT A BELL ON HER COLLAR.
BESIDES, WHAT MAGE WORTH HIS SALT WOULD OVERLOOK A FONT OF MAGICAL ENERGY LIKE THAT GATE?
So that's why...

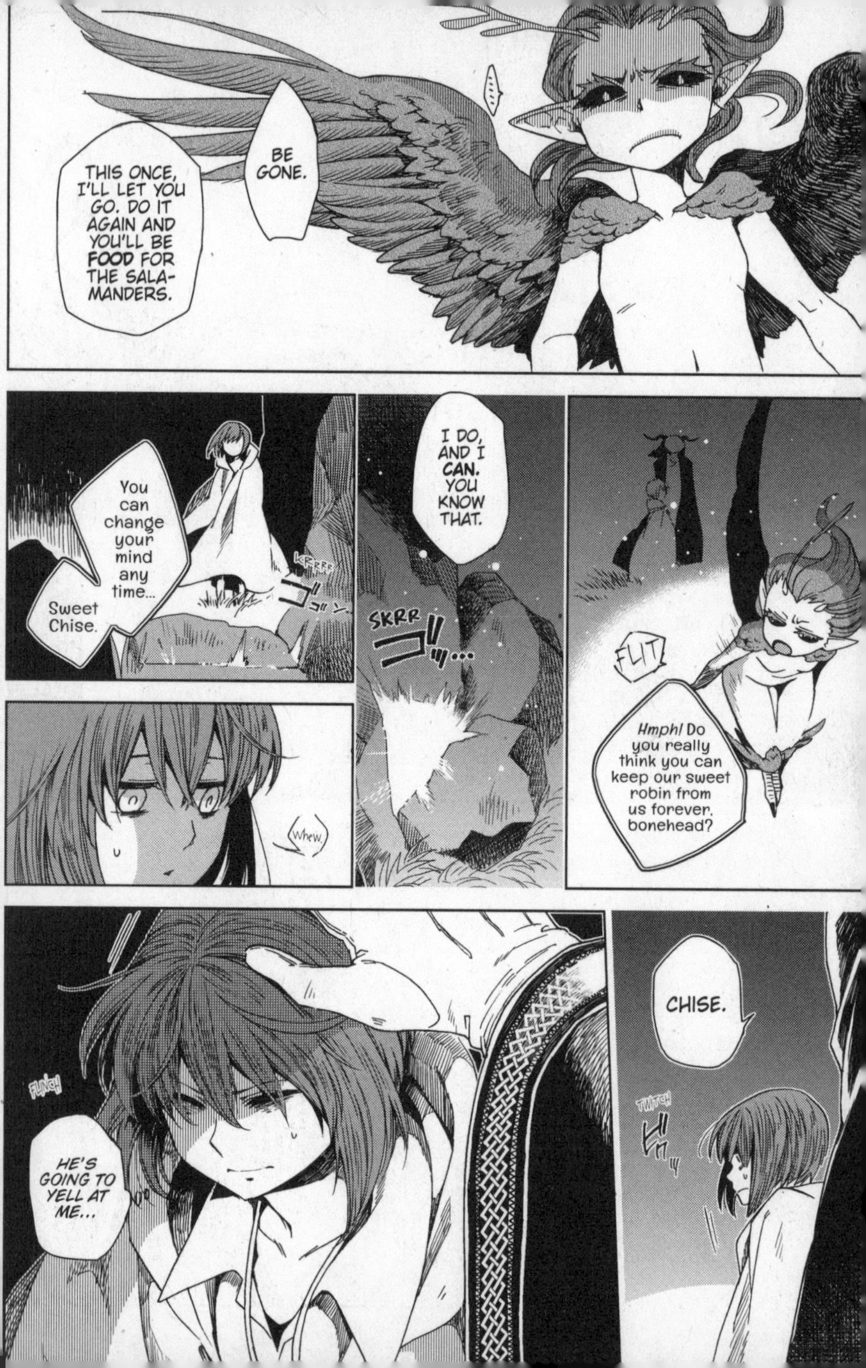
...
BE GONE.
THIS ONCE, I'LL LET YOU GO. DO IT AGAIN AND YOU'LL BE **FOOD** FOR THE SALA-MANDERS.
FLIT
Hmph! Do you really think you can keep our sweet robin from us forever, bonehead?
I DO, AND I **CAN.** YOU KNOW THAT.
SKRR
You can change your mind any time... Sweet Chise.
KRRRR
Whew.
CHISE.
TWITCH
FLINCH
HE'S GOING TO YELL AT ME...

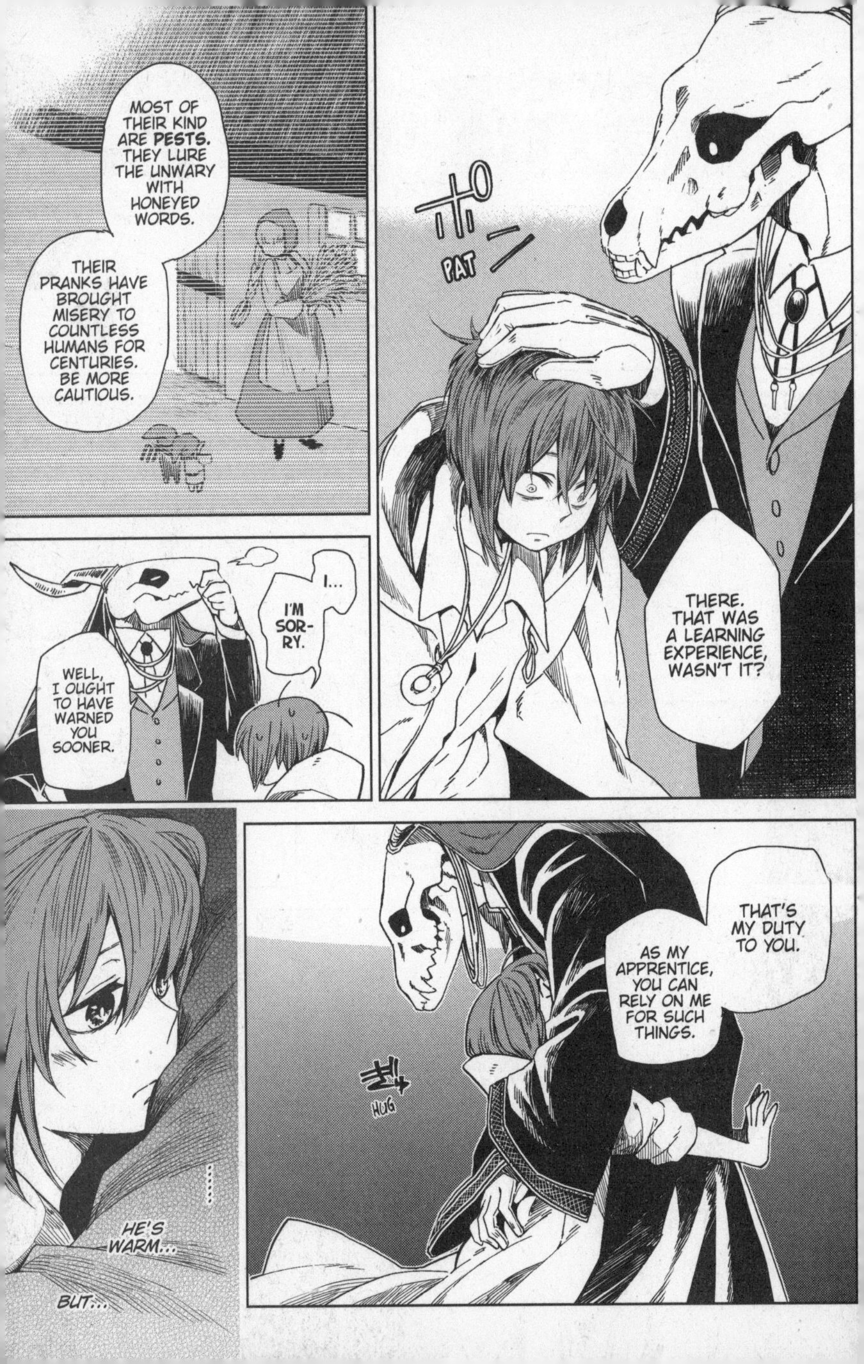
PAT
THERE. THAT WAS A LEARNING EXPERIENCE, WASN'T IT?
MOST OF THEIR KIND ARE **PESTS.** THEY LURE THE UNWARY WITH HONEYED WORDS.
THEIR PRANKS HAVE BROUGHT MISERY TO COUNTLESS HUMANS FOR CENTURIES. BE MORE CAUTIOUS.
I... I'M SOR-RY.
WELL, I OUGHT TO HAVE WARNED YOU SOONER.
THAT'S MY DUTY TO YOU.
AS MY APPRENTICE, YOU CAN RELY ON ME FOR SUCH THINGS.
HUG
......
HE'S WARM...
BUT...

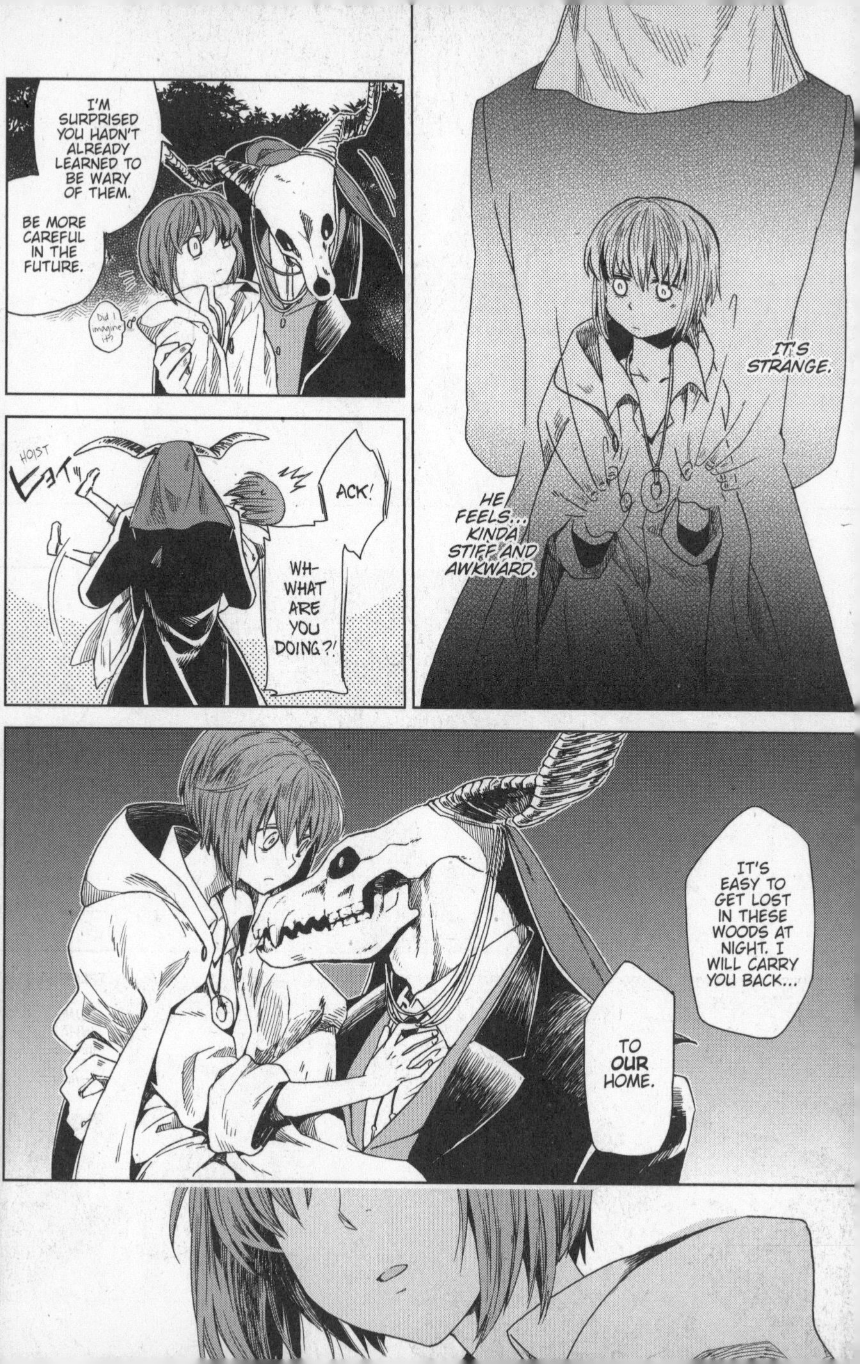
IT'S STRANGE.
HE FEELS... KINDA STIFF AND AWKWARD.
I'M SURPRISED YOU HADN'T ALREADY LEARNED TO BE WARY OF THEM.
BE MORE CAREFUL IN THE FUTURE.
Did I imagine it?
HOIST
ヒョイッ
ACK!
WH-WHAT ARE YOU DOING?!
IT'S EASY TO GET LOST IN THESE WOODS AT NIGHT. I WILL CARRY YOU BACK...
TO **OUR** HOME.

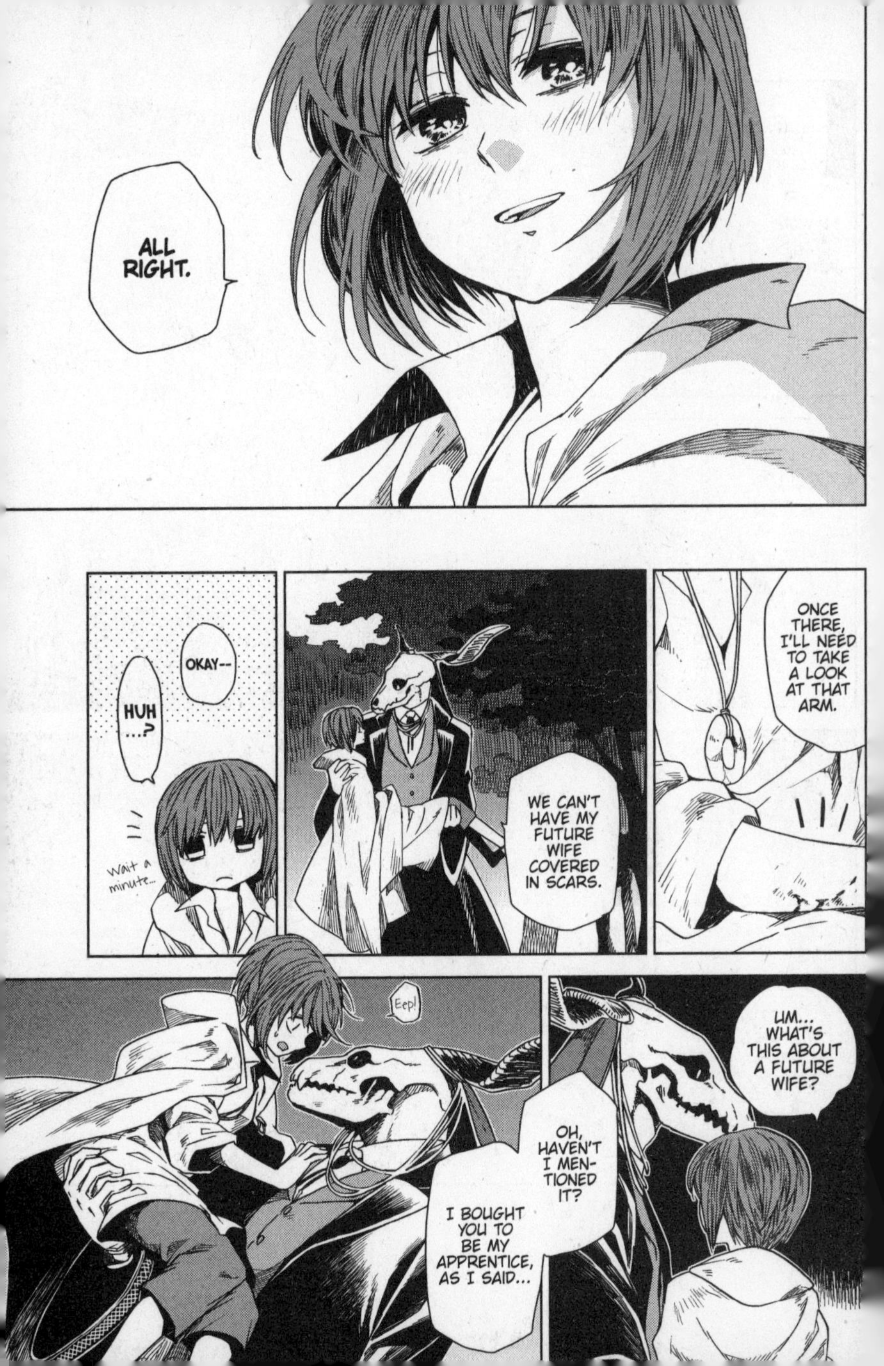
ALL RIGHT.
ONCE THERE, I'LL NEED TO TAKE A LOOK AT THAT ARM.
WE CAN'T HAVE MY FUTURE WIFE COVERED IN SCARS.
OKAY--
HUH ...?
Wait a minute...
UM... WHAT'S THIS ABOUT A FUTURE WIFE?
OH, HAVEN'T I MEN-TIONED IT?
I BOUGHT YOU TO BE MY APPRENTICE, AS I SAID...
Eep!

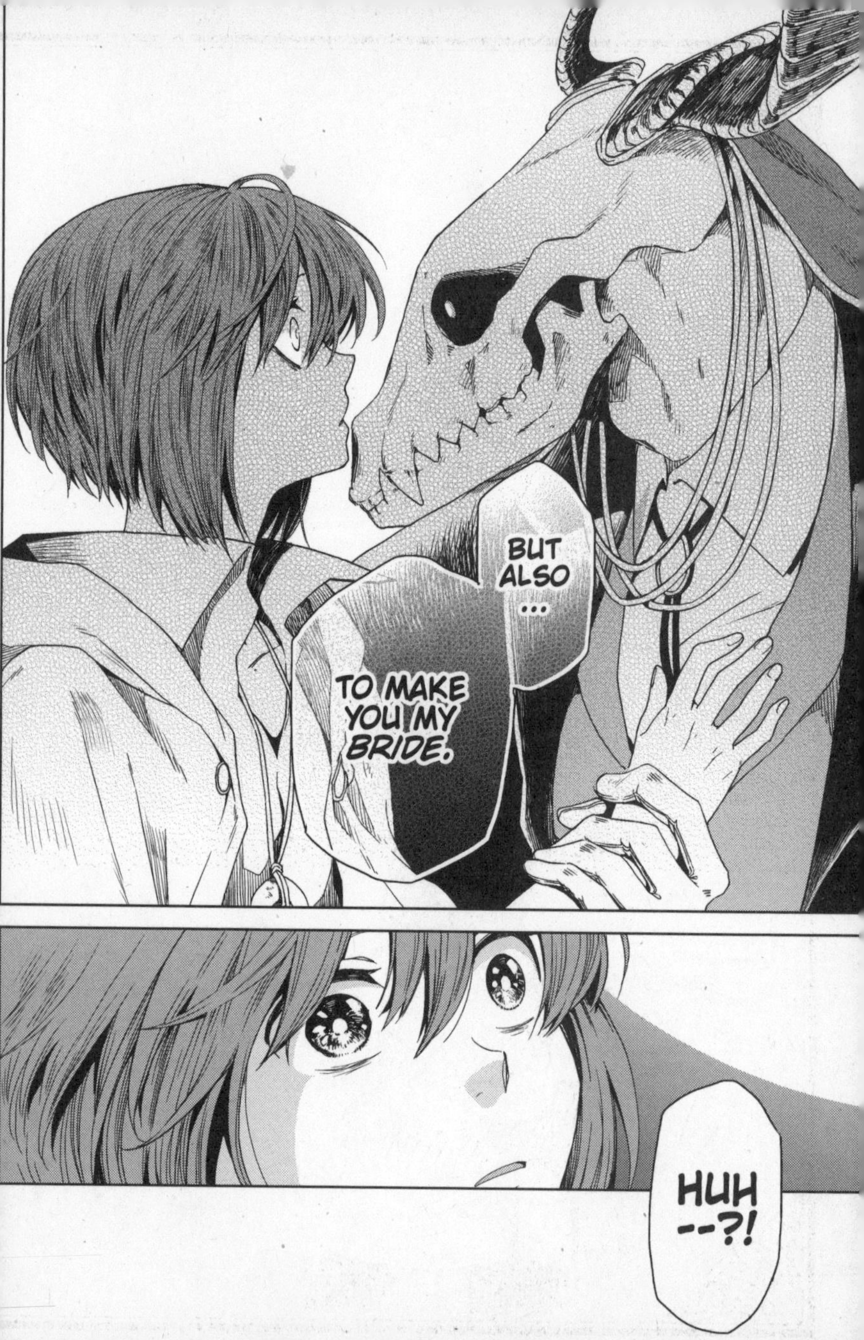
BUT ALSO ...
TO MAKE YOU MY BRIDE.
HUH --?!

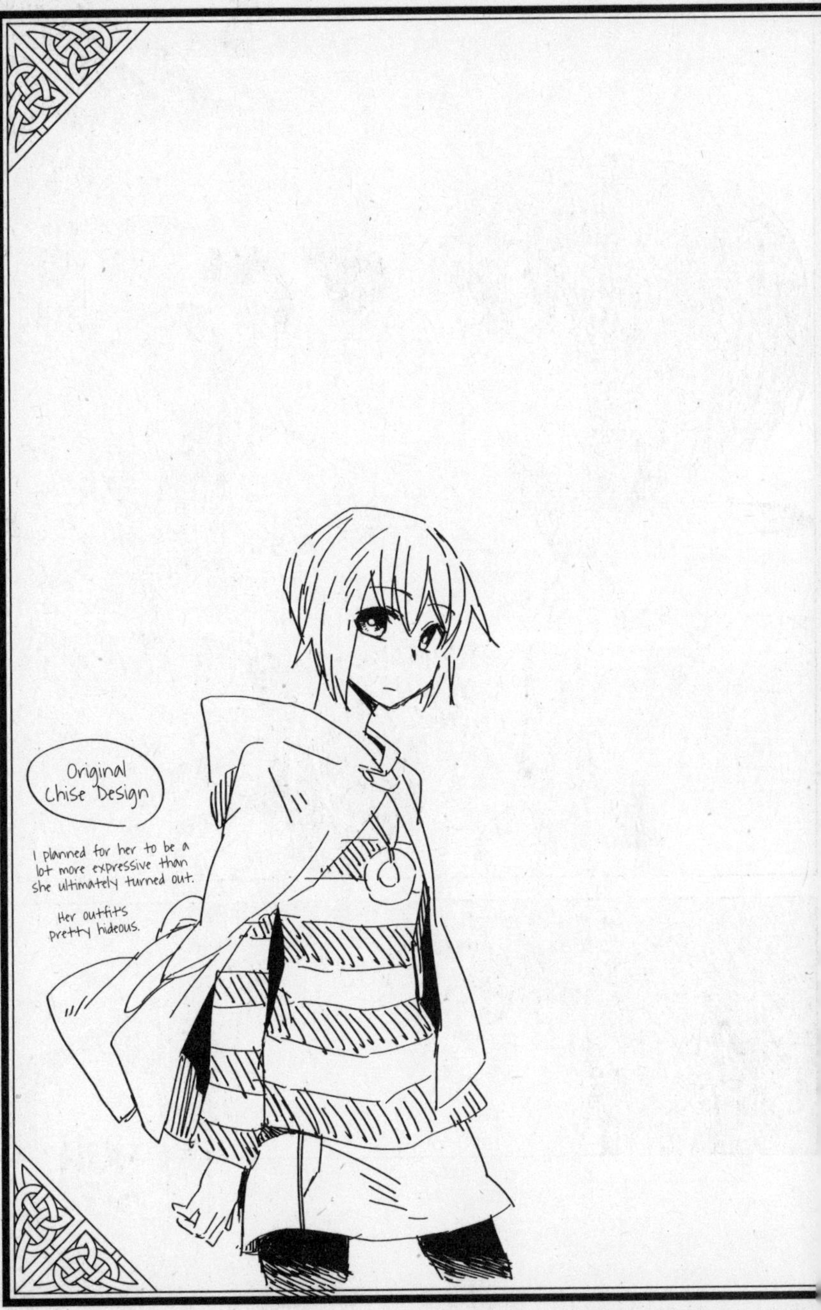
Original Chise Design
I planned for her to be a lot more expressive than she ultimately turned out.
Her outfit's pretty hideous.

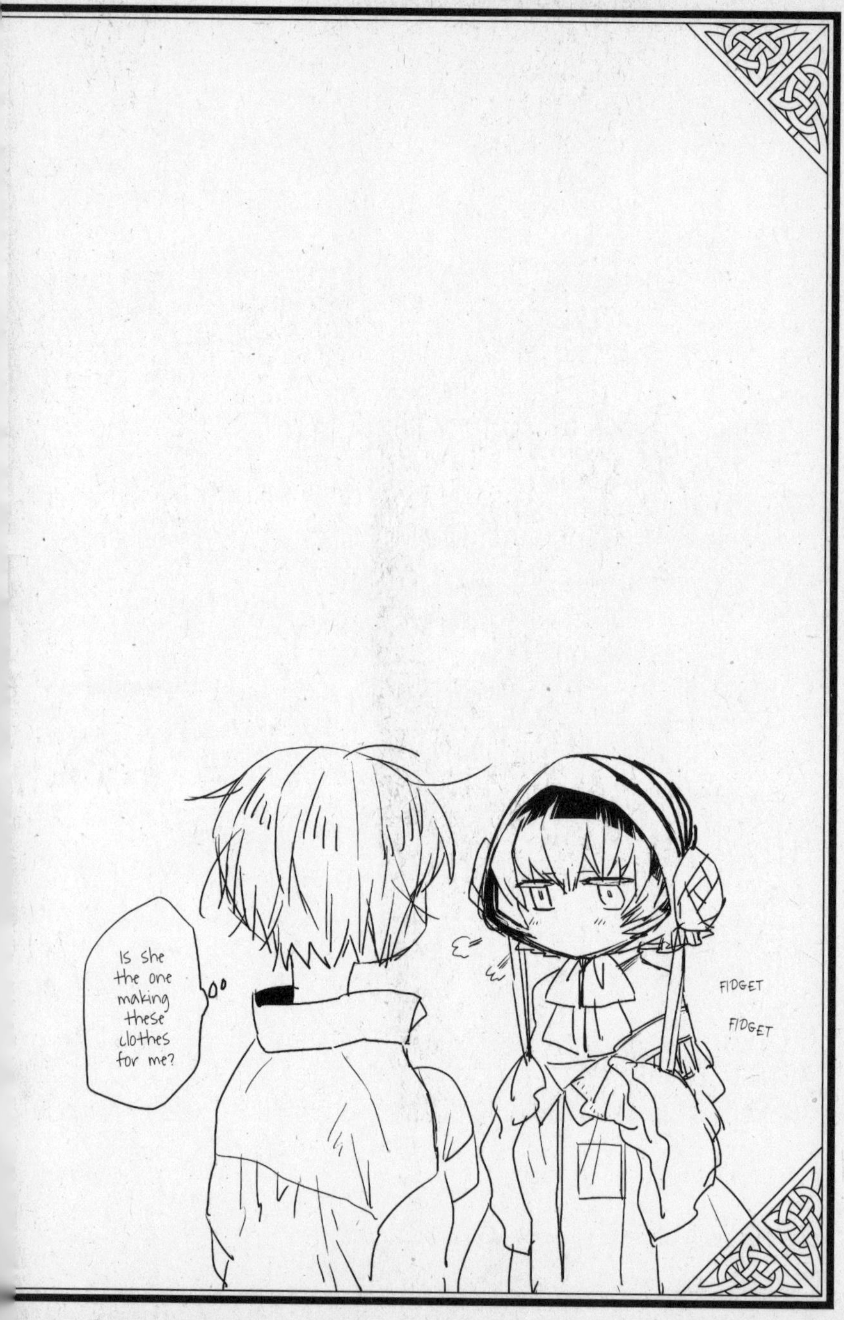
FIDGET
FIDGET
Is she the one making these clothes for me?

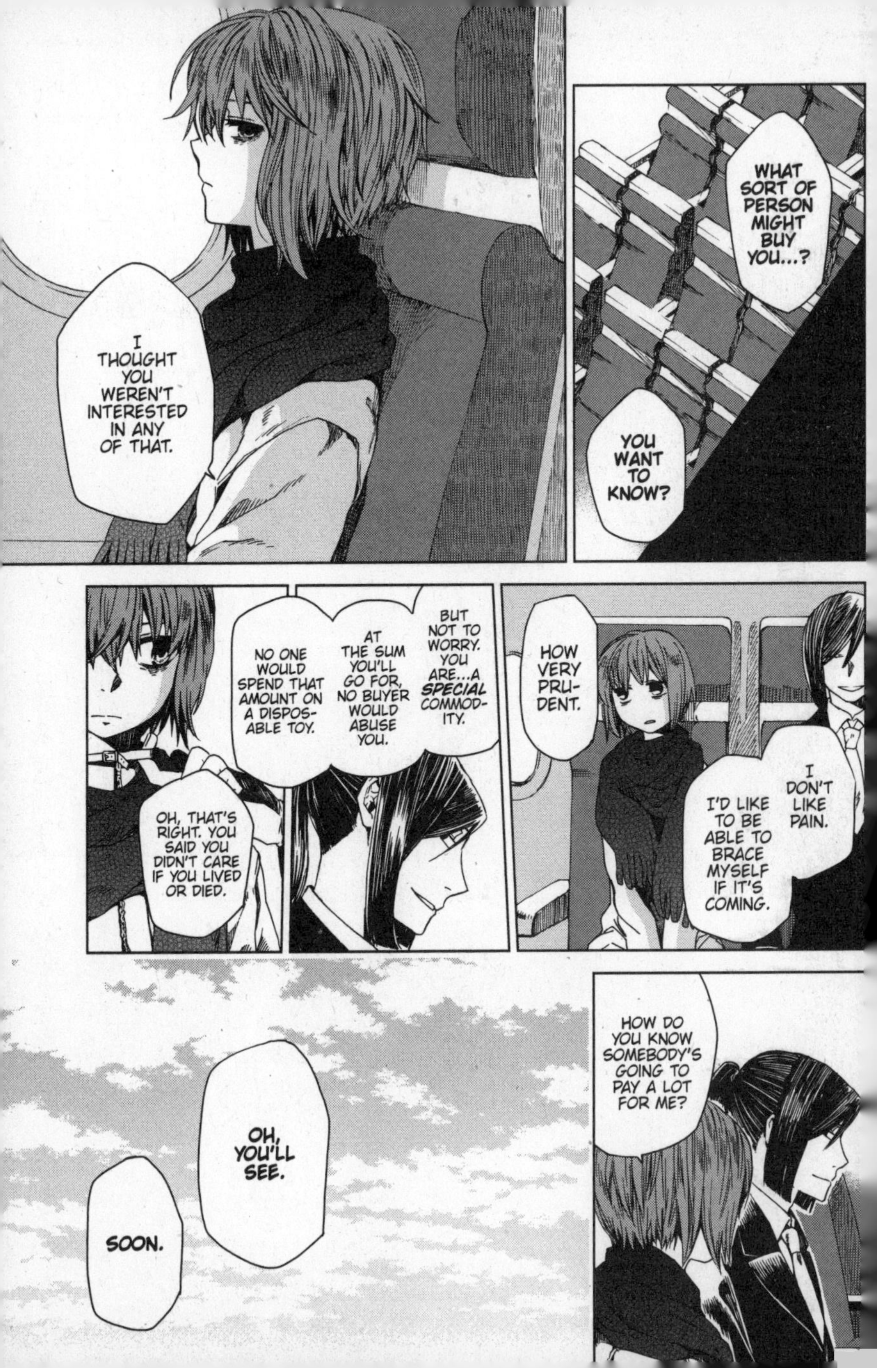
WHAT SORT OF PERSON MIGHT BUY YOU...?
YOU WANT TO KNOW?
I THOUGHT YOU WEREN'T INTERESTED IN ANY OF THAT.
HOW VERY PRUDENT.
I DON'T LIKE PAIN.
I'D LIKE TO BE ABLE TO BRACE MYSELF IF IT'S COMING.
BUT NOT TO WORRY. YOU ARE...A *SPECIAL* COMMODITY.
AT THE SUM YOU'LL GO FOR, NO BUYER WOULD ABUSE YOU.
NO ONE WOULD SPEND THAT AMOUNT ON A DISPOSABLE TOY.
OH, THAT'S RIGHT. YOU SAID YOU DIDN'T CARE IF YOU LIVED OR DIED.
HOW DO YOU KNOW SOMEBODY'S GOING TO PAY A LOT FOR ME?
OH, YOU'LL SEE.
SOON.

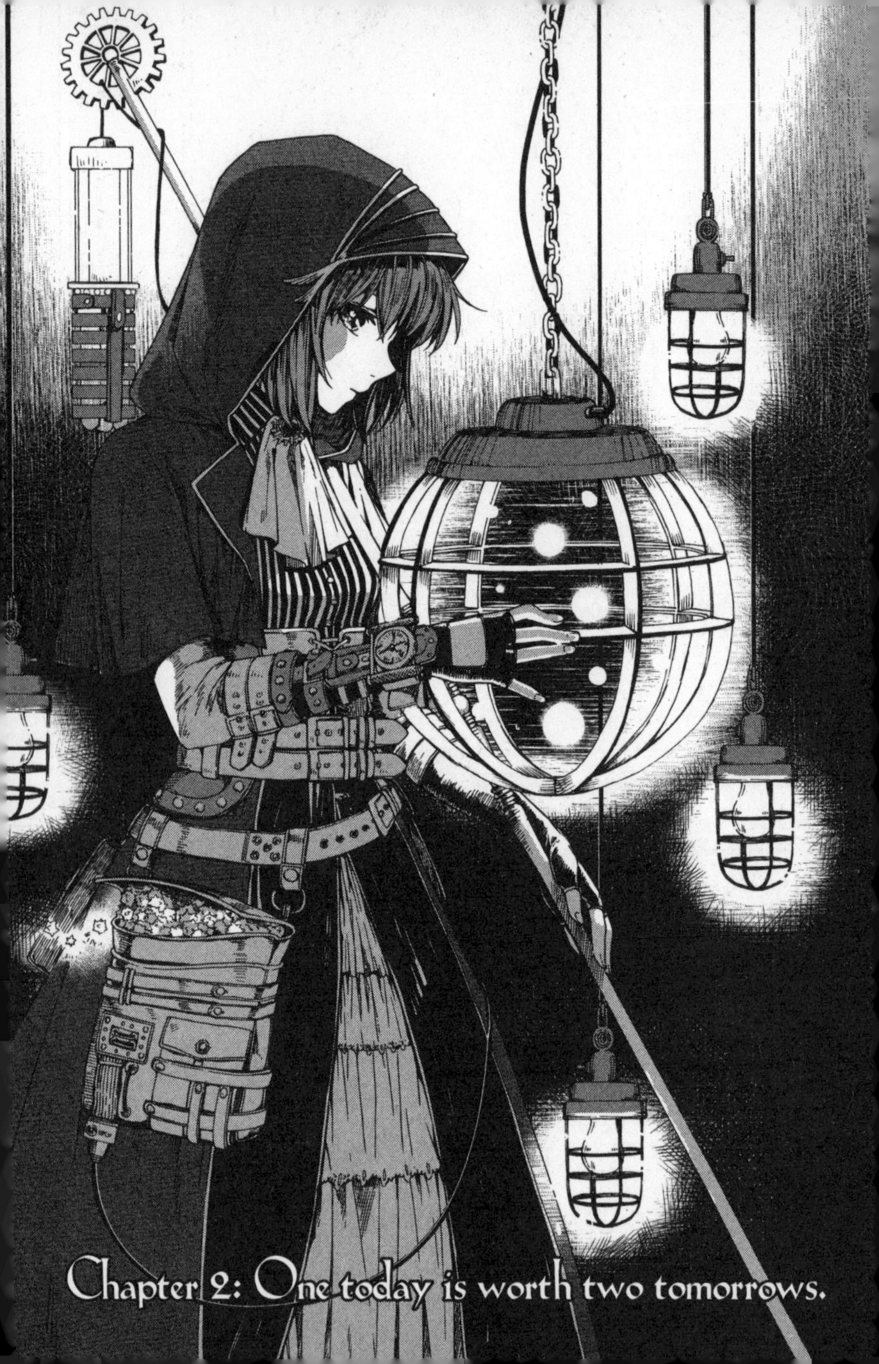
Chapter 2: One today is worth two tomorrows.

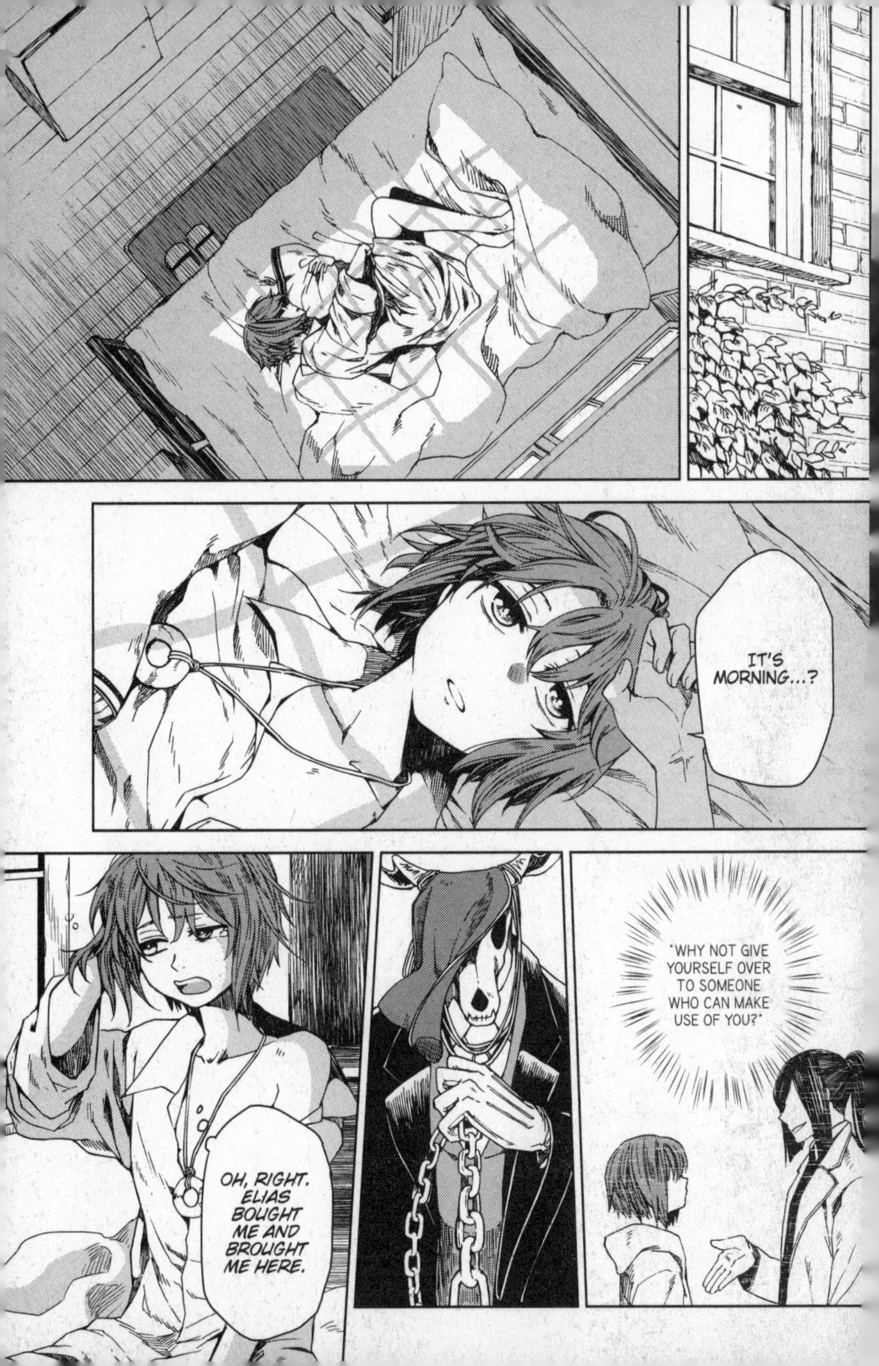
IT'S MORNING...?
"WHY NOT GIVE YOURSELF OVER TO SOMEONE WHO CAN MAKE USE OF YOU?"
OH, RIGHT. ELIAS BOUGHT ME AND BROUGHT ME HERE.

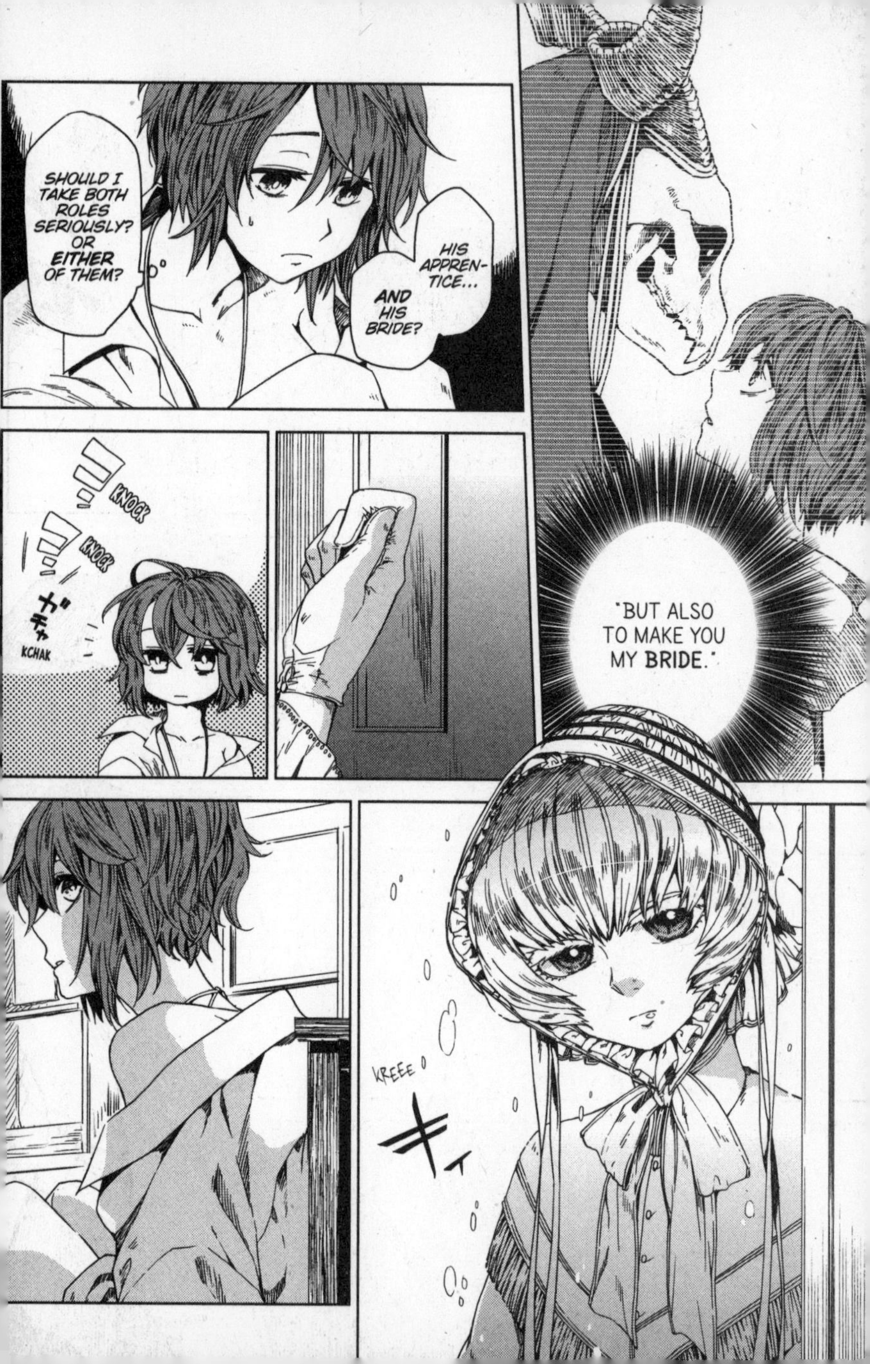
"BUT ALSO TO MAKE YOU MY BRIDE."
HIS APPRENTICE...
AND HIS BRIDE?
SHOULD I TAKE BOTH ROLES SERIOUSLY? OR EITHER OF THEM?
KNOCK
KNOCK
ガチャ
KCHAK
キィ
KREEE

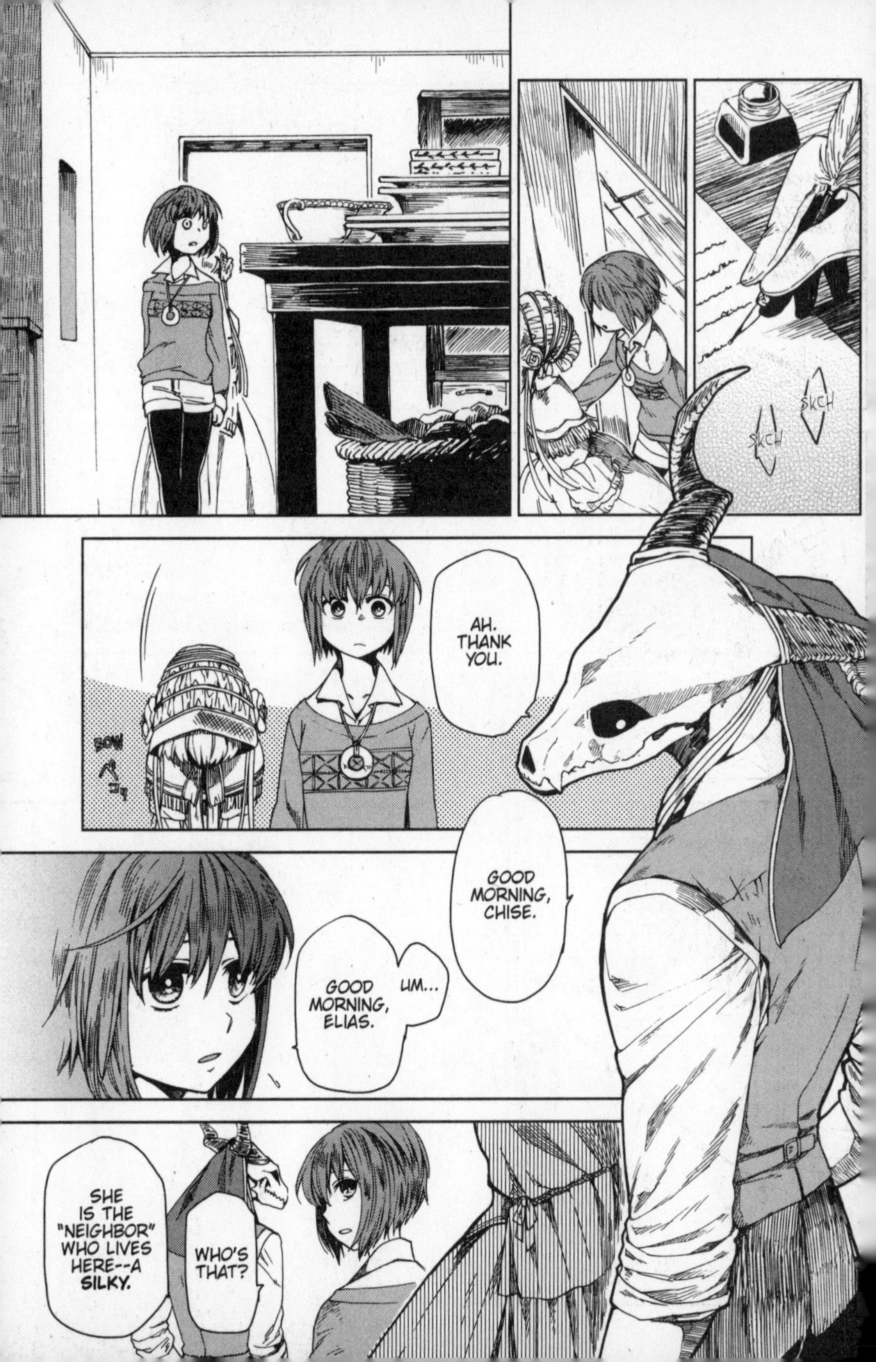
SKCH
SKCH
AH. THANK YOU.
BOW
GOOD MORNING, CHISE.
UM...
GOOD MORNING, ELIAS.
WHO'S THAT?
SHE IS THE "NEIGHBOR" WHO LIVES HERE--A **SILKY.**

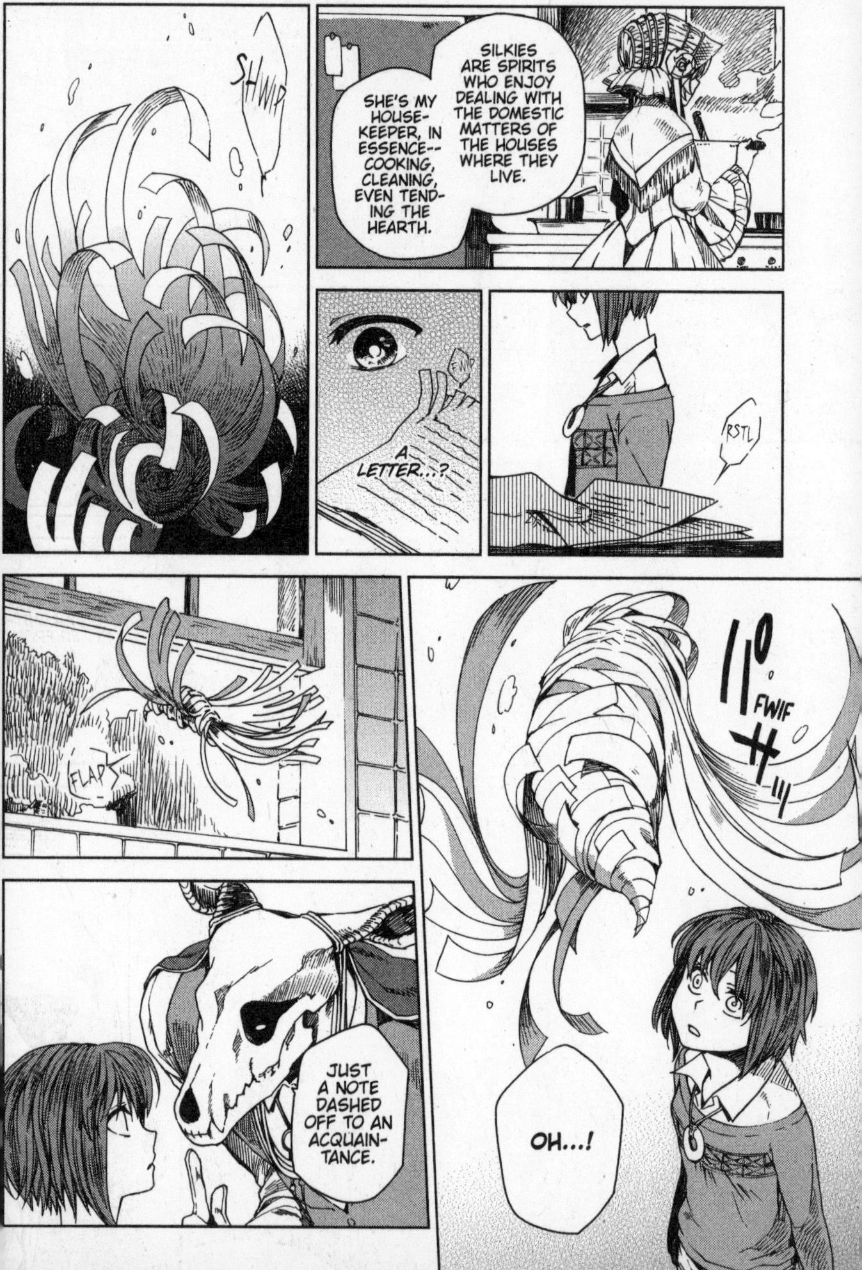
SHWIP
SILKIES ARE SPIRITS WHO ENJOY DEALING WITH THE DOMESTIC MATTERS OF THE HOUSES WHERE THEY LIVE.
SHE'S MY HOUSE-KEEPER, IN ESSENCE--COOKING, CLEANING, EVEN TEND-ING THE HEARTH.
RSTL
A LETTER...?
FLAP
FWIF
OH...!
JUST A NOTE DASHED OFF TO AN ACQUAIN-TANCE.

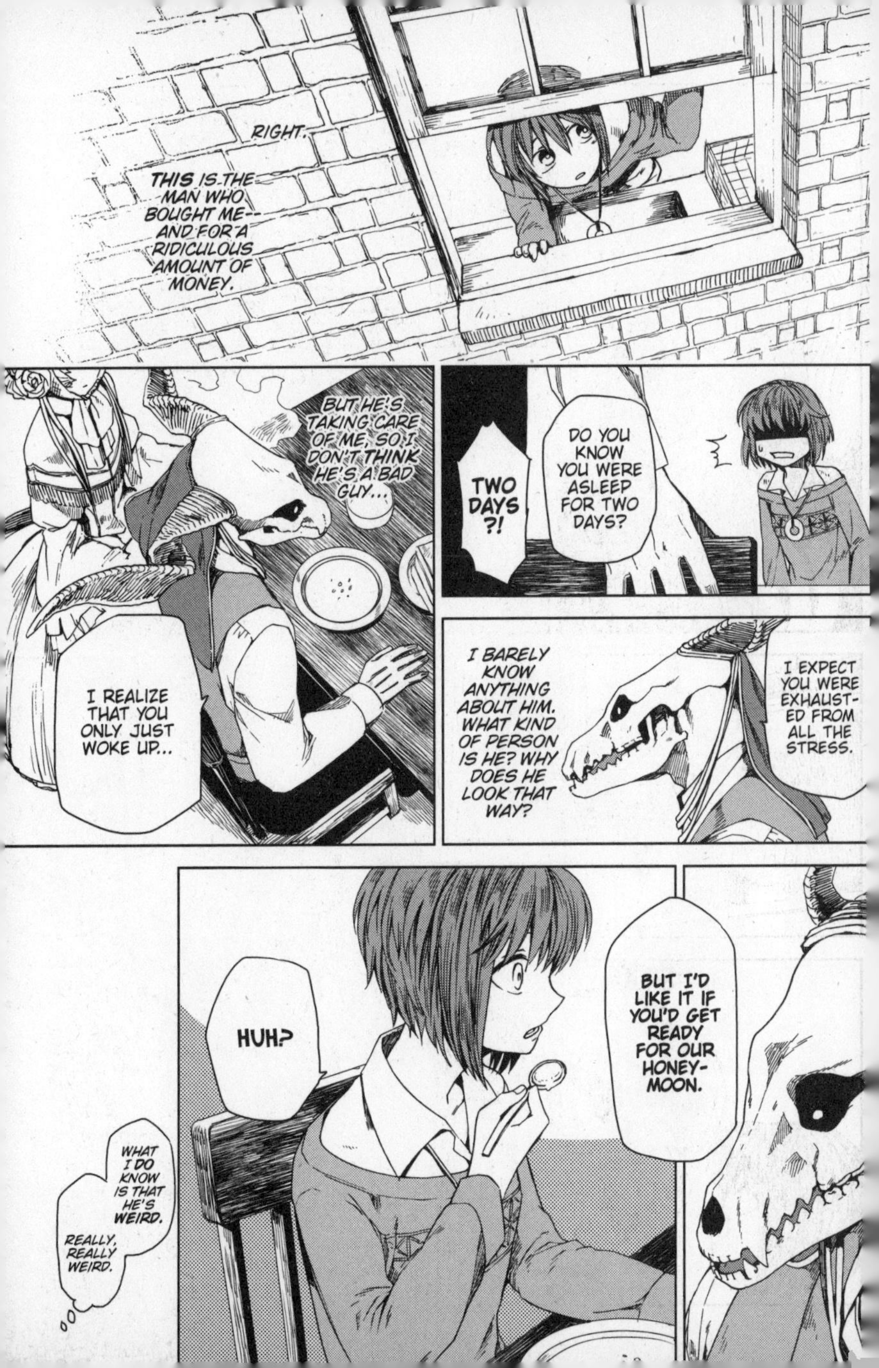
RIGHT.
THIS IS THE MAN WHO BOUGHT ME--AND FOR A RIDICULOUS AMOUNT OF MONEY.
DO YOU KNOW YOU WERE ASLEEP FOR TWO DAYS?
TWO DAYS?!
I EXPECT YOU WERE EXHAUST-ED FROM ALL THE STRESS.
I BARELY KNOW ANYTHING ABOUT HIM. WHAT KIND OF PERSON IS HE? WHY DOES HE LOOK THAT WAY?
BUT HE'S TAKING CARE OF ME, SO I DON'T THINK HE'S A BAD GUY...
I REALIZE THAT YOU ONLY JUST WOKE UP...
BUT I'D LIKE IT IF YOU'D GET READY FOR OUR HONEY-MOON.
HUH?
WHAT I DO KNOW IS THAT HE'S WEIRD.
REALLY, REALLY WEIRD.

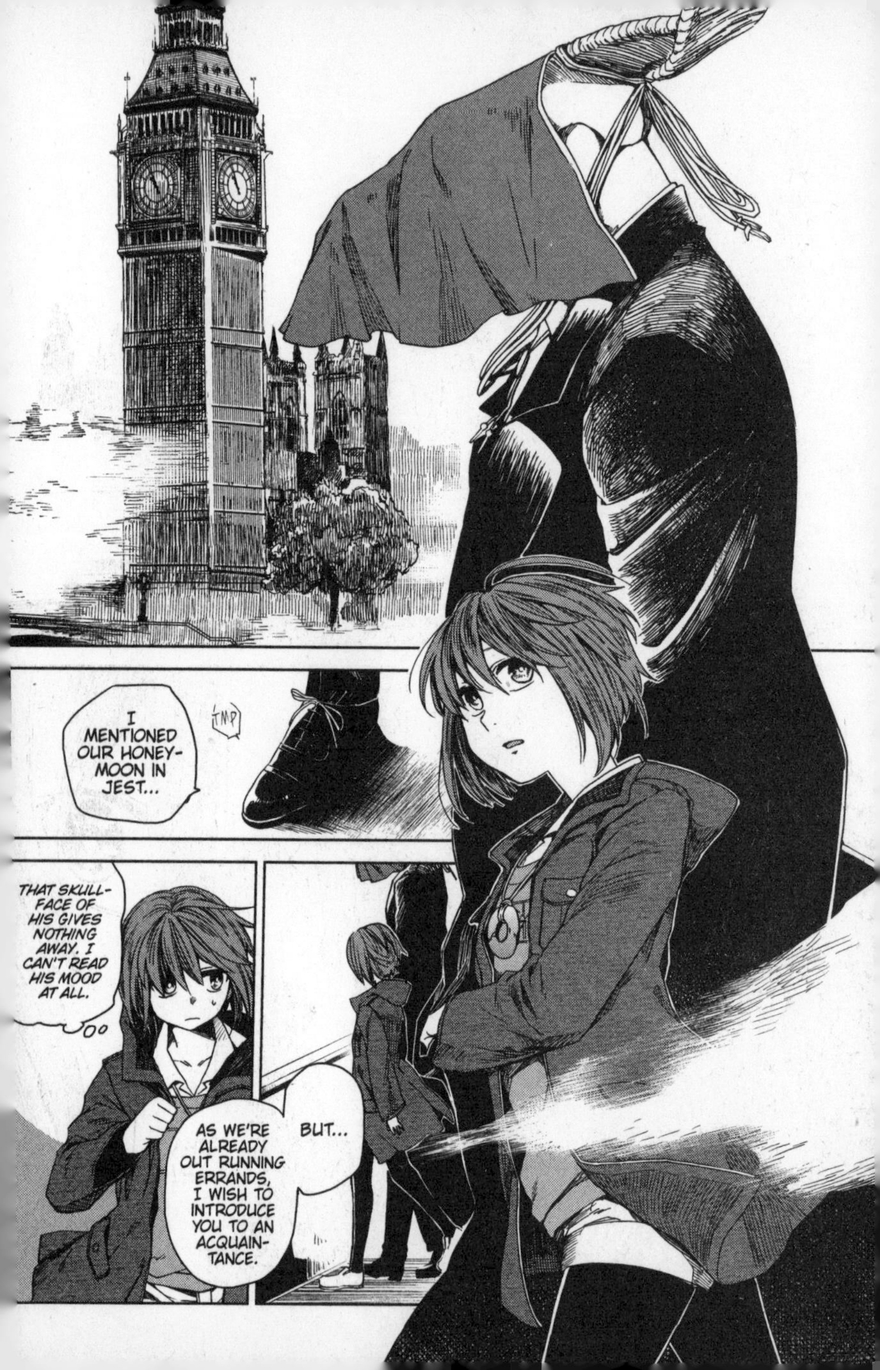
TMP
I MENTIONED OUR HONEY-MOON IN JEST...
BUT...
AS WE'RE ALREADY OUT RUNNING ERRANDS, I WISH TO INTRODUCE YOU TO AN ACQUAIN-TANCE.
THAT SKULL-FACE OF HIS GIVES NOTHING AWAY. I CAN'T READ HIS MOOD AT ALL.

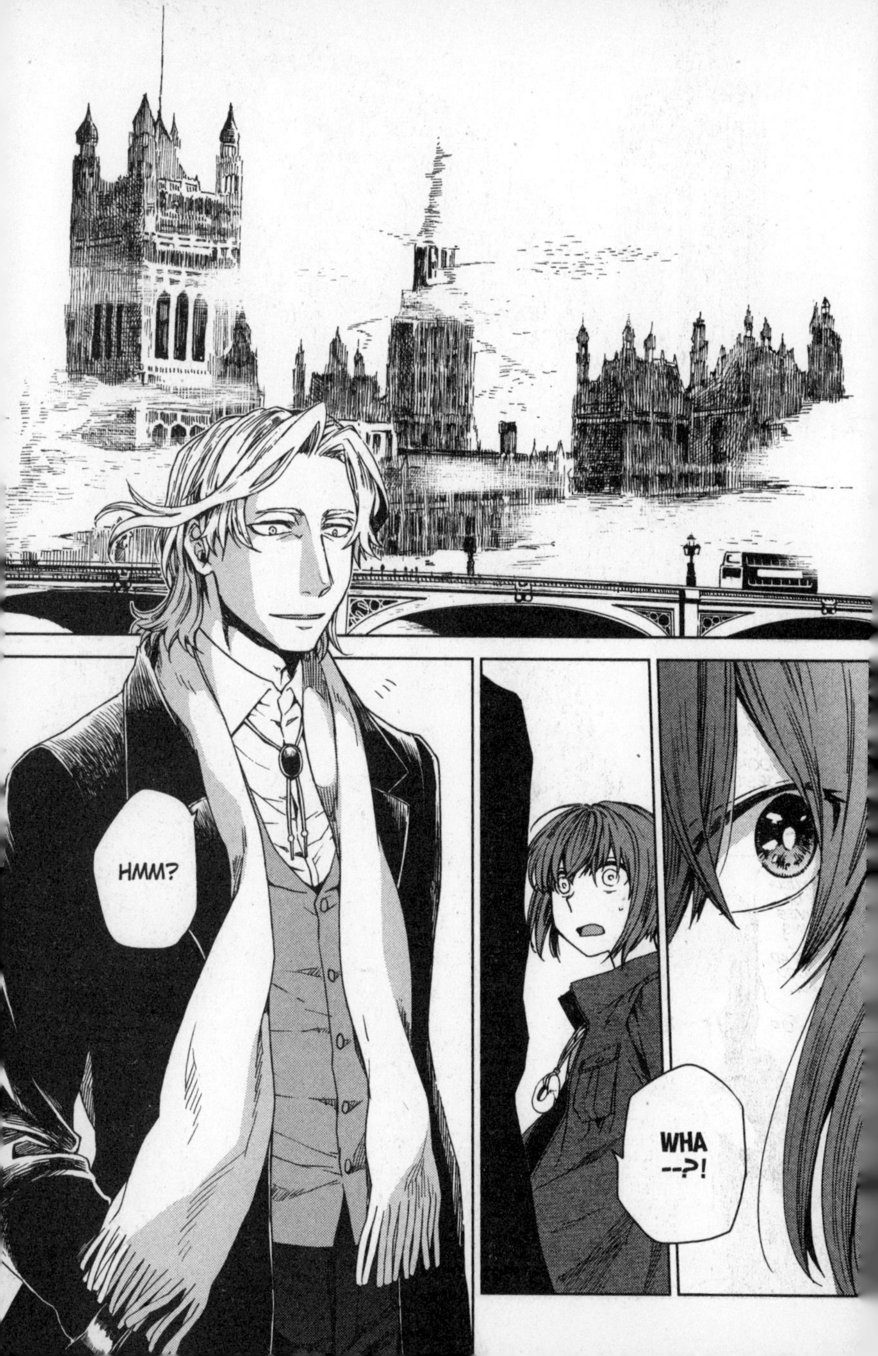
WHA --?!
HMM?

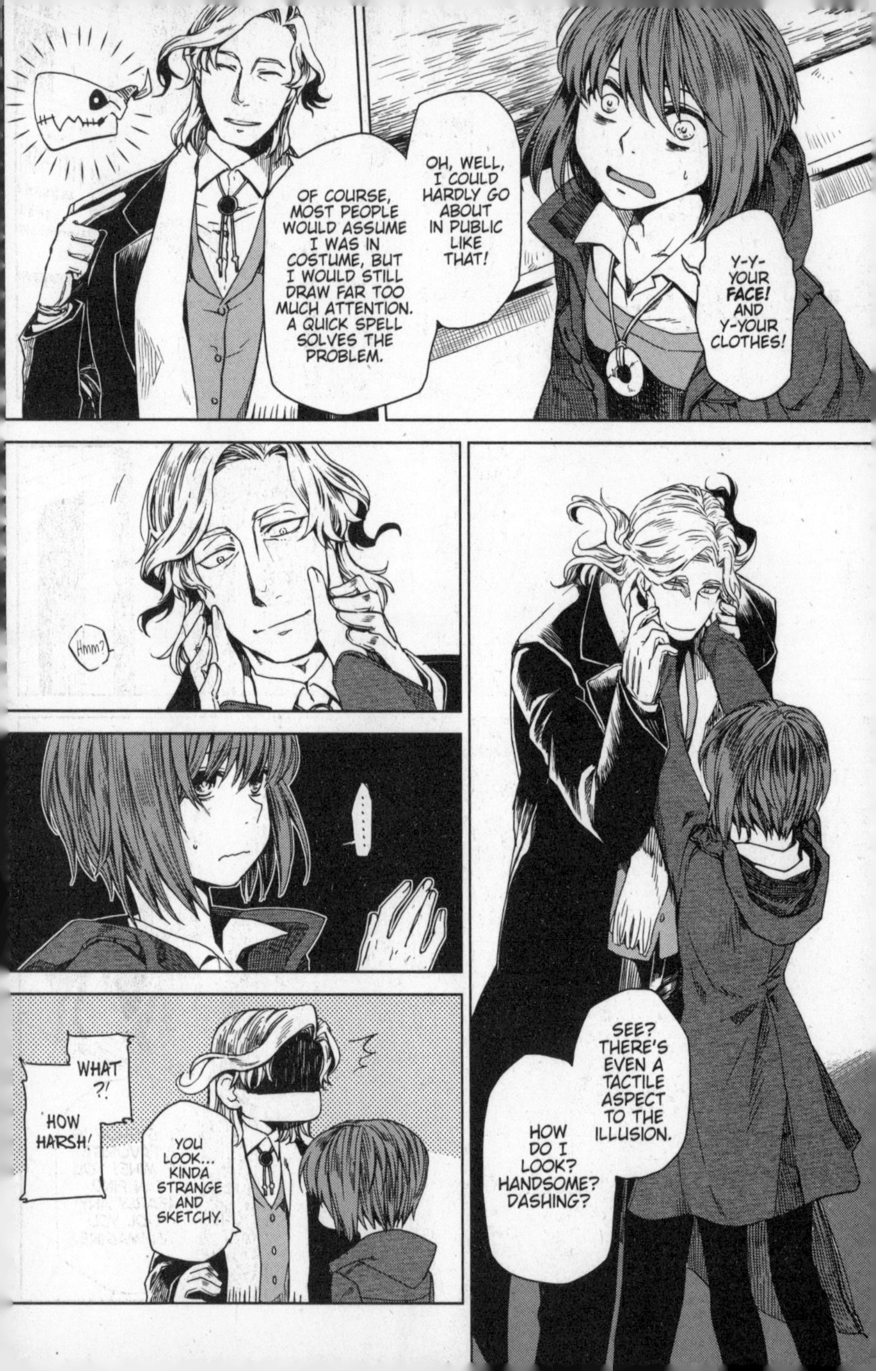
Y-Y-YOUR FACE! AND Y-YOUR CLOTHES!
OH, WELL, I COULD HARDLY GO ABOUT IN PUBLIC LIKE THAT!
OF COURSE, MOST PEOPLE WOULD ASSUME I WAS IN COSTUME, BUT I WOULD STILL DRAW FAR TOO MUCH ATTENTION. A QUICK SPELL SOLVES THE PROBLEM.
SEE? THERE'S EVEN A TACTILE ASPECT TO THE ILLUSION.
HOW DO I LOOK? HANDSOME? DASHING?
Hmm?
...
YOU LOOK... KINDA STRANGE AND SKETCHY.
WHAT?! HOW HARSH!

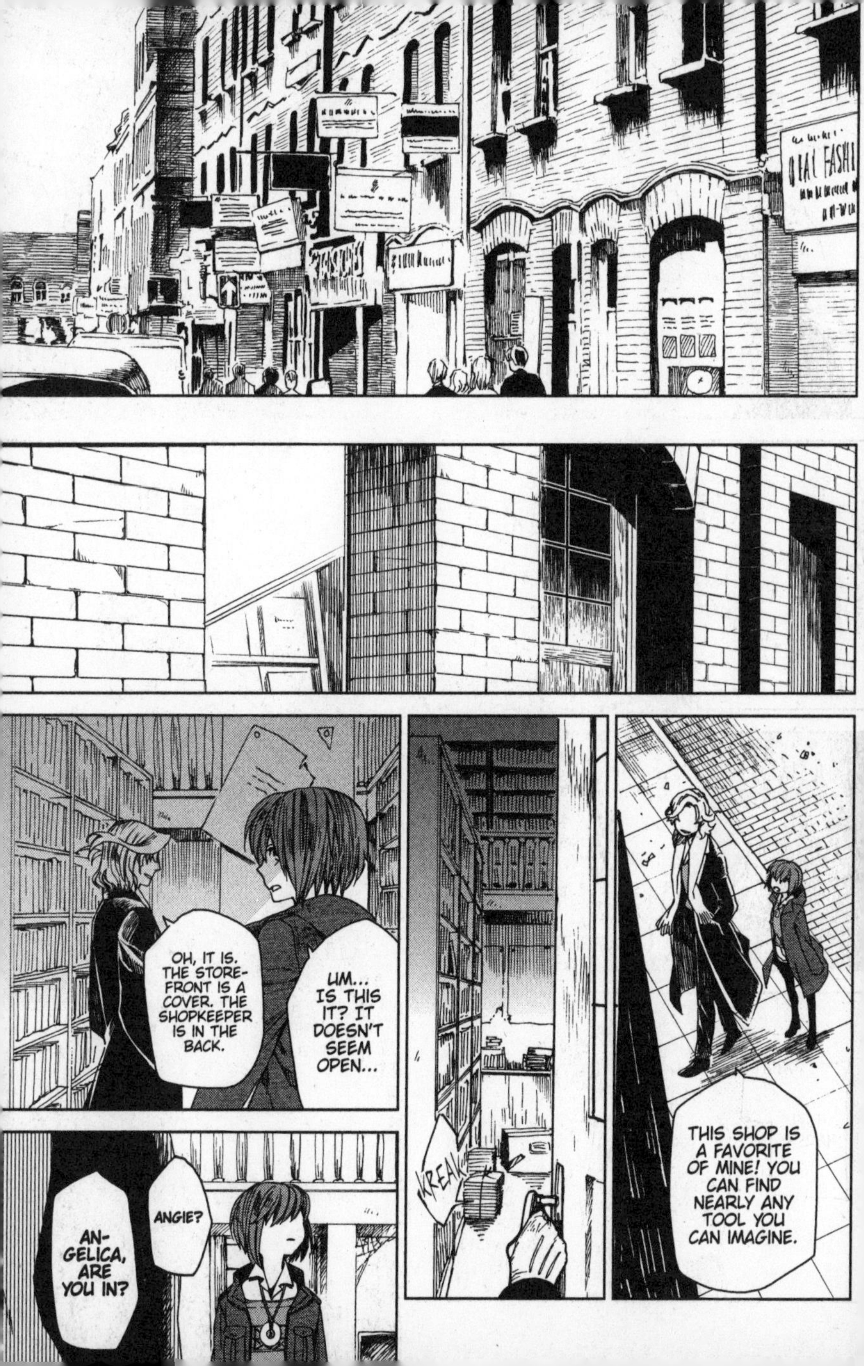
THIS SHOP IS A FAVORITE OF MINE! YOU CAN FIND NEARLY ANY TOOL YOU CAN IMAGINE.
KREAK
UM... IS THIS IT? IT DOESN'T SEEM OPEN...
OH, IT IS. THE STORE-FRONT IS A COVER. THE SHOPKEEPER IS IN THE BACK.
ANGIE?
AN-GELICA, ARE YOU IN?

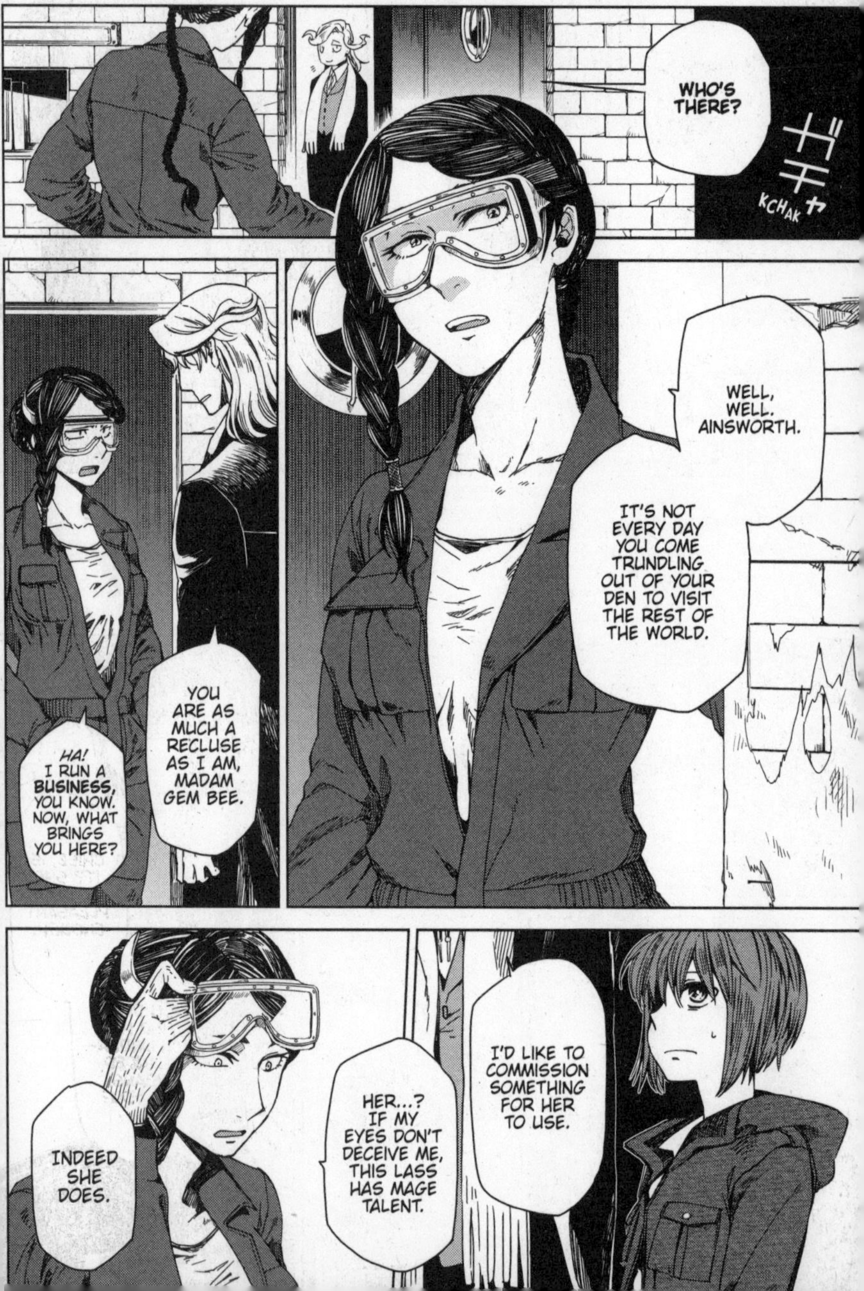
WHO'S THERE?
ガチャ
KCHAK
WELL, WELL. AINSWORTH.
IT'S NOT EVERY DAY YOU COME TRUNDLING OUT OF YOUR DEN TO VISIT THE REST OF THE WORLD.
YOU ARE AS MUCH A RECLUSE AS I AM, MADAM GEM BEE.
HA! I RUN A BUSINESS, YOU KNOW. NOW, WHAT BRINGS YOU HERE?
I'D LIKE TO COMMISSION SOMETHING FOR HER TO USE.
HER...? IF MY EYES DON'T DECEIVE ME, THIS LASS HAS MAGE TALENT.
INDEED SHE DOES.

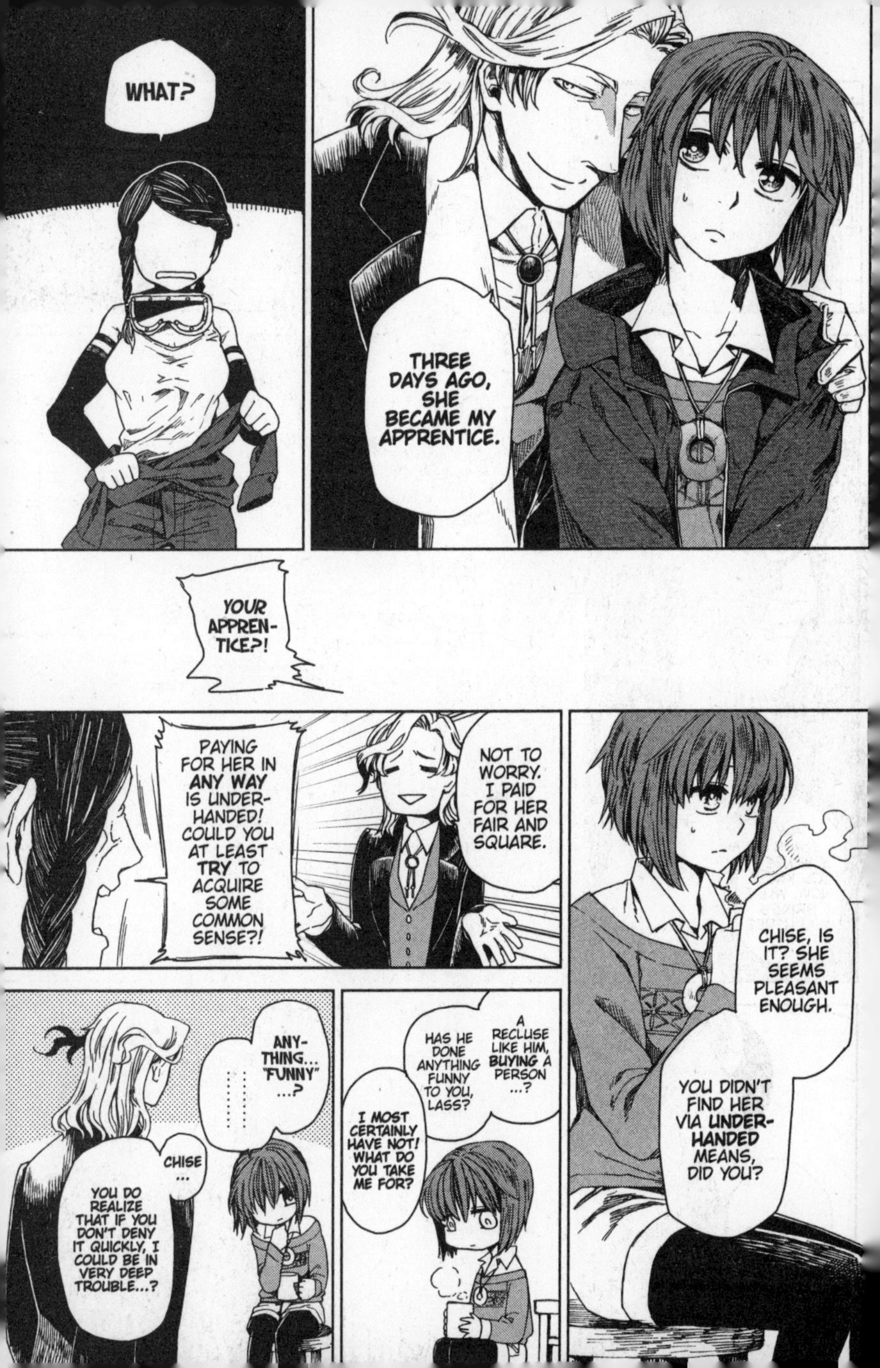
THREE DAYS AGO, SHE BECAME MY APPRENTICE.
WHAT?
YOUR APPREN-TICE?!
CHISE, IS IT? SHE SEEMS PLEASANT ENOUGH.
YOU DIDN'T FIND HER VIA UNDER-HANDED MEANS, DID YOU?
NOT TO WORRY. I PAID FOR HER FAIR AND SQUARE.
PAYING FOR HER IN ANY WAY IS UNDER-HANDED! COULD YOU AT LEAST TRY TO ACQUIRE SOME COMMON SENSE?!
A RECLUSE LIKE HIM, BUYING A PERSON ...?
HAS HE DONE ANYTHING FUNNY TO YOU, LASS?
I MOST CERTAINLY HAVE NOT! WHAT DO YOU TAKE ME FOR?
ANY-THING... "FUNNY" ...?
......
CHISE ...
YOU DO REALIZE THAT IF YOU DON'T DENY IT QUICKLY, I COULD BE IN VERY DEEP TROUBLE...?

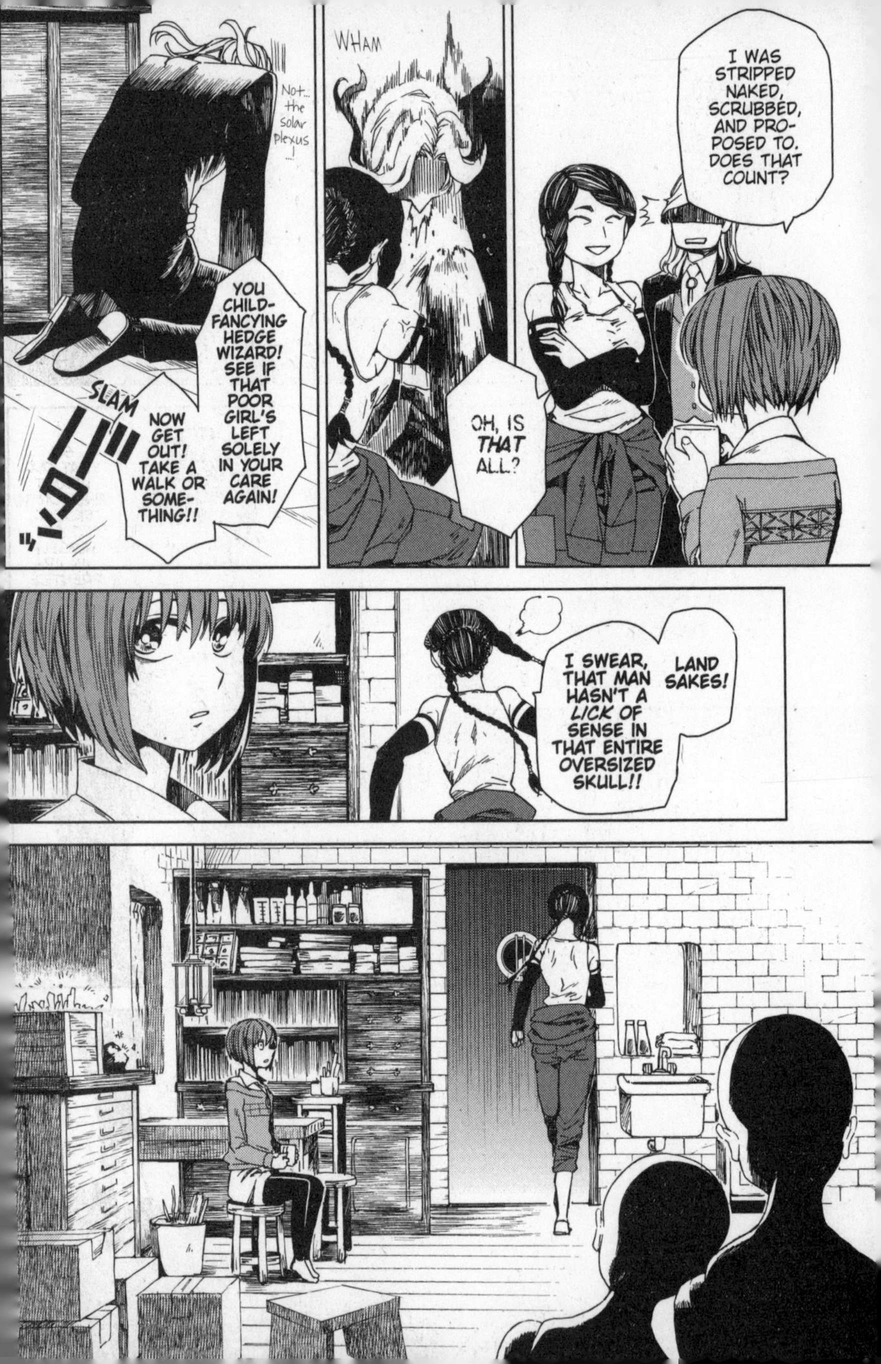
I WAS STRIPPED NAKED, SCRUBBED, AND PRO-POSED TO. DOES THAT COUNT?
OH, IS THAT ALL?
WHAM
YOU CHILD-FANCYING HEDGE WIZARD! SEE IF THAT POOR GIRL'S LEFT SOLELY IN YOUR CARE AGAIN!
NOW GET OUT! TAKE A WALK OR SOME-THING!!
SLAM
Not... the solar plexus...!
LAND SAKES!
I SWEAR, THAT MAN HASN'T A LICK OF SENSE IN THAT ENTIRE OVERSIZED SKULL!!

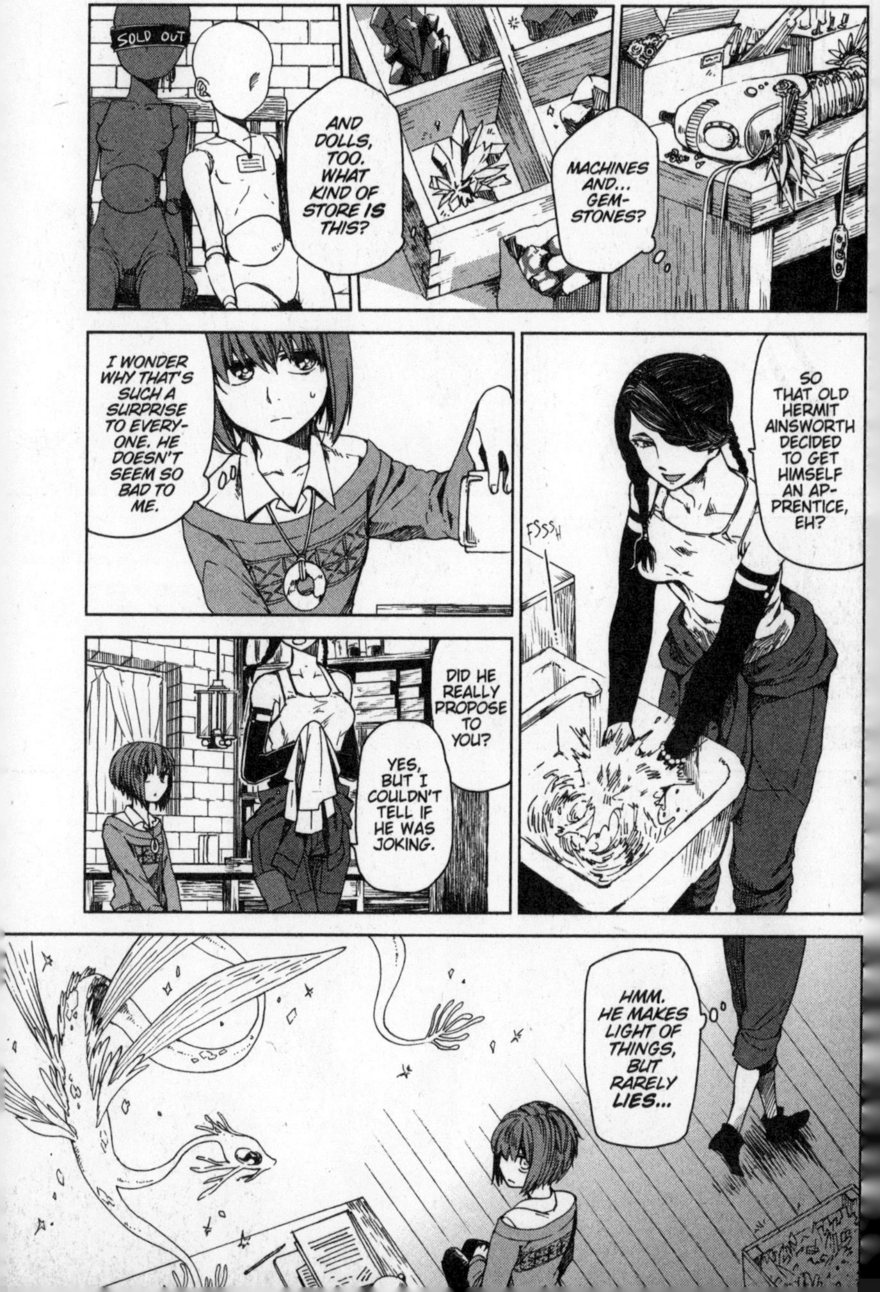
MACHINES AND... GEM-STONES?
AND DOLLS, TOO. WHAT KIND OF STORE IS THIS?
SOLD OUT
SO THAT OLD HERMIT AINSWORTH DECIDED TO GET HIMSELF AN AP-PRENTICE, EH?
FSSSH
I WONDER WHY THAT'S SUCH A SURPRISE TO EVERY-ONE. HE DOESN'T SEEM SO BAD TO ME.
DID HE REALLY PROPOSE TO YOU?
YES, BUT I COULDN'T TELL IF HE WAS JOKING.
HMM. HE MAKES LIGHT OF THINGS, BUT RARELY LIES...

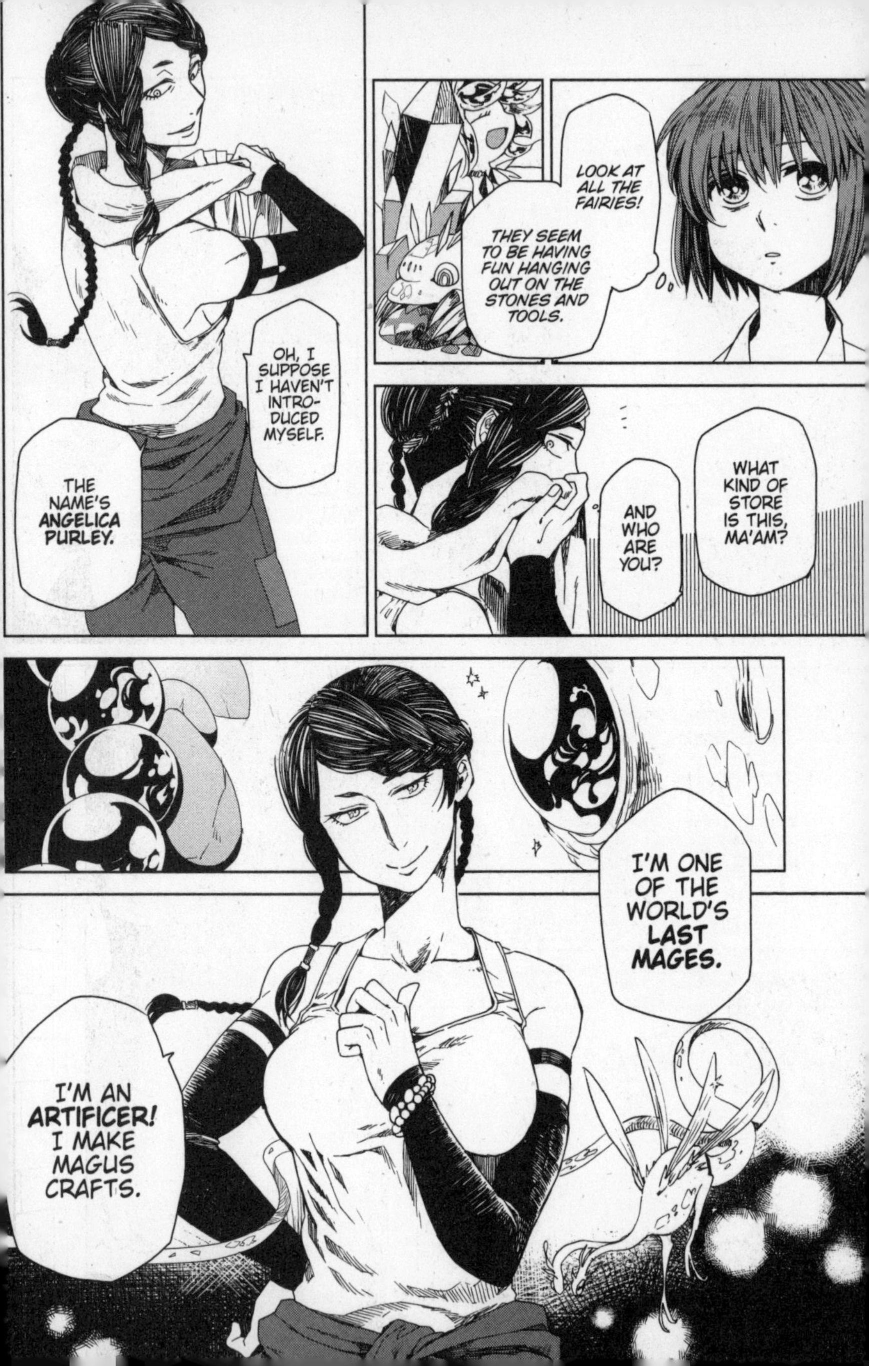
LOOK AT ALL THE FAIRIES!
THEY SEEM TO BE HAVING FUN HANGING OUT ON THE STONES AND TOOLS.
WHAT KIND OF STORE IS THIS, MA'AM?
AND WHO ARE YOU?
OH, I SUPPOSE I HAVEN'T INTRODUCED MYSELF.
THE NAME'S ANGELICA PURLEY.
I'M ONE OF THE WORLD'S LAST MAGES.
I'M AN ARTIFICER! I MAKE MAGUS CRAFTS.

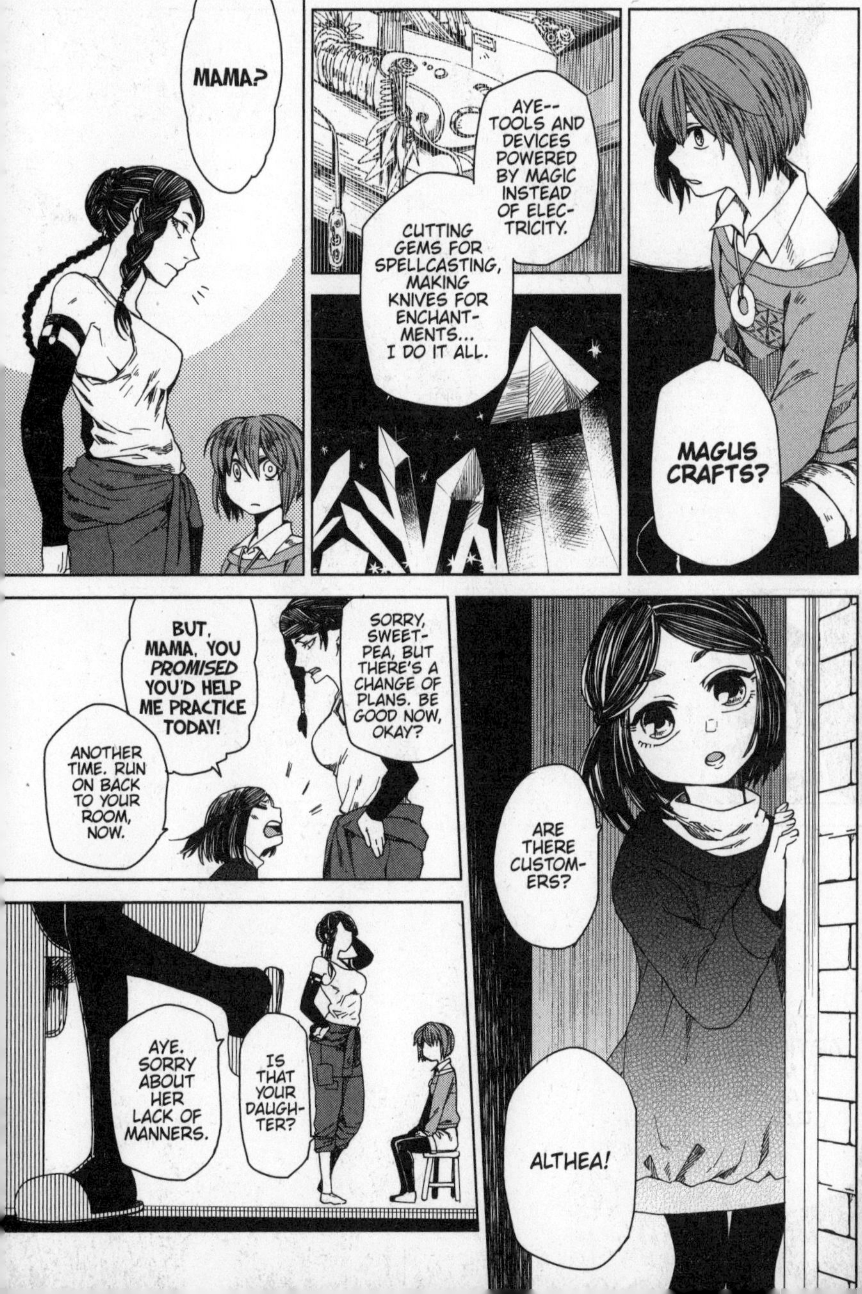
MAGUS CRAFTS?
AYE-- TOOLS AND DEVICES POWERED BY MAGIC INSTEAD OF ELEC-TRICITY.
CUTTING GEMS FOR SPELLCASTING, MAKING KNIVES FOR ENCHANT-MENTS... I DO IT ALL.
MAMA?
ARE THERE CUSTOM-ERS?
ALTHEA!
SORRY, SWEET-PEA, BUT THERE'S A CHANGE OF PLANS. BE GOOD NOW, OKAY?
BUT, MAMA, YOU *PROMISED* YOU'D HELP ME PRACTICE TODAY!
ANOTHER TIME. RUN ON BACK TO YOUR ROOM, NOW.
IS THAT YOUR DAUGH-TER?
AYE. SORRY ABOUT HER LACK OF MANNERS.

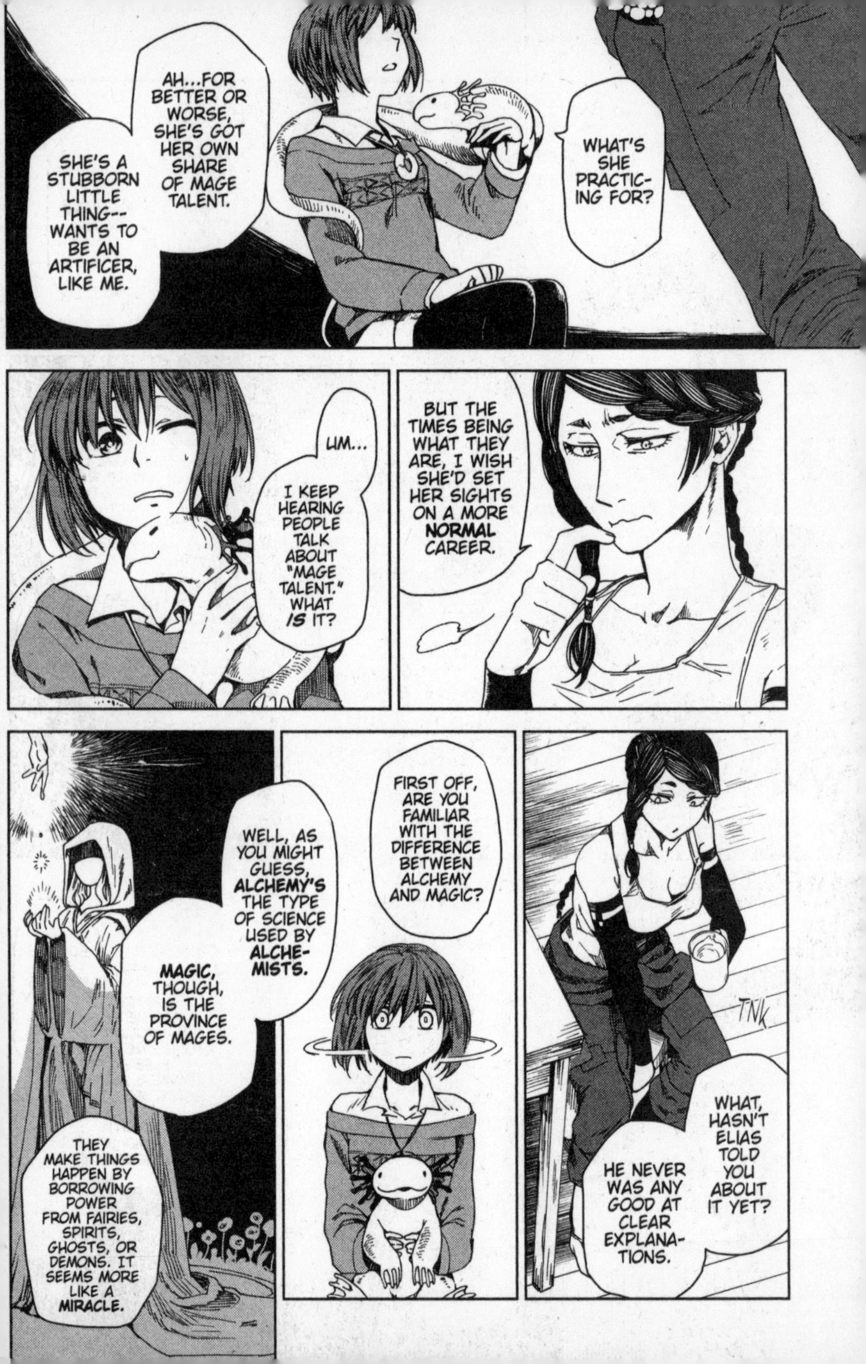
WHAT'S SHE PRACTICING FOR?
AH...FOR BETTER OR WORSE, SHE'S GOT HER OWN SHARE OF MAGE TALENT.
SHE'S A STUBBORN LITTLE THING--WANTS TO BE AN ARTIFICER, LIKE ME.
BUT THE TIMES BEING WHAT THEY ARE, I WISH SHE'D SET HER SIGHTS ON A MORE NORMAL CAREER.
UM...
I KEEP HEARING PEOPLE TALK ABOUT "MAGE TALENT." WHAT IS IT?
TNK
WHAT, HASN'T ELIAS TOLD YOU ABOUT IT YET?
HE NEVER WAS ANY GOOD AT CLEAR EXPLANATIONS.
FIRST OFF, ARE YOU FAMILIAR WITH THE DIFFERENCE BETWEEN ALCHEMY AND MAGIC?
WELL, AS YOU MIGHT GUESS, ALCHEMY'S THE TYPE OF SCIENCE USED BY ALCHEMISTS.
MAGIC, THOUGH, IS THE PROVINCE OF MAGES.
THEY MAKE THINGS HAPPEN BY BORROWING POWER FROM FAIRIES, SPIRITS, GHOSTS, OR DEMONS. IT SEEMS MORE LIKE A MIRACLE.

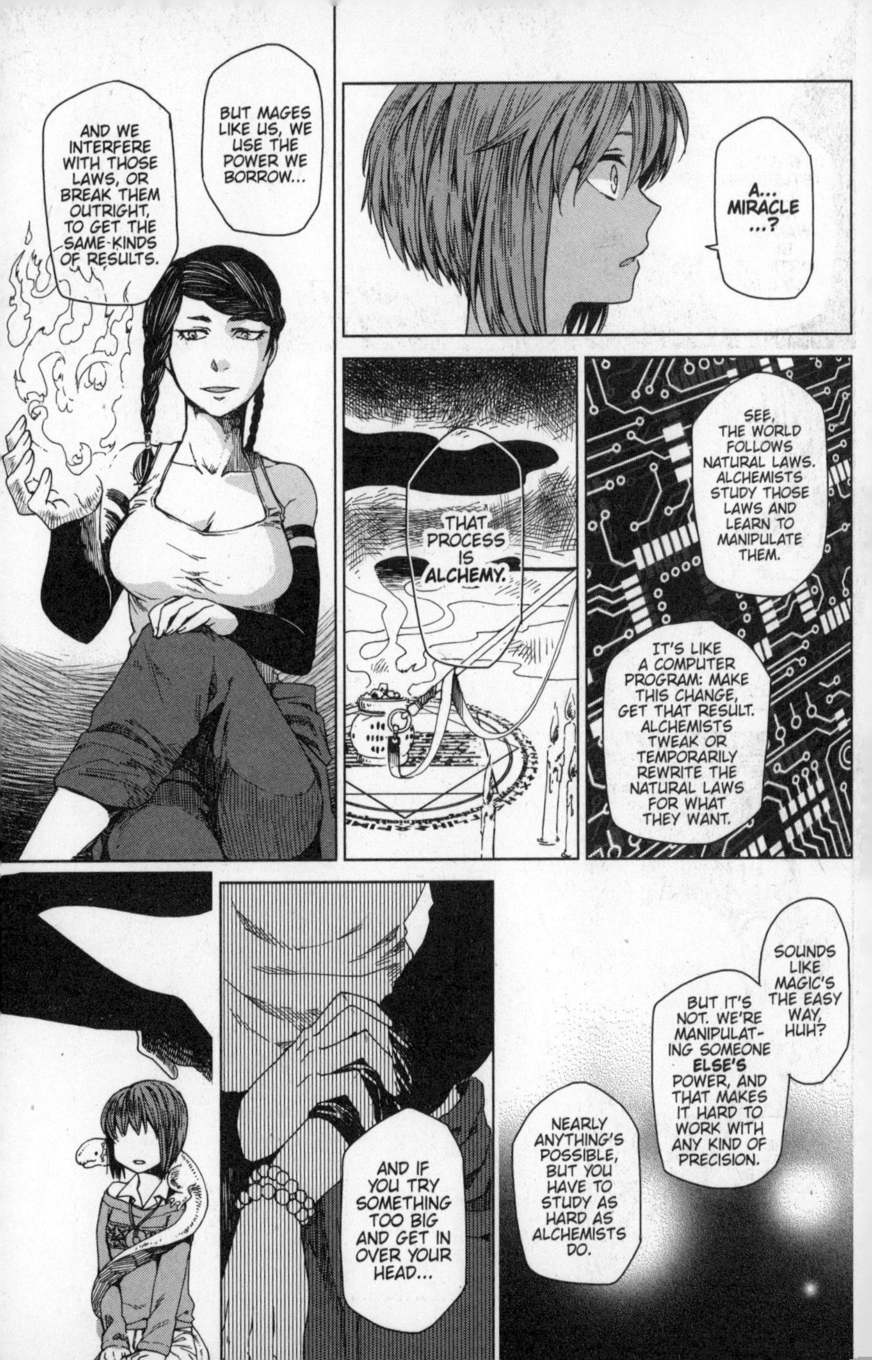
A... MIRACLE ...?
SEE, THE WORLD FOLLOWS NATURAL LAWS. ALCHEMISTS STUDY THOSE LAWS AND LEARN TO MANIPULATE THEM.
IT'S LIKE A COMPUTER PROGRAM: MAKE THIS CHANGE, GET THAT RESULT. ALCHEMISTS TWEAK OR TEMPORARILY REWRITE THE NATURAL LAWS FOR WHAT THEY WANT.
THAT PROCESS IS ALCHEMY.
BUT MAGES LIKE US, WE USE THE POWER WE BORROW...
AND WE INTERFERE WITH THOSE LAWS, OR BREAK THEM OUTRIGHT, TO GET THE SAME KINDS OF RESULTS.
SOUNDS LIKE MAGIC'S THE EASY WAY, HUH?
BUT IT'S NOT. WE'RE MANIPULATING SOMEONE ELSE'S POWER, AND THAT MAKES IT HARD TO WORK WITH ANY KIND OF PRECISION.
NEARLY ANYTHING'S POSSIBLE, BUT YOU HAVE TO STUDY AS HARD AS ALCHEMISTS DO.
AND IF YOU TRY SOMETHING TOO BIG AND GET IN OVER YOUR HEAD...

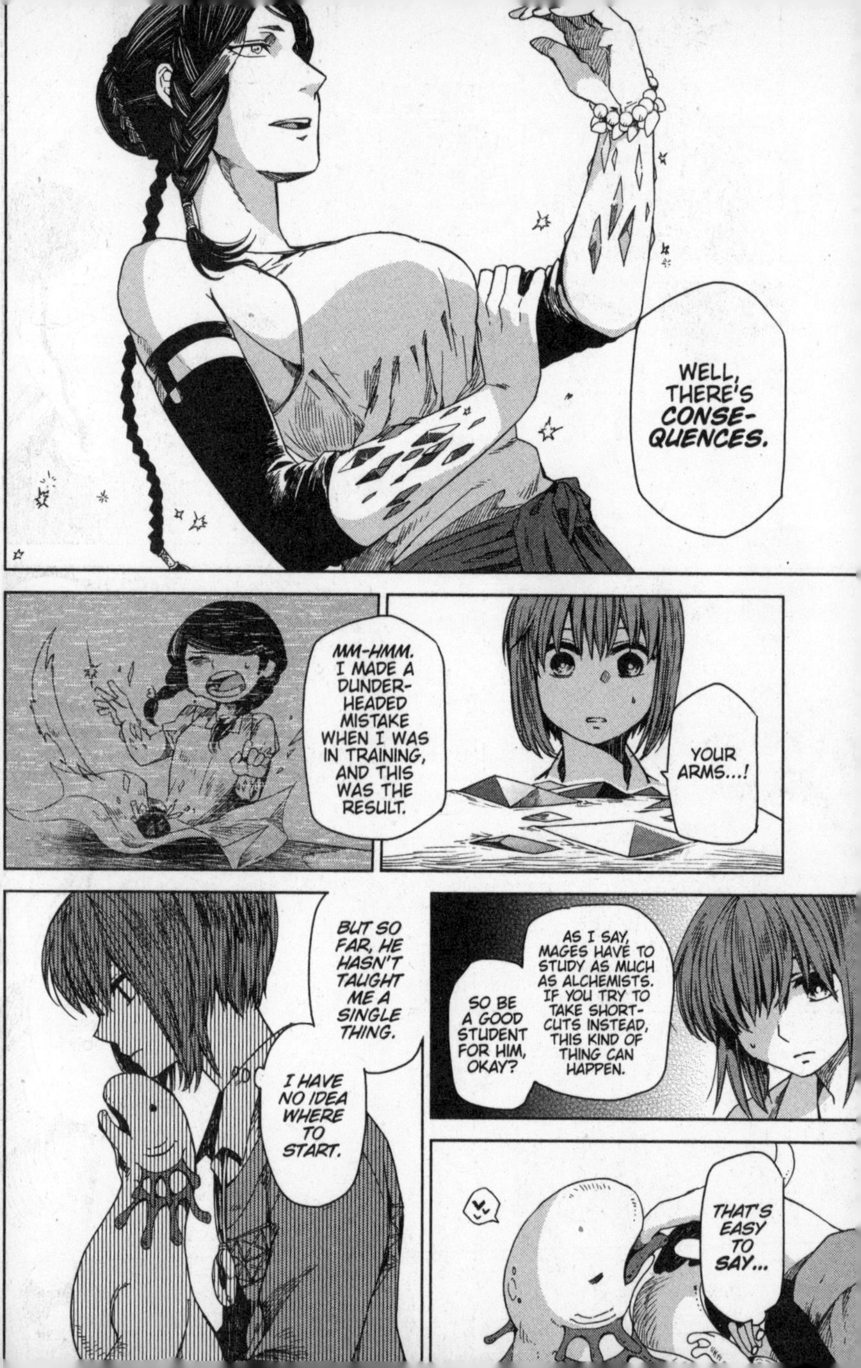
WELL, THERE'S CONSEQUENCES.
YOUR ARMS...!
MM-HMM. I MADE A DUNDER-HEADED MISTAKE WHEN I WAS IN TRAINING, AND THIS WAS THE RESULT.
AS I SAY, MAGES HAVE TO STUDY AS MUCH AS ALCHEMISTS. IF YOU TRY TO TAKE SHORT-CUTS INSTEAD, THIS KIND OF THING CAN HAPPEN.
SO BE A GOOD STUDENT FOR HIM, OKAY?
THAT'S EASY TO SAY...
BUT SO FAR, HE HASN'T TAUGHT ME A SINGLE THING.
I HAVE NO IDEA WHERE TO START.

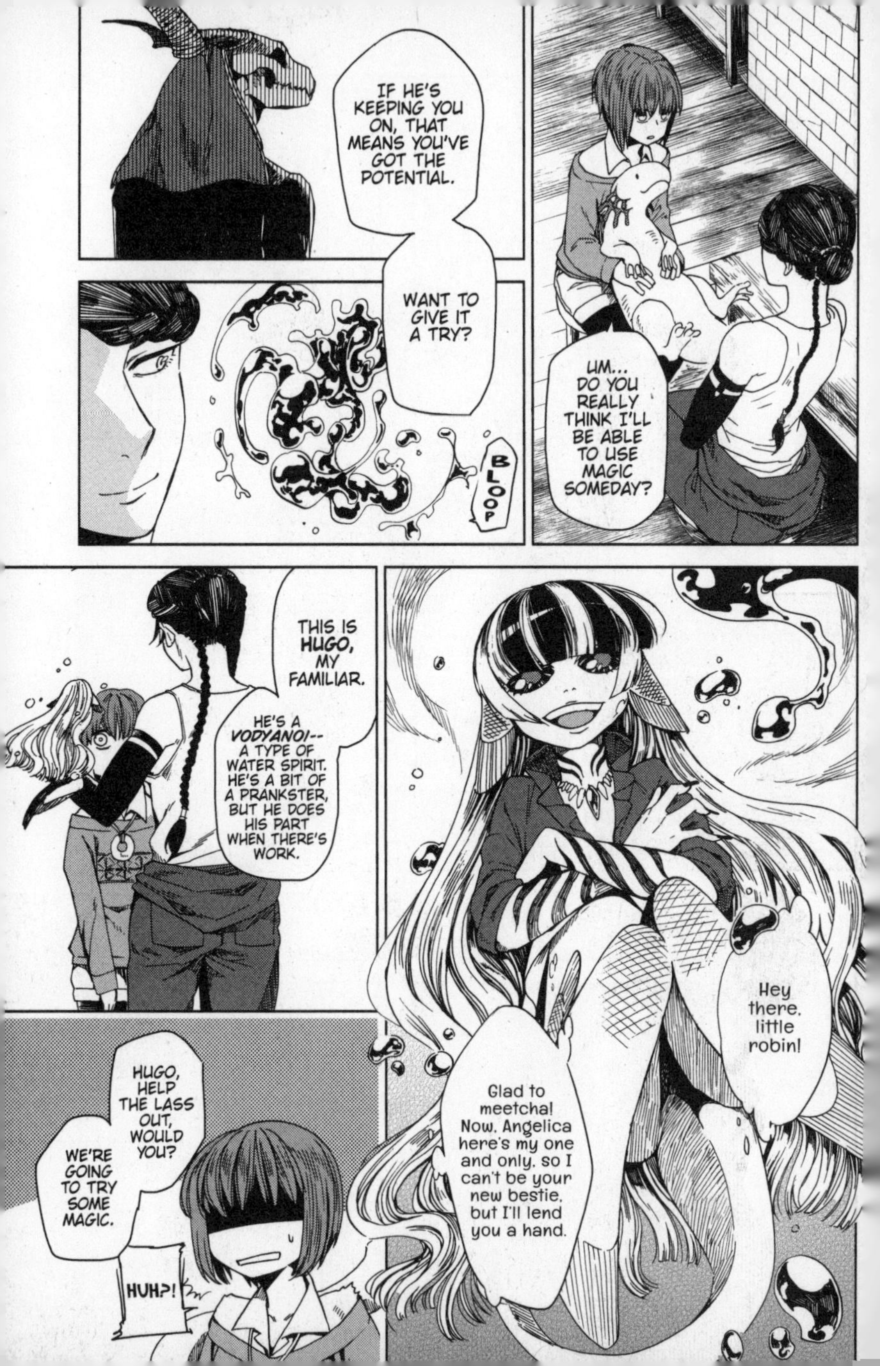

UM... DO YOU REALLY THINK I'LL BE ABLE TO USE MAGIC SOMEDAY?
IF HE'S KEEPING YOU ON, THAT MEANS YOU'VE GOT THE POTENTIAL.
WANT TO GIVE IT A TRY?
BLOOP
Hey there, little robin!
Glad to meetcha! Now, Angelica here's my one and only, so I can't be your new bestie, but I'll lend you a hand.
THIS IS **HUGO**, MY FAMILIAR.
HE'S A ***VODYANOI***--A TYPE OF WATER SPIRIT. HE'S A BIT OF A PRANKSTER, BUT HE DOES HIS PART WHEN THERE'S WORK.
HUGO, HELP THE LASS OUT, WOULD YOU?
WE'RE GOING TO TRY SOME MAGIC.
HUH?!

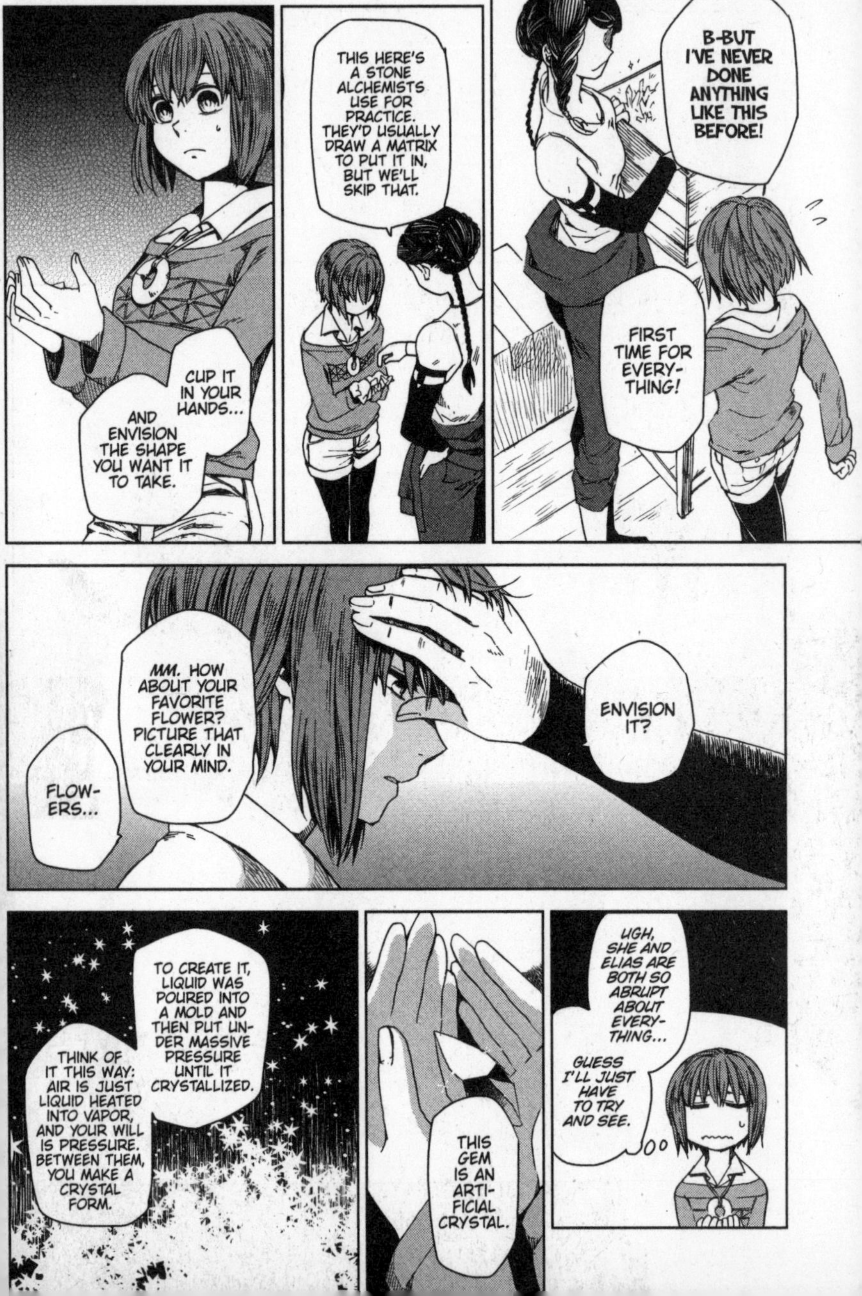
B-BUT I'VE NEVER DONE ANYTHING LIKE THIS BEFORE!
FIRST TIME FOR EVERY-THING!
THIS HERE'S A STONE ALCHEMISTS USE FOR PRACTICE. THEY'D USUALLY DRAW A MATRIX TO PUT IT IN, BUT WE'LL SKIP THAT.
CUP IT IN YOUR HANDS...
AND ENVISION THE SHAPE YOU WANT IT TO TAKE.
ENVISION IT?
MM. HOW ABOUT YOUR FAVORITE FLOWER? PICTURE THAT CLEARLY IN YOUR MIND.
FLOW-ERS...
UGH, SHE AND ELIAS ARE BOTH SO ABRUPT ABOUT EVERY-THING...
GUESS I'LL JUST HAVE TO TRY AND SEE.
THIS GEM IS AN ARTI-FICIAL CRYSTAL.
TO CREATE IT, LIQUID WAS POURED INTO A MOLD AND THEN PUT UN-DER MASSIVE PRESSURE UNTIL IT CRYSTALLIZED.
THINK OF IT THIS WAY: AIR IS JUST LIQUID HEATED INTO VAPOR, AND YOUR WILL IS PRESSURE. BETWEEN THEM, YOU MAKE A CRYSTAL FORM.

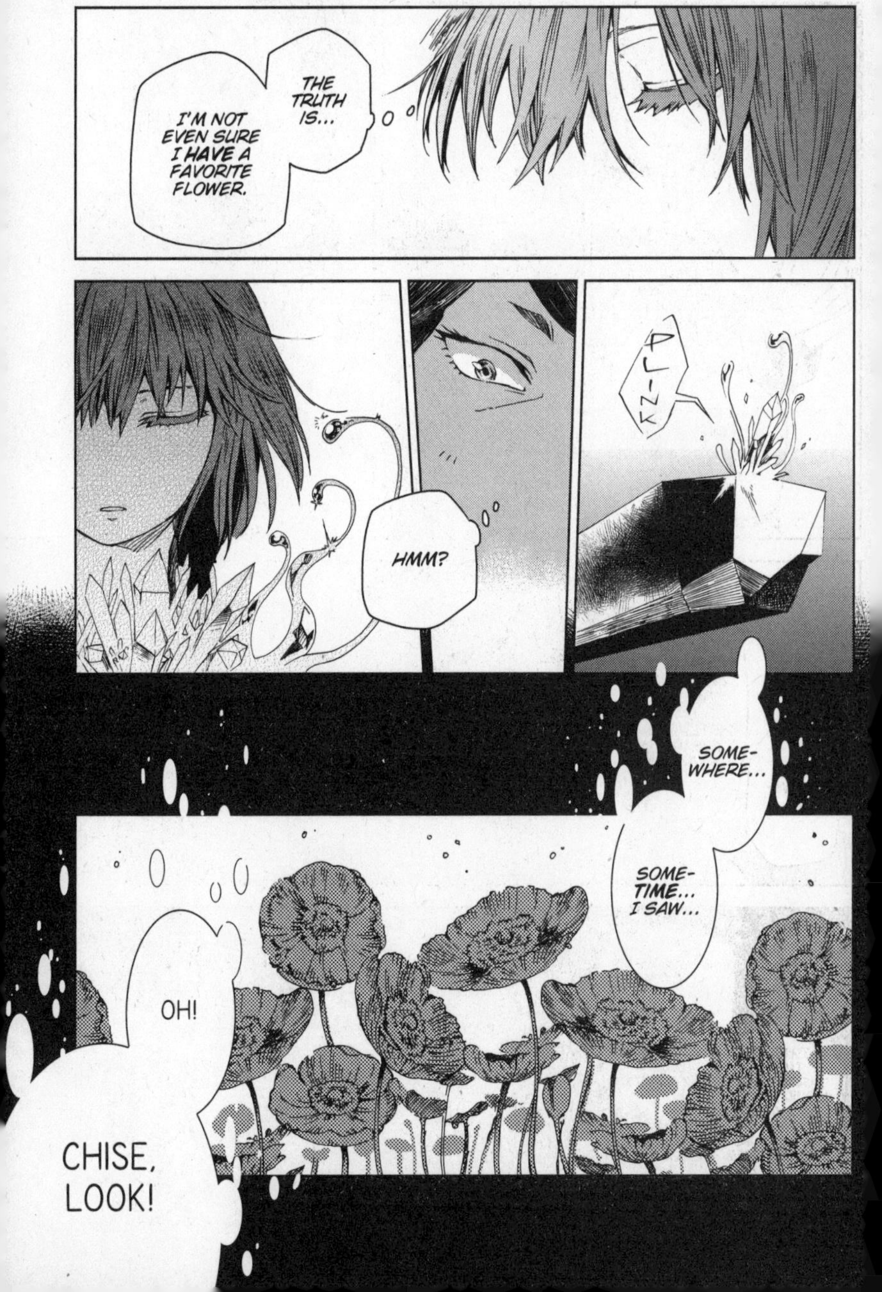
THE TRUTH IS...
I'M NOT EVEN SURE I HAVE A FAVORITE FLOWER.
PLINK
HMM?
SOME-WHERE...
SOME-TIME... I SAW...
OH!
CHISE, LOOK!

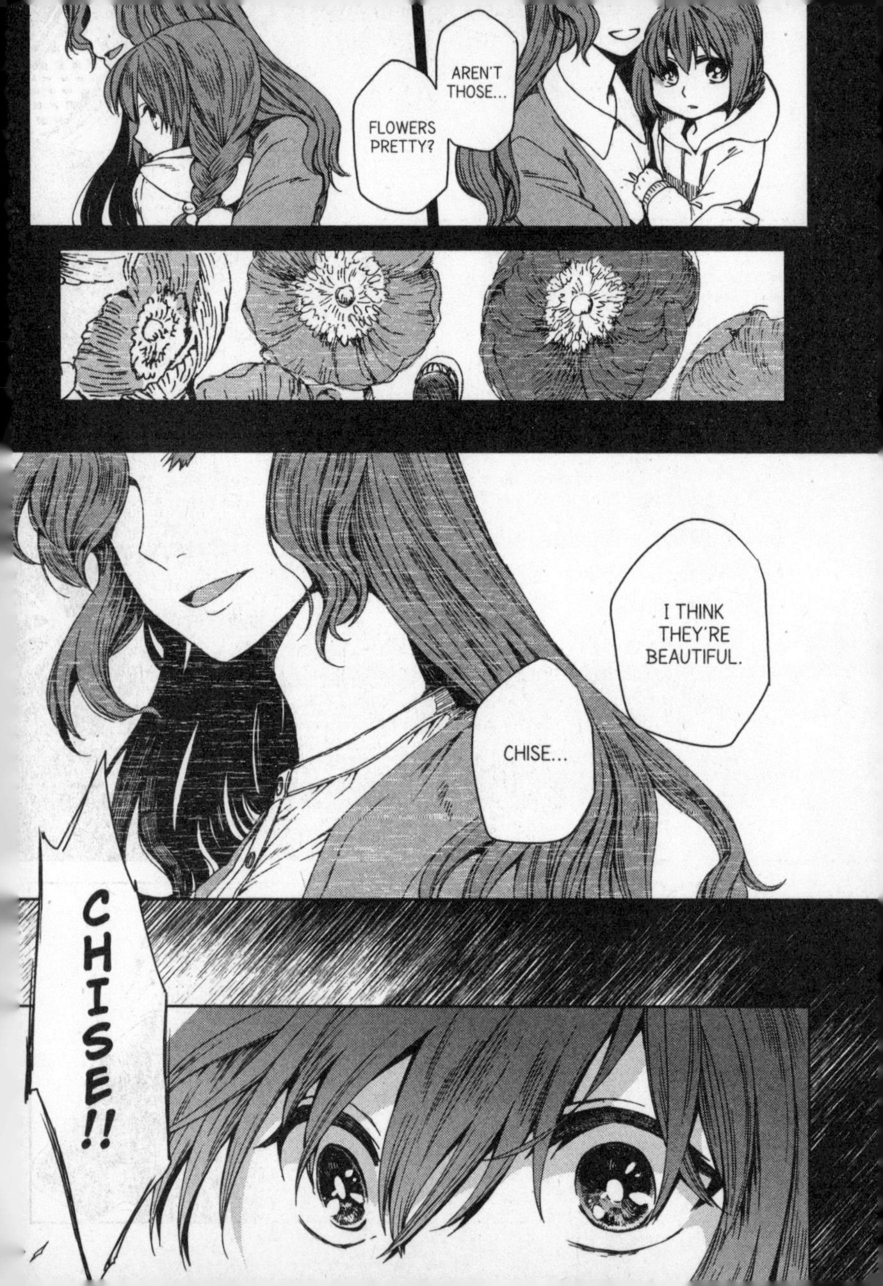
AREN'T THOSE...
FLOWERS PRETTY?
I THINK THEY'RE BEAUTIFUL.
CHISE...
CHISE!!

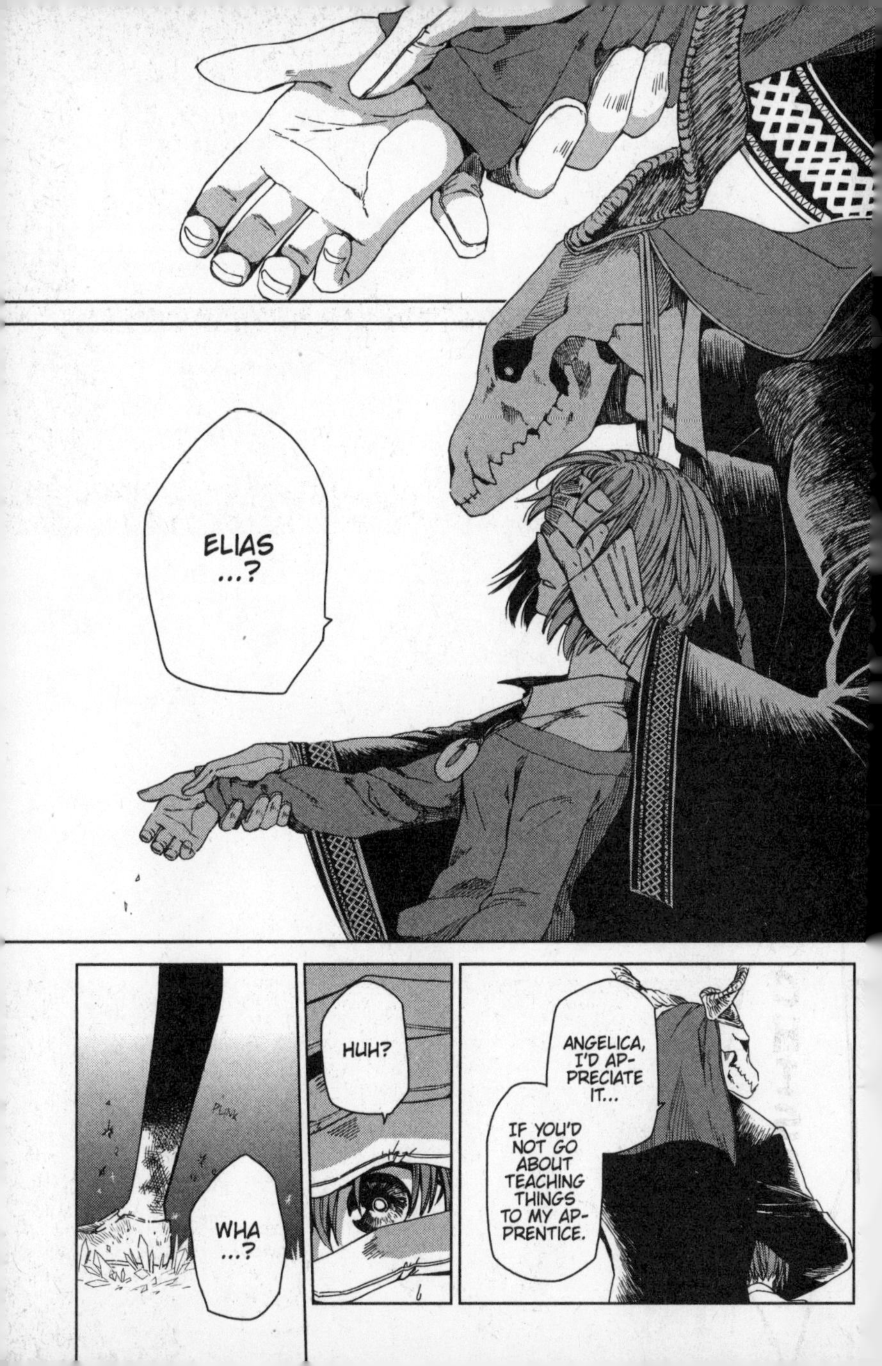
ELIAS ...?
ANGELICA, I'D AP-PRECIATE IT...
IF YOU'D NOT GO ABOUT TEACHING THINGS TO MY AP-PRENTICE.
HUH?
PLINK
WHA ...?

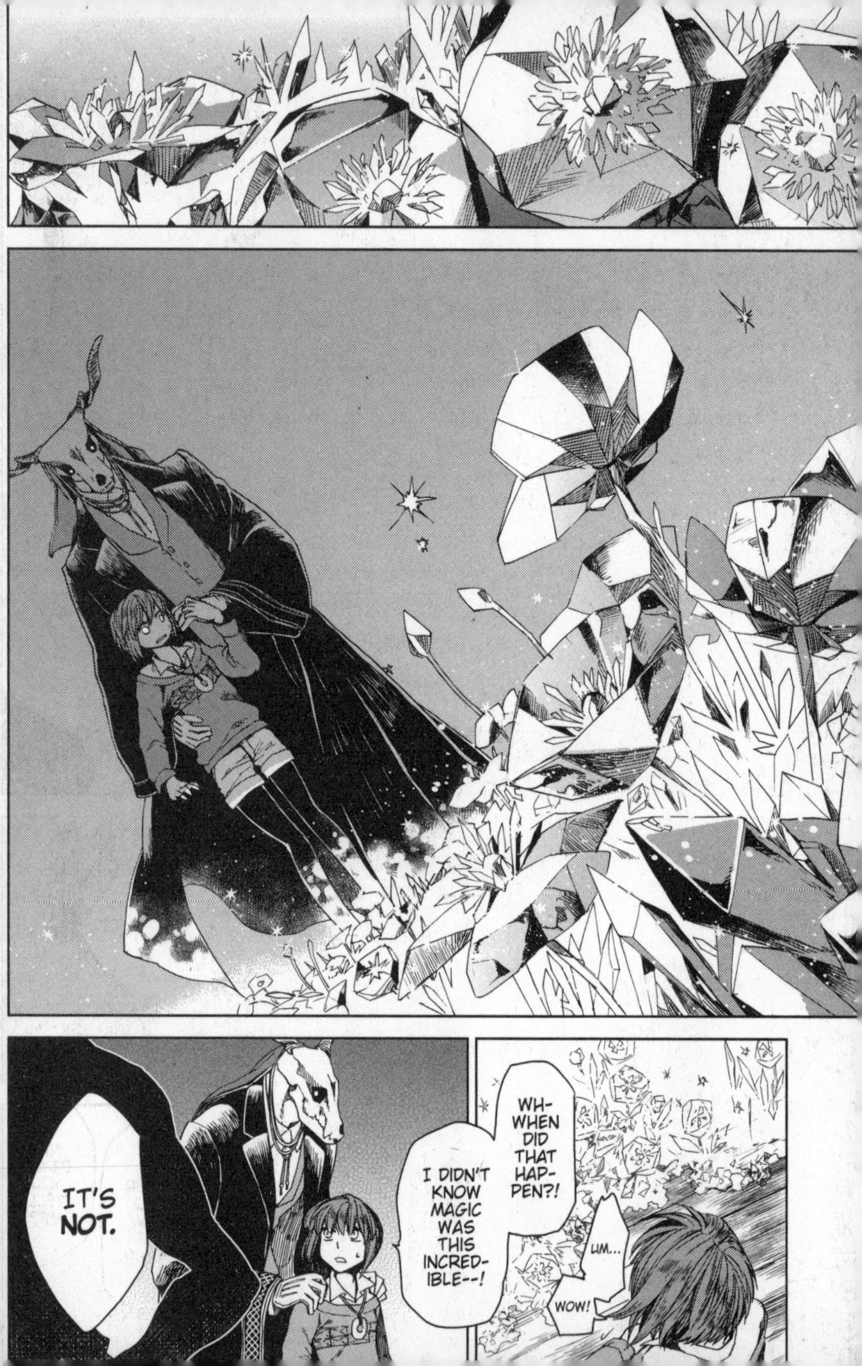
WH-WHEN DID THAT HAPPEN?!
I DIDN'T KNOW MAGIC WAS THIS INCREDIBLE--!
UM...
WOW!
IT'S NOT.

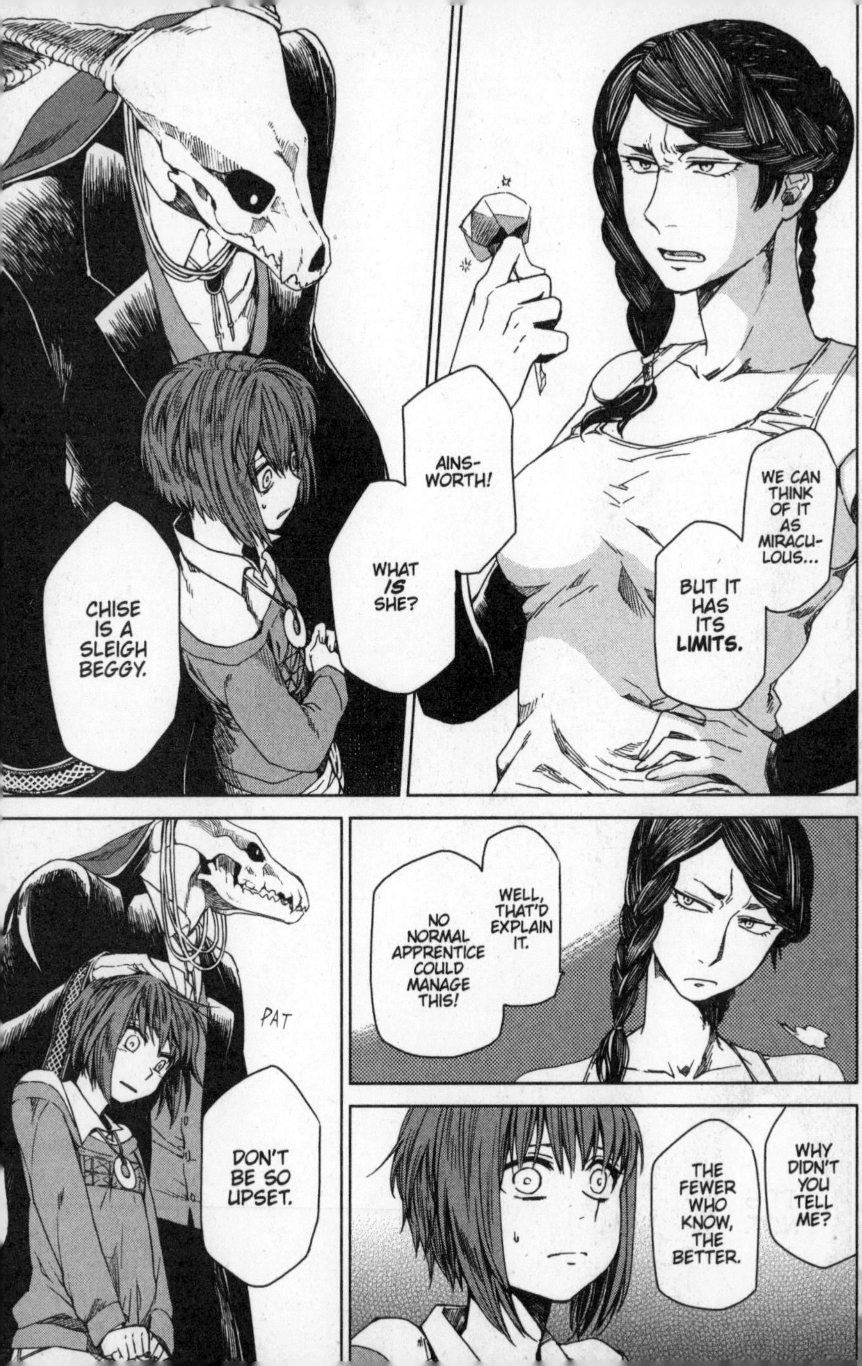
WE CAN THINK OF IT AS MIRACULOUS...
BUT IT HAS ITS LIMITS.
AINSWORTH!
WHAT *IS* SHE?
CHISE IS A SLEIGH BEGGY.
WELL, THAT'D EXPLAIN IT.
NO NORMAL APPRENTICE COULD MANAGE THIS!
WHY DIDN'T YOU TELL ME?
THE FEWER WHO KNOW, THE BETTER.
PAT
DON'T BE SO UPSET.

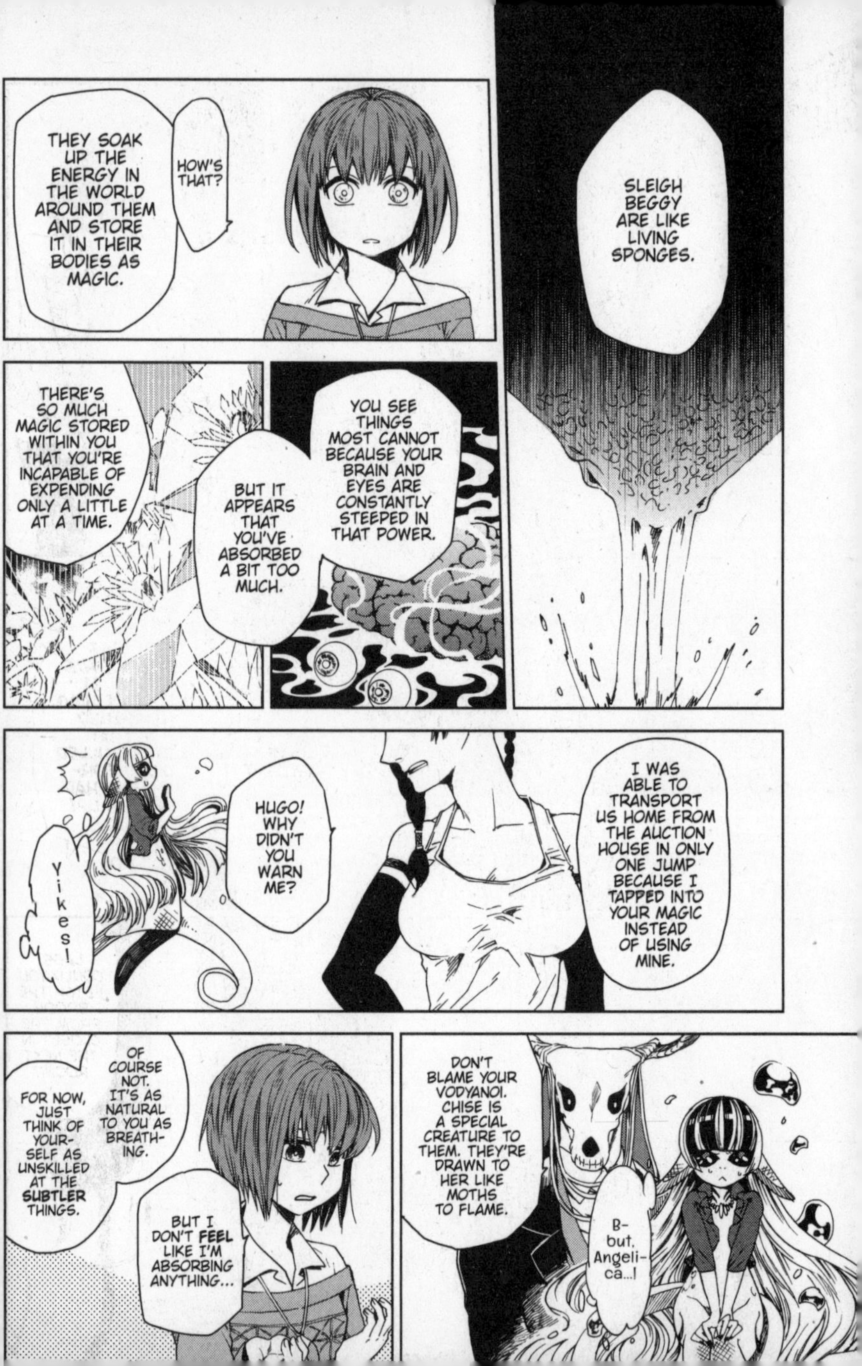
SLEIGH BEGGY ARE LIKE LIVING SPONGES.
HOW'S THAT?
THEY SOAK UP THE ENERGY IN THE WORLD AROUND THEM AND STORE IT IN THEIR BODIES AS MAGIC.
YOU SEE THINGS MOST CANNOT BECAUSE YOUR BRAIN AND EYES ARE CONSTANTLY STEEPED IN THAT POWER.
BUT IT APPEARS THAT YOU'VE ABSORBED A BIT TOO MUCH.
THERE'S SO MUCH MAGIC STORED WITHIN YOU THAT YOU'RE INCAPABLE OF EXPENDING ONLY A LITTLE AT A TIME.
I WAS ABLE TO TRANSPORT US HOME FROM THE AUCTION HOUSE IN ONLY ONE JUMP BECAUSE I TAPPED INTO YOUR MAGIC INSTEAD OF USING MINE.
HUGO! WHY DIDN'T YOU WARN ME?
Yikes!
DON'T BLAME YOUR VODYANOI. CHISE IS A SPECIAL CREATURE TO THEM. THEY'RE DRAWN TO HER LIKE MOTHS TO FLAME.
B-but, Angelica...!
OF COURSE NOT. IT'S AS NATURAL TO YOU AS BREATH-ING.
FOR NOW, JUST THINK OF YOUR-SELF AS UNSKILLED AT THE **SUBTLER** THINGS.
BUT I DON'T **FEEL** LIKE I'M ABSORBING ANYTHING...

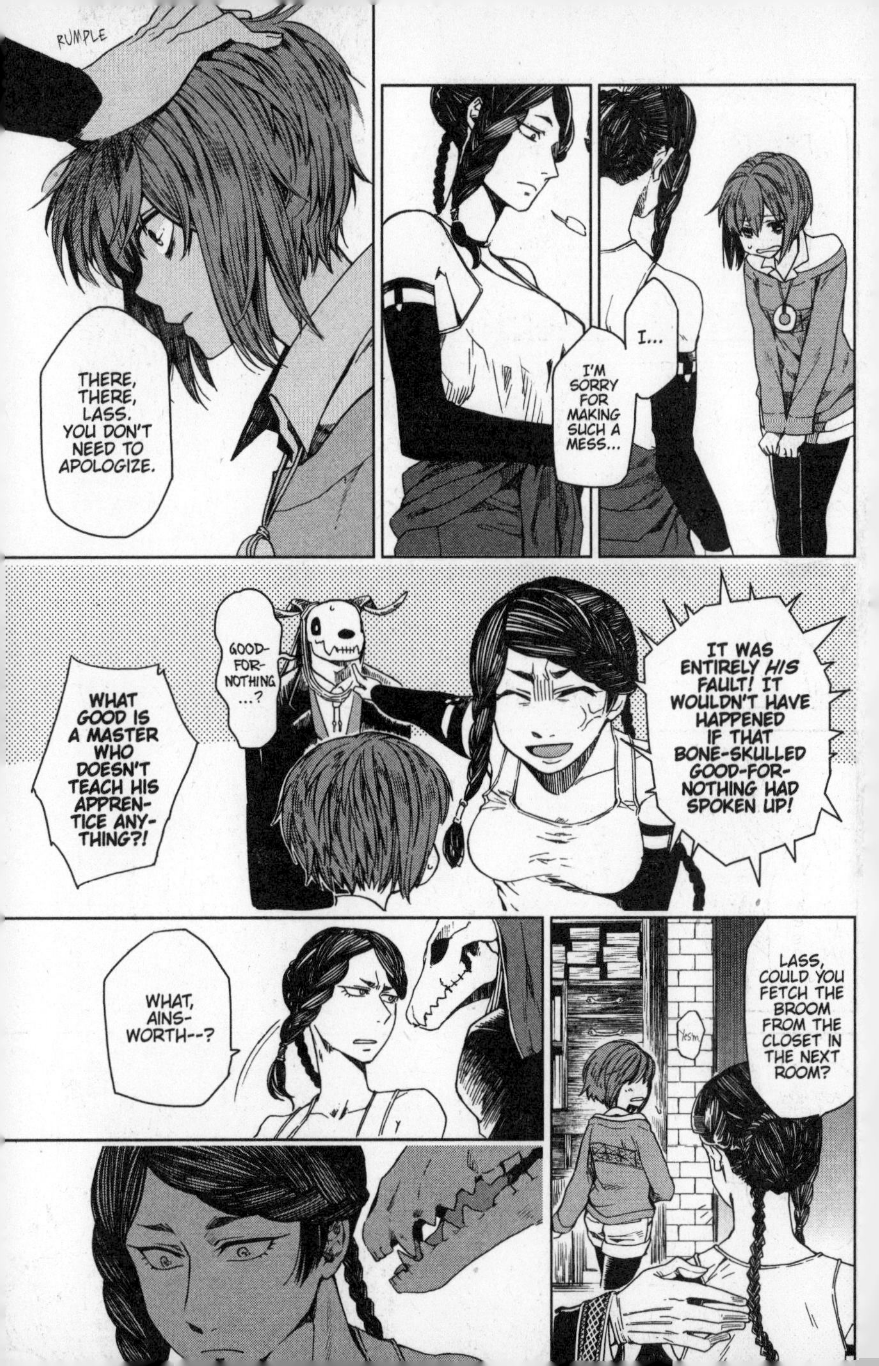
I...
I'M SORRY FOR MAKING SUCH A MESS...
RUMPLE
THERE, THERE, LASS. YOU DON'T NEED TO APOLOGIZE.
IT WAS ENTIRELY *HIS* FAULT! IT WOULDN'T HAVE HAPPENED IF THAT BONE-SKULLED GOOD-FOR-NOTHING HAD SPOKEN UP!
GOOD-FOR-NOTHING ...?
WHAT GOOD IS A MASTER WHO DOESN'T TEACH HIS APPRENTICE ANYTHING?!
LASS, COULD YOU FETCH THE BROOM FROM THE CLOSET IN THE NEXT ROOM?
Yes'm
WHAT, AINSWORTH--?

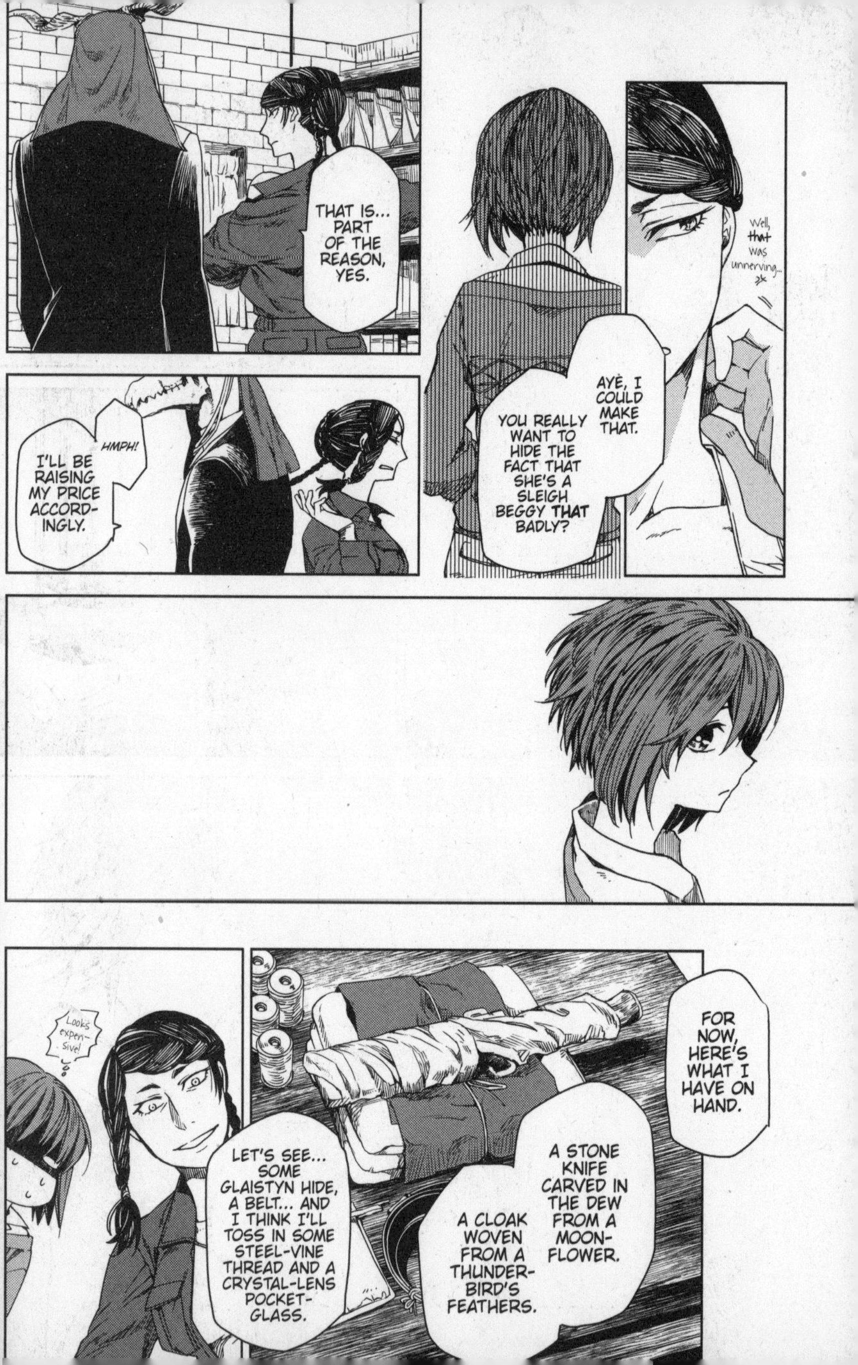
Well, that was unnerving...
AYE, I COULD MAKE THAT.
YOU REALLY WANT TO HIDE THE FACT THAT SHE'S A SLEIGH BEGGY THAT BADLY?
THAT IS... PART OF THE REASON, YES.
HMPH!
I'LL BE RAISING MY PRICE ACCORDINGLY.
FOR NOW, HERE'S WHAT I HAVE ON HAND.
A STONE KNIFE CARVED IN THE DEW FROM A MOONFLOWER.
A CLOAK WOVEN FROM A THUNDERBIRD'S FEATHERS.
LET'S SEE... SOME GLAISTYN HIDE, A BELT... AND I THINK I'LL TOSS IN SOME STEEL-VINE THREAD AND A CRYSTAL-LENS POCKETGLASS.
Looks expensive!

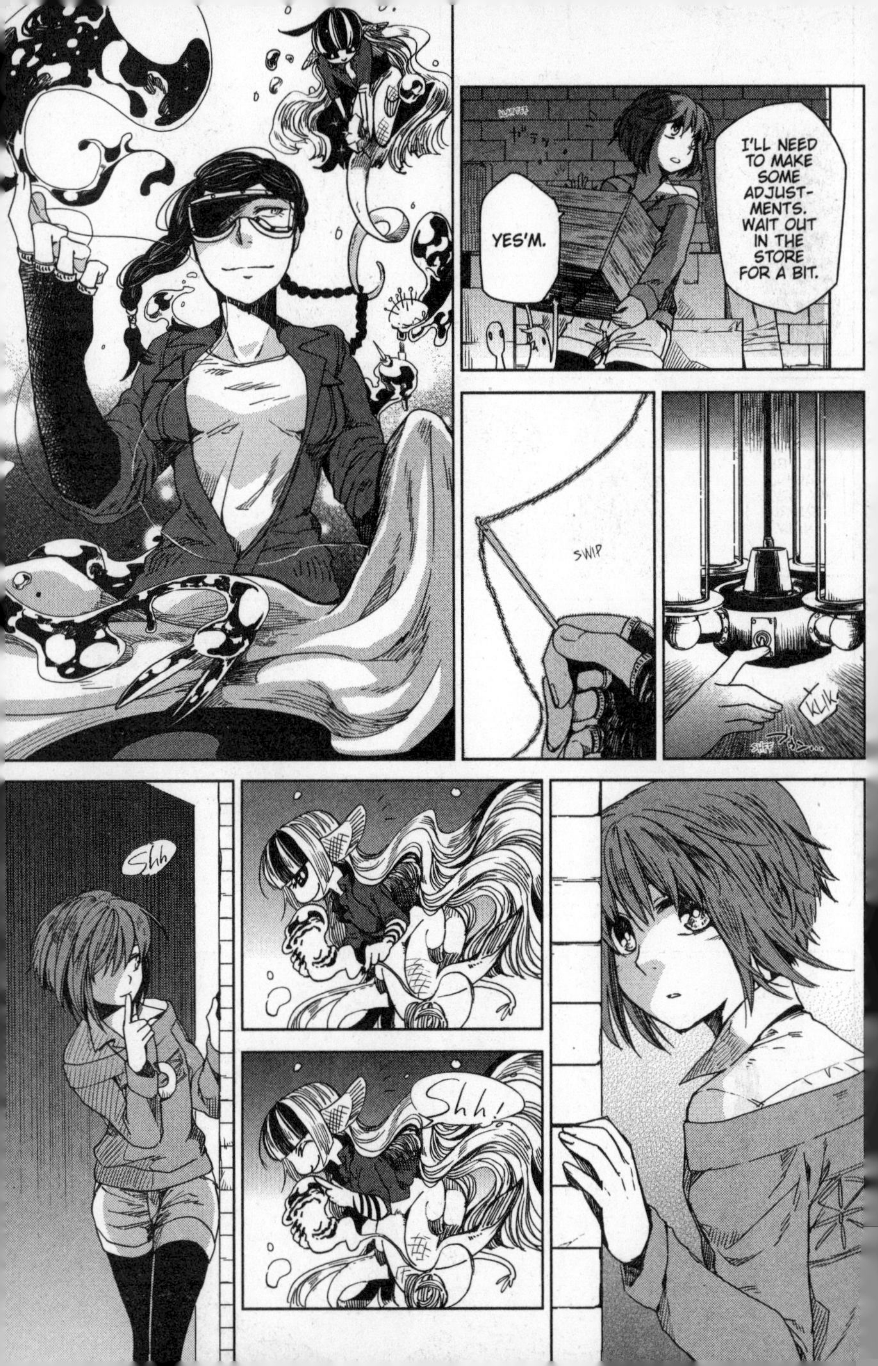
I'LL NEED TO MAKE SOME ADJUST-MENTS. WAIT OUT IN THE STORE FOR A BIT.
YES'M.
KLIK
SWIP
Shh!
Shh

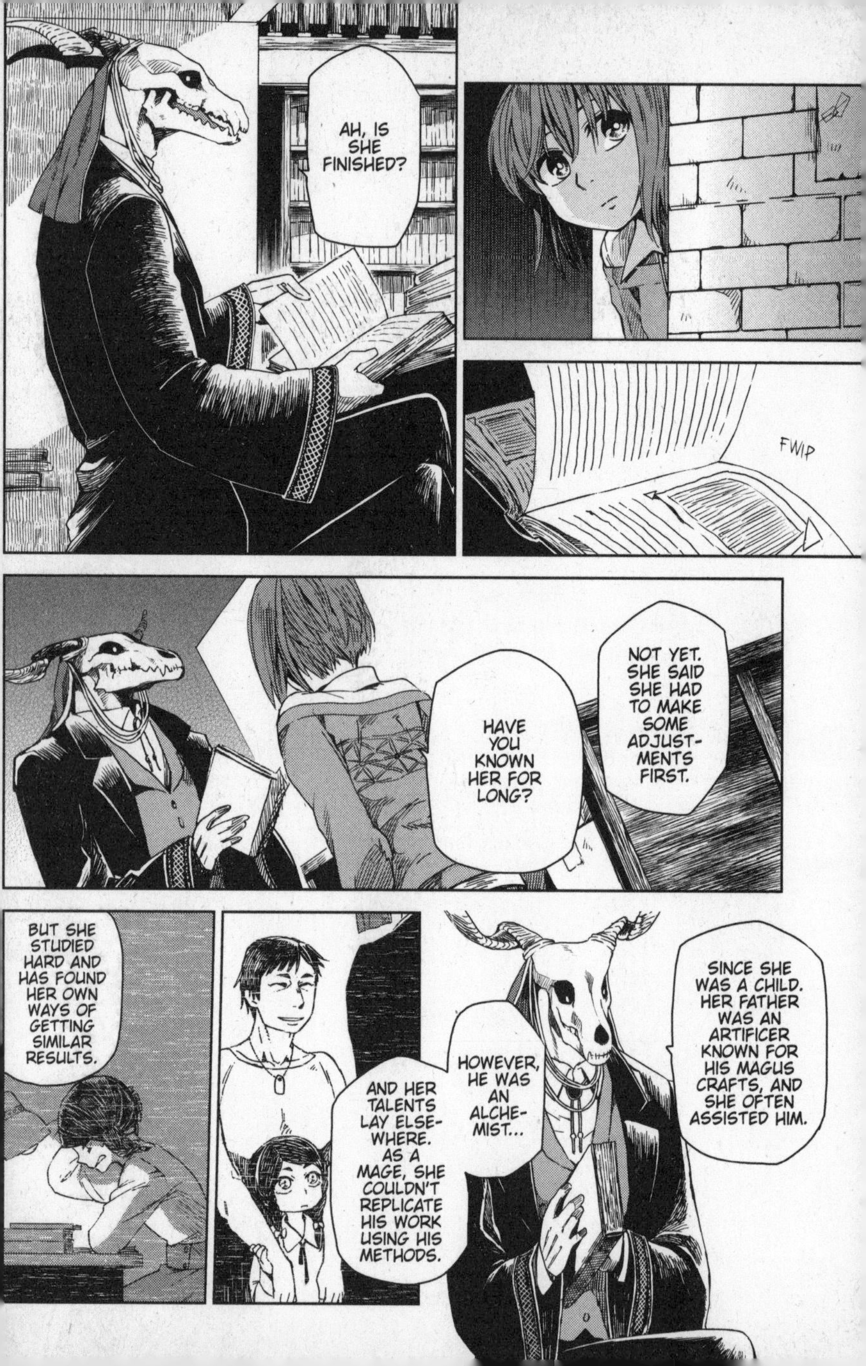
FWIP
AH, IS SHE FINISHED?
NOT YET. SHE SAID SHE HAD TO MAKE SOME ADJUST-MENTS FIRST.
HAVE YOU KNOWN HER FOR LONG?
SINCE SHE WAS A CHILD. HER FATHER WAS AN ARTIFICER KNOWN FOR HIS MAGUS CRAFTS, AND SHE OFTEN ASSISTED HIM.
HOWEVER, HE WAS AN ALCHE-MIST...
AND HER TALENTS LAY ELSE-WHERE. AS A MAGE, SHE COULDN'T REPLICATE HIS WORK USING HIS METHODS.
BUT SHE STUDIED HARD AND HAS FOUND HER OWN WAYS OF GETTING SIMILAR RESULTS.

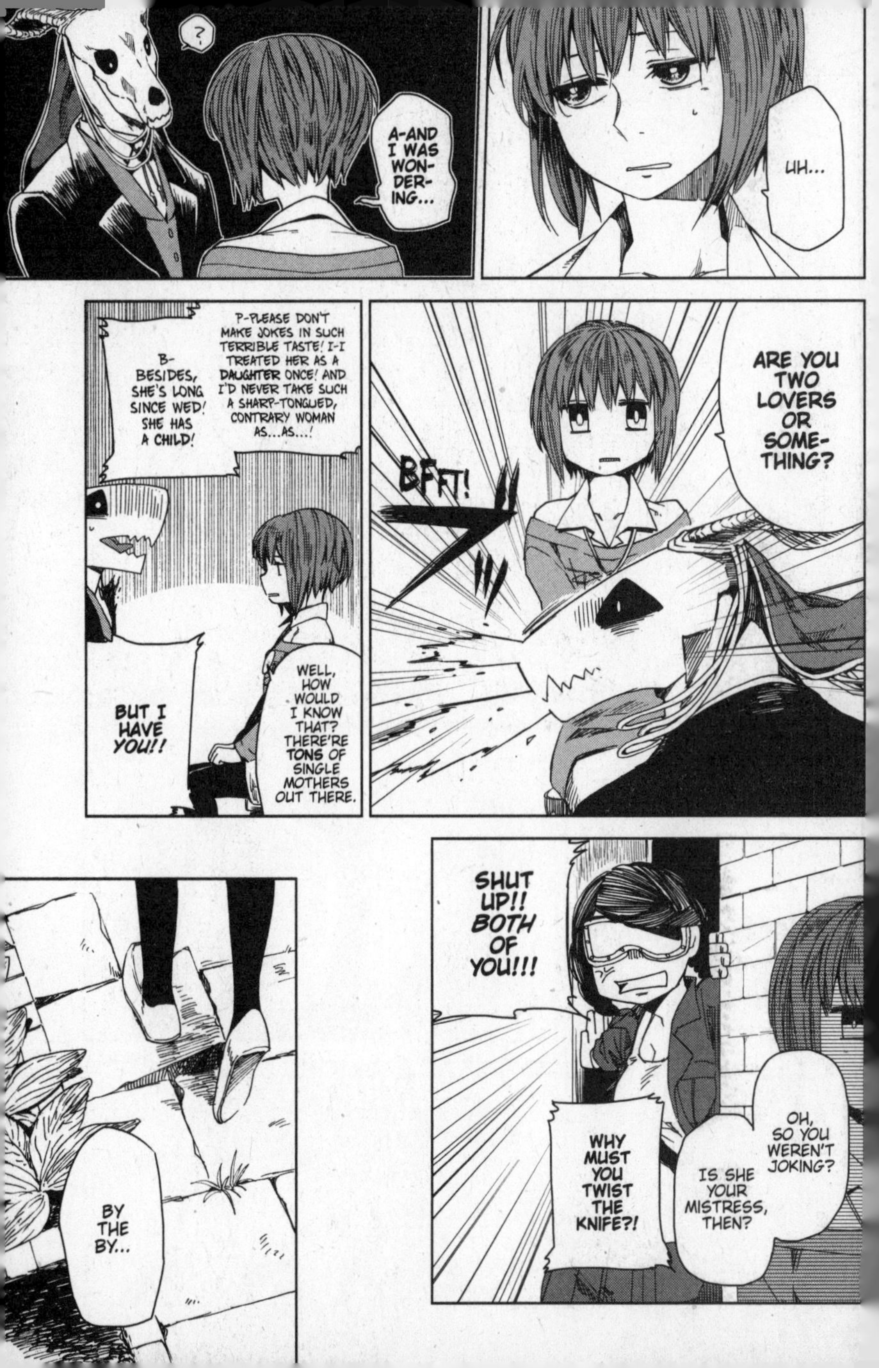
UH...
?
A-AND I WAS WON-DER-ING...
ARE YOU TWO LOVERS OR SOME-THING?
BFFT!
P-PLEASE DON'T MAKE JOKES IN SUCH TERRIBLE TASTE! I-I TREATED HER AS A DAUGHTER ONCE! AND I'D NEVER TAKE SUCH A SHARP-TONGUED, CONTRARY WOMAN AS...AS...!
B-BESIDES, SHE'S LONG SINCE WED! SHE HAS A CHILD!
WELL, HOW WOULD I KNOW THAT? THERE'RE TONS OF SINGLE MOTHERS OUT THERE.
BUT I HAVE YOU!!
SHUT UP!! BOTH OF YOU!!!
OH, SO YOU WEREN'T JOKING?
IS SHE YOUR MISTRESS, THEN?
WHY MUST YOU TWIST THE KNIFE?!
BY THE BY...

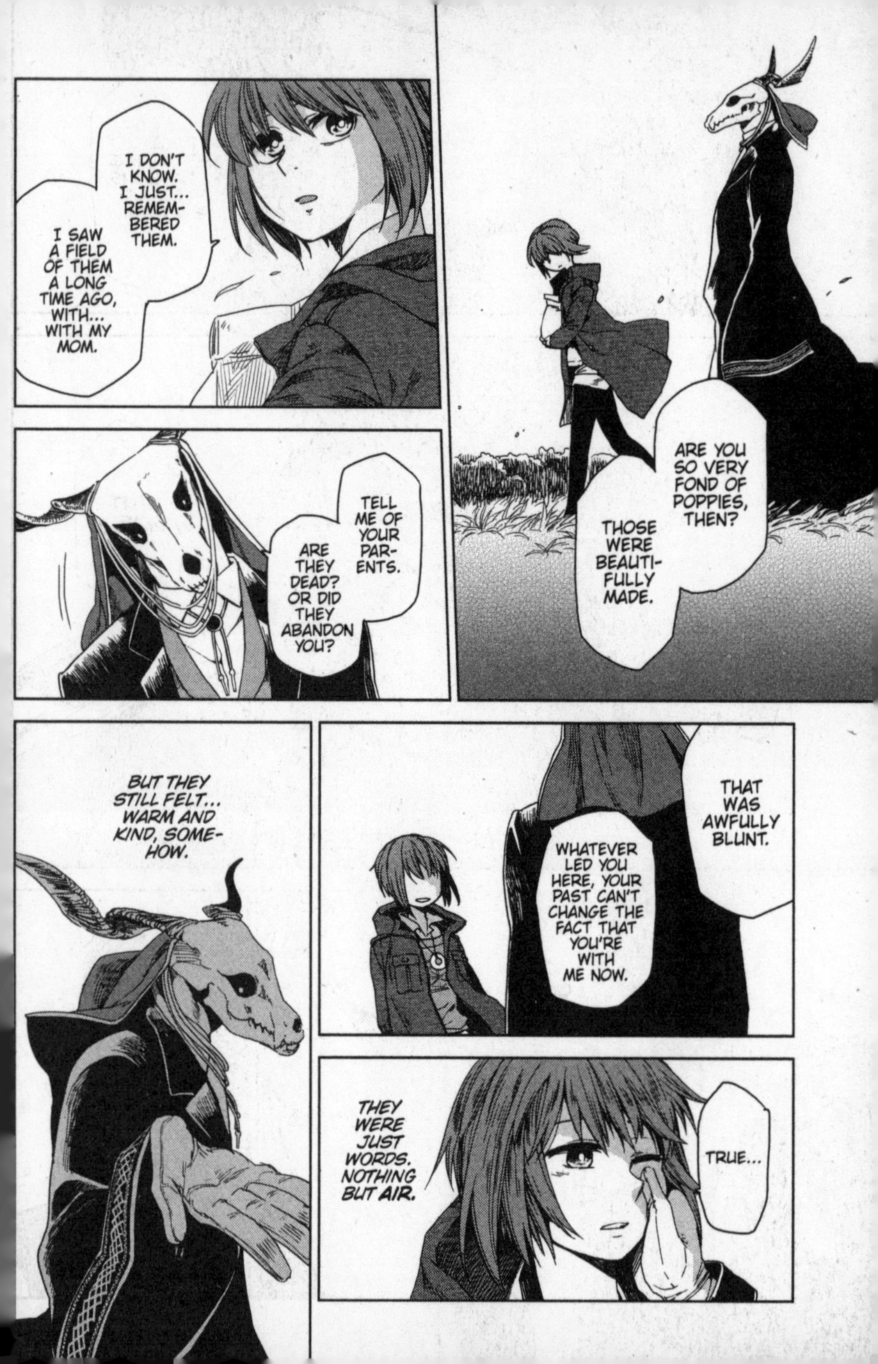
ARE YOU SO VERY FOND OF POPPIES, THEN?
THOSE WERE BEAUTIFULLY MADE.
I DON'T KNOW. I JUST... REMEMBERED THEM.
I SAW A FIELD OF THEM A LONG TIME AGO, WITH... WITH MY MOM.
TELL ME OF YOUR PARENTS.
ARE THEY DEAD? OR DID THEY ABANDON YOU?
THAT WAS AWFULLY BLUNT.
WHATEVER LED YOU HERE, YOUR PAST CAN'T CHANGE THE FACT THAT YOU'RE WITH ME NOW.
TRUE...
THEY WERE JUST WORDS. NOTHING BUT AIR.
BUT THEY STILL FELT... WARM AND KIND, SOMEHOW.

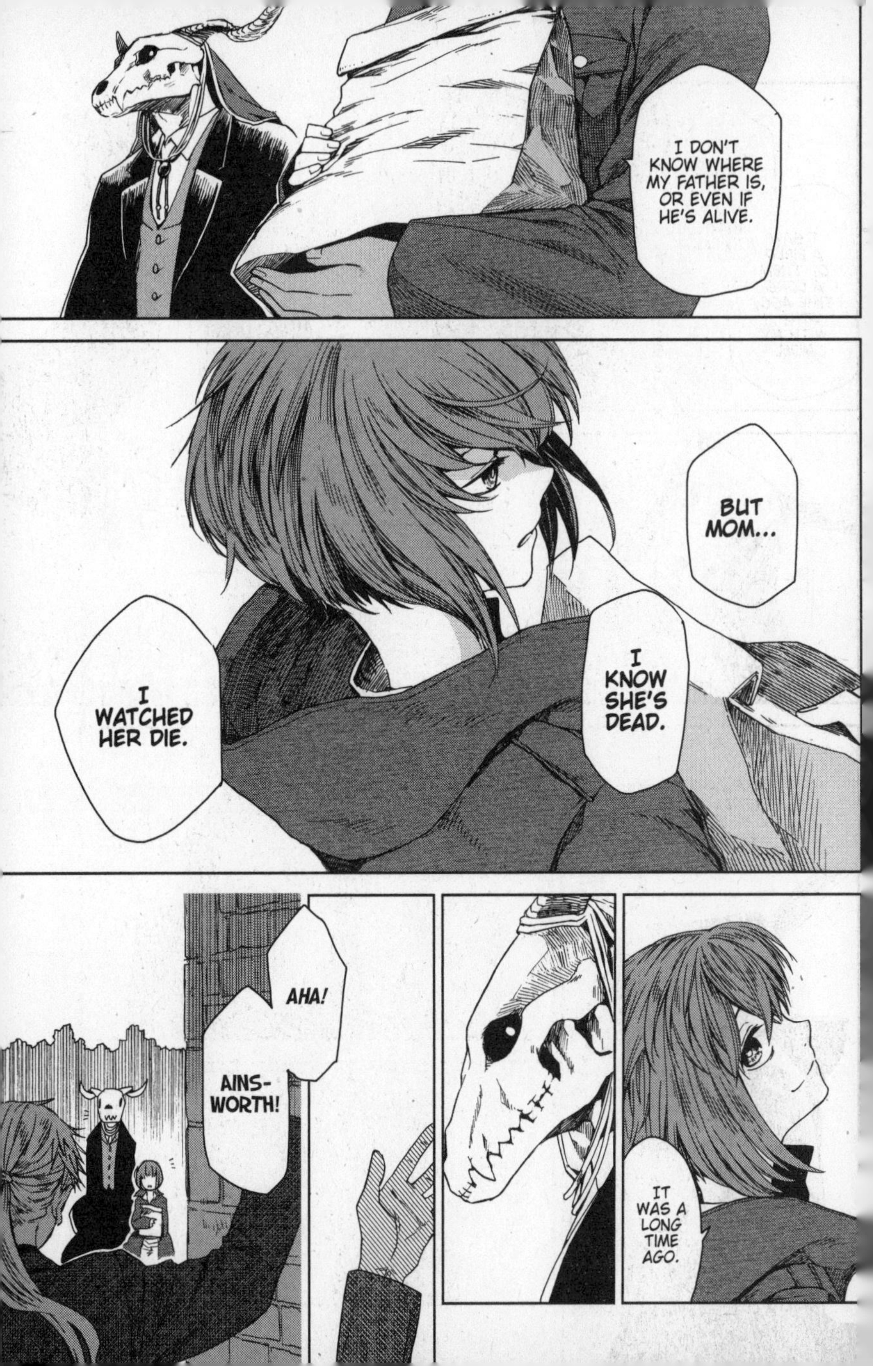
I DON'T KNOW WHERE MY FATHER IS, OR EVEN IF HE'S ALIVE.
BUT MOM...
I KNOW SHE'S DEAD.
I WATCHED HER DIE.
IT WAS A LONG TIME AGO.
AHA!
AINS-WORTH!

I WROTE AND TOLD YOU WHEN I'D BE ARRIVING!
WHY ARE YOU ALWAYS OUT OF THE HOUSE WHEN I COME CALLING? WHAT KIND OF HERMIT ARE YOU?
EVEN I HAVE THE OCCASIONAL ERRAND. BESIDES, YOU'RE HARDLY EVER EAGER TO COME SEE ME.
A PRIEST ...?
WELL, YOUR MAID SEEMS TO HATE ME, SO I WASN'T EVEN ALLOWED TO WAIT INSIDE. I'VE BEEN STANDING AROUND OUT HERE.
OH, HULLO. YOU MUST BE HIS NEW APPRENTICE, CHISE.
MY NAME IS SIMON CULLUM.
I STOPPED BY TO ASK YOU FOR HELP-- BOTH OF YOU.

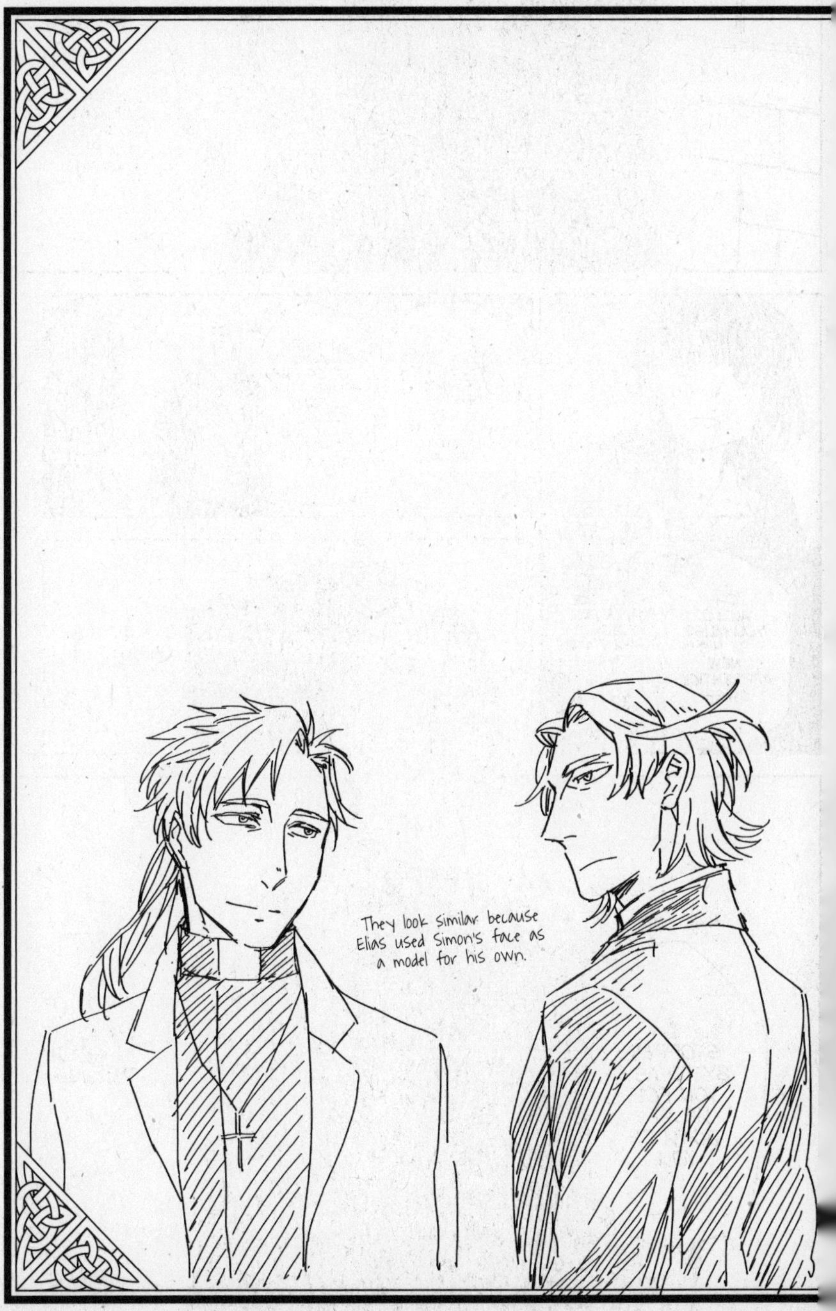
They look similar because Elias used Simon's face as a model for his own.

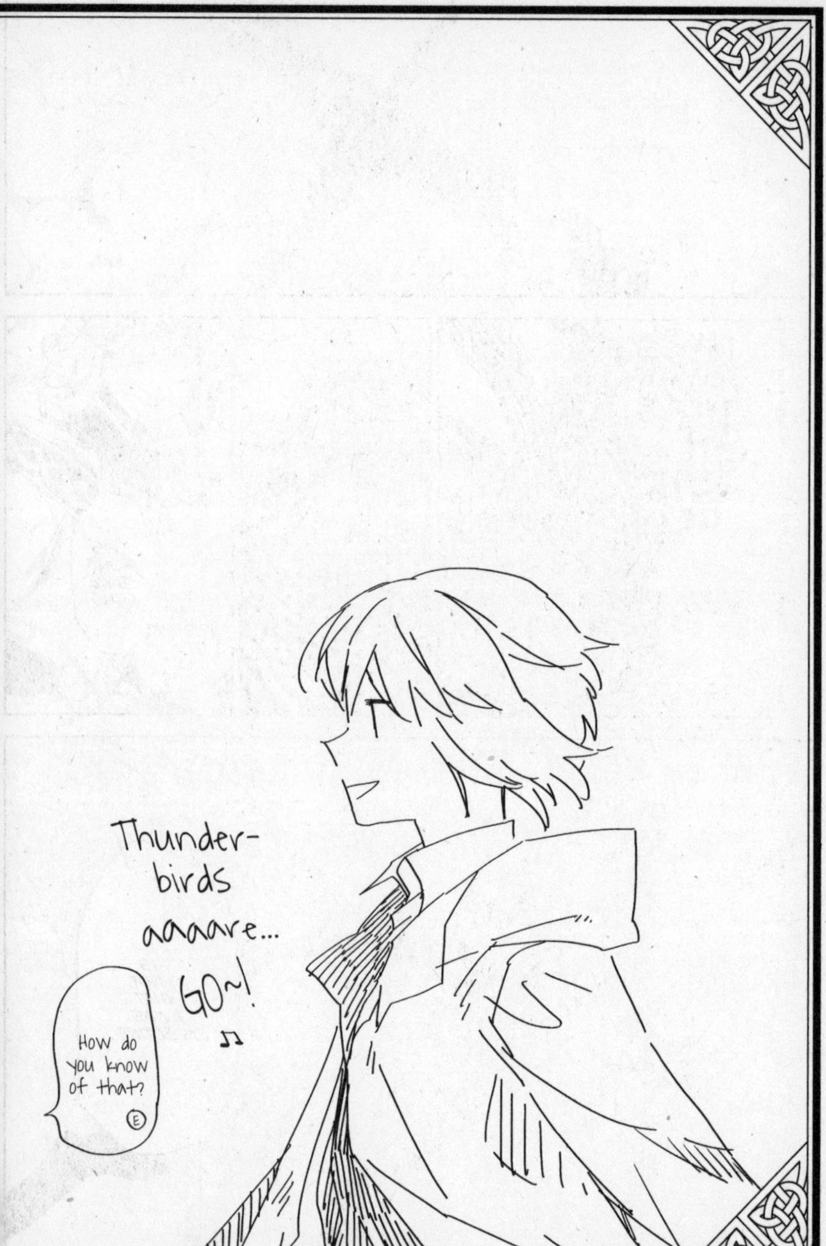
Thunder-birds aaaare... GO~!
How do you know of that? Ⓔ

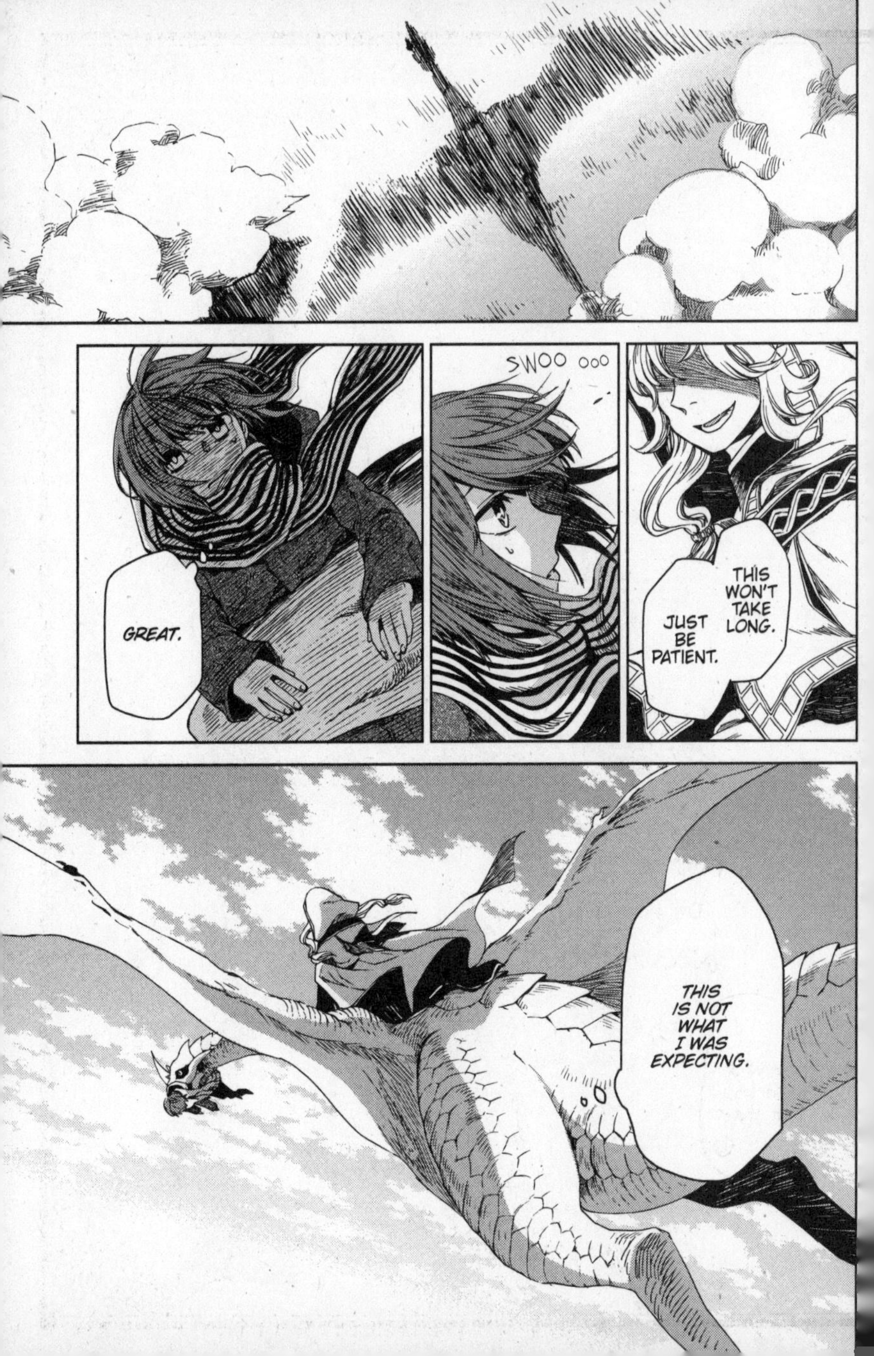
THIS WON'T TAKE LONG.
JUST BE PATIENT.
SWOO ooo
GREAT.
THIS IS NOT WHAT I WAS EXPECTING.

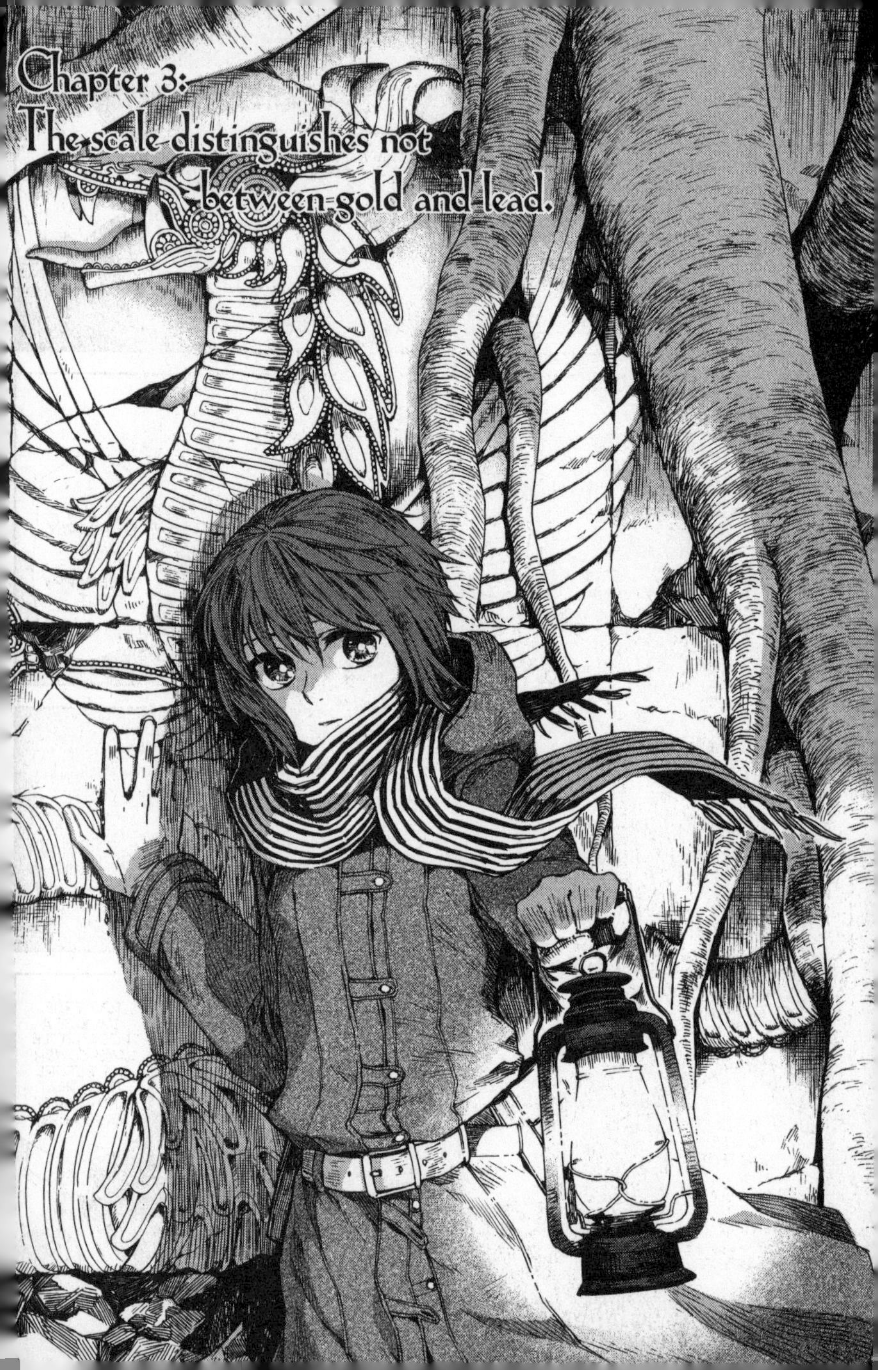
Chapter 3:
The scale distinguishes not between gold and lead.

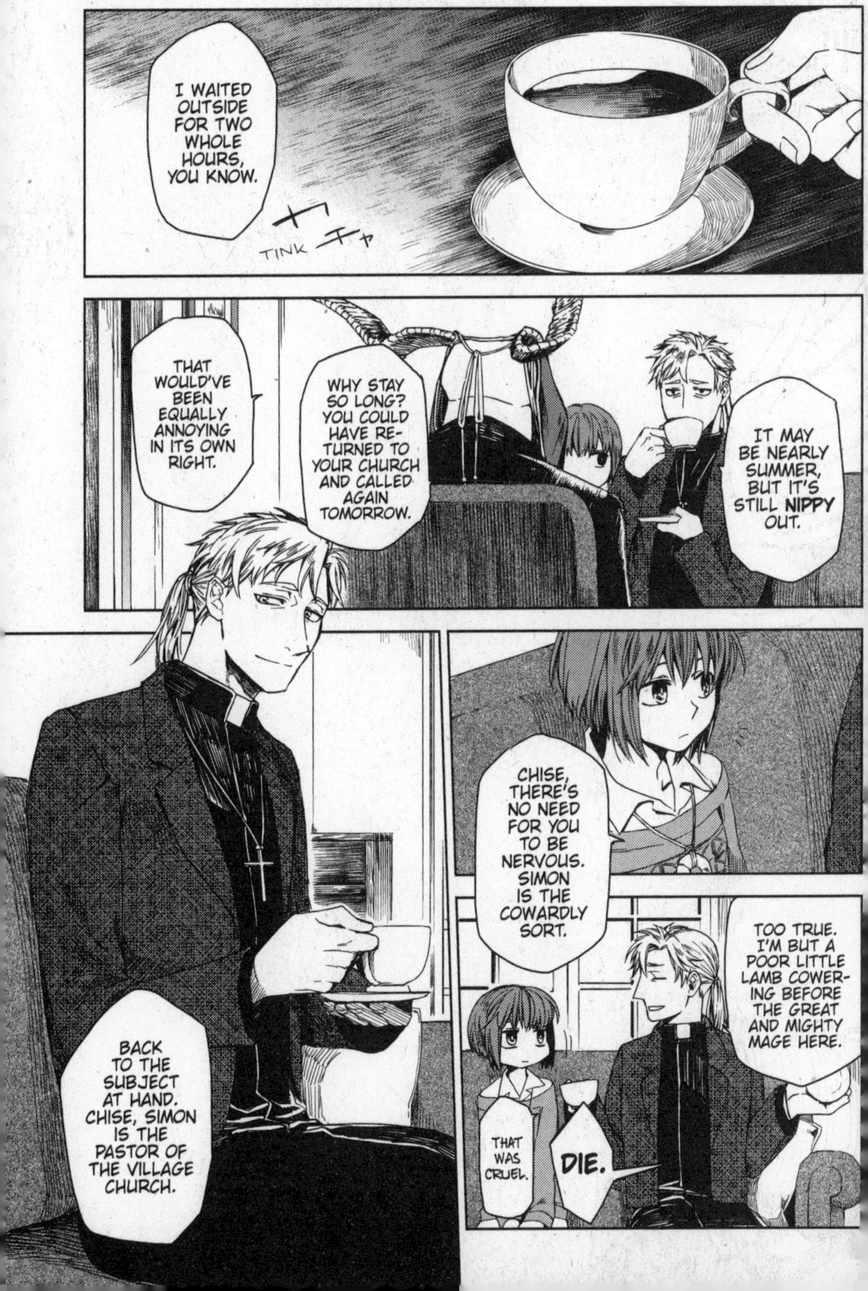
I WAITED OUTSIDE FOR TWO WHOLE HOURS, YOU KNOW.
TINK
IT MAY BE NEARLY SUMMER, BUT IT'S STILL **NIPPY** OUT.
WHY STAY SO LONG? YOU COULD HAVE RE-TURNED TO YOUR CHURCH AND CALLED AGAIN TOMORROW.
THAT WOULD'VE BEEN EQUALLY ANNOYING IN ITS OWN RIGHT.
CHISE, THERE'S NO NEED FOR YOU TO BE NERVOUS. SIMON IS THE COWARDLY SORT.
TOO TRUE. I'M BUT A POOR LITTLE LAMB COWER-ING BEFORE THE GREAT AND MIGHTY MAGE HERE.
DIE.
THAT WAS CRUEL.
BACK TO THE SUBJECT AT HAND. CHISE, SIMON IS THE PASTOR OF THE VILLAGE CHURCH.

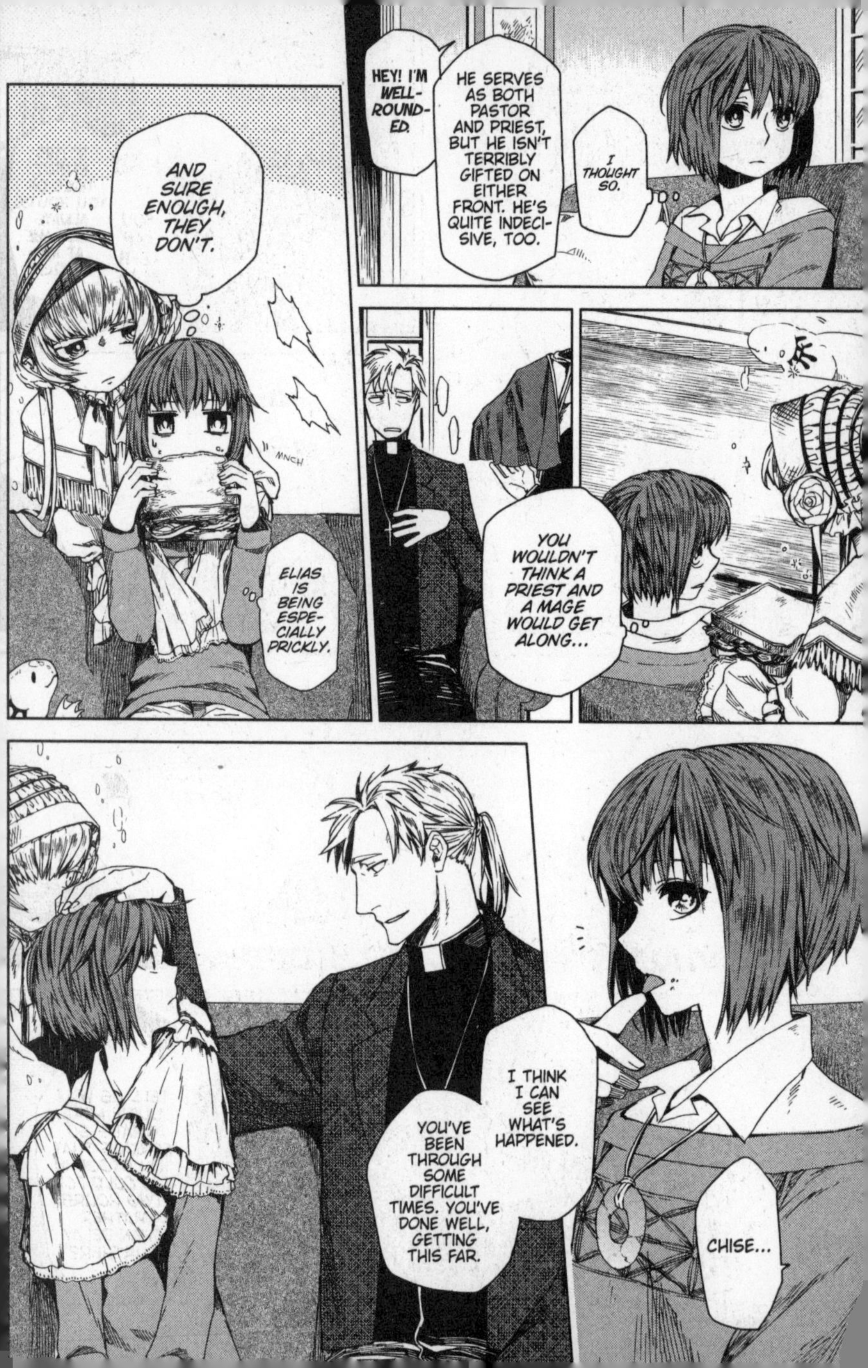

I THOUGHT SO.
HE SERVES AS BOTH PASTOR AND PRIEST, BUT HE ISN'T TERRIBLY GIFTED ON EITHER FRONT. HE'S QUITE INDECISIVE, TOO.
HEY! I'M WELL-ROUNDED.
YOU WOULDN'T THINK A PRIEST AND A MAGE WOULD GET ALONG...
AND SURE ENOUGH, THEY DON'T.
MNCH
ELIAS IS BEING ESPECIALLY PRICKLY.
CHISE...
I THINK I CAN SEE WHAT'S HAPPENED.
YOU'VE BEEN THROUGH SOME DIFFICULT TIMES. YOU'VE DONE WELL, GETTING THIS FAR.

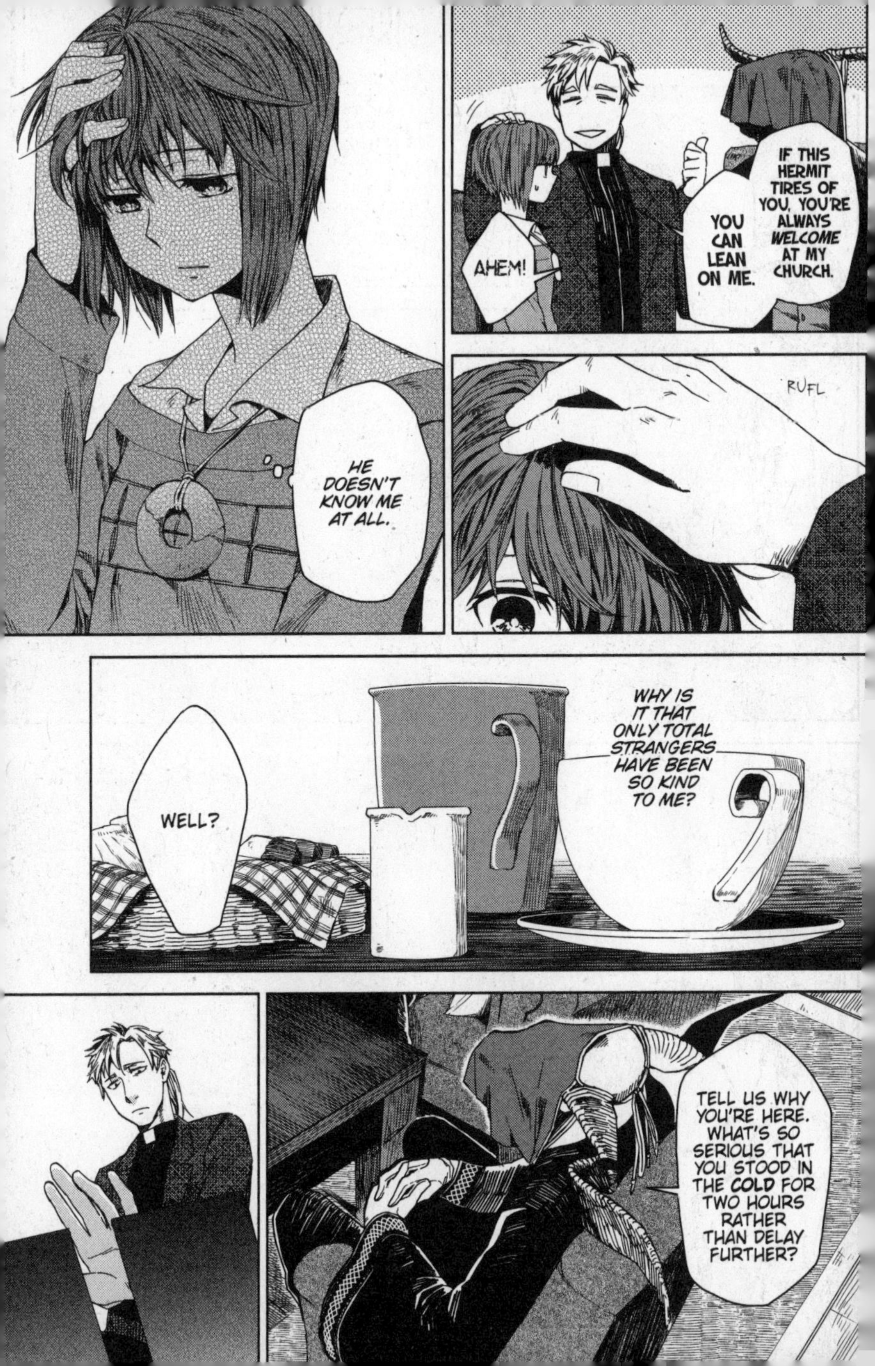
IF THIS HERMIT TIRES OF YOU, YOU'RE ALWAYS WELCOME AT MY CHURCH.
YOU CAN LEAN ON ME.
AHEM!
RUFL
HE DOESN'T KNOW ME AT ALL.
WHY IS IT THAT ONLY TOTAL STRANGERS HAVE BEEN SO KIND TO ME?
WELL?
TELL US WHY YOU'RE HERE. WHAT'S SO SERIOUS THAT YOU STOOD IN THE COLD FOR TWO HOURS RATHER THAN DELAY FURTHER?

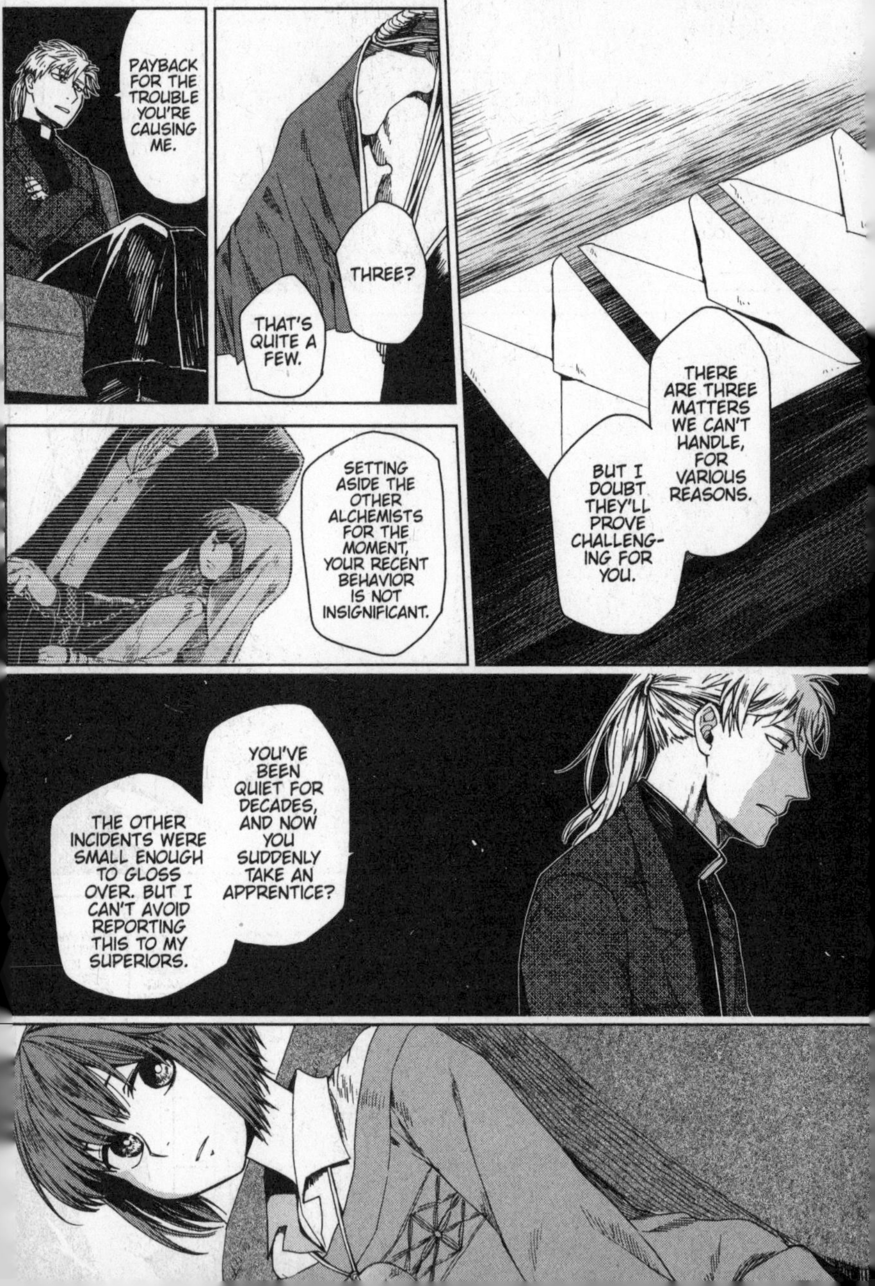
THERE ARE THREE MATTERS WE CAN'T HANDLE, FOR VARIOUS REASONS.
BUT I DOUBT THEY'LL PROVE CHALLENG-ING FOR YOU.
THREE?
THAT'S QUITE A FEW.
PAYBACK FOR THE TROUBLE YOU'RE CAUSING ME.
SETTING ASIDE THE OTHER ALCHEMISTS FOR THE MOMENT, YOUR RECENT BEHAVIOR IS NOT INSIGNIFICANT.
YOU'VE BEEN QUIET FOR DECADES, AND NOW YOU SUDDENLY TAKE AN APPRENTICE?
THE OTHER INCIDENTS WERE SMALL ENOUGH TO GLOSS OVER. BUT I CAN'T AVOID REPORTING THIS TO MY SUPERIORS.

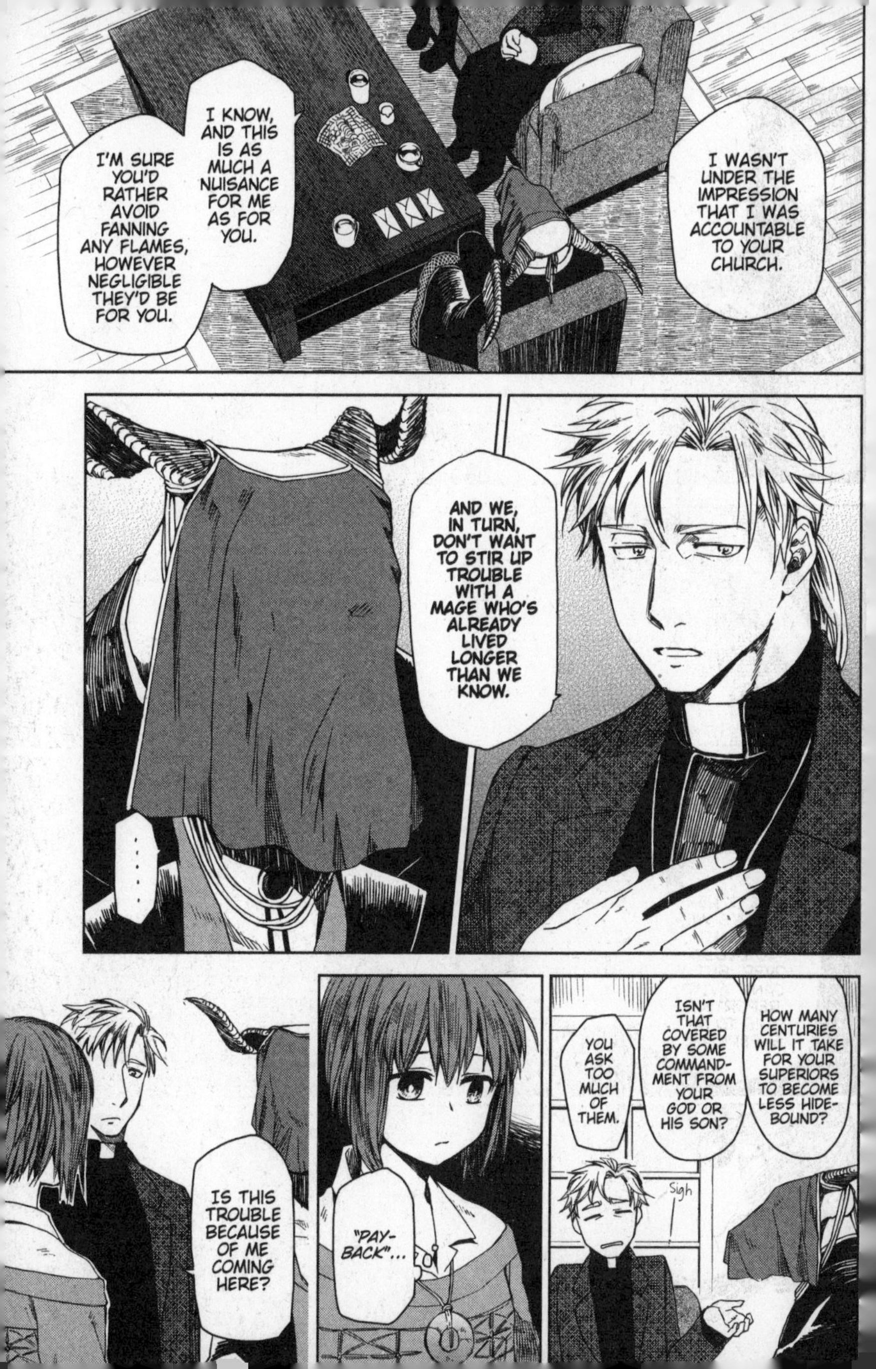
I WASN'T UNDER THE IMPRESSION THAT I WAS ACCOUNTABLE TO YOUR CHURCH.
I KNOW, AND THIS IS AS MUCH A NUISANCE FOR ME AS FOR YOU.
I'M SURE YOU'D RATHER AVOID FANNING ANY FLAMES, HOWEVER NEGLIGIBLE THEY'D BE FOR YOU.
AND WE, IN TURN, DON'T WANT TO STIR UP TROUBLE WITH A MAGE WHO'S ALREADY LIVED LONGER THAN WE KNOW.
.....
HOW MANY CENTURIES WILL IT TAKE FOR YOUR SUPERIORS TO BECOME LESS HIDE-BOUND?
ISN'T THAT COVERED BY SOME COMMAND-MENT FROM YOUR GOD OR HIS SON?
YOU ASK TOO MUCH OF THEM.
Sigh
"PAY-BACK"...
IS THIS TROUBLE BECAUSE OF ME COMING HERE?

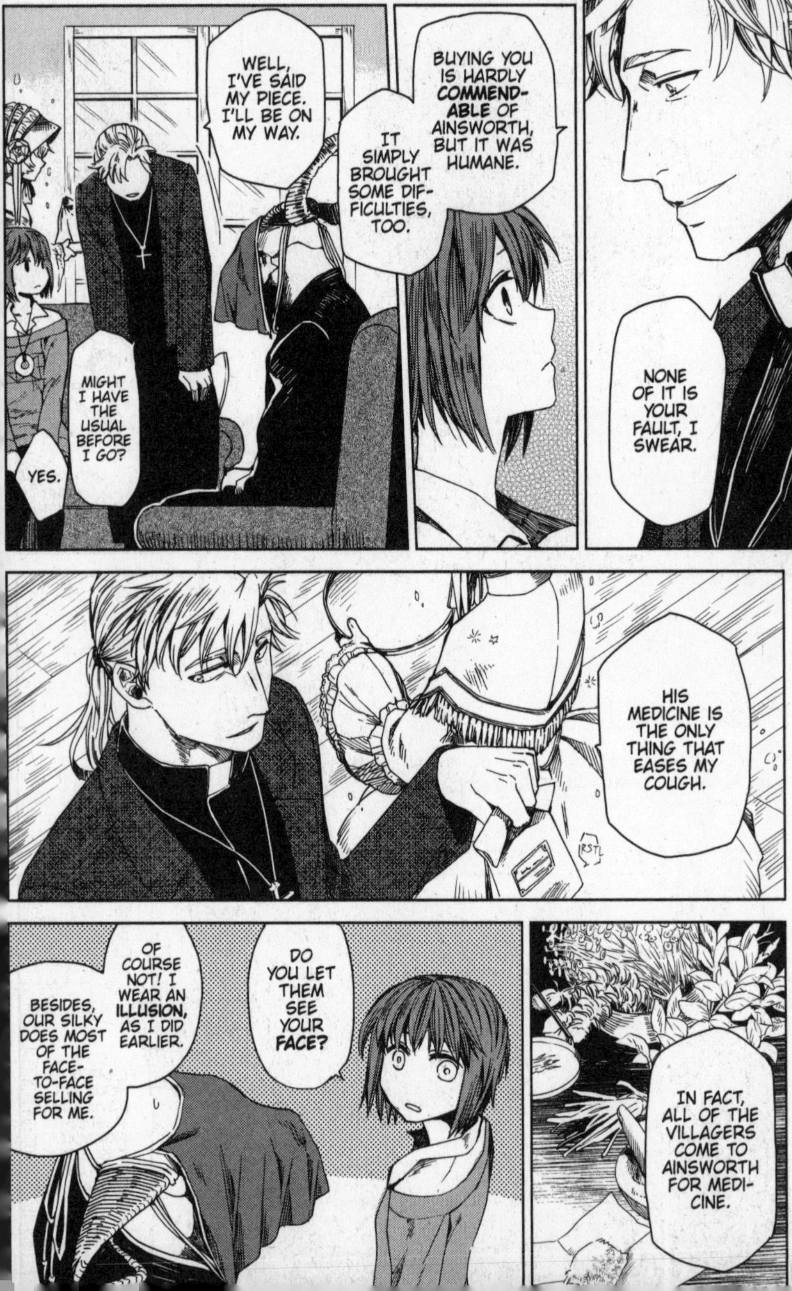
NONE OF IT IS YOUR FAULT, I SWEAR.
BUYING YOU IS HARDLY COMMENDABLE OF AINSWORTH, BUT IT WAS HUMANE.
IT SIMPLY BROUGHT SOME DIFFICULTIES, TOO.
WELL, I'VE SAID MY PIECE. I'LL BE ON MY WAY.
MIGHT I HAVE THE USUAL BEFORE I GO?
YES.
HIS MEDICINE IS THE ONLY THING THAT EASES MY COUGH.
RSTL
IN FACT, ALL OF THE VILLAGERS COME TO AINSWORTH FOR MEDICINE.
DO YOU LET THEM SEE YOUR FACE?
OF COURSE NOT! I WEAR AN ILLUSION, AS I DID EARLIER.
BESIDES, OUR SILKY DOES MOST OF THE FACE-TO-FACE SELLING FOR ME.

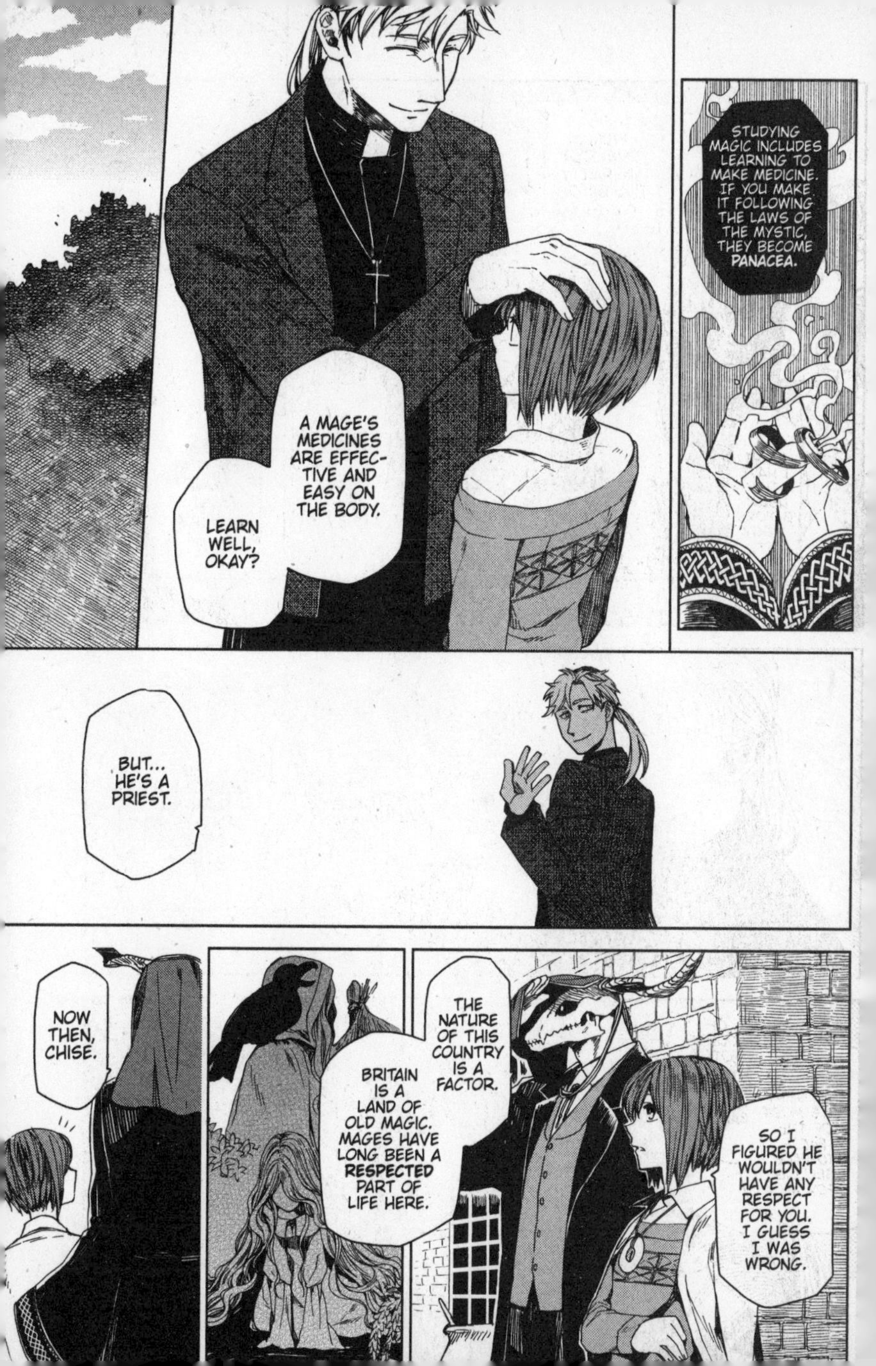
STUDYING MAGIC INCLUDES LEARNING TO MAKE MEDICINE. IF YOU MAKE IT FOLLOWING THE LAWS OF THE MYSTIC, THEY BECOME **PANACEA.**
A MAGE'S MEDICINES ARE EFFECTIVE AND EASY ON THE BODY.
LEARN WELL, OKAY?
BUT... HE'S A PRIEST.
SO I FIGURED HE WOULDN'T HAVE ANY RESPECT FOR YOU. I GUESS I WAS WRONG.
THE NATURE OF THIS COUNTRY IS A FACTOR.
BRITAIN IS A LAND OF OLD MAGIC. MAGES HAVE LONG BEEN A **RESPECTED** PART OF LIFE HERE.
NOW THEN, CHISE.

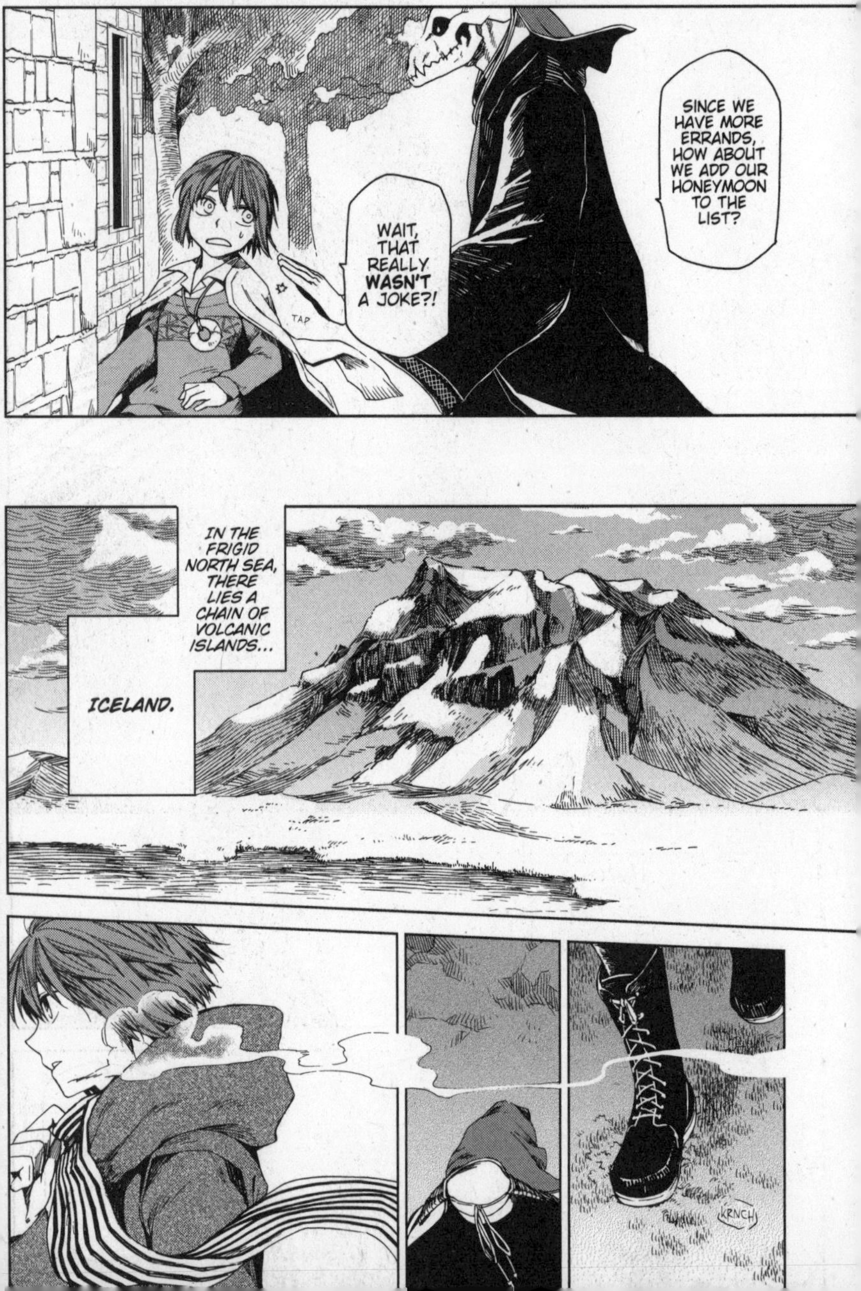
SINCE WE HAVE MORE ERRANDS, HOW ABOUT WE ADD OUR HONEYMOON TO THE LIST?
WAIT, THAT REALLY WASN'T A JOKE?!
TAP
IN THE FRIGID NORTH SEA, THERE LIES A CHAIN OF VOLCANIC ISLANDS...
ICELAND.
KRNCH

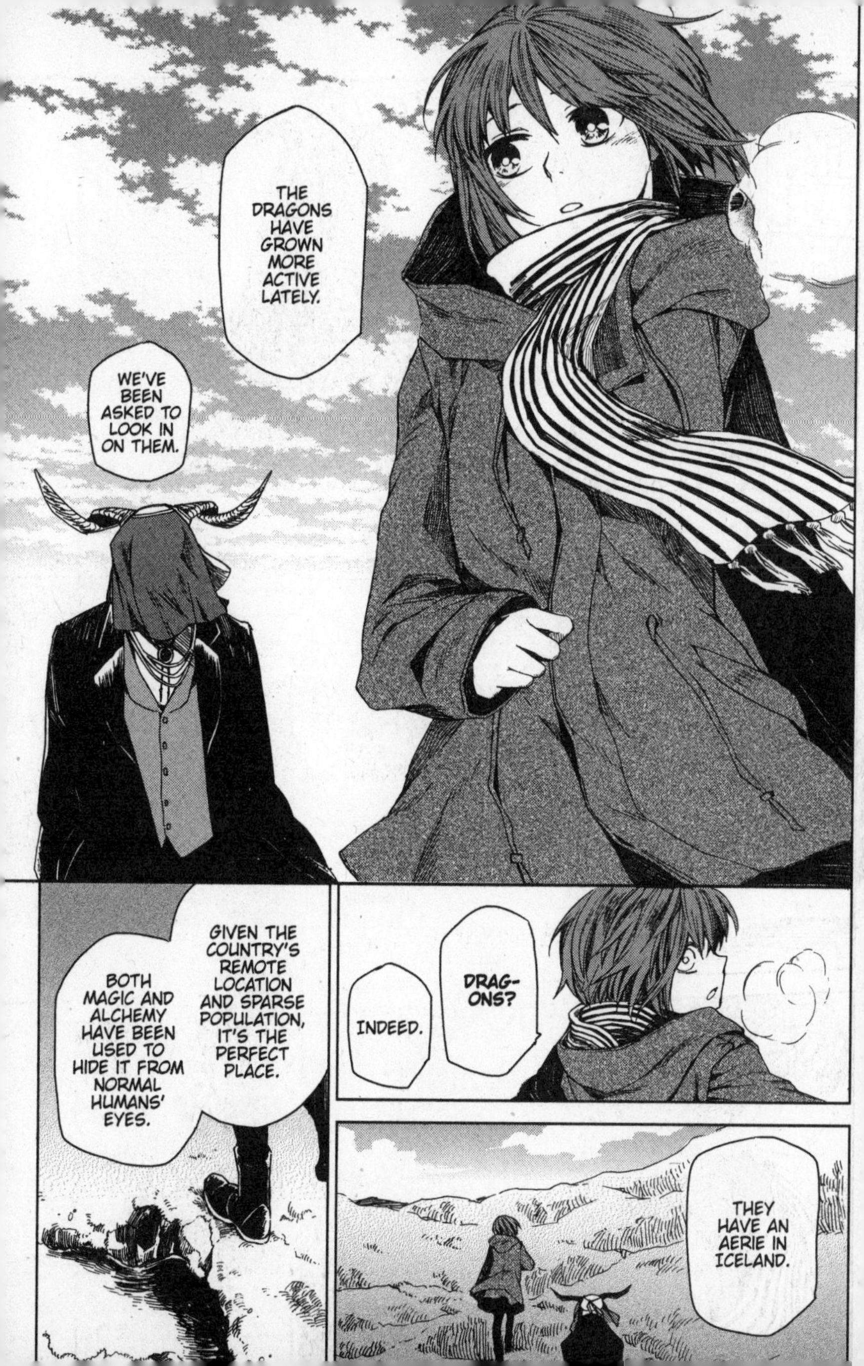
THE DRAGONS HAVE GROWN MORE ACTIVE LATELY.
WE'VE BEEN ASKED TO LOOK IN ON THEM.
DRAG-ONS?
INDEED.
THEY HAVE AN AERIE IN ICELAND.
GIVEN THE COUNTRY'S REMOTE LOCATION AND SPARSE POPULATION, IT'S THE PERFECT PLACE.
BOTH MAGIC AND ALCHEMY HAVE BEEN USED TO HIDE IT FROM NORMAL HUMANS' EYES.

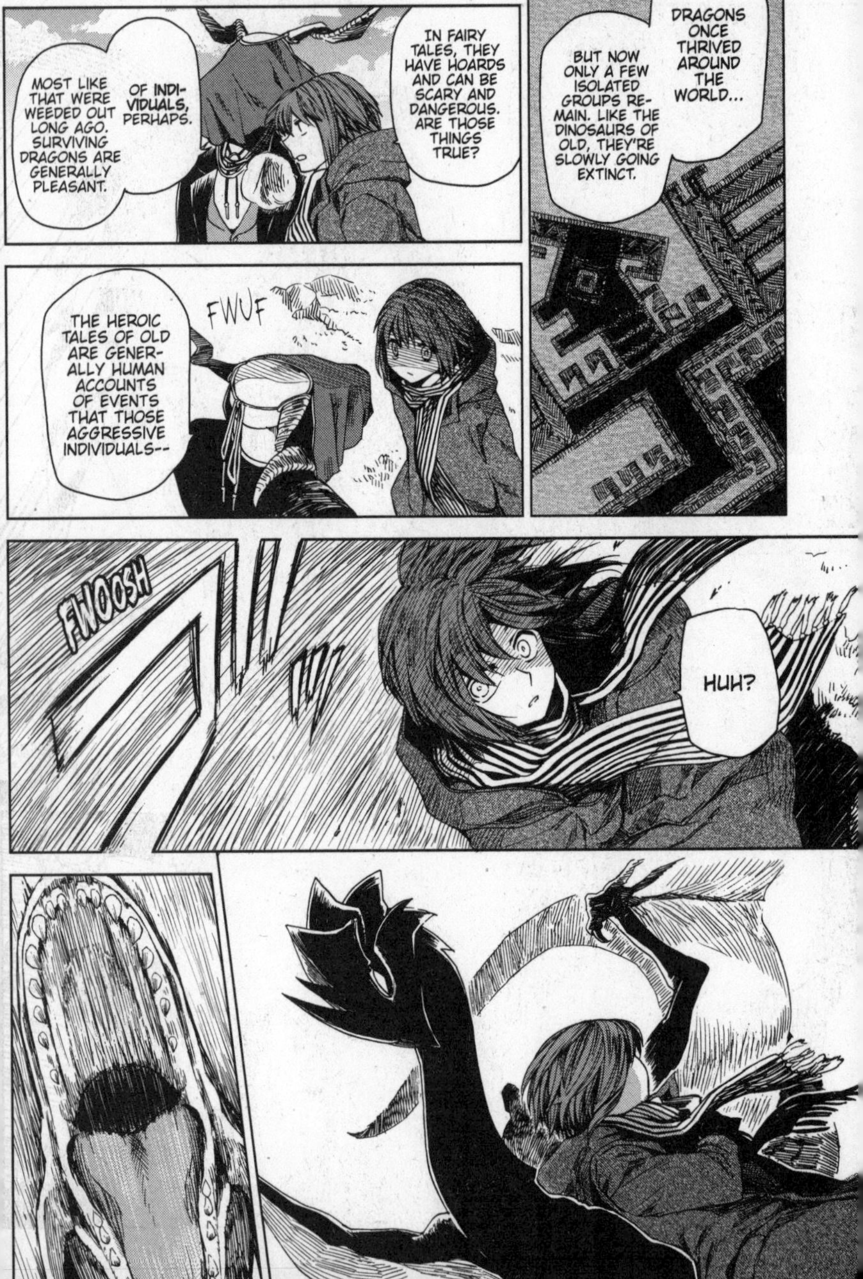
DRAGONS ONCE THRIVED AROUND THE WORLD...
BUT NOW ONLY A FEW ISOLATED GROUPS RE-MAIN. LIKE THE DINOSAURS OF OLD, THEY'RE SLOWLY GOING EXTINCT.
IN FAIRY TALES, THEY HAVE HOARDS AND CAN BE SCARY AND DANGEROUS. ARE THOSE THINGS TRUE?
OF INDI-VIDUALS, PERHAPS.
MOST LIKE THAT WERE WEEDED OUT LONG AGO. SURVIVING DRAGONS ARE GENERALLY PLEASANT.
FWUF
THE HEROIC TALES OF OLD ARE GENER-ALLY HUMAN ACCOUNTS OF EVENTS THAT THOSE AGGRESSIVE INDIVIDUALS--
HUH?
FWOOSH

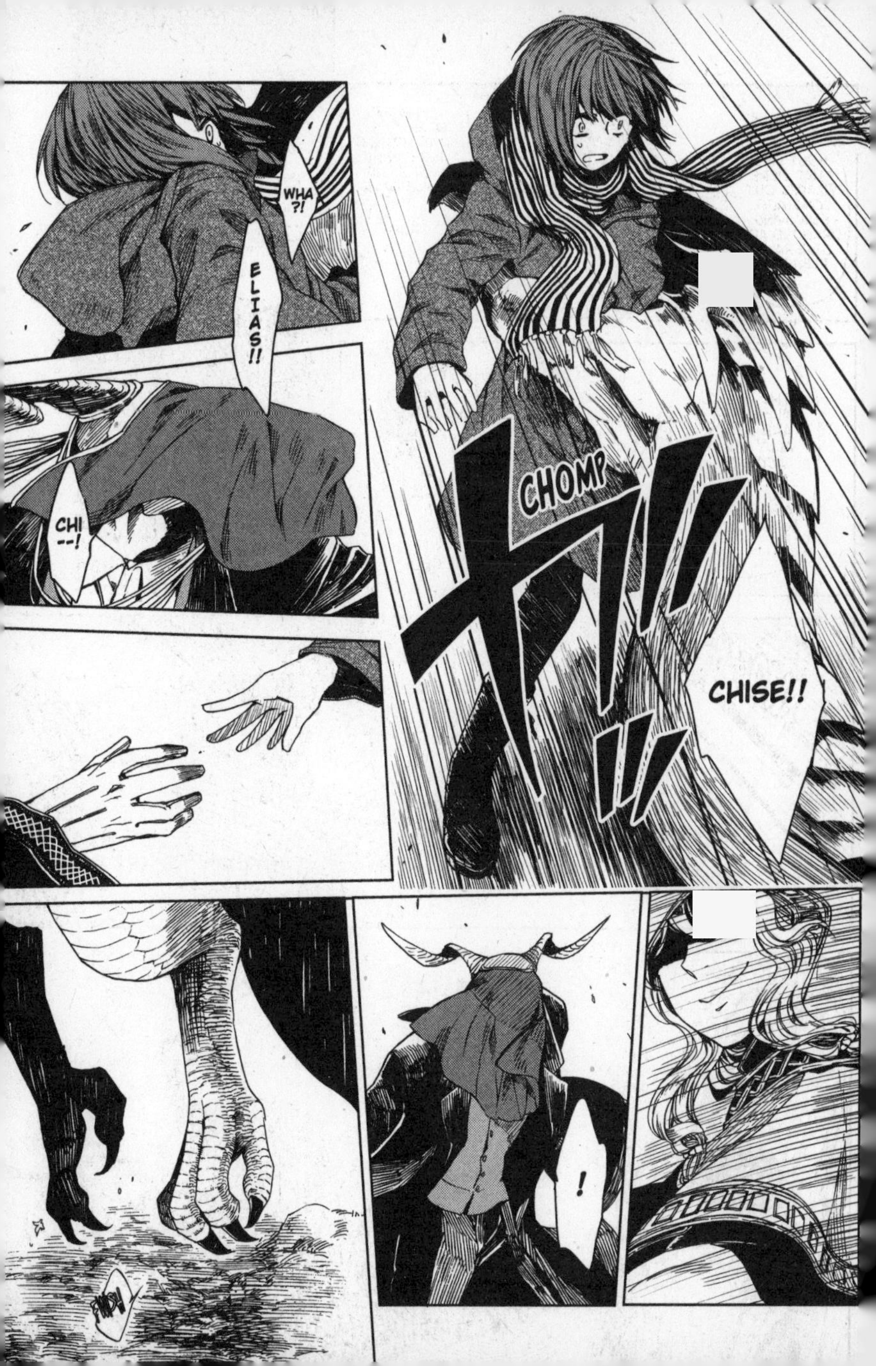
CHOMP
CHISE!!
WHA?!
ELIAS!!
CHI--!
!

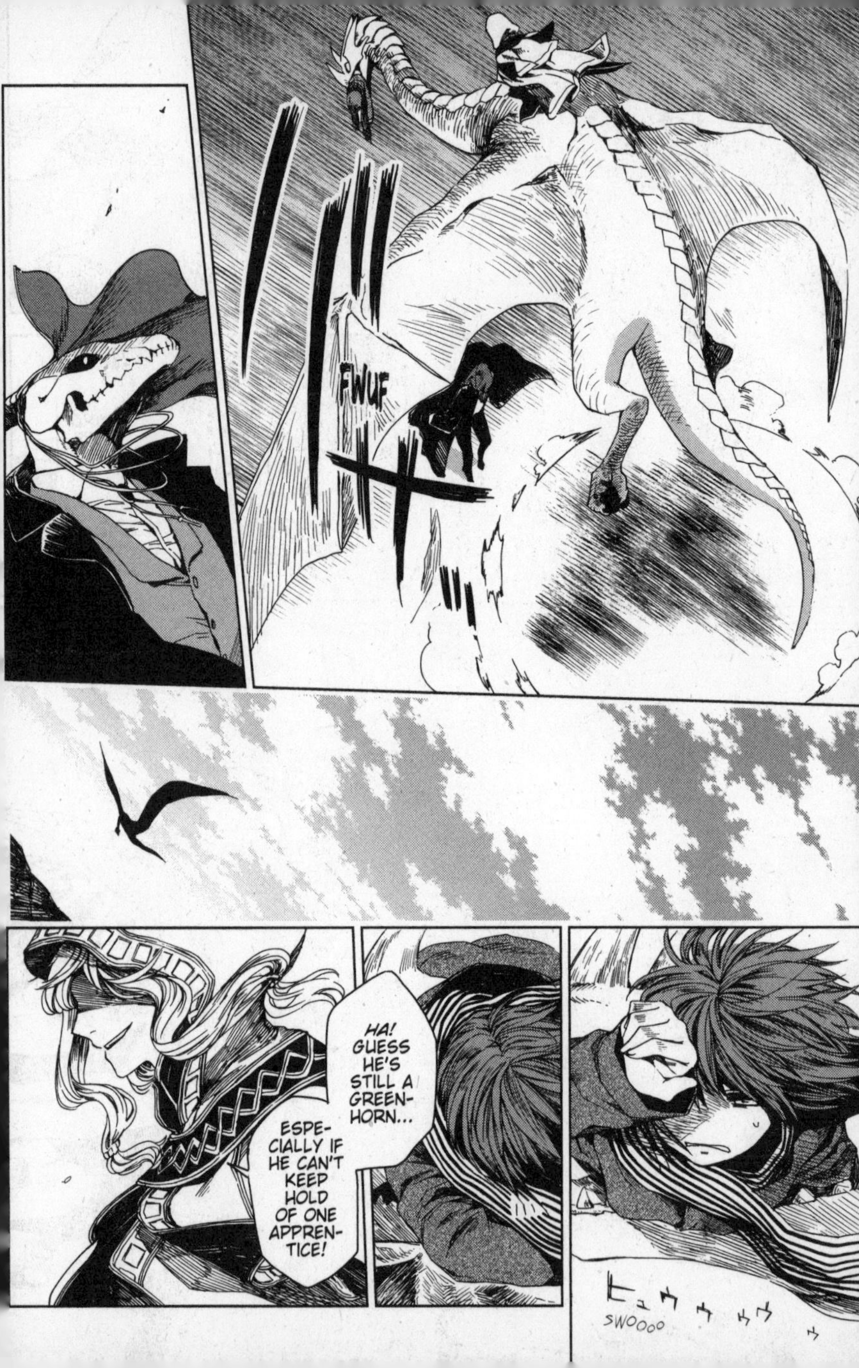
FWUF
SWOOOO
HA! GUESS HE'S STILL A GREEN-HORN...
ESPE-CIALLY IF HE CAN'T KEEP HOLD OF ONE APPREN-TICE!

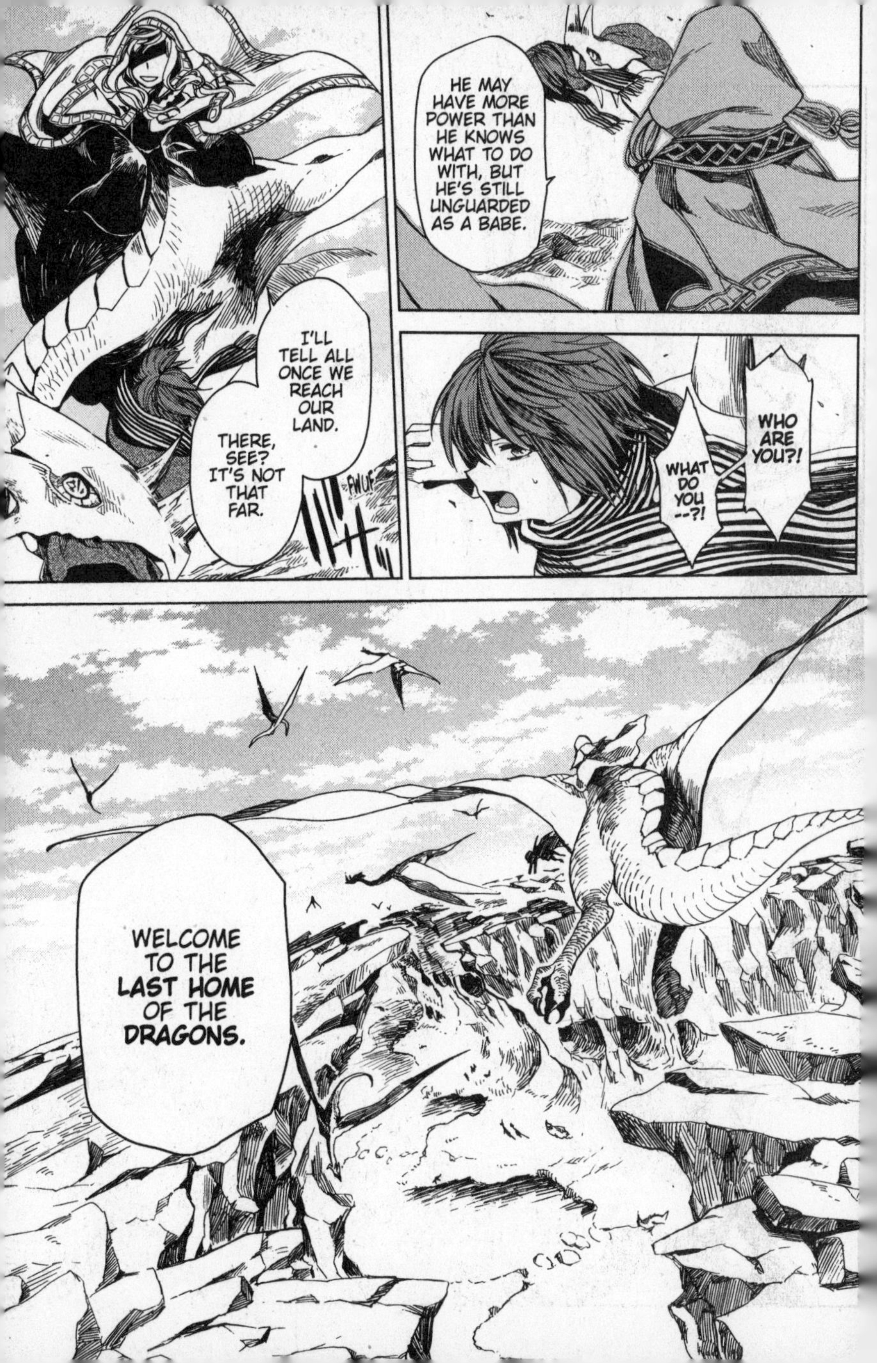
HE MAY HAVE MORE POWER THAN HE KNOWS WHAT TO DO WITH, BUT HE'S STILL UNGUARDED AS A BABE.
WHO ARE YOU?!
WHAT DO YOU --?!
I'LL TELL ALL ONCE WE REACH OUR LAND.
THERE, SEE? IT'S NOT THAT FAR.
WELCOME TO THE LAST HOME OF THE DRAGONS.

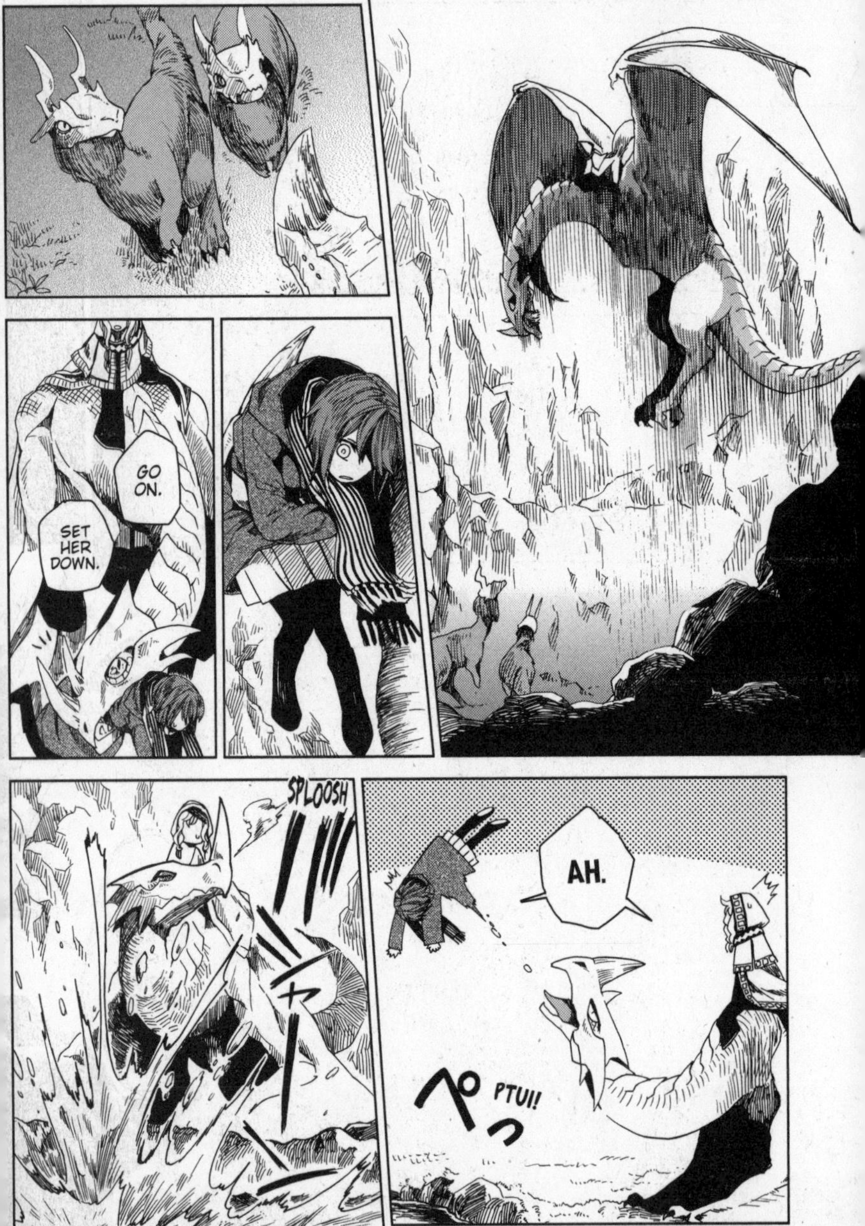
GO ON.
SET HER DOWN.
AH.
ペっ
PTUI!
SPLOOSH

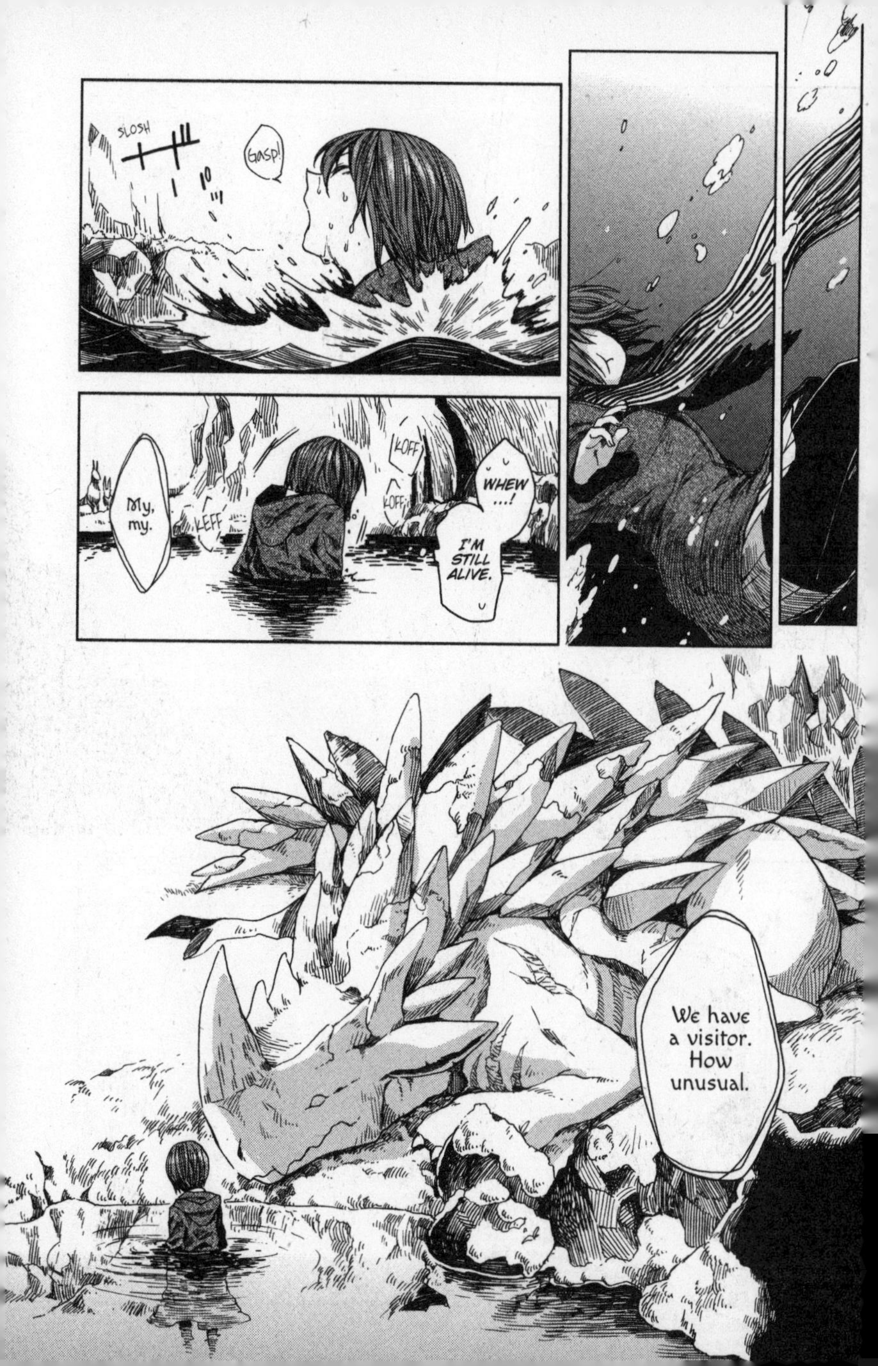
SLOSH
Gasp!
KOFF
KOFF
KEFF
WHEW...!
I'M STILL ALIVE.
My, my.
We have a visitor. How unusual.

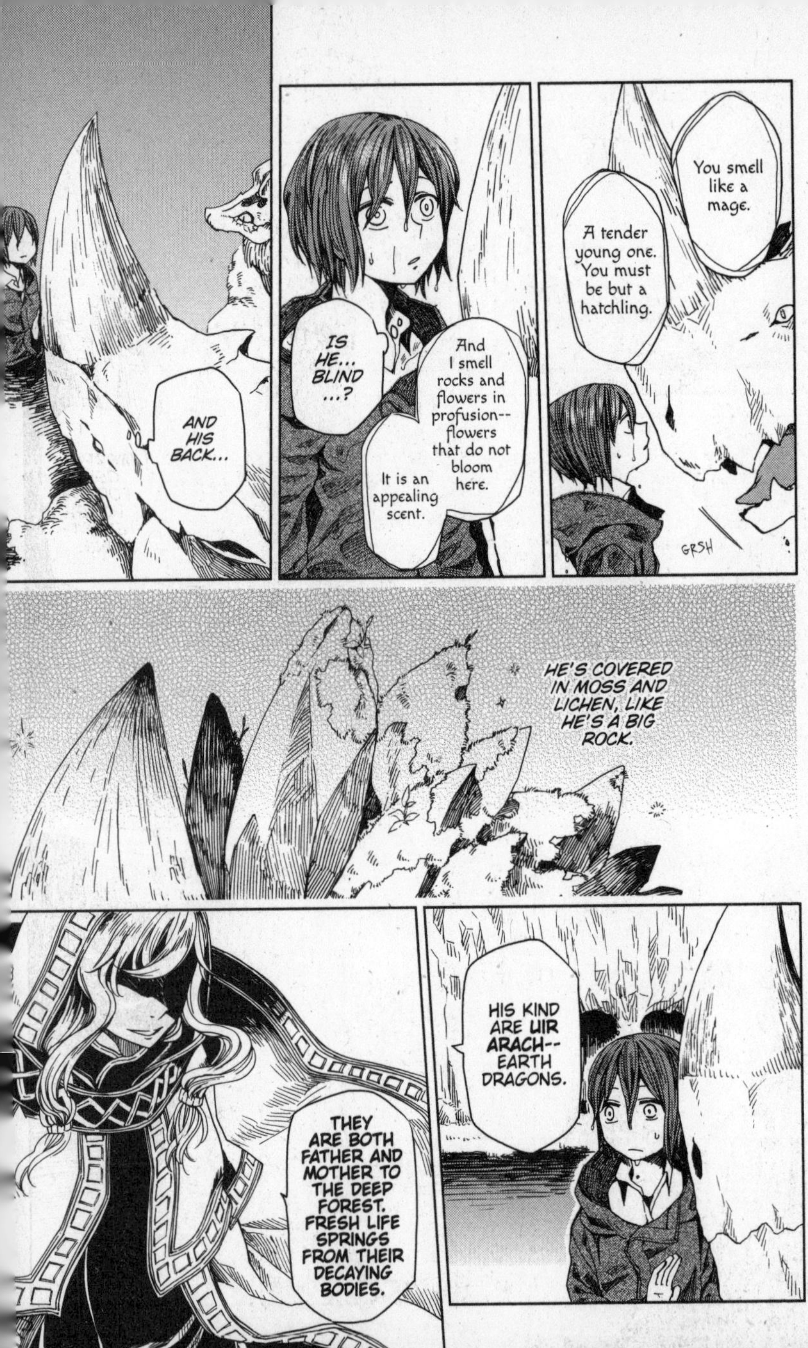
You smell like a mage.
A tender young one. You must be but a hatchling.
GRSH
And I smell rocks and flowers in profusion--flowers that do not bloom here.
It is an appealing scent.
IS HE... BLIND ...?
AND HIS BACK...
HE'S COVERED IN MOSS AND LICHEN, LIKE HE'S A BIG ROCK.
HIS KIND ARE **UIR ARACH**--EARTH DRAGONS.
THEY ARE BOTH FATHER AND MOTHER TO THE DEEP FOREST. FRESH LIFE SPRINGS FROM THEIR DECAYING BODIES.

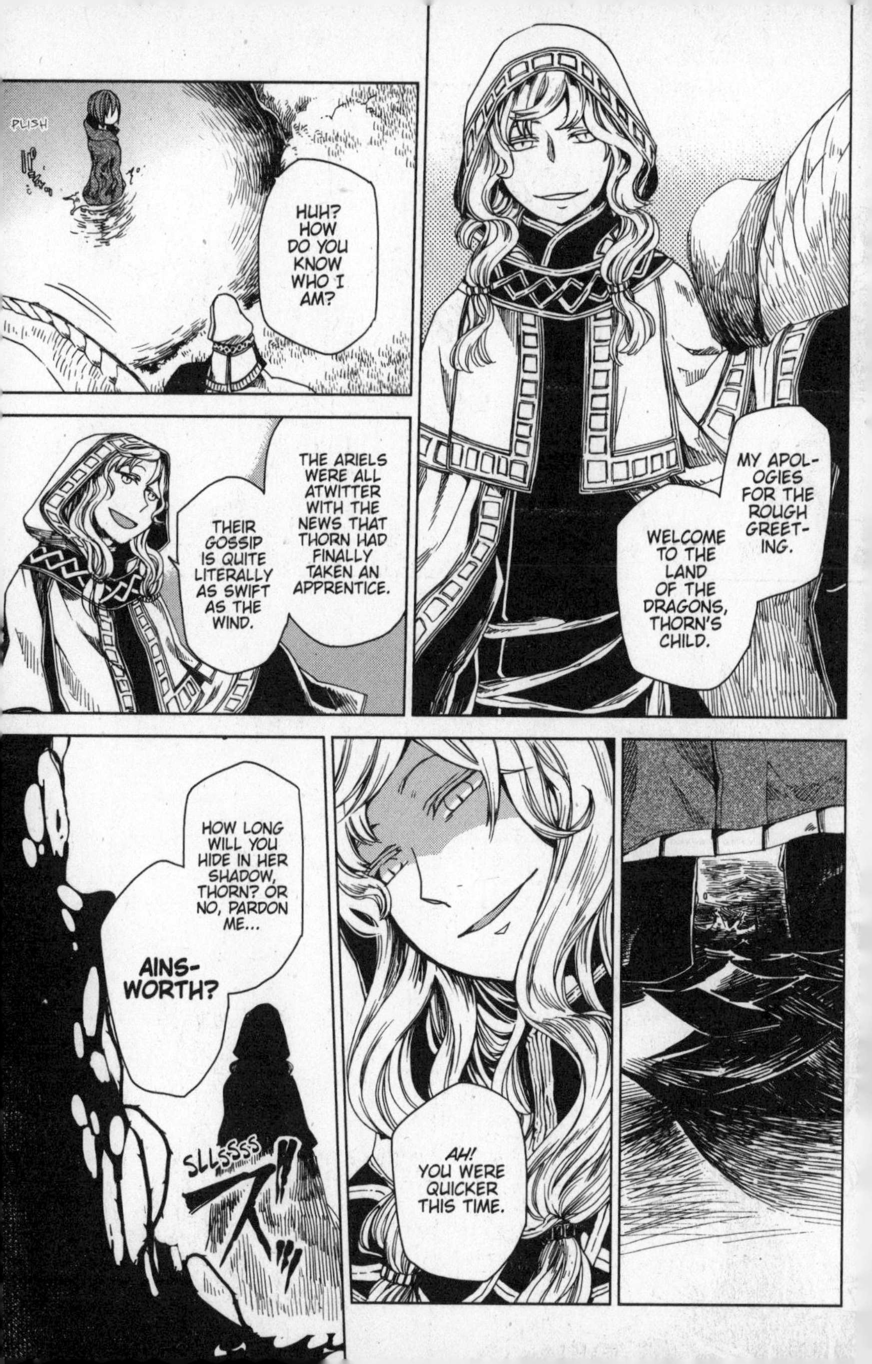
MY APOLOGIES FOR THE ROUGH GREETING.
WELCOME TO THE LAND OF THE DRAGONS, THORN'S CHILD.
HUH? HOW DO YOU KNOW WHO I AM?
PUSH
THE ARIELS WERE ALL ATWITTER WITH THE NEWS THAT THORN HAD FINALLY TAKEN AN APPRENTICE.
THEIR GOSSIP IS QUITE LITERALLY AS SWIFT AS THE WIND.
AH! YOU WERE QUICKER THIS TIME.
HOW LONG WILL YOU HIDE IN HER SHADOW, THORN? OR NO, PARDON ME...
AINSWORTH?
SLLSSSS

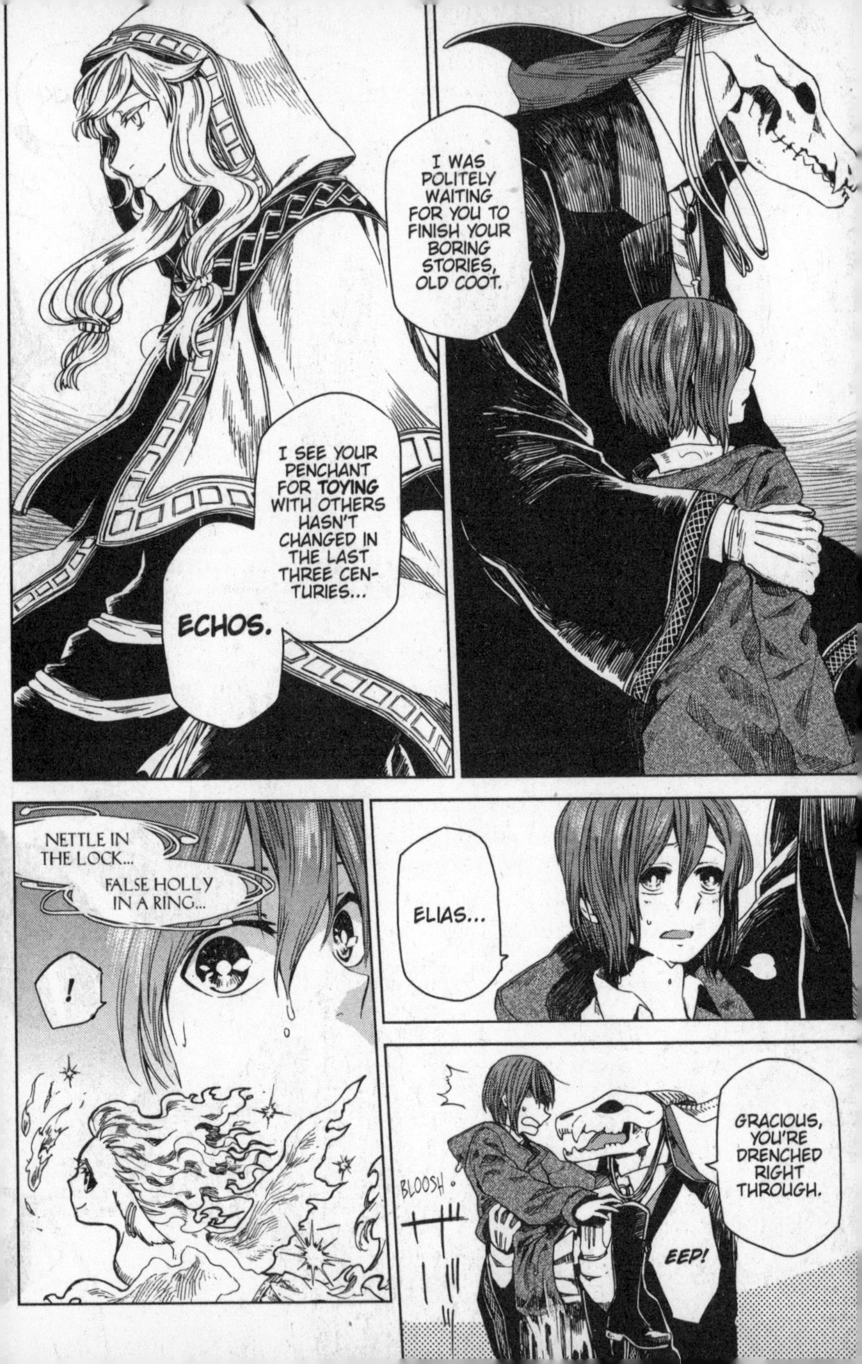

I WAS POLITELY WAITING FOR YOU TO FINISH YOUR BORING STORIES, OLD COOT.
I SEE YOUR PENCHANT FOR TOYING WITH OTHERS HASN'T CHANGED IN THE LAST THREE CENTURIES...
ECHOS.
ELIAS...
GRACIOUS, YOU'RE DRENCHED RIGHT THROUGH.
BLOOSH
EEP!
NETTLE IN THE LOCK...
FALSE HOLLY IN A RING...
!

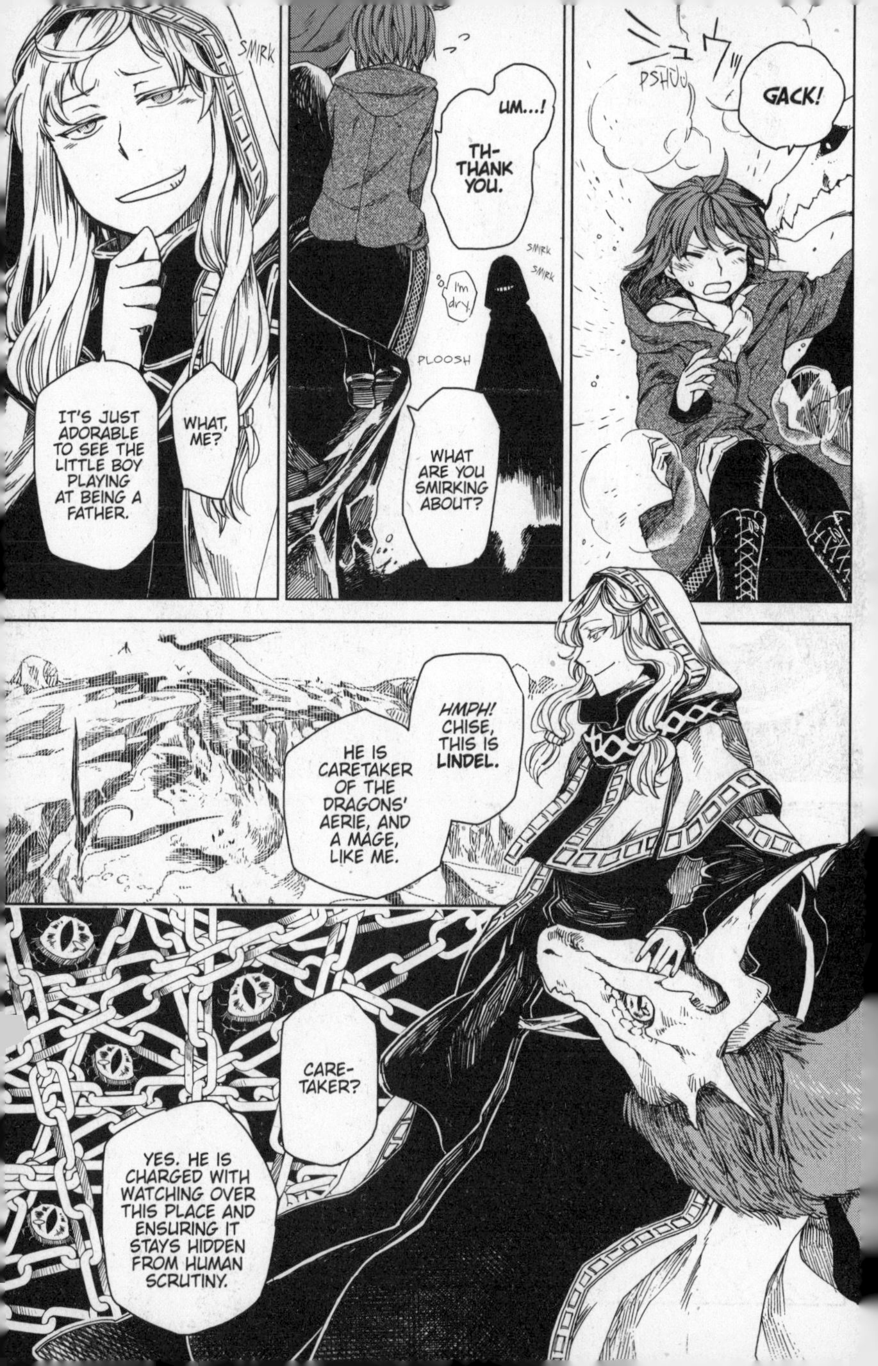
シュウッ
PSHUU
GACK!
UM...!
TH-THANK YOU.
SMIRK
SMIRK
I'm dry.
PLOOSH
WHAT ARE YOU SMIRKING ABOUT?
SMIRK
WHAT, ME?
IT'S JUST ADORABLE TO SEE THE LITTLE BOY PLAYING AT BEING A FATHER.
HMPH! CHISE, THIS IS LINDEL.
HE IS CARETAKER OF THE DRAGONS' AERIE, AND A MAGE, LIKE ME.
CARE-TAKER?
YES. HE IS CHARGED WITH WATCHING OVER THIS PLACE AND ENSURING IT STAYS HIDDEN FROM HUMAN SCRUTINY.

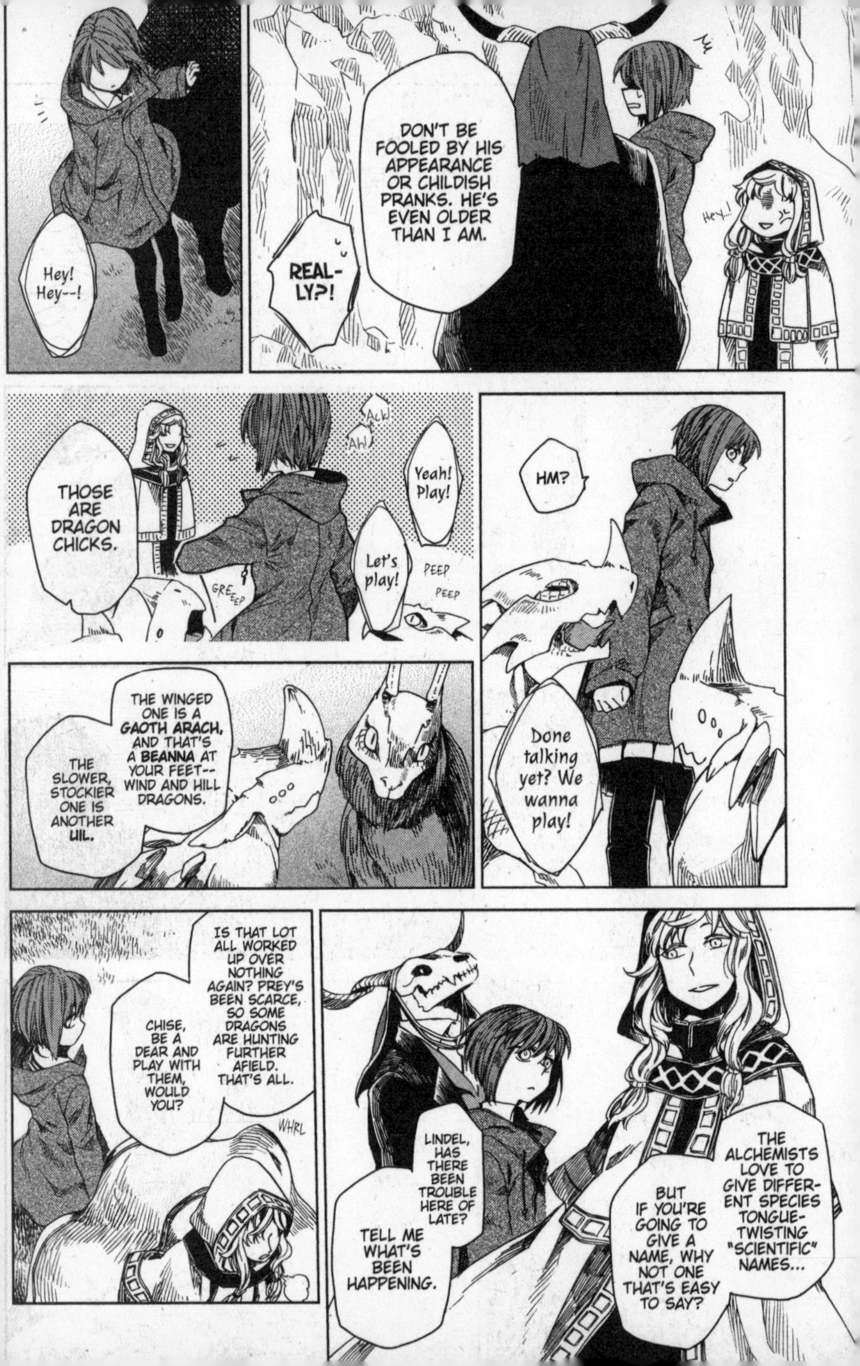
Hey...!
DON'T BE FOOLED BY HIS APPEARANCE OR CHILDISH PRANKS. HE'S EVEN OLDER THAN I AM.
REAL-LY?!
Hey! Hey--!
HM?
Done talking yet? We wanna play!
Ack!
Ah!
Yeah! Play!
Let's play!
PEEP
PEEP
THOSE ARE DRAGON CHICKS.
GREEEP
THE WINGED ONE IS A **GAOTH ARACH**, AND THAT'S A **BEANNA** AT YOUR FEET-- WIND AND HILL DRAGONS.
THE SLOWER, STOCKIER ONE IS ANOTHER **UIL**.
THE ALCHEMISTS LOVE TO GIVE DIFFER-ENT SPECIES TONGUE-TWISTING "SCIENTIFIC" NAMES...
BUT IF YOU'RE GOING TO GIVE A NAME, WHY NOT ONE THAT'S EASY TO SAY?
LINDEL, HAS THERE BEEN TROUBLE HERE OF LATE?
TELL ME WHAT'S BEEN HAPPENING.
IS THAT LOT ALL WORKED UP OVER NOTHING AGAIN? PREY'S BEEN SCARCE, SO SOME DRAGONS ARE HUNTING FURTHER AFIELD. THAT'S ALL.
CHISE, BE A DEAR AND PLAY WITH THEM, WOULD YOU?
WHRL

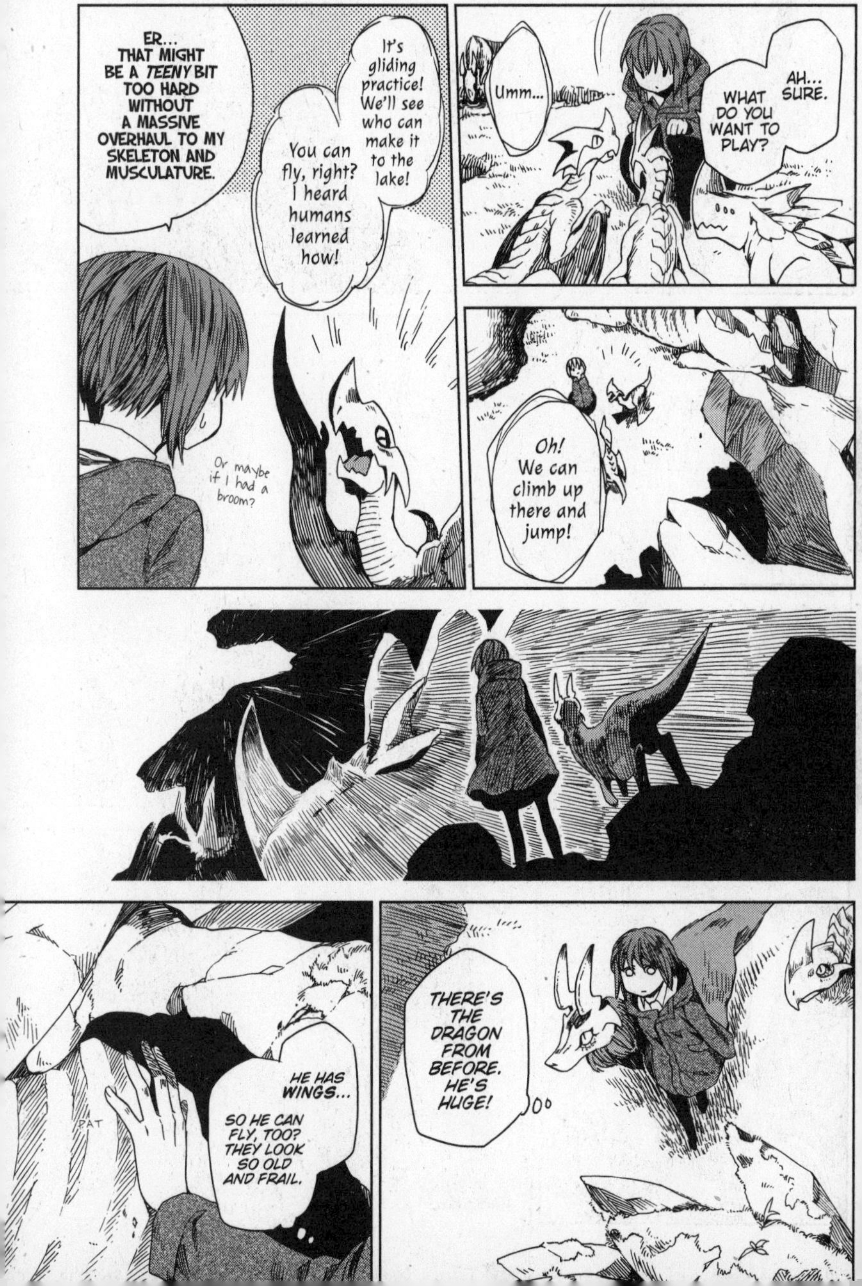
AH... SURE. WHAT DO YOU WANT TO PLAY?
Umm...
Oh! We can climb up there and jump!
It's gliding practice! We'll see who can make it to the lake!
You can fly, right? I heard humans learned how!
ER... THAT MIGHT BE A *TEENY* BIT TOO HARD WITHOUT A MASSIVE OVERHAUL TO MY SKELETON AND MUSCULATURE.
Or maybe if I had a broom?
THERE'S THE DRAGON FROM BEFORE. HE'S HUGE!
HE HAS WINGS... SO HE CAN FLY, TOO? THEY LOOK SO OLD AND FRAIL.
PAT

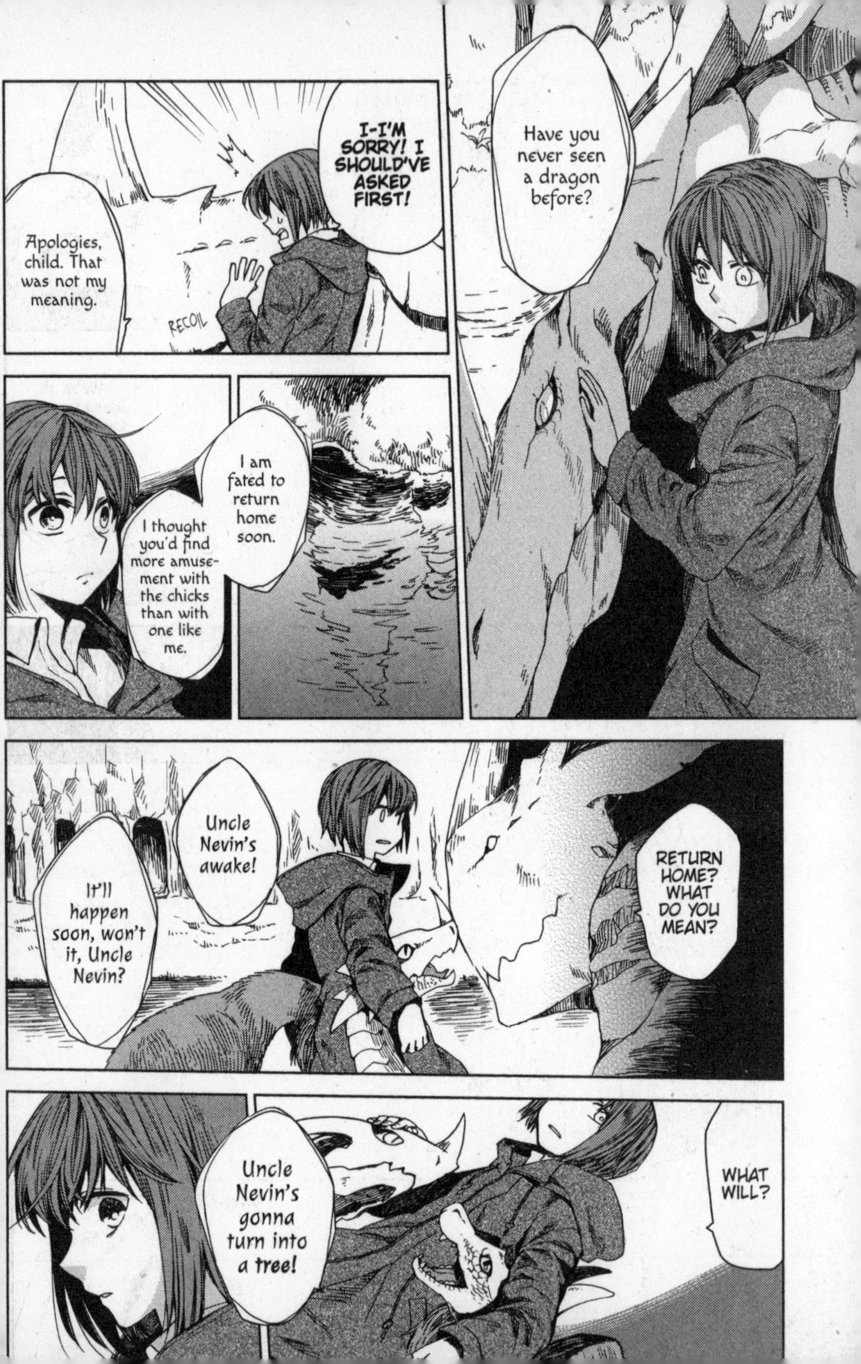
Have you never seen a dragon before?
I-I'M SORRY! I SHOULD'VE ASKED FIRST!
RECOIL
Apologies, child. That was not my meaning.
I am fated to return home soon.
I thought you'd find more amusement with the chicks than with one like me.
RETURN HOME? WHAT DO YOU MEAN?
Uncle Nevin's awake!
It'll happen soon, won't it, Uncle Nevin?
WHAT WILL?
Uncle Nevin's gonna turn into a tree!

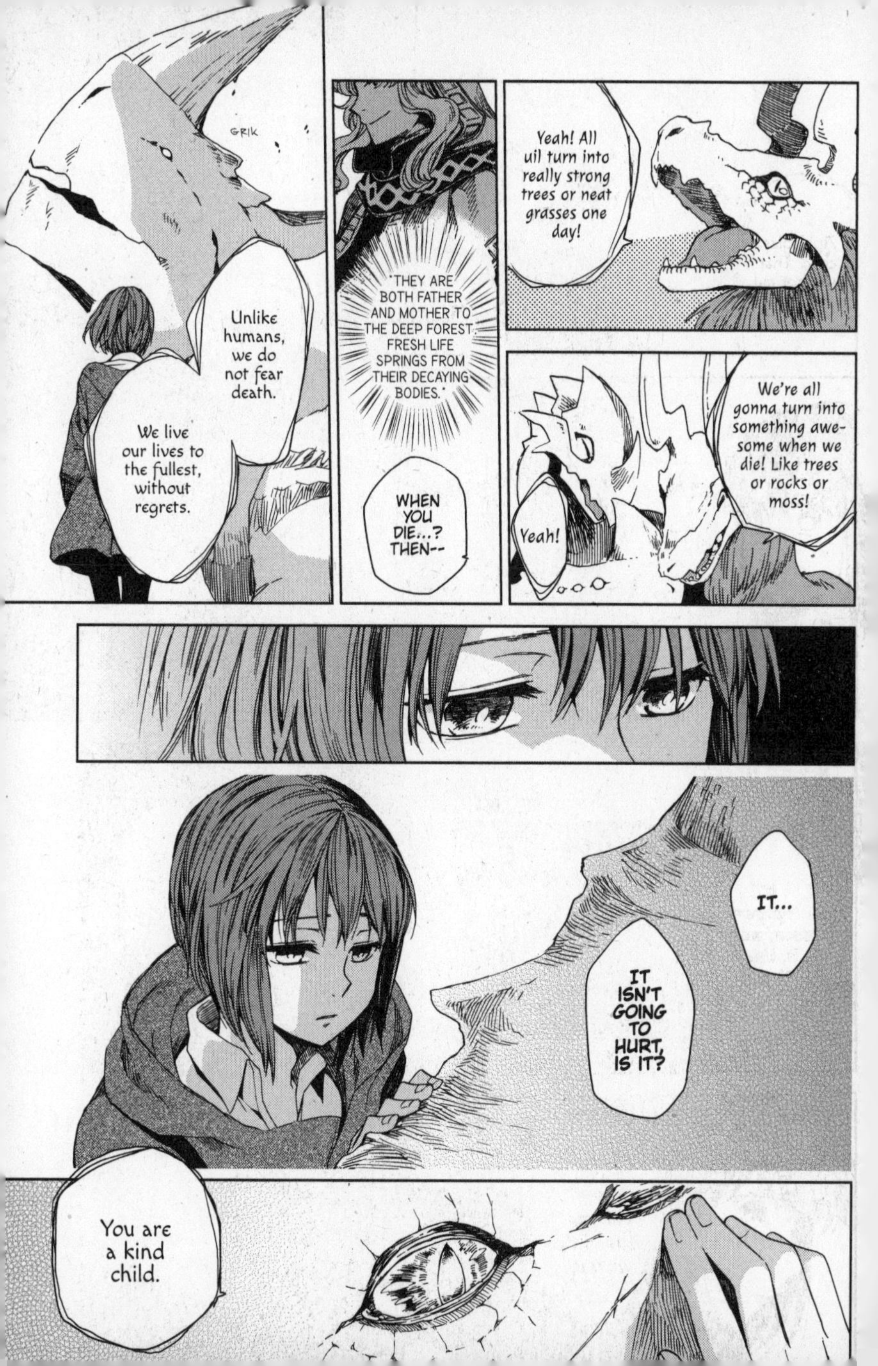
Yeah! All uil turn into really strong trees or neat grasses one day!
We're all gonna turn into something awe-some when we die! Like trees or rocks or moss!
Yeah!
"THEY ARE BOTH FATHER AND MOTHER TO THE DEEP FOREST. FRESH LIFE SPRINGS FROM THEIR DECAYING BODIES."
WHEN YOU DIE...? THEN--
GRIK
Unlike humans, we do not fear death.
We live our lives to the fullest, without regrets.
IT...
IT ISN'T GOING TO HURT, IS IT?
You are a kind child.

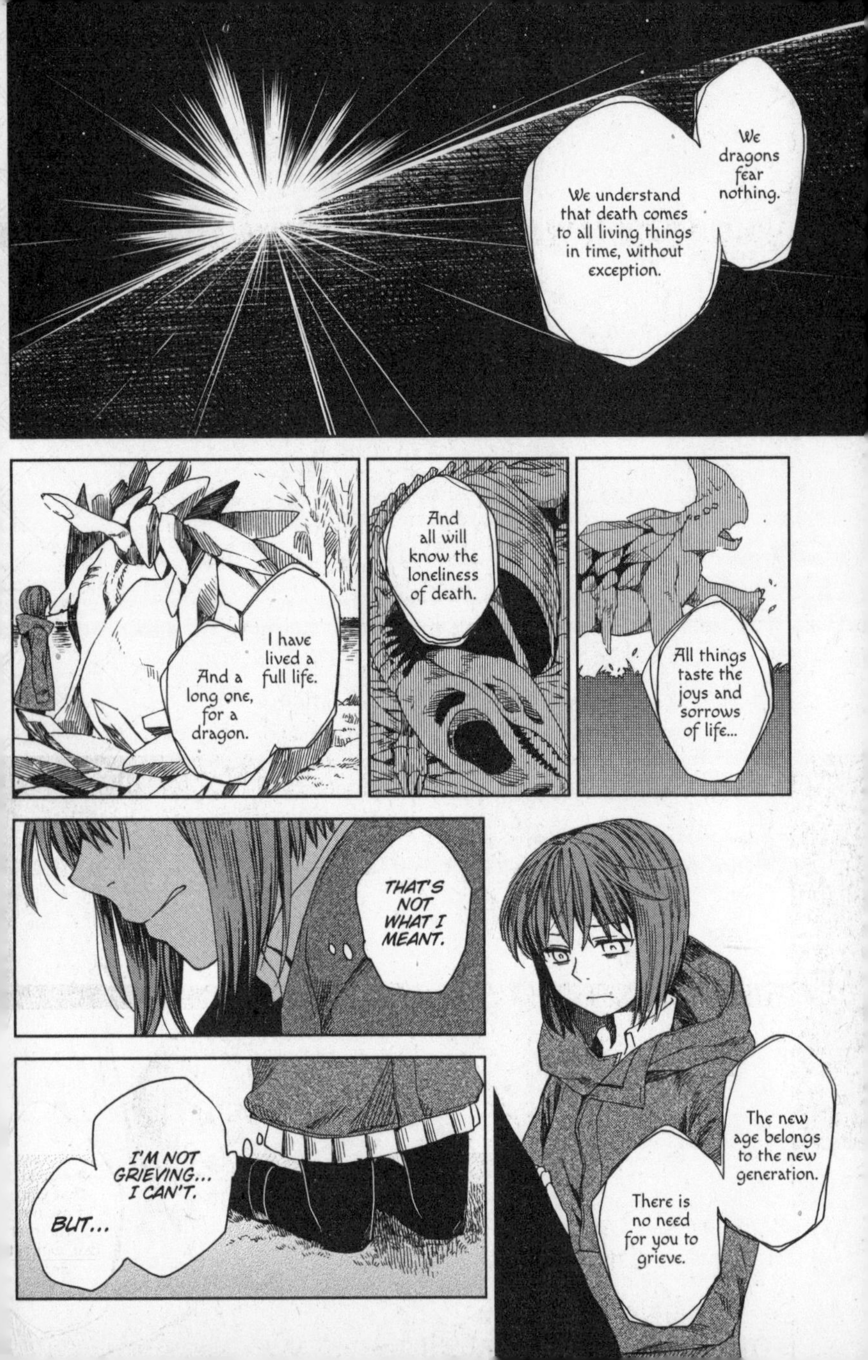
We dragons fear nothing.
We understand that death comes to all living things in time, without exception.
All things taste the joys and sorrows of life...
And all will know the loneliness of death.
I have lived a full life.
And a long one, for a dragon.
The new age belongs to the new generation.
There is no need for you to grieve.
THAT'S NOT WHAT I MEANT.
I'M NOT GRIEVING... I CAN'T.
BUT...

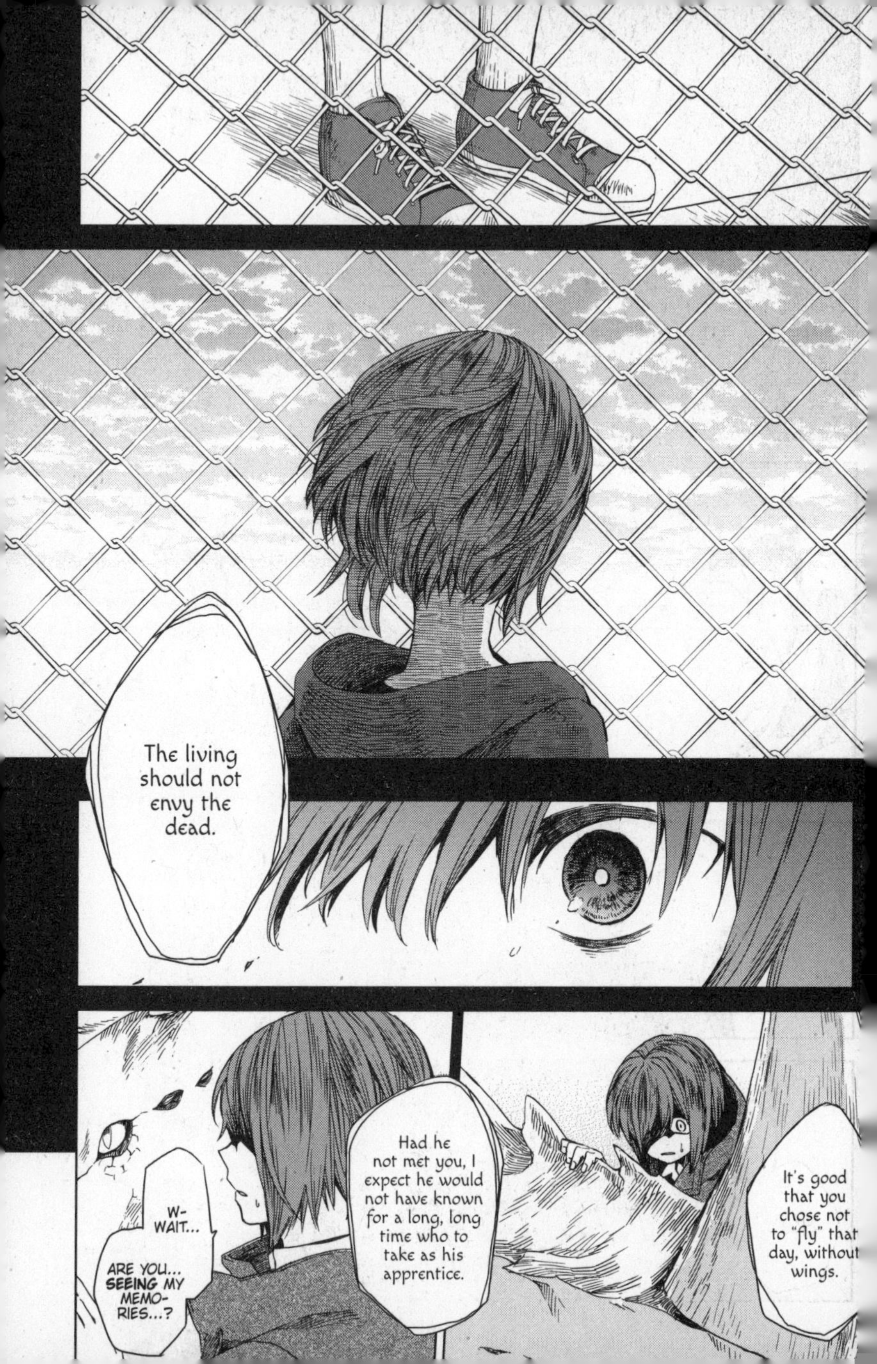
The living should not envy the dead.
It's good that you chose not to "fly" that day, without wings.
Had he not met you, I expect he would not have known for a long, long time who to take as his apprentice.
W-WAIT...
ARE YOU... **SEEING** MY MEMO-RIES...?

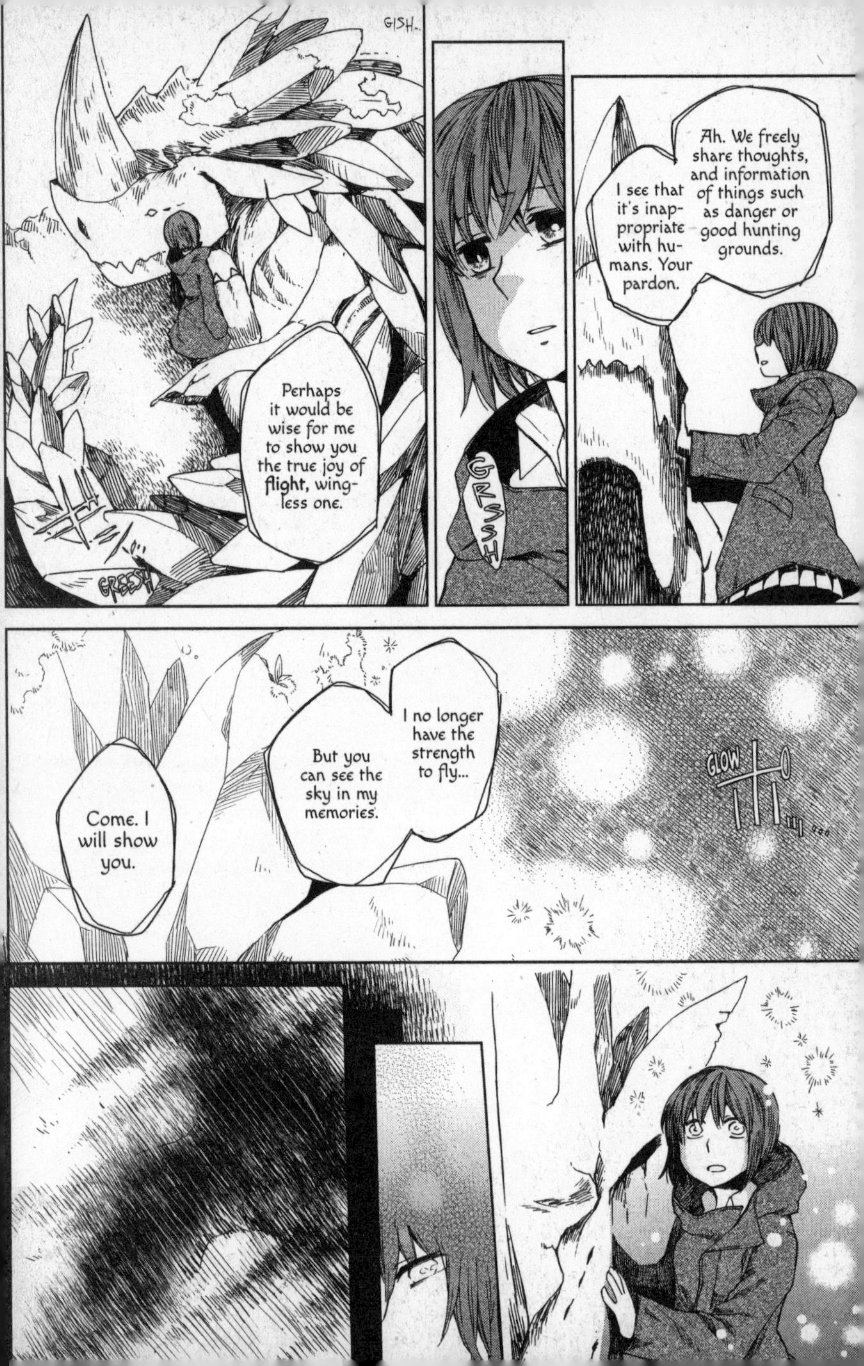
Ah. We freely share thoughts, and information of things such as danger or good hunting grounds.
I see that it's inappropriate with humans. Your pardon.
GRSSH
GISH..
Perhaps it would be wise for me to show you the true joy of **flight**, wingless one.
GREESH
GLOW
I no longer have the strength to fly...
But you can see the sky in my memories.
Come. I will show you.

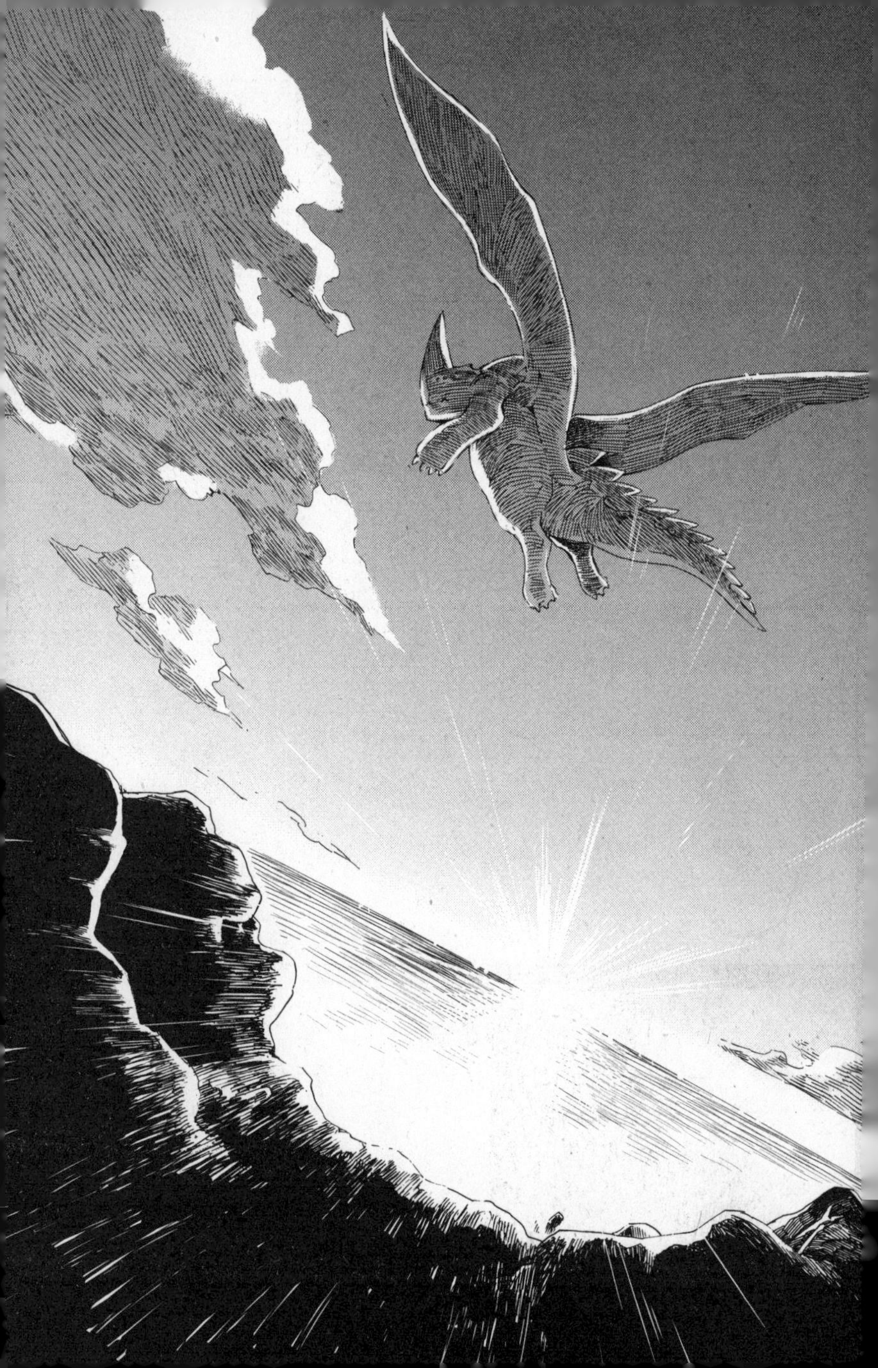

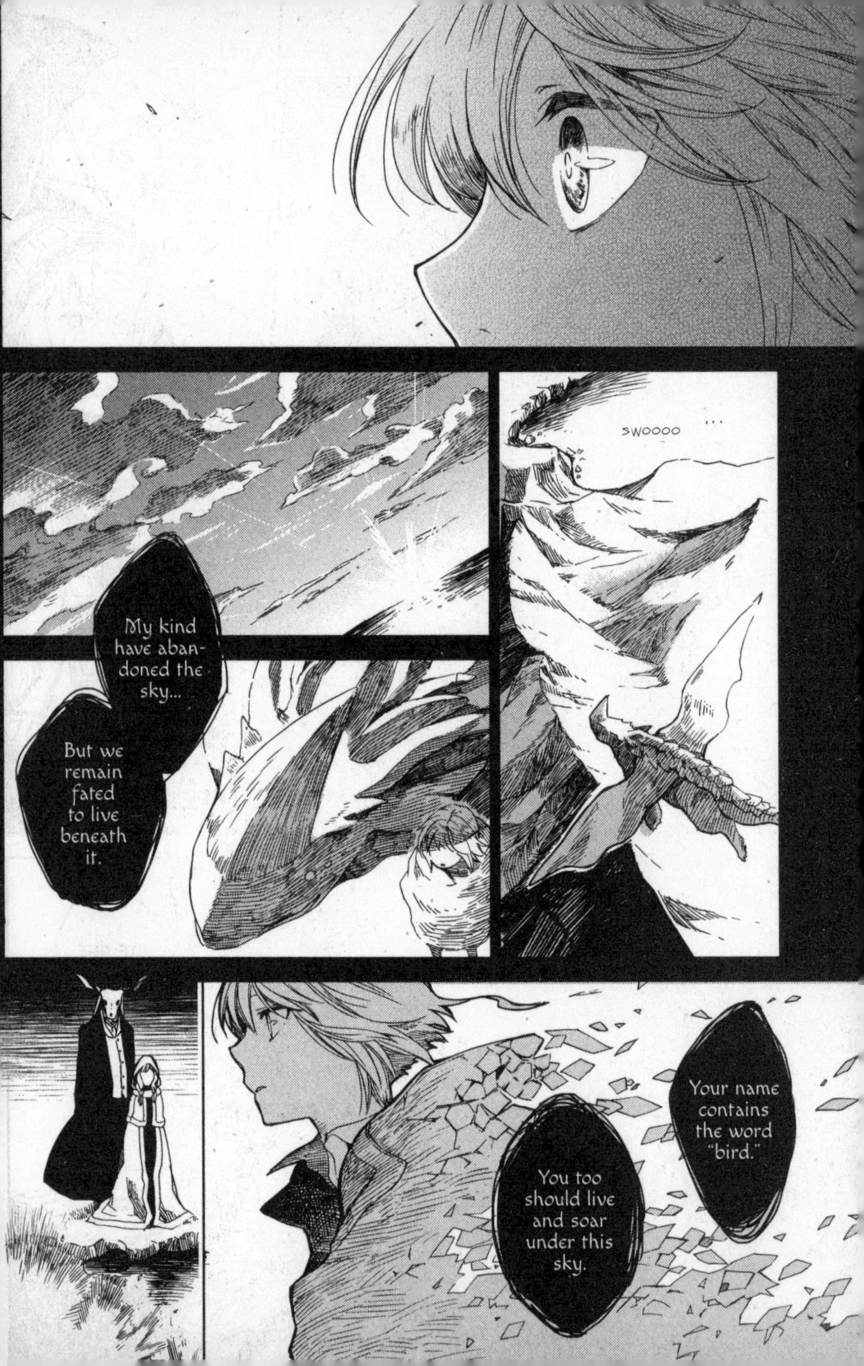
SWOOOO ...
My kind have aban- doned the sky...
But we remain fated to live beneath it.
Your name contains the word "bird."
You too should live and soar under this sky.

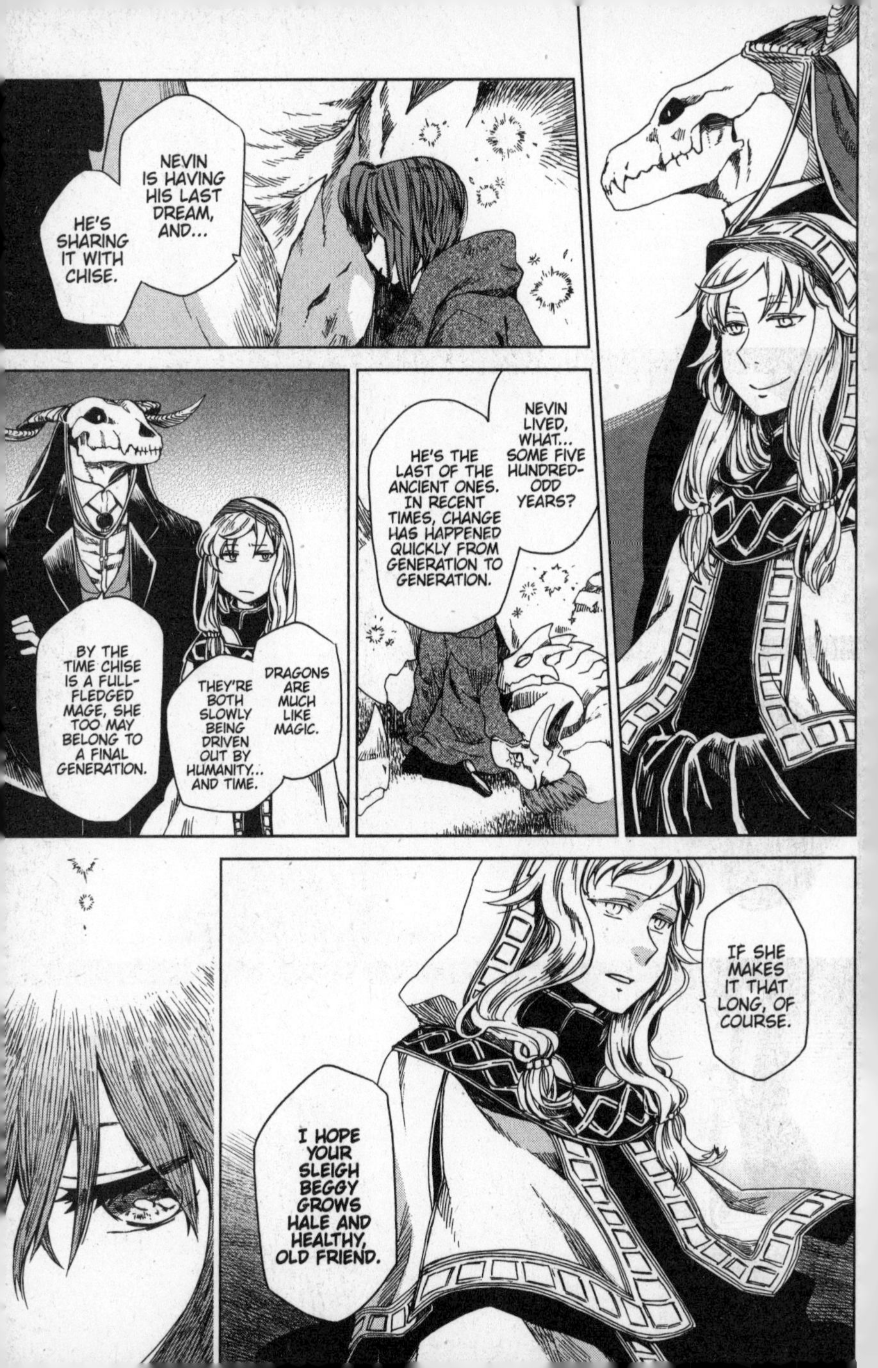
NEVIN IS HAVING HIS LAST DREAM, AND...
HE'S SHARING IT WITH CHISE.
NEVIN LIVED, WHAT... SOME FIVE HUNDRED-ODD YEARS?
HE'S THE LAST OF THE ANCIENT ONES. IN RECENT TIMES, CHANGE HAS HAPPENED QUICKLY FROM GENERATION TO GENERATION.
DRAGONS ARE MUCH LIKE MAGIC.
THEY'RE BOTH SLOWLY BEING DRIVEN OUT BY HUMANITY... AND TIME.
BY THE TIME CHISE IS A FULL-FLEDGED MAGE, SHE TOO MAY BELONG TO A FINAL GENERATION.
IF SHE MAKES IT THAT LONG, OF COURSE.
I HOPE YOUR SLEIGH BEGGY GROWS HALE AND HEALTHY, OLD FRIEND.

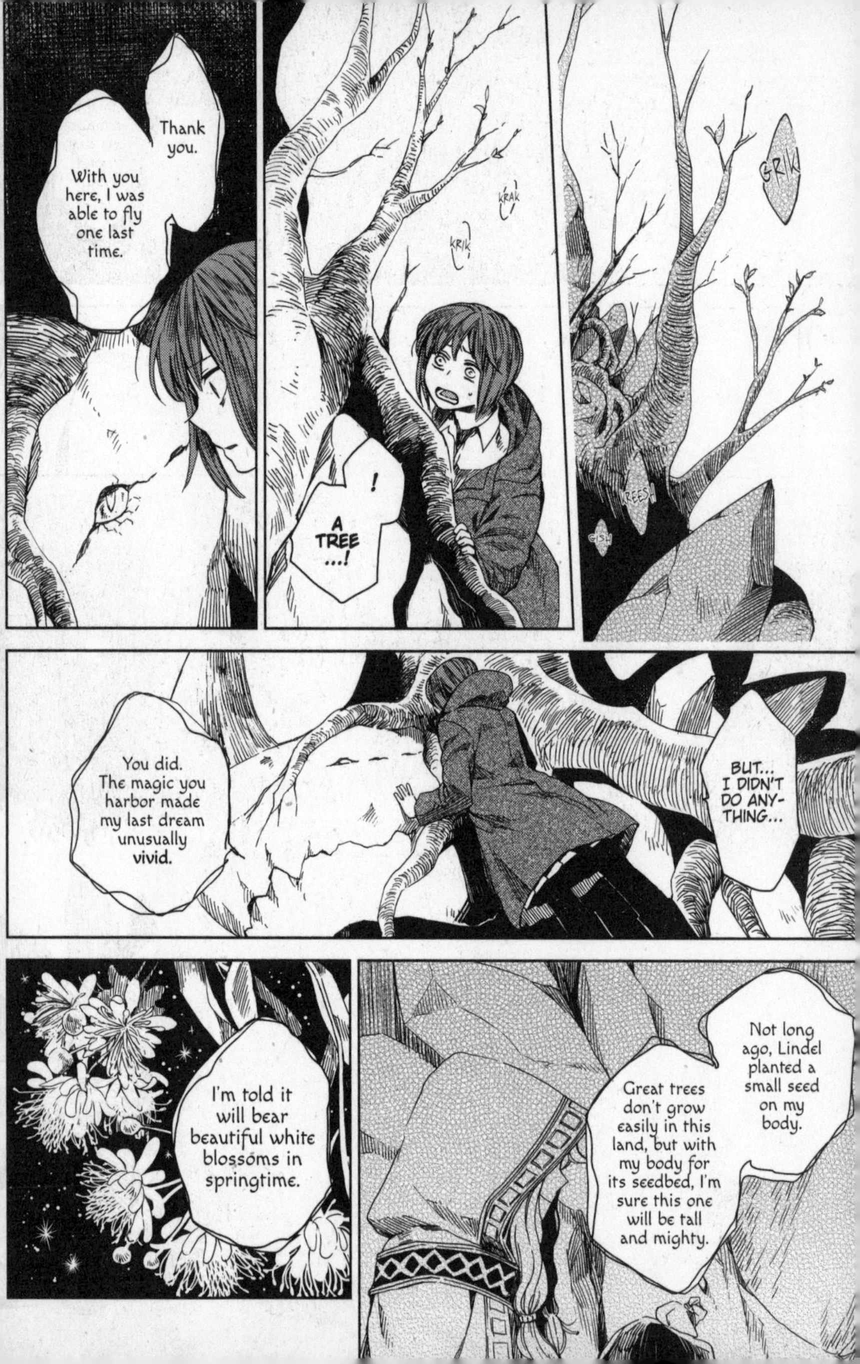
GRIK
KREESH
KRAK
KRIK
!
A TREE ...!
Thank you.
With you here, I was able to fly one last time.
BUT... I DIDN'T DO ANYTHING...
You did. The magic you harbor made my last dream unusually **vivid.**
Not long ago, Lindel planted a small seed on my body.
Great trees don't grow easily in this land, but with my body for its seedbed, I'm sure this one will be tall and mighty.
I'm told it will bear beautiful white blossoms in springtime.

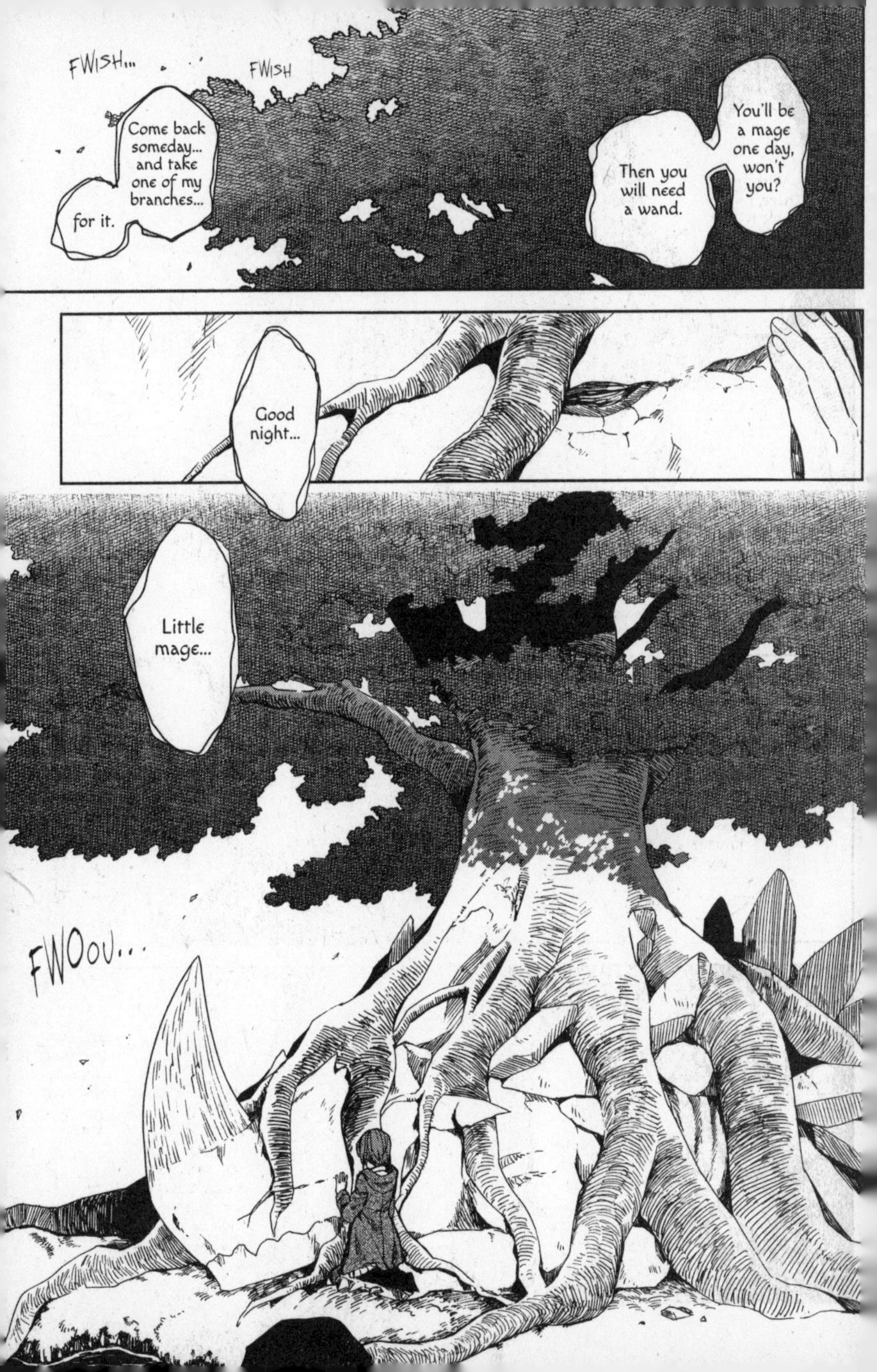
You'll be a mage one day, won't you?
Then you will need a wand.
FWISH
FWISH...
Come back someday... and take one of my branches...
for it.
Good night...
Little mage...
FWOou...

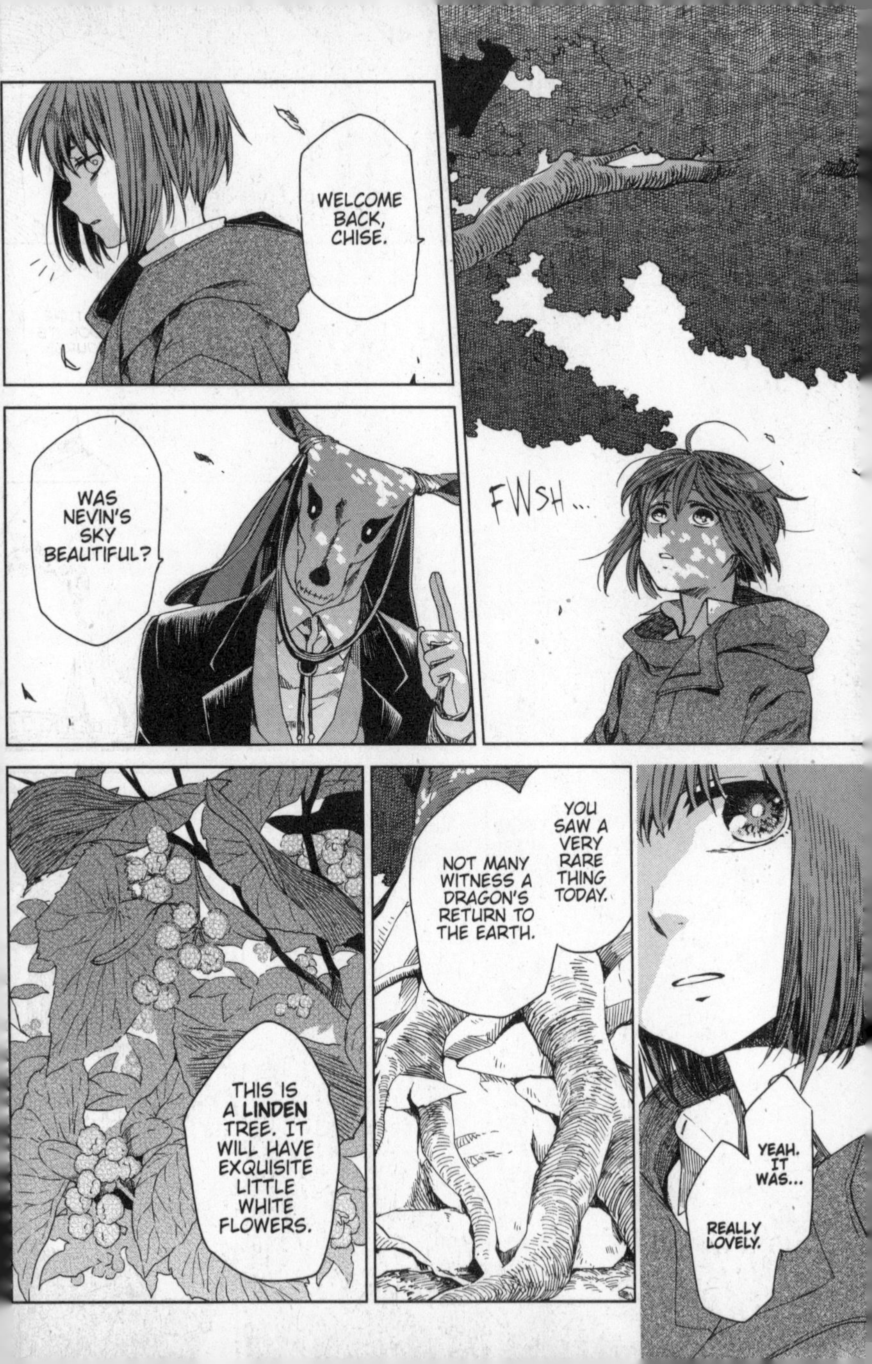
FWSH...
WELCOME BACK, CHISE.
WAS NEVIN'S SKY BEAUTIFUL?
YEAH. IT WAS...
REALLY LOVELY.
YOU SAW A VERY RARE THING TODAY.
NOT MANY WITNESS A DRAGON'S RETURN TO THE EARTH.
THIS IS A **LINDEN** TREE. IT WILL HAVE EXQUISITE LITTLE WHITE FLOWERS.

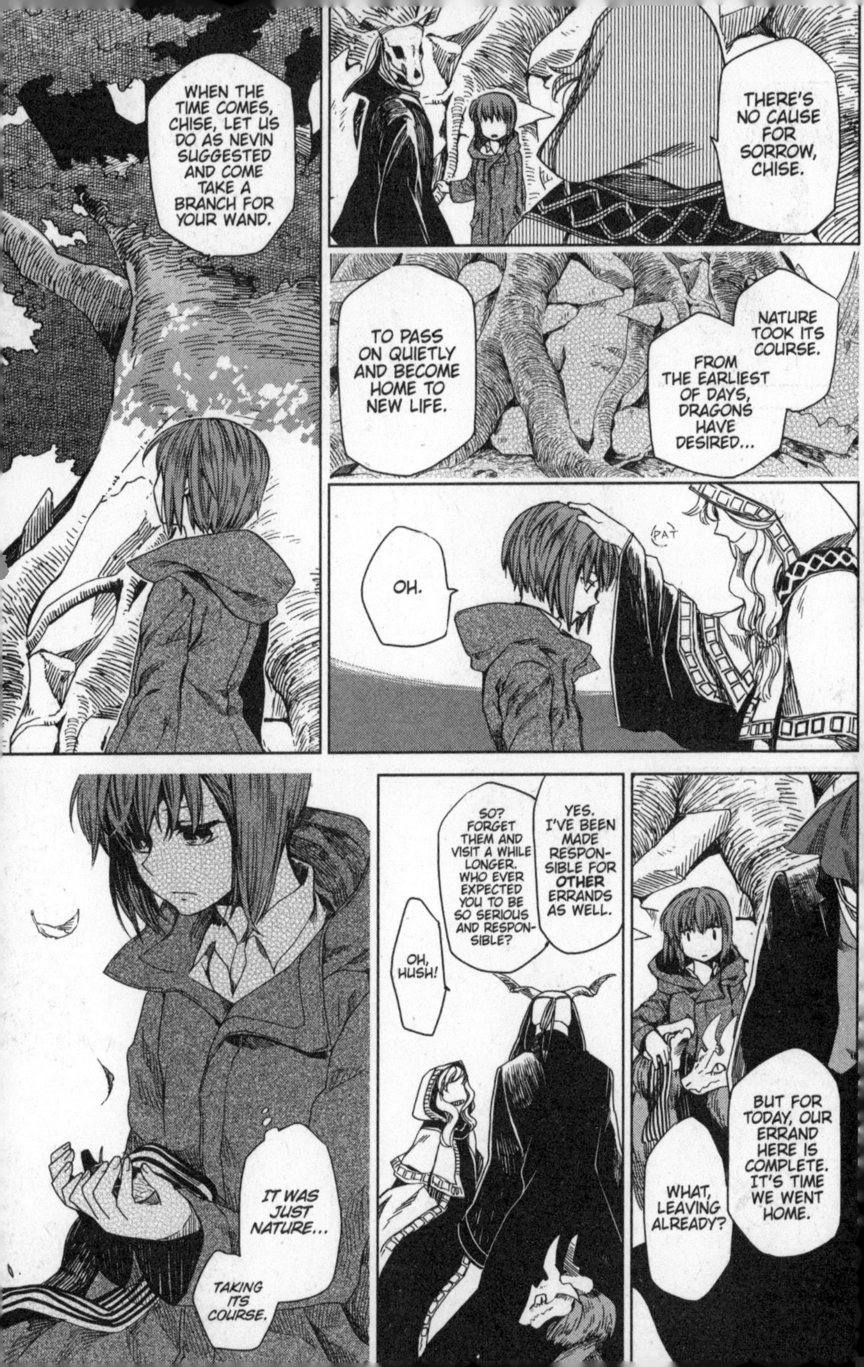
THERE'S NO CAUSE FOR SORROW, CHISE.
NATURE TOOK ITS COURSE.
FROM THE EARLIEST OF DAYS, DRAGONS HAVE DESIRED...
TO PASS ON QUIETLY AND BECOME HOME TO NEW LIFE.
PAT
OH.
WHEN THE TIME COMES, CHISE, LET US DO AS NEVIN SUGGESTED AND COME TAKE A BRANCH FOR YOUR WAND.
BUT FOR TODAY, OUR ERRAND HERE IS COMPLETE. IT'S TIME WE WENT HOME.
WHAT, LEAVING ALREADY?
YES. I'VE BEEN MADE RESPONSIBLE FOR OTHER ERRANDS AS WELL.
SO? FORGET THEM AND VISIT A WHILE LONGER. WHO EVER EXPECTED YOU TO BE SO SERIOUS AND RESPONSIBLE?
OH, HUSH!
IT WAS JUST NATURE...
TAKING ITS COURSE.

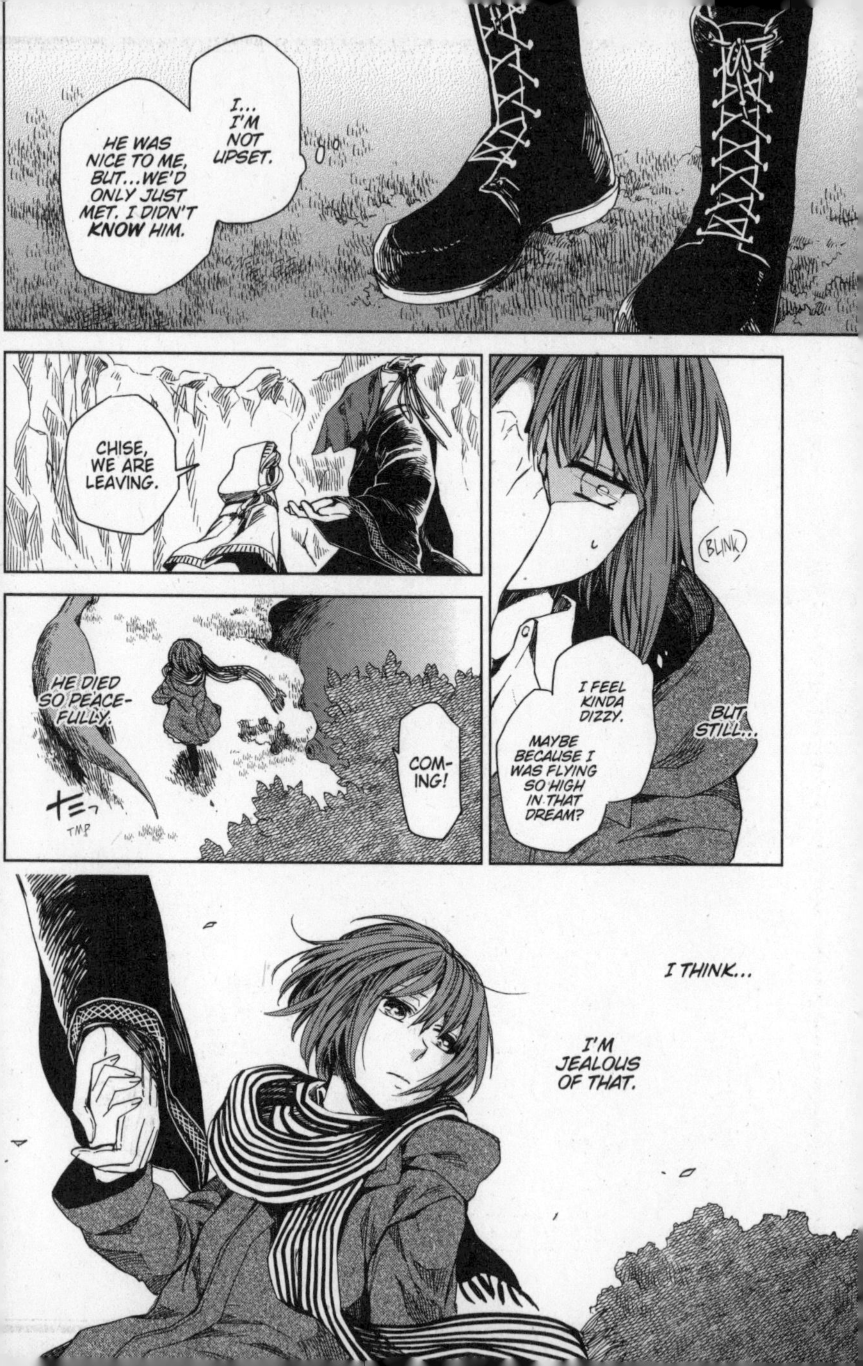
I... I'M NOT UPSET.
HE WAS NICE TO ME, BUT...WE'D ONLY JUST MET. I DIDN'T KNOW HIM.
(BLINK)
BUT STILL...
I FEEL KINDA DIZZY.
MAYBE BECAUSE I WAS FLYING SO HIGH IN THAT DREAM?
CHISE, WE ARE LEAVING.
COMING!
HE DIED SO PEACEFULLY.
TMP
I THINK...
I'M JEALOUS OF THAT.

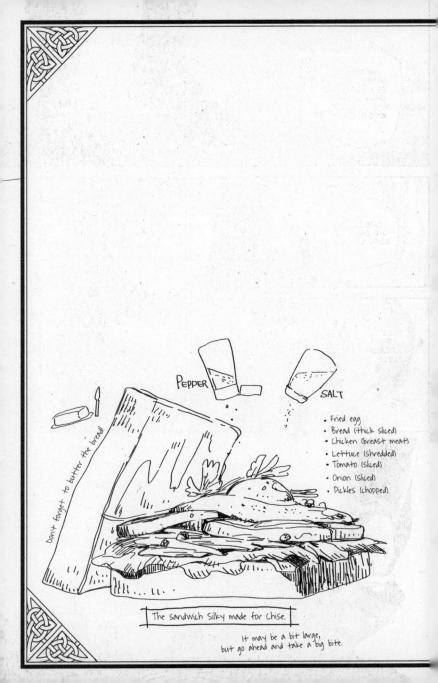

PEPPER

SALT

Don't forget to butter the bread

- Fried egg
- Bread (thick sliced)
- Chicken (breast meat)
- Lettuce (shredded)
- Tomato (sliced)
- Onion (sliced)
- Pickles (chopped)

The sandwich Silky made for Chise.

It may be a bit large,
but go ahead and take a big bite.

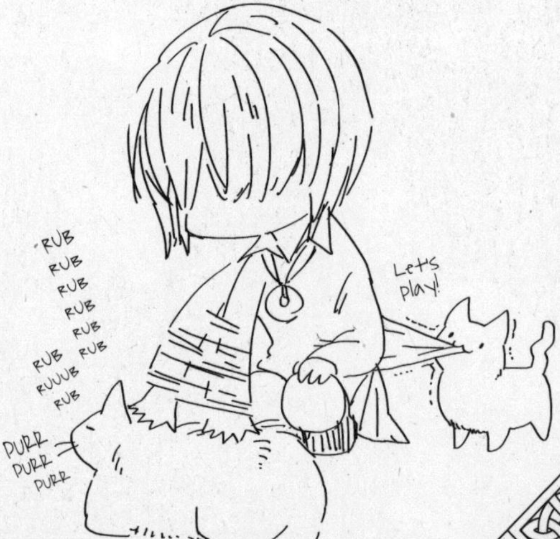
Let's play!
RUB RUB RUB RUB RUB RUB
RUB RUUUB RUB
PURR PURR PURR

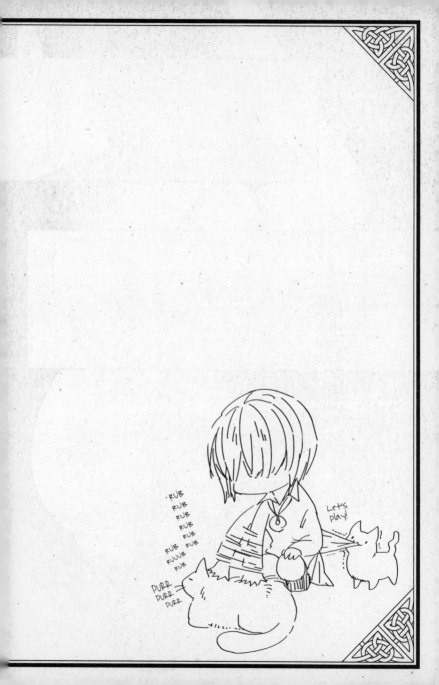

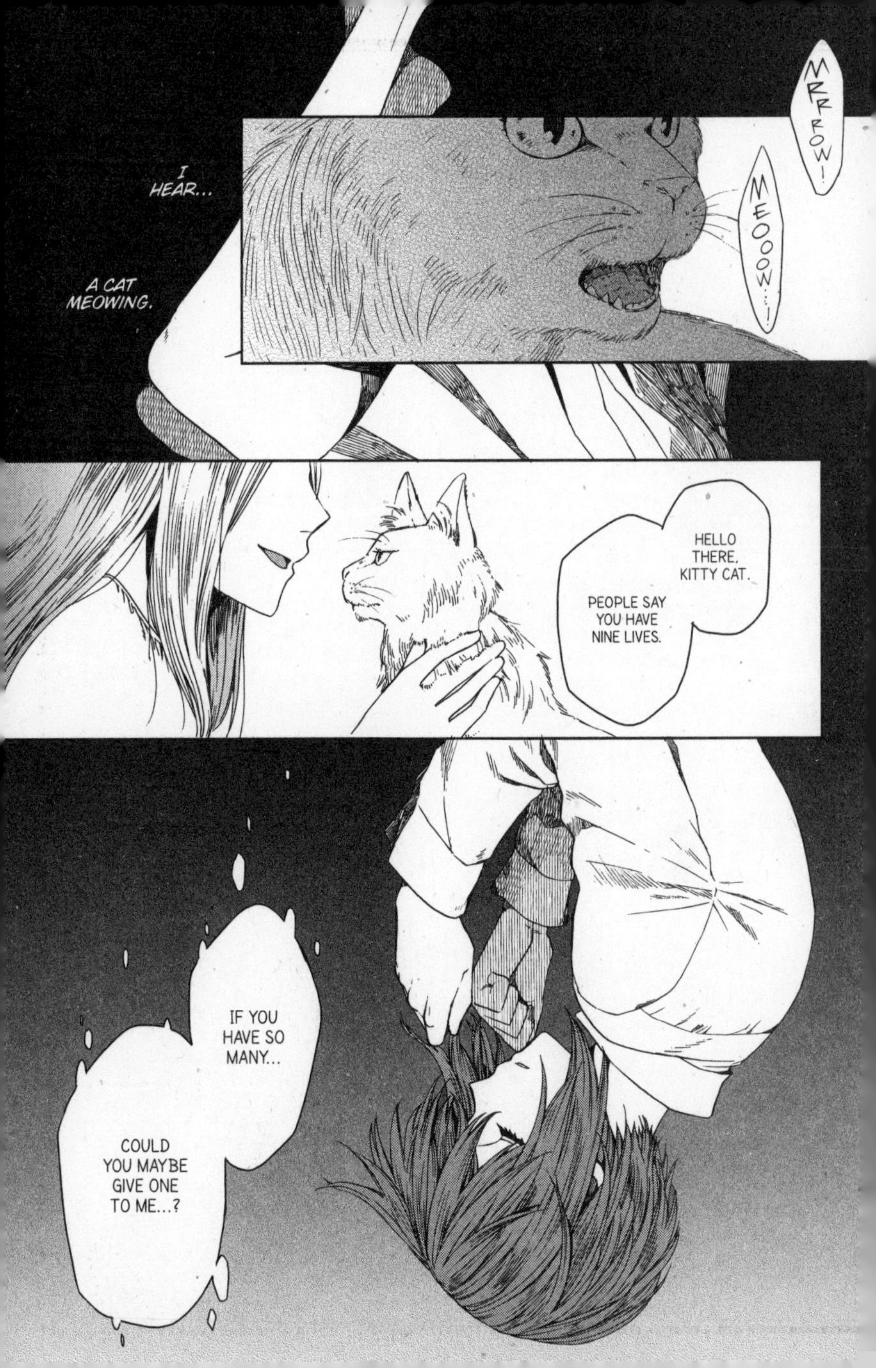
MRRROW!
MEOOOW...!
I HEAR...
A CAT MEOWING.
HELLO THERE, KITTY CAT.
PEOPLE SAY YOU HAVE NINE LIVES.
IF YOU HAVE SO MANY...
COULD YOU MAYBE GIVE ONE TO ME...?

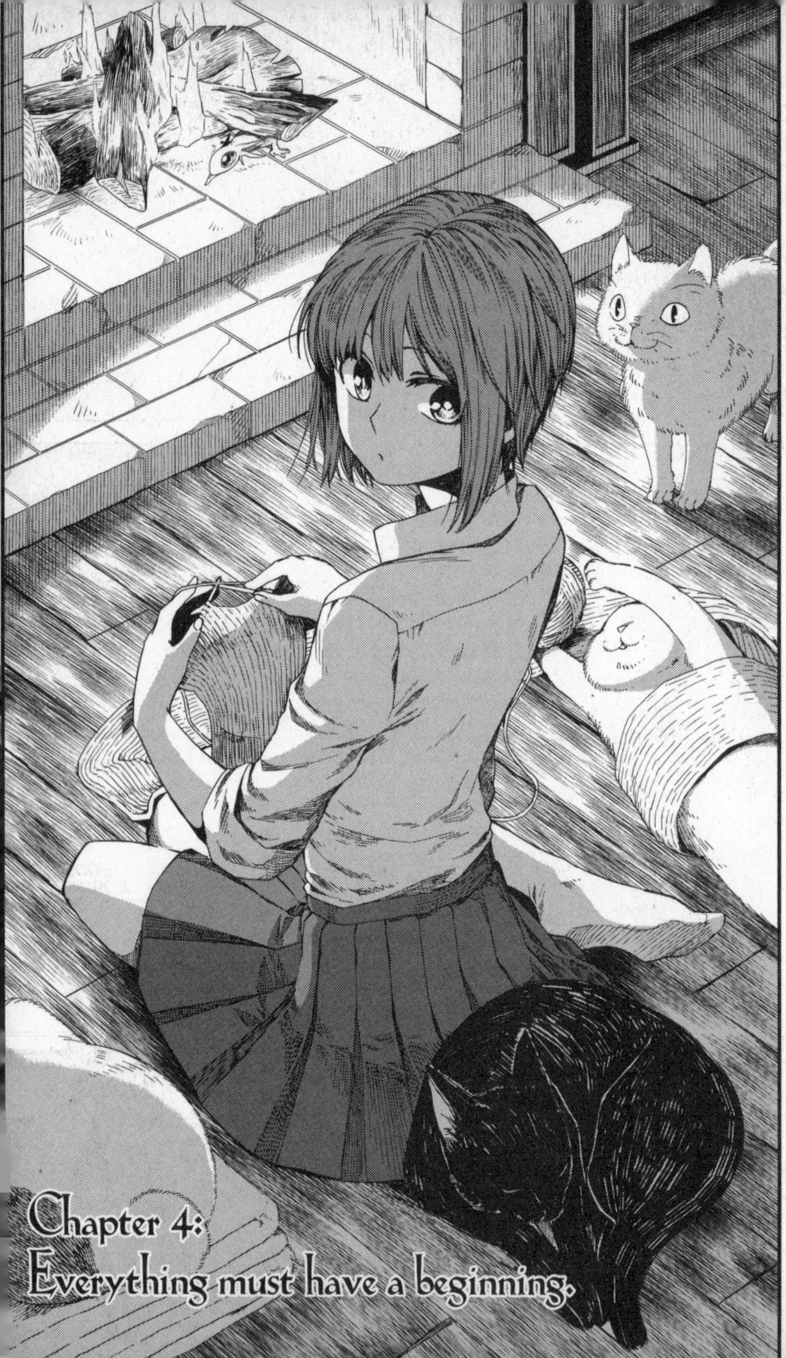
Chapter 4:
Everything must have a beginning.

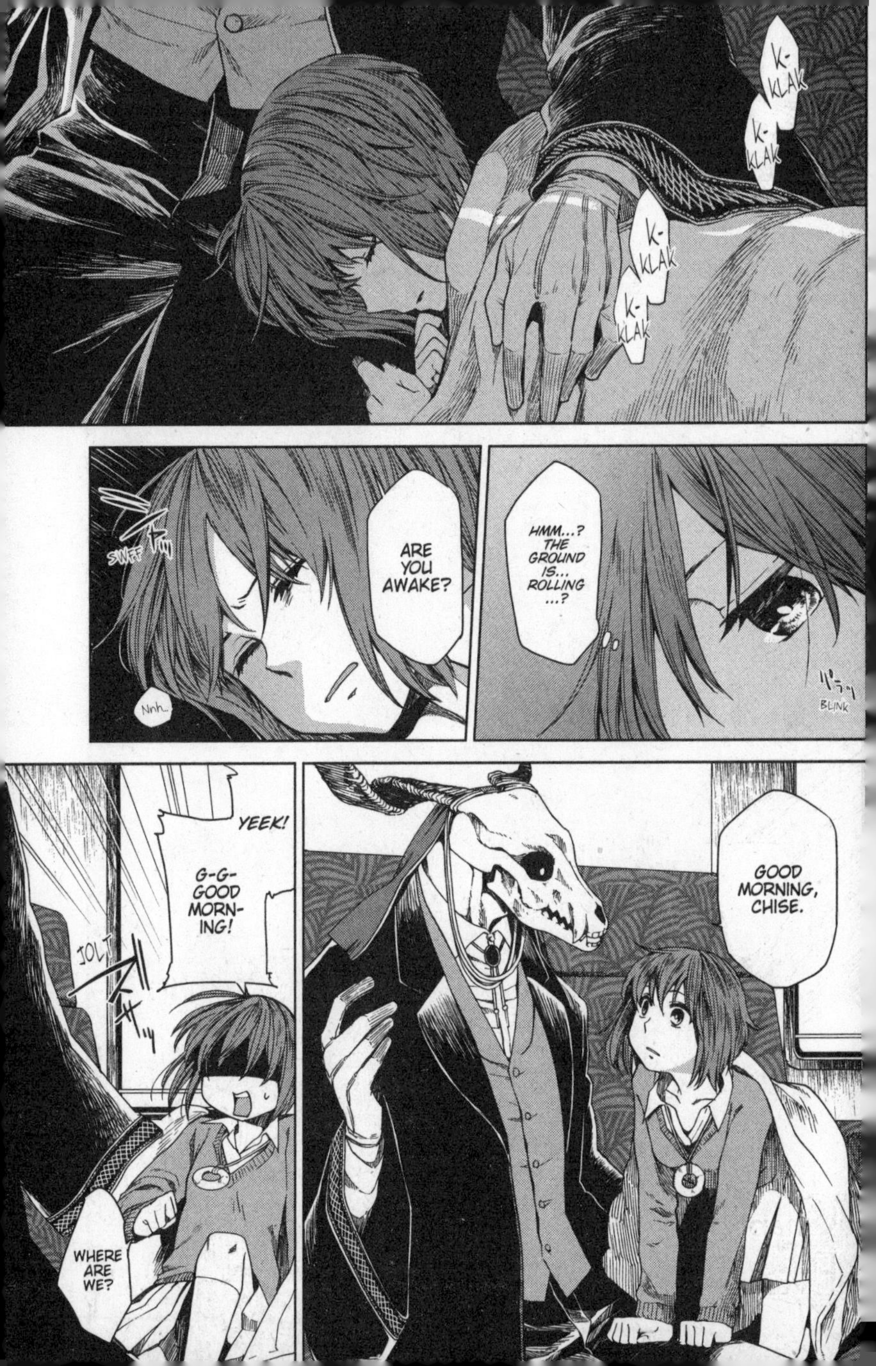
K-KLAK
K-KLAK
K-KLAK
K-KLAK
HMM...? THE GROUND IS... ROLLING ...?
BLINK
ARE YOU AWAKE?
SWFF
Nnh...
GOOD MORNING, CHISE.
YEEK!
G-G-GOOD MORNING!
JOLT
WHERE ARE WE?

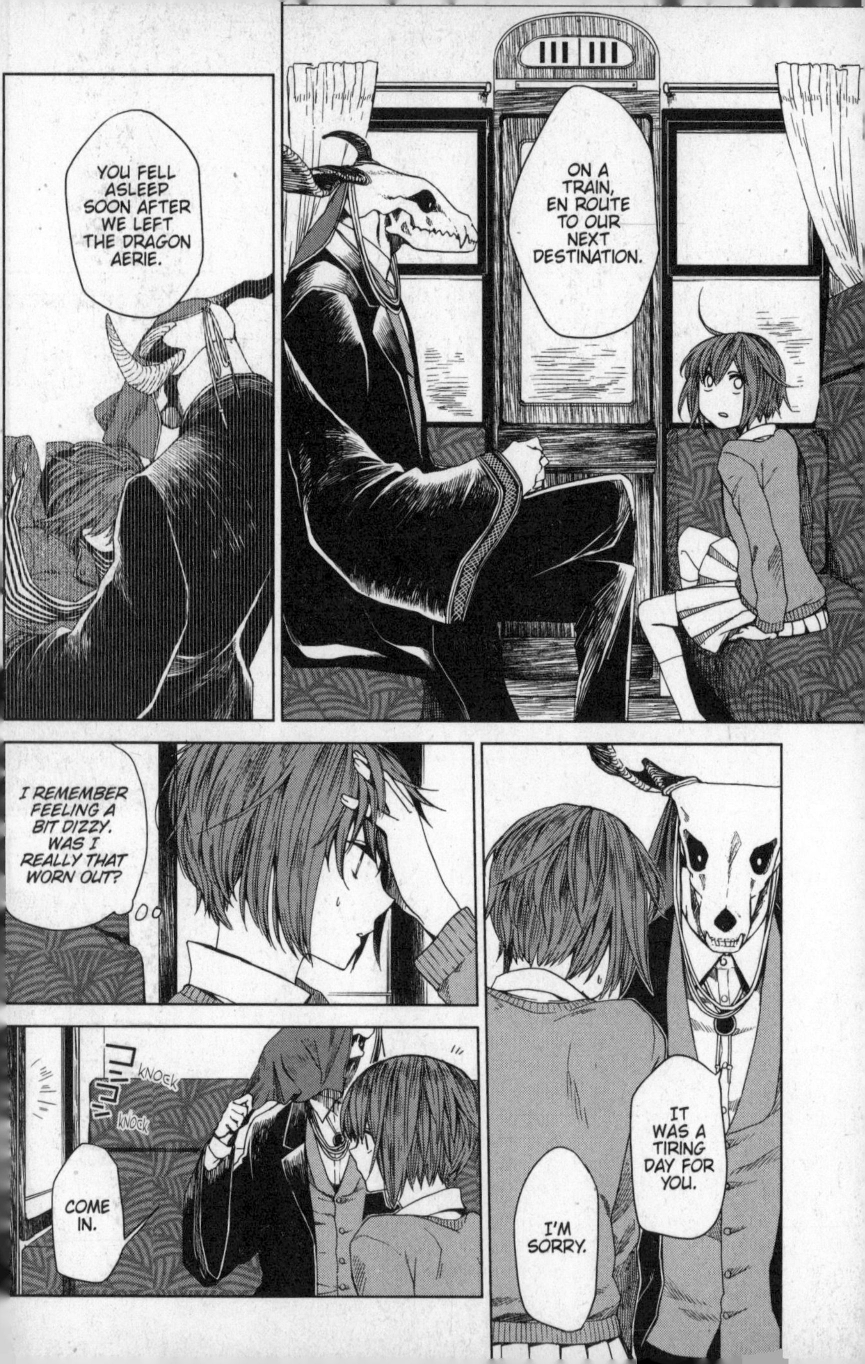
ON A TRAIN, EN ROUTE TO OUR NEXT DESTINATION.
YOU FELL ASLEEP SOON AFTER WE LEFT THE DRAGON AERIE.
IT WAS A TIRING DAY FOR YOU.
I'M SORRY.
I REMEMBER FEELING A BIT DIZZY. WAS I REALLY THAT WORN OUT?
KNOCK
KNOCK
COME IN.

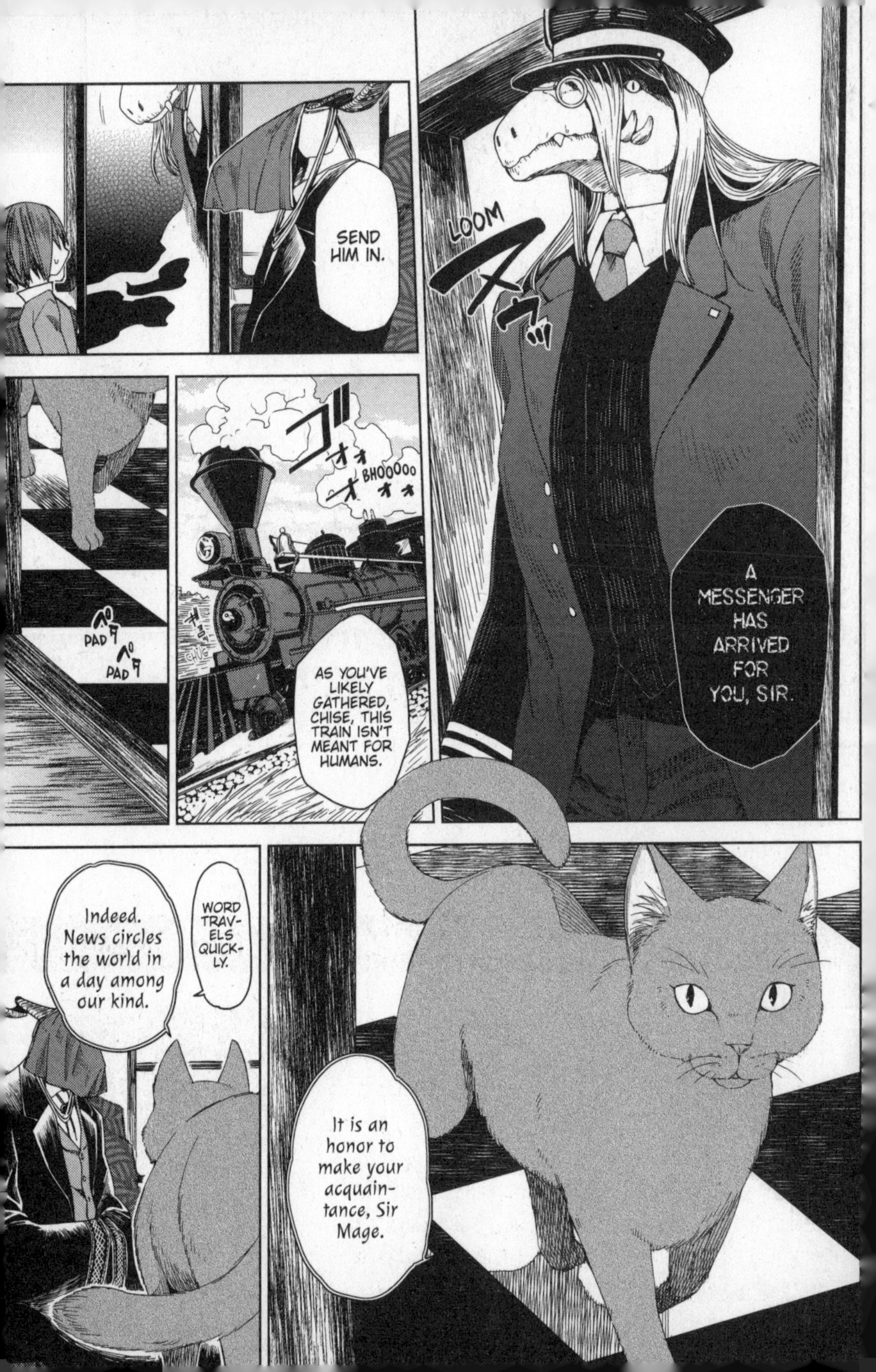
LOOM
A MESSENGER HAS ARRIVED FOR YOU, SIR.
SEND HIM IN.
BHOOOOO
CHUG
AS YOU'VE LIKELY GATHERED, CHISE, THIS TRAIN ISN'T MEANT FOR HUMANS.
PAD
PAD
It is an honor to make your acquaintance, Sir Mage.
WORD TRAVELS QUICKLY.
Indeed. News circles the world in a day among our kind.

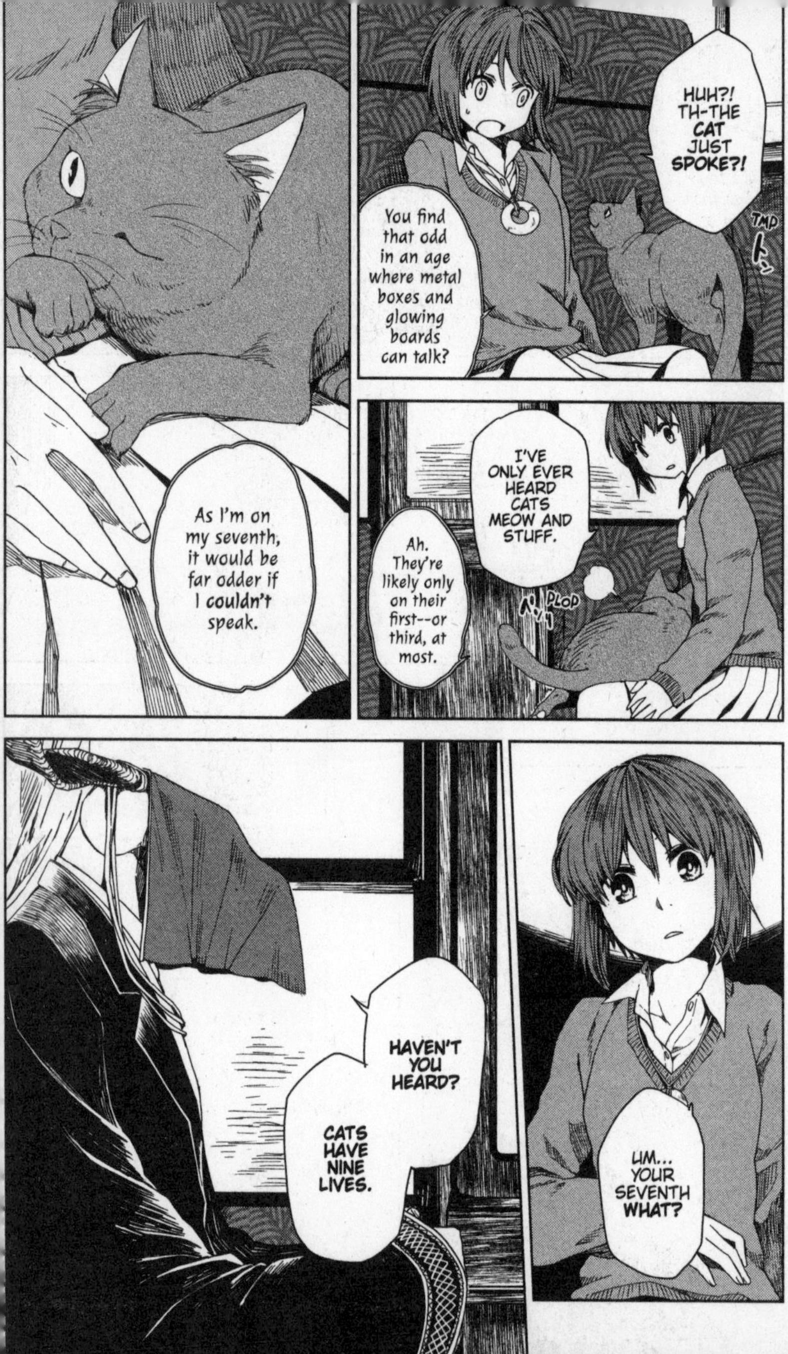
HUH?! TH-THE CAT JUST SPOKE?!
TMP
You find that odd in an age where metal boxes and glowing boards can talk?
I'VE ONLY EVER HEARD CATS MEOW AND STUFF.
Ah. They're likely only on their first--or third, at most.
PLOP
As I'm on my seventh, it would be far odder if I couldn't speak.
UM... YOUR SEVENTH WHAT?
HAVEN'T YOU HEARD?
CATS HAVE NINE LIVES.

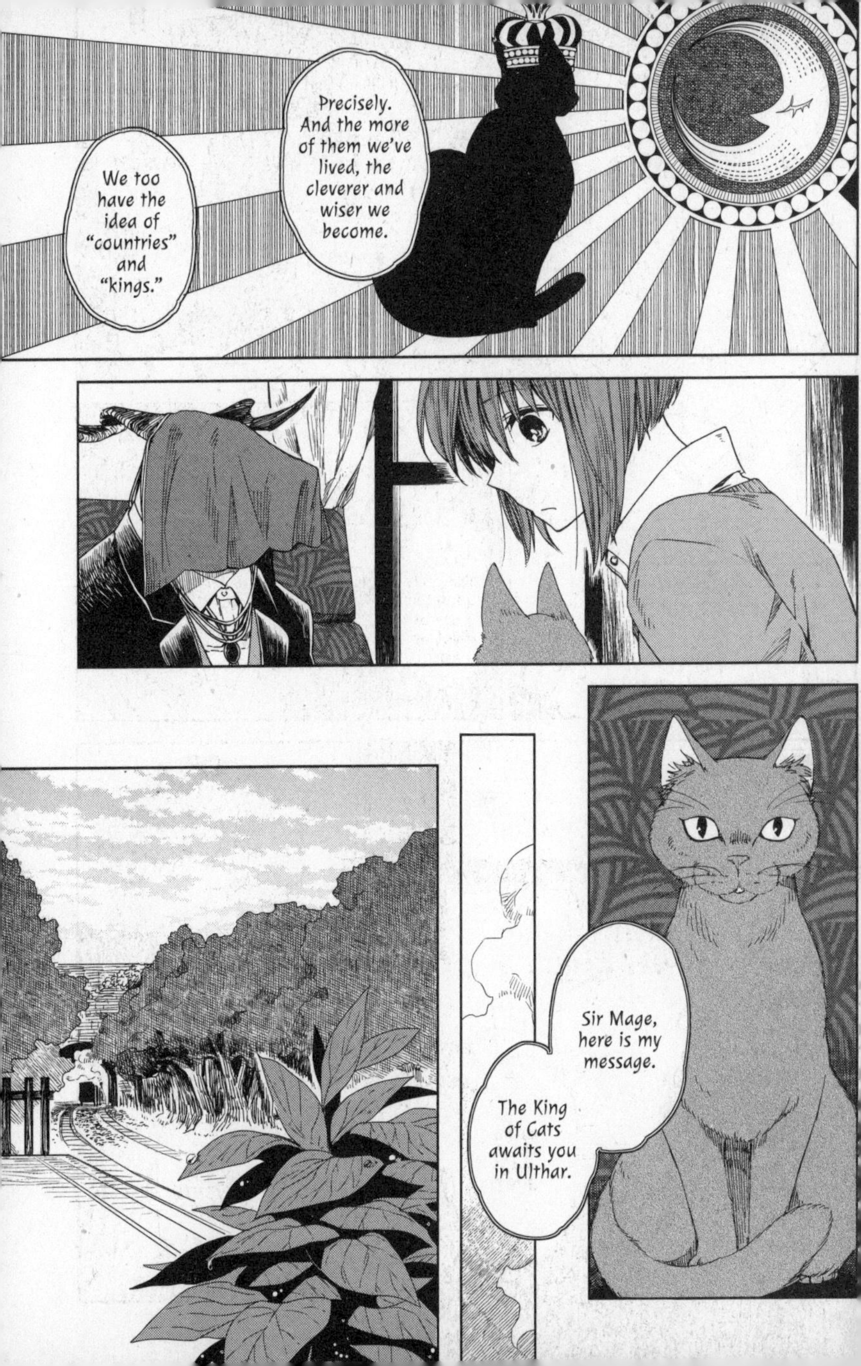
Precisely. And the more of them we've lived, the cleverer and wiser we become.
We too have the idea of "countries" and "kings."
Sir Mage, here is my message.
The King of Cats awaits you in Ulthar.

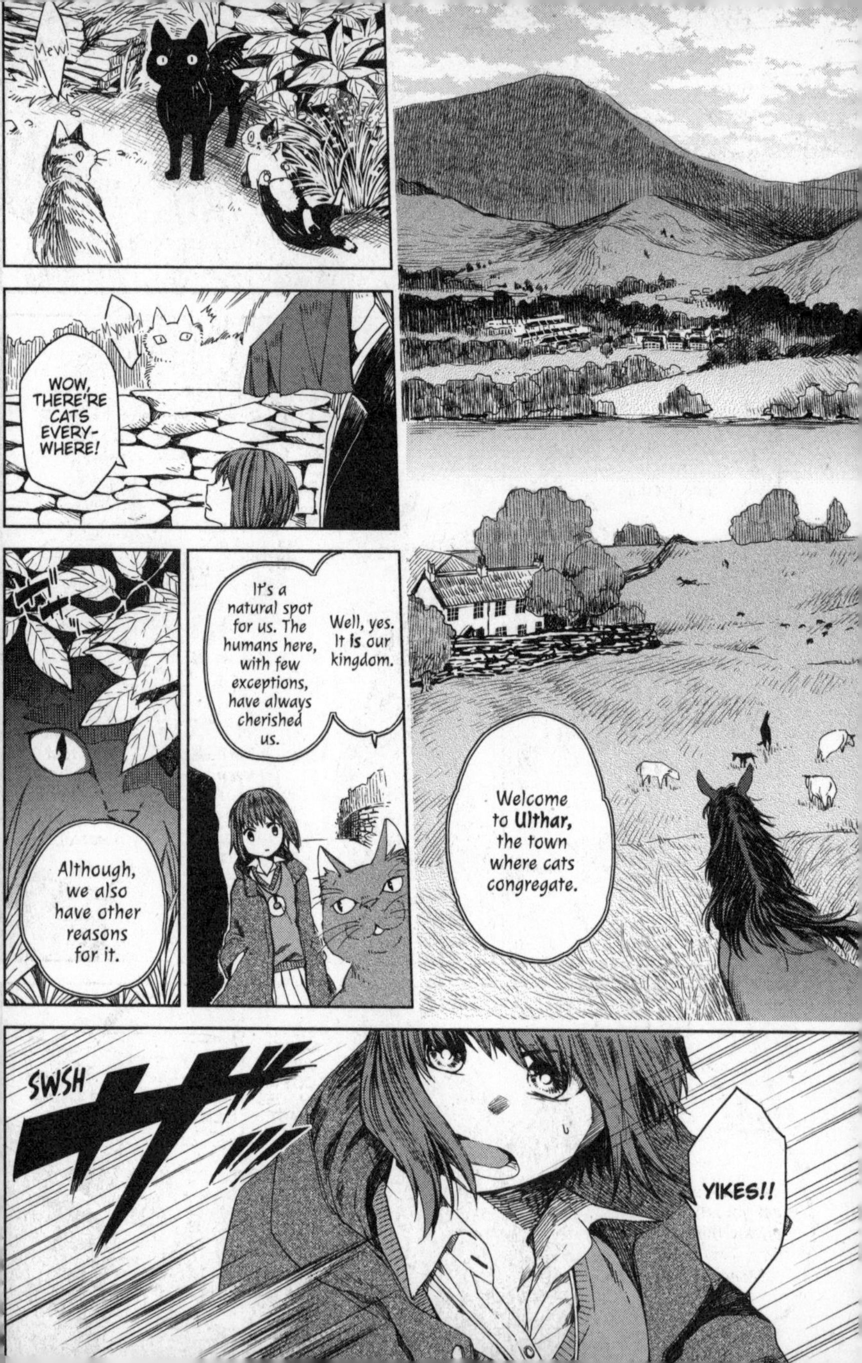
Welcome to Ulthar, the town where cats congregate.
Mew!
Myowr!
WOW, THERE'RE CATS EVERY-WHERE!
Well, yes. It is our kingdom.
It's a natural spot for us. The humans here, with few exceptions, have always cherished us.
Although, we also have other reasons for it.
YIKES!!
SWSH

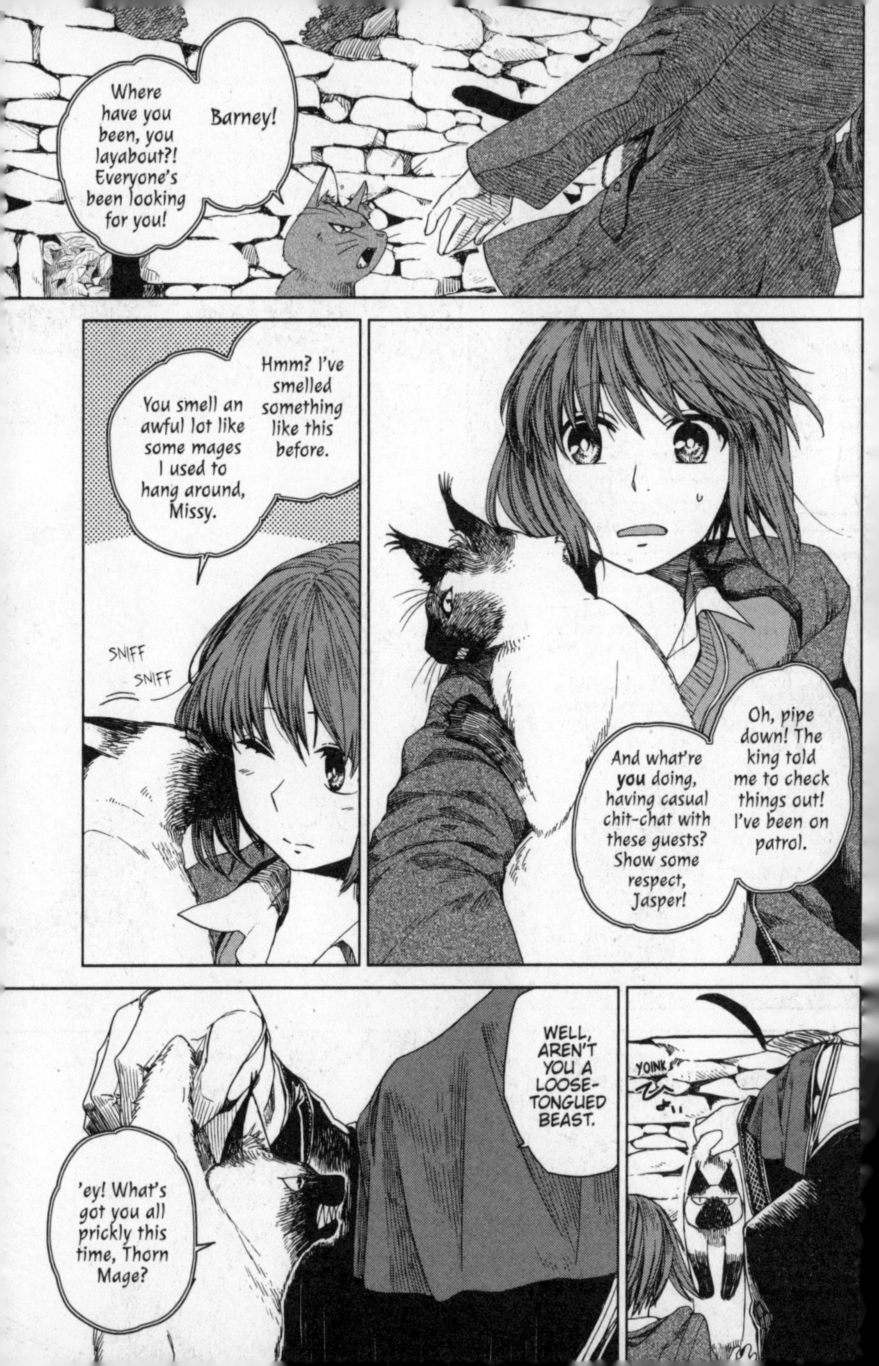
Barney!
Where have you been, you layabout?! Everyone's been looking for you!
Oh, pipe down! The king told me to check things out! I've been on patrol.
And what're **you** doing, having casual chit-chat with these guests? Show some respect, Jasper!
Hmm? I've smelled something like this before.
You smell an awful lot like some mages I used to hang around, Missy.
SNIFF
SNIFF
YOINK
WELL, AREN'T YOU A LOOSE-TONGUED BEAST.
'ey! What's got you all prickly this time, Thorn Mage?

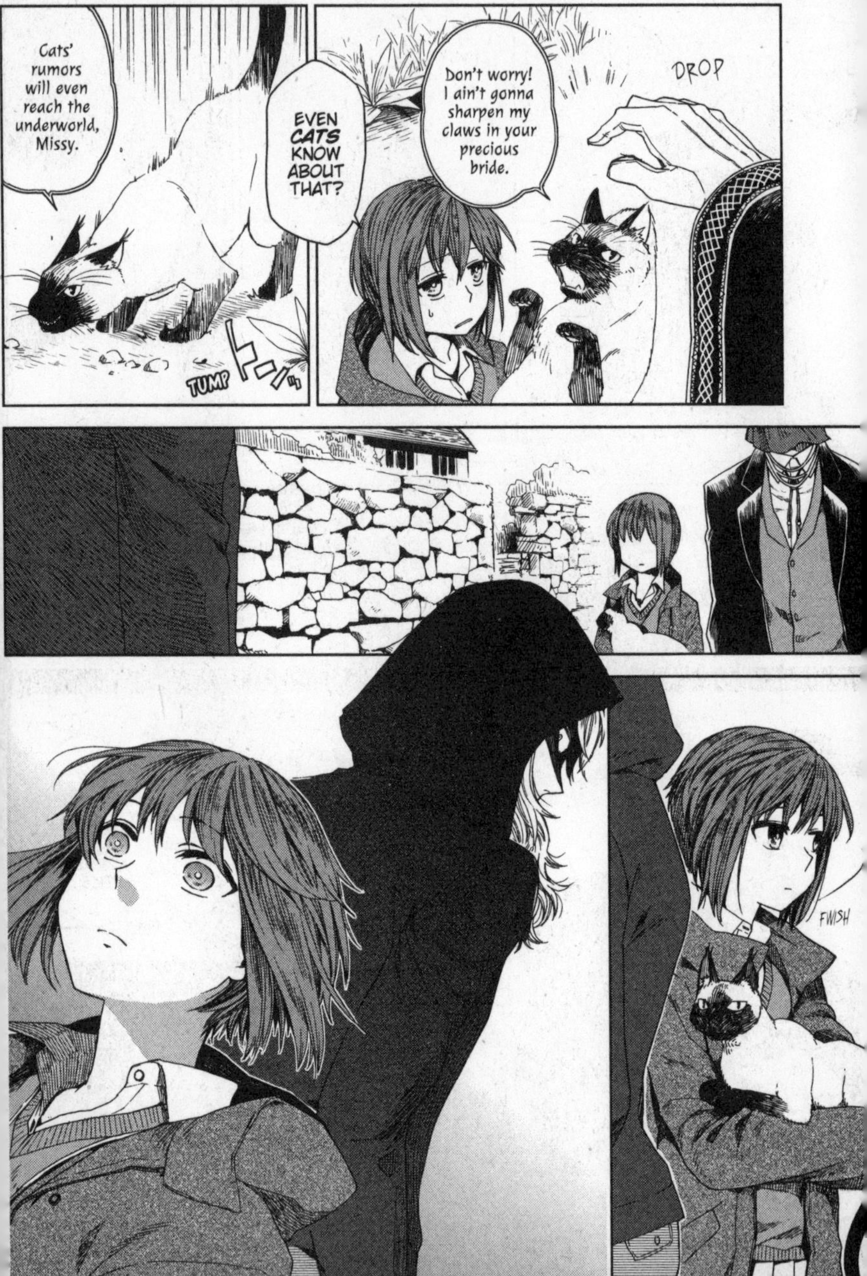
DROP
Don't worry! I ain't gonna sharpen my claws in your precious bride.
EVEN CATS KNOW ABOUT THAT?
Cats' rumors will even reach the underworld, Missy.
TUMP
FWISH

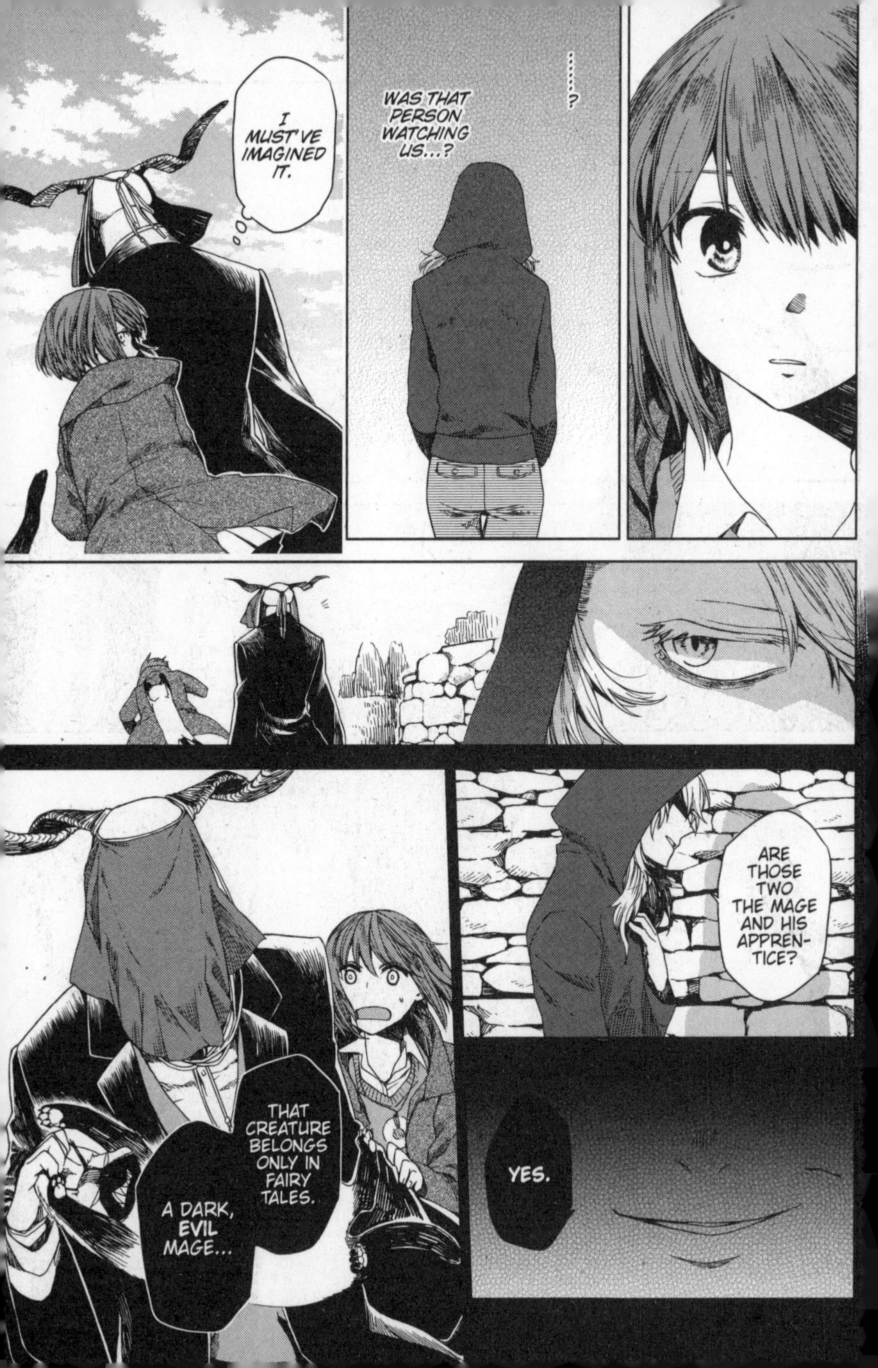
......?
WAS THAT PERSON WATCHING US...?
I MUST'VE IMAGINED IT.
ARE THOSE TWO THE MAGE AND HIS APPREN- TICE?
YES.
THAT CREATURE BELONGS ONLY IN FAIRY TALES.
A DARK, EVIL MAGE...

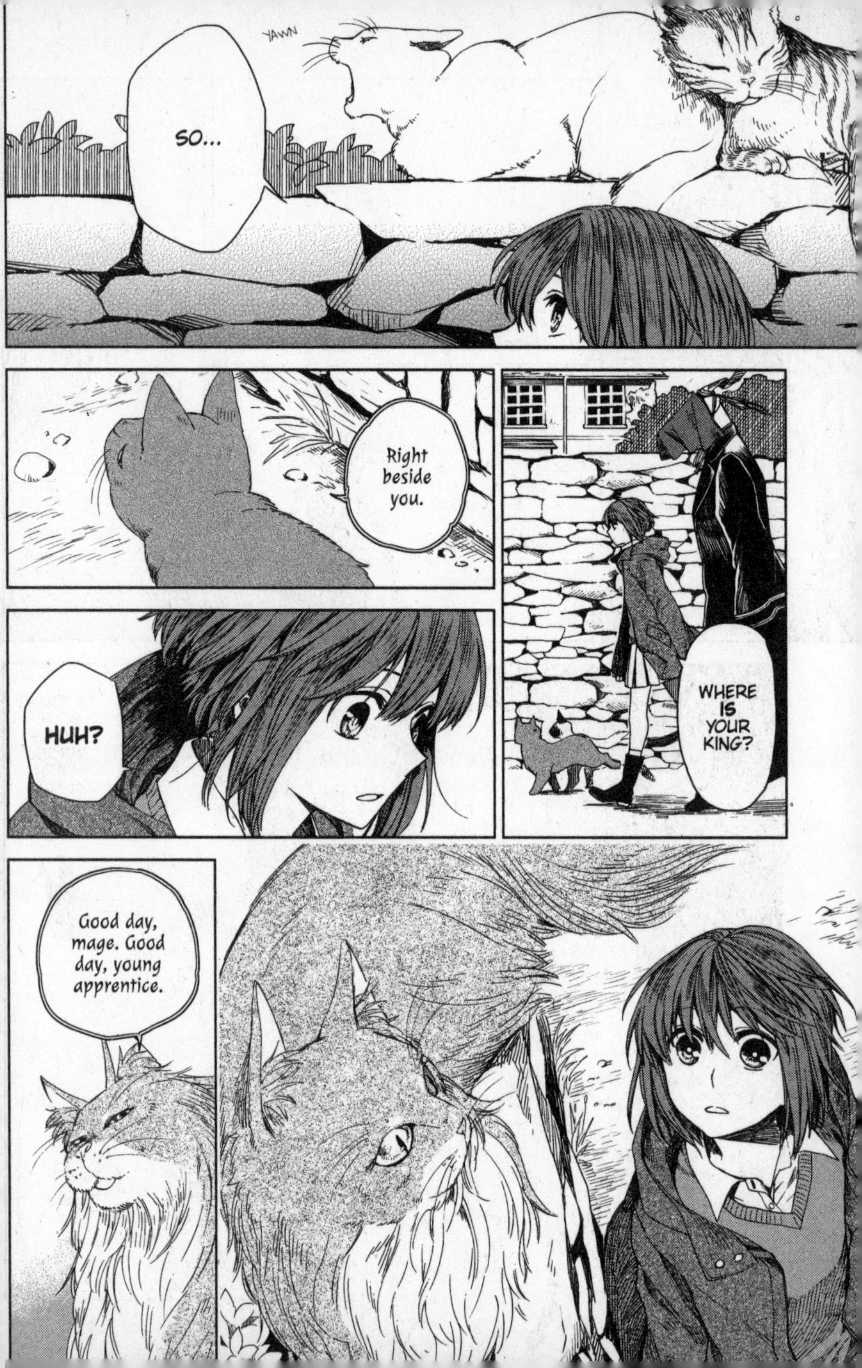
YAWN
SO...
WHERE IS YOUR KING?
Right beside you.
HUH?
Good day, mage. Good day, young apprentice.

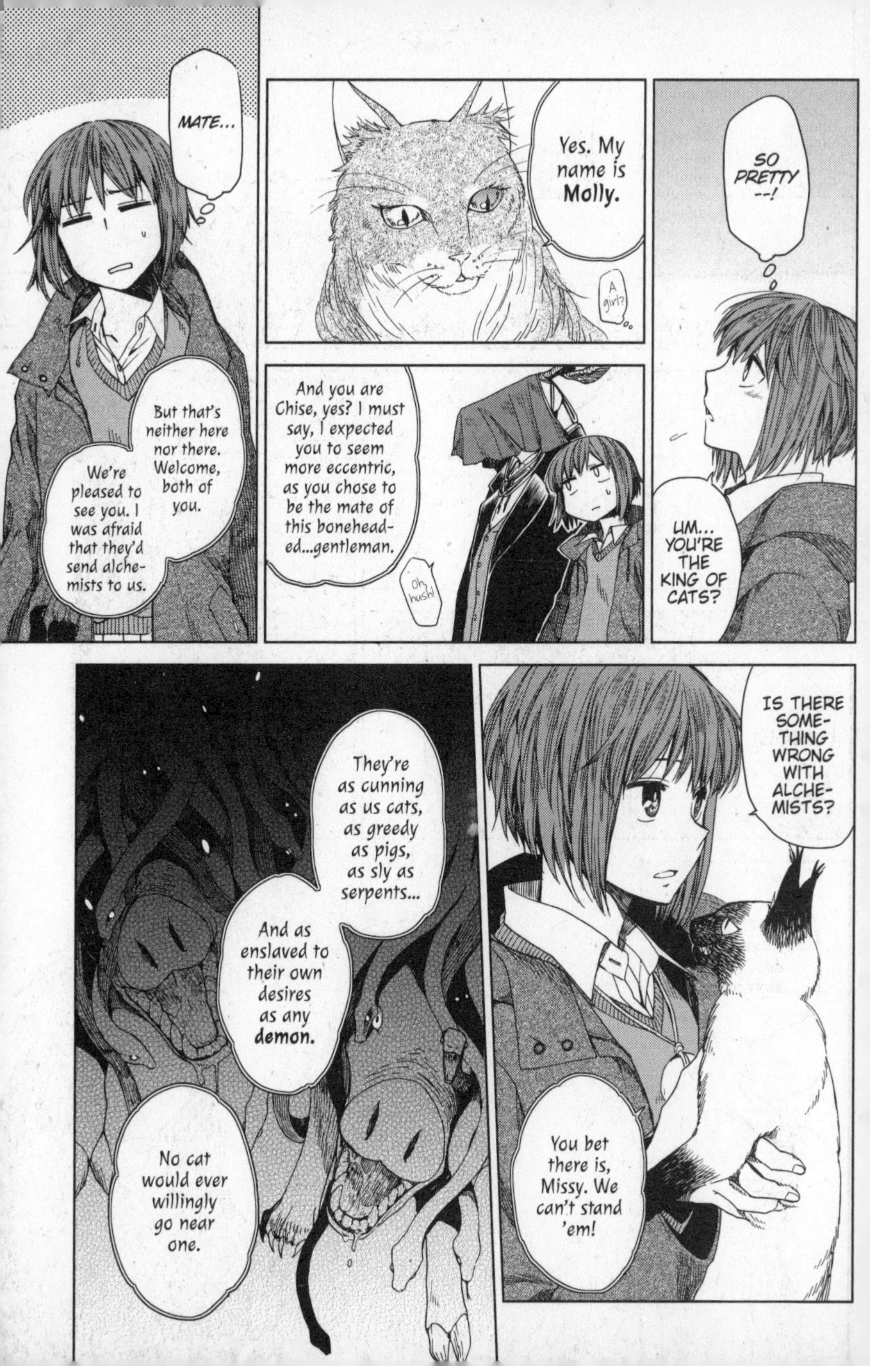
SO PRETTY --!
UM... YOU'RE THE KING OF CATS?
Yes. My name is **Molly.**
A girl?
And you are Chise, yes? I must say, I expected you to seem more eccentric, as you chose to be the mate of this boneheaded-ed...gentleman.
Oh, hush!
MATE...
But that's neither here nor there. Welcome, both of you.
We're pleased to see you. I was afraid that they'd send alche-mists to us.
IS THERE SOME-THING WRONG WITH ALCHE-MISTS?
You bet there is, Missy. We can't stand 'em!
They're as cunning as us cats, as greedy as pigs, as sly as serpents...
And as enslaved to their own desires as any **demon.**
No cat would ever willingly go near one.

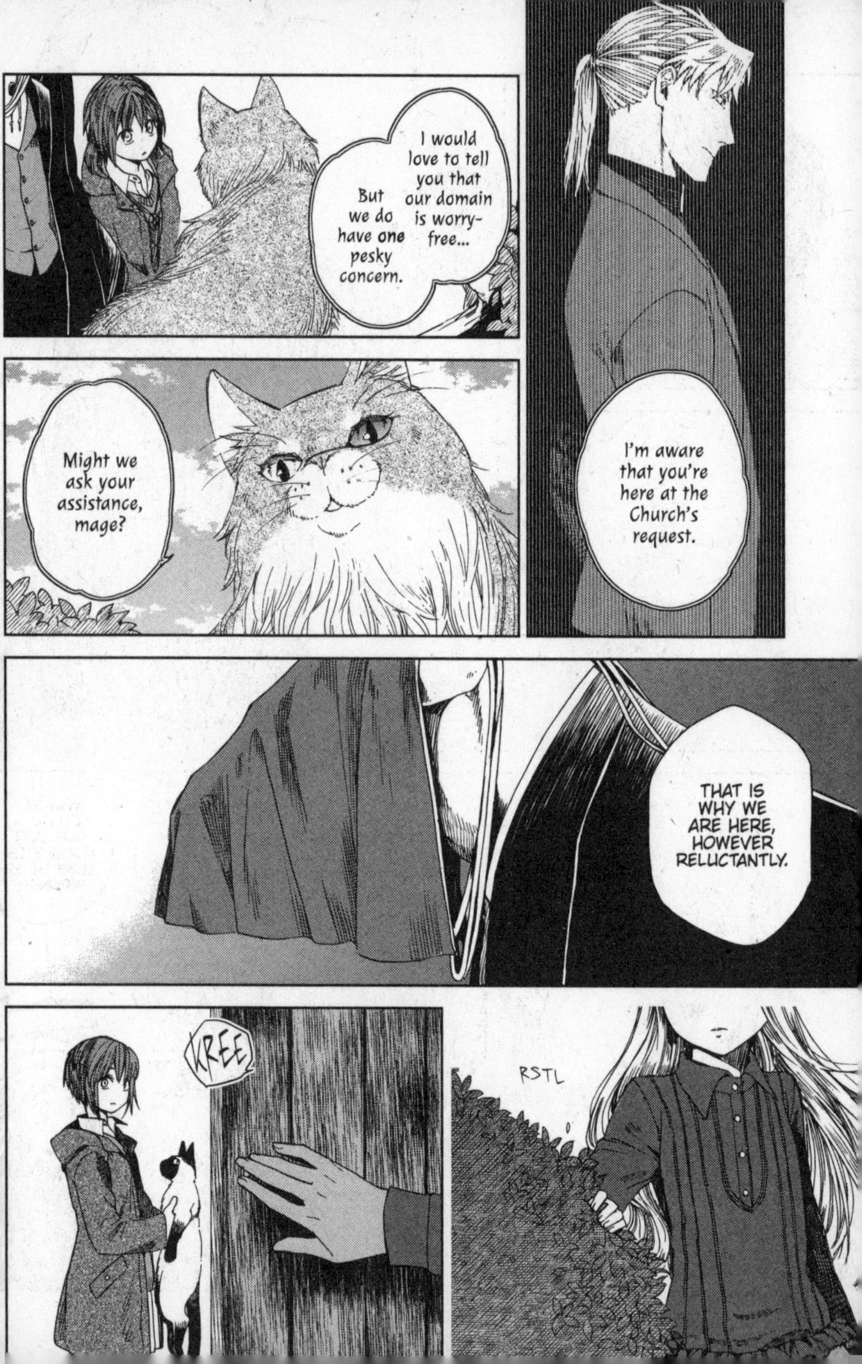
I'm aware that you're here at the Church's request.
I would love to tell you that our domain is worry-free...
But we do have one pesky concern.
Might we ask your assistance, mage?
THAT IS WHY WE ARE HERE, HOWEVER RELUCTANTLY.
RSTL
KREE

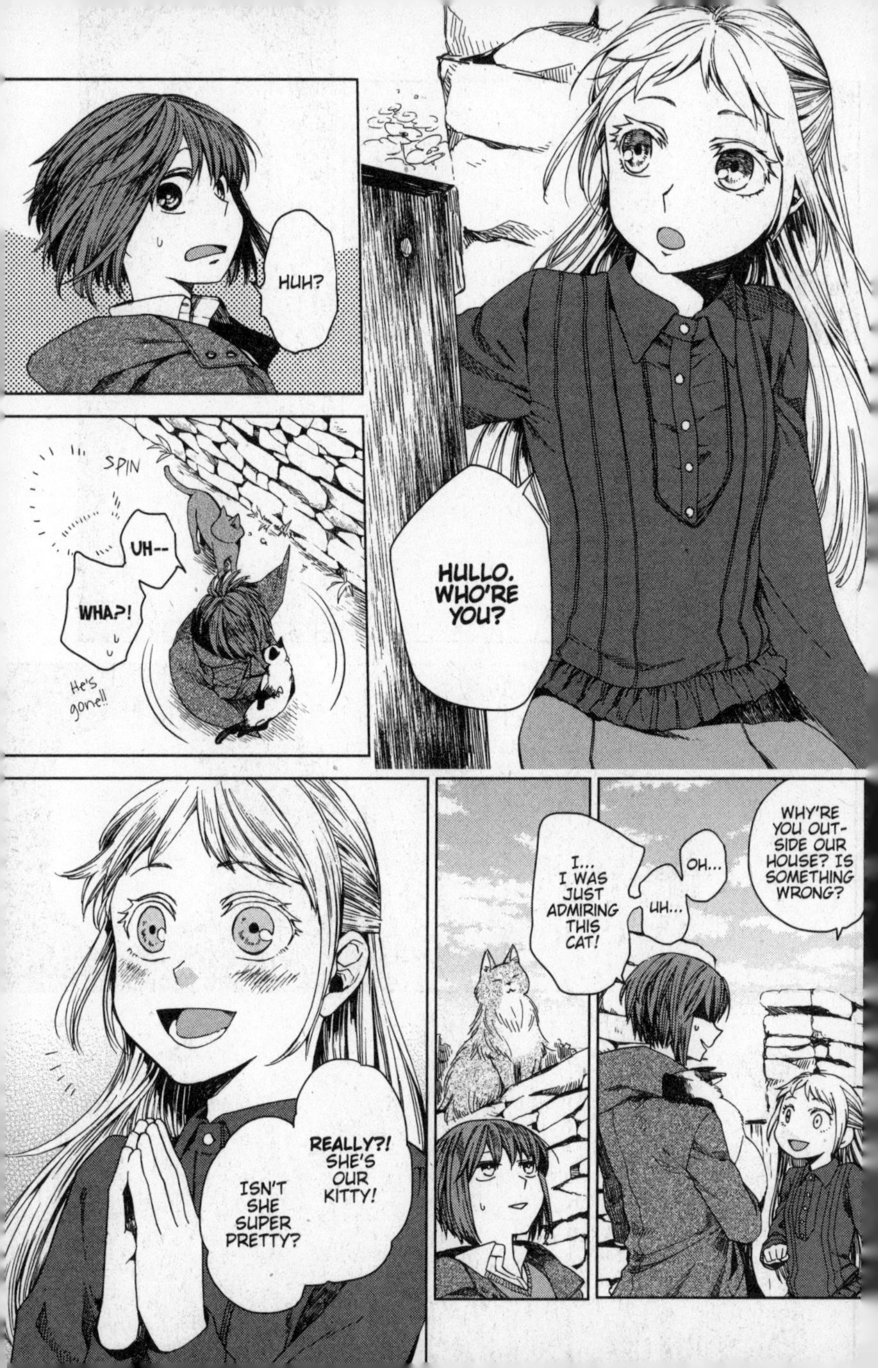
HULLO. WHO'RE YOU?
HUH?
SPIN
UH--
WHA?!
He's gone!!
WHY'RE YOU OUT-SIDE OUR HOUSE? IS SOMETHING WRONG?
OH...
UH...
I... I WAS JUST ADMIRING THIS CAT!
REALLY?! SHE'S OUR KITTY!
ISN'T SHE SUPER PRETTY?

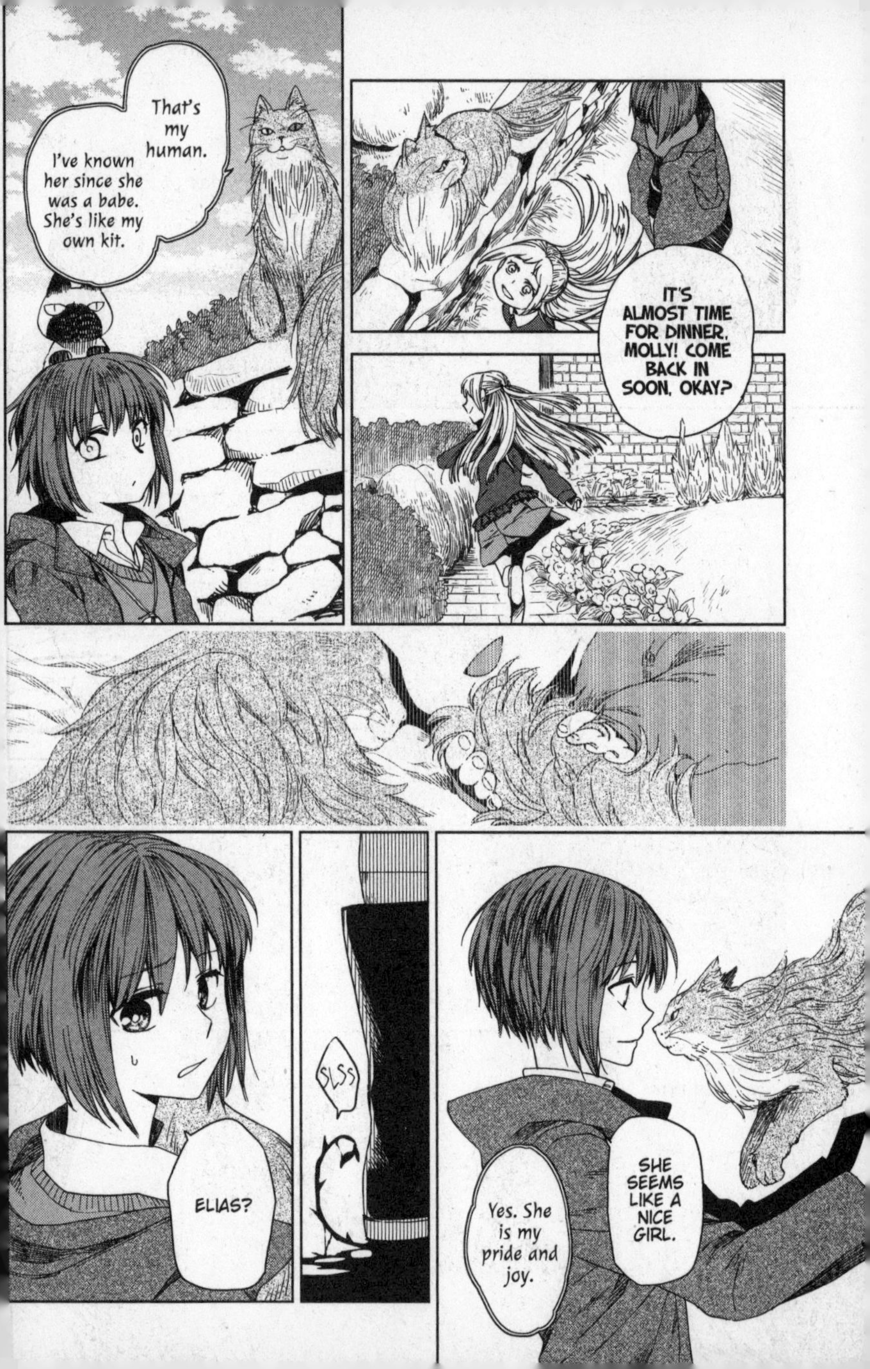
IT'S ALMOST TIME FOR DINNER, MOLLY! COME BACK IN SOON, OKAY?
That's my human.
I've known her since she was a babe. She's like my own kit.
SHE SEEMS LIKE A NICE GIRL.
Yes. She is my pride and joy.
SLSS
ELIAS?

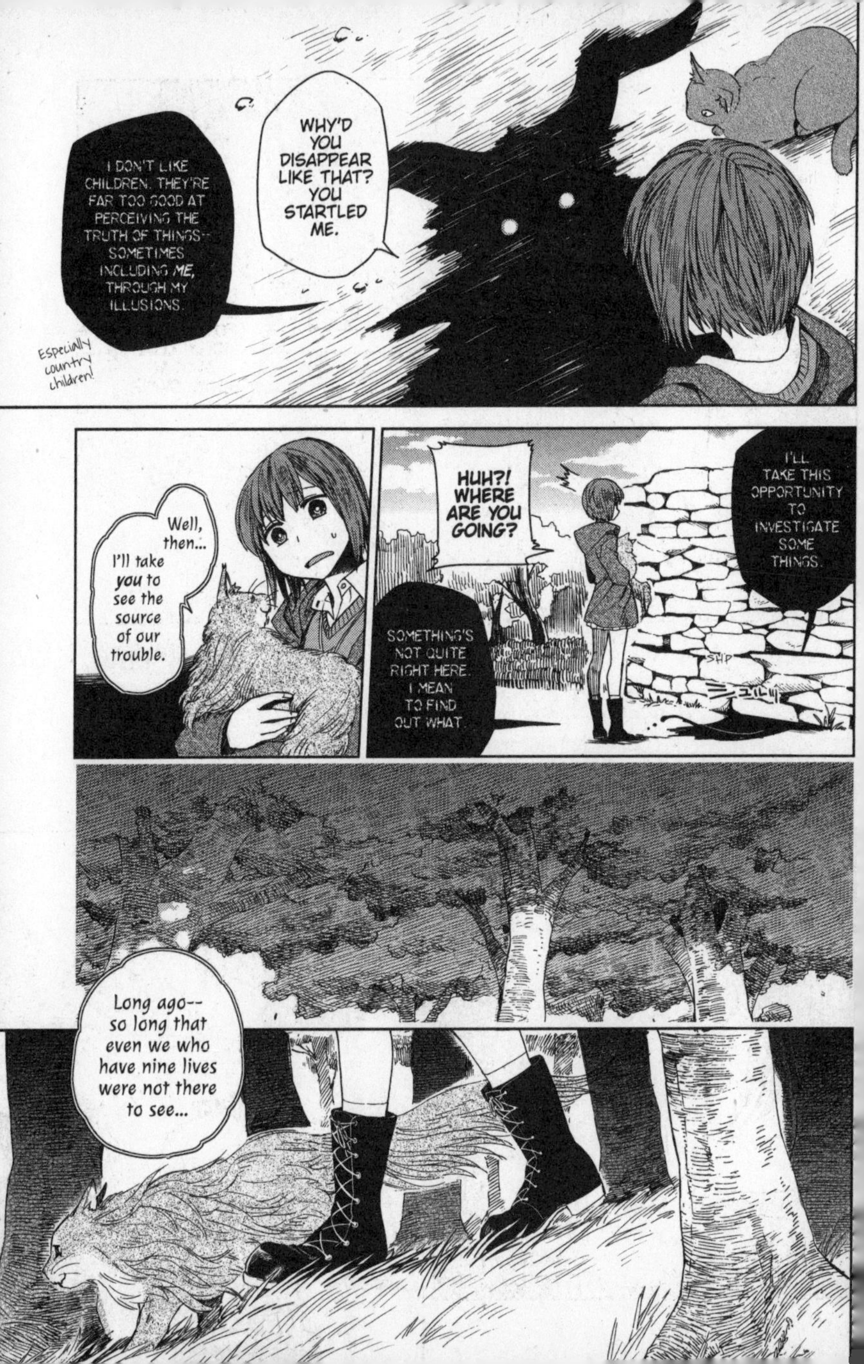
WHY'D YOU DISAPPEAR LIKE THAT? YOU STARTLED ME.
I DON'T LIKE CHILDREN. THEY'RE FAR TOO GOOD AT PERCEIVING THE TRUTH OF THINGS-- SOMETIMES INCLUDING *ME*, THROUGH MY ILLUSIONS.
Especially country children!
I'LL TAKE THIS OPPORTUNITY TO INVESTIGATE SOME THINGS.
SHP
HUH?! WHERE ARE YOU GOING?
SOMETHING'S NOT QUITE RIGHT HERE. I MEAN TO FIND OUT WHAT.
Well, then... I'll take *you* to see the source of our trouble.
Long ago-- so long that even we who have nine lives were not there to see...

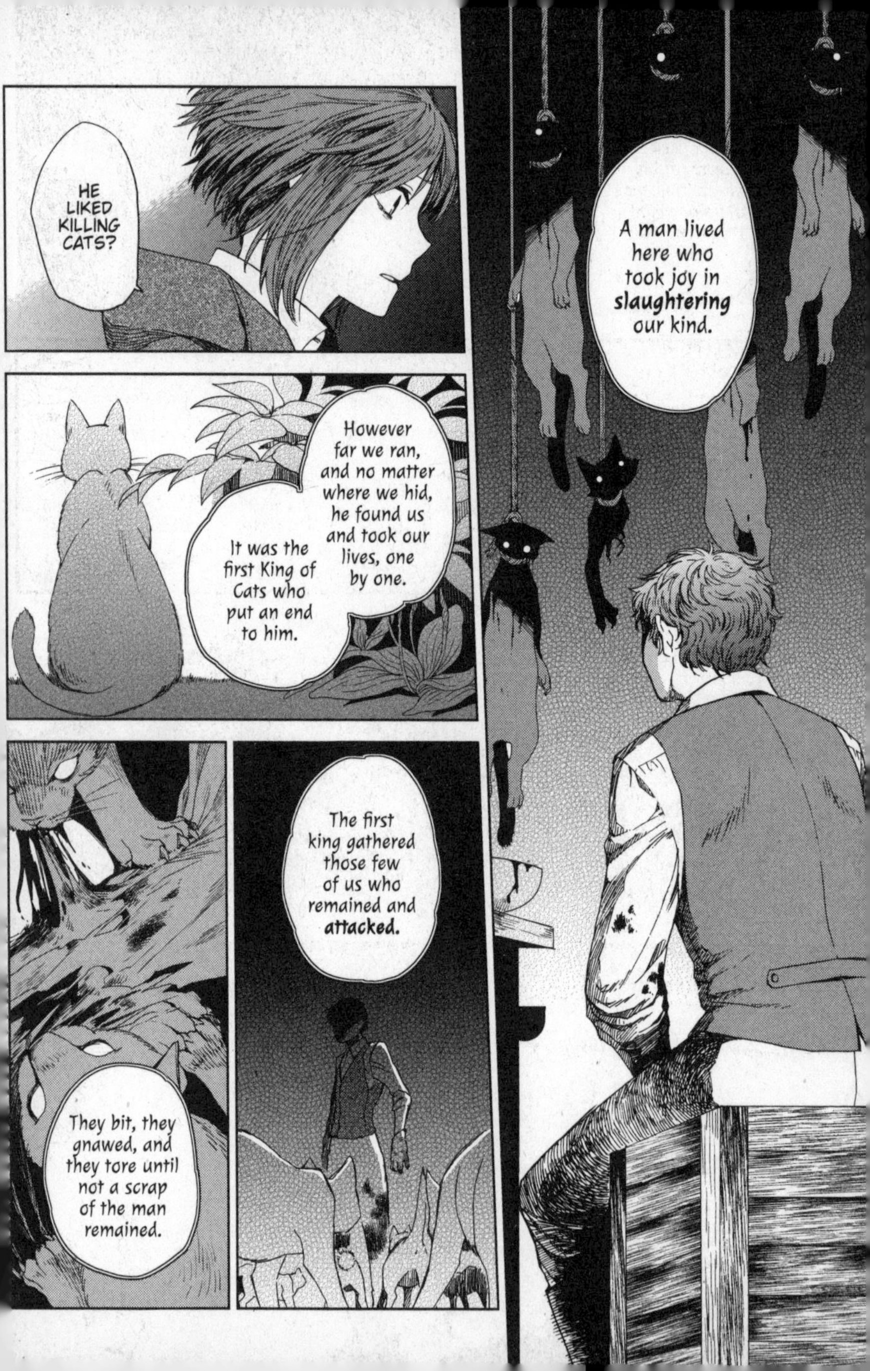
A man lived here who took joy in **slaughtering** our kind.
HE LIKED KILLING CATS?
However far we ran, and no matter where we hid, he found us and took our lives, one by one.
It was the first King of Cats who put an end to him.
The first king gathered those few of us who remained and **attacked.**
They bit, they gnawed, and they tore until not a scrap of the man remained.

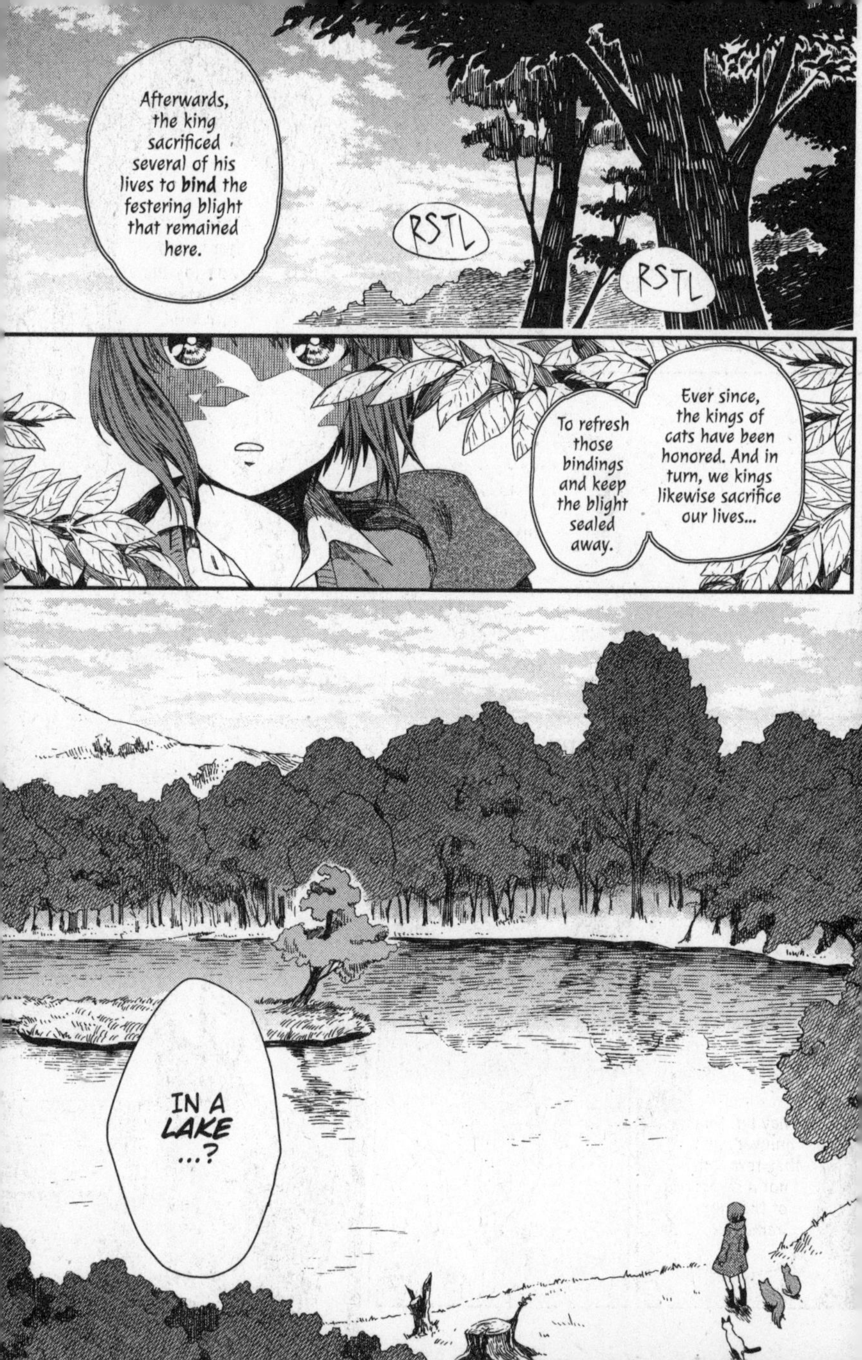
Afterwards, the king sacrificed several of his lives to **bind** the festering blight that remained here.
RSTL
RSTL
Ever since, the kings of cats have been honored. And in turn, we kings likewise sacrifice our lives...
To refresh those bindings and keep the blight sealed away.
IN A LAKE ...?

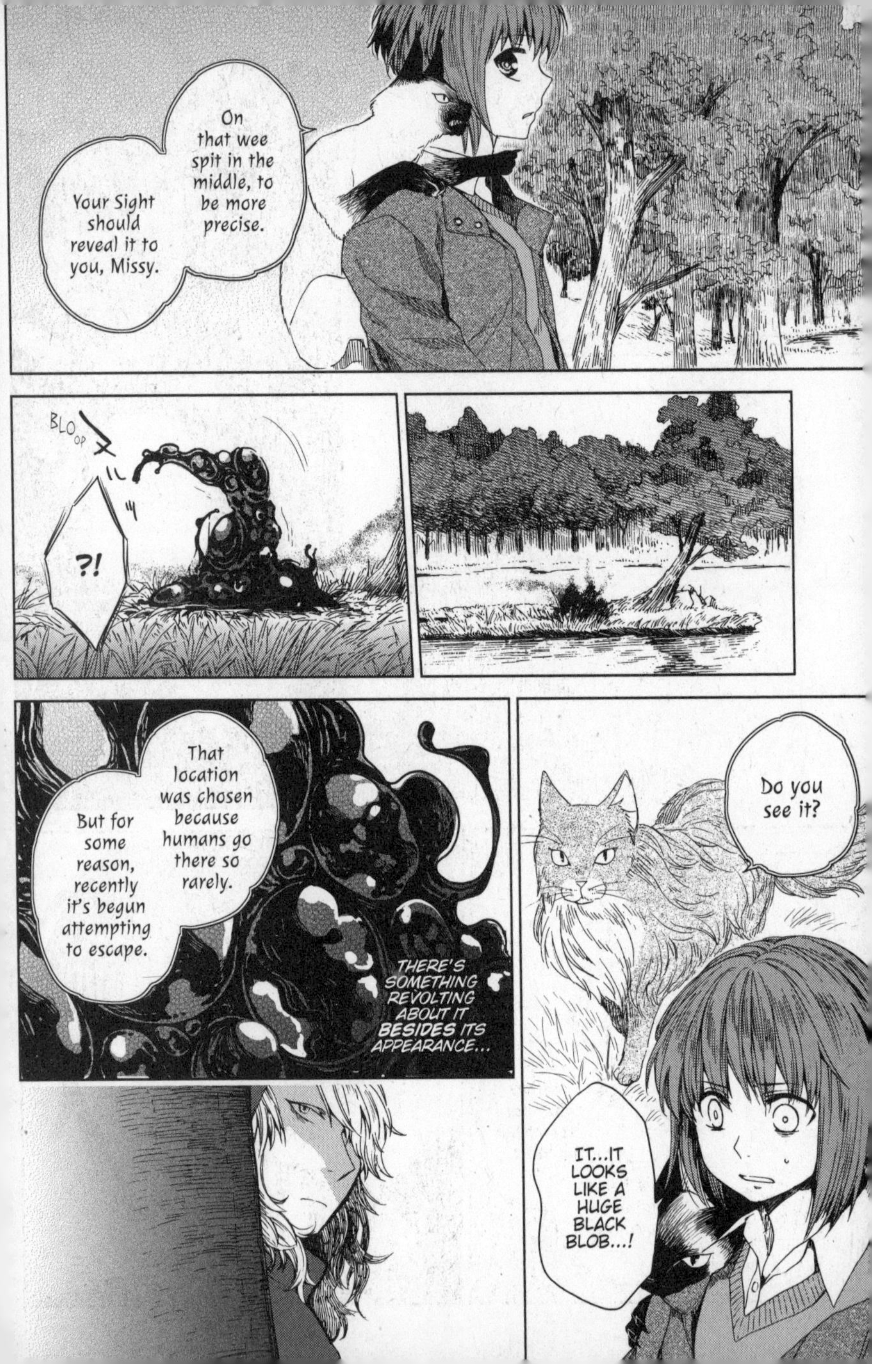
On that wee spit in the middle, to be more precise.
Your Sight should reveal it to you, Missy.
BLOOP
?!
Do you see it?
IT...IT LOOKS LIKE A HUGE BLACK BLOB...!
That location was chosen because humans go there so rarely.
But for some reason, recently it's begun attempting to escape.
THERE'S SOMETHING REVOLTING ABOUT IT BESIDES ITS APPEARANCE...

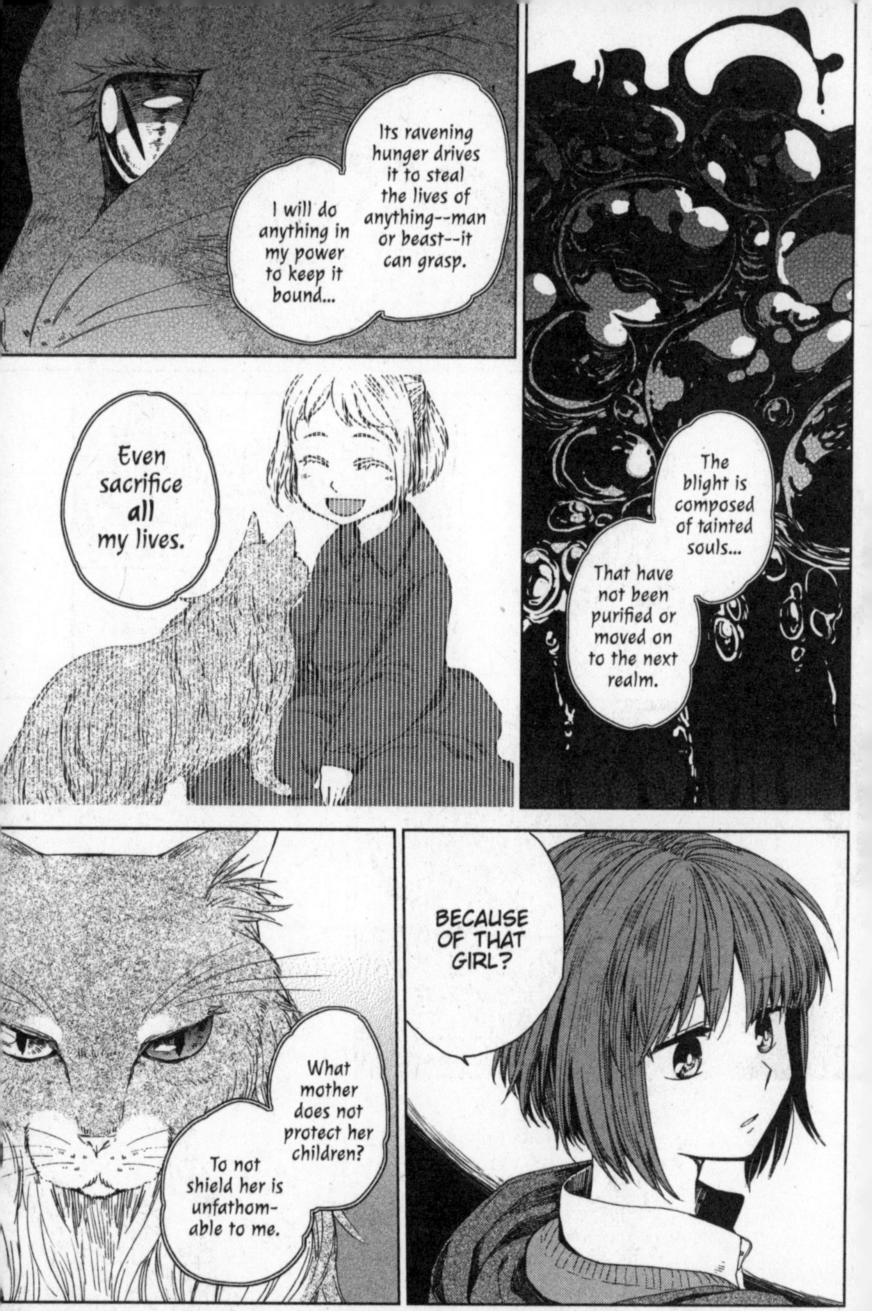
The blight is composed of tainted souls...
That have not been purified or moved on to the next realm.
Its ravening hunger drives it to steal the lives of anything--man or beast--it can grasp.
I will do anything in my power to keep it bound...
Even sacrifice all my lives.
BECAUSE OF THAT GIRL?
What mother does not protect her children?
To not shield her is unfathomable to me.

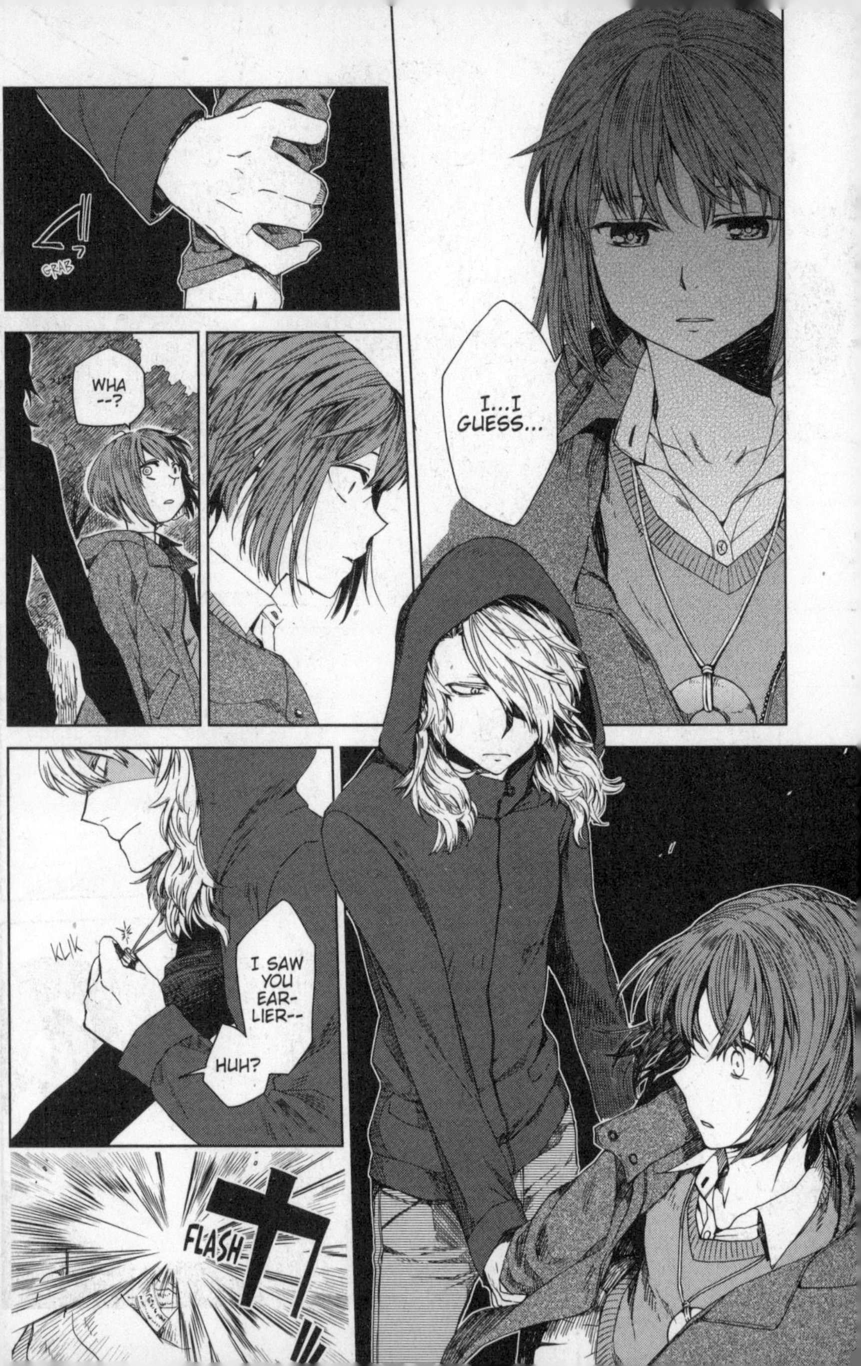
I...I GUESS...
GRAB
WHA --?
I SAW YOU EAR-LIER--
KLIK
HUH?
FLASH

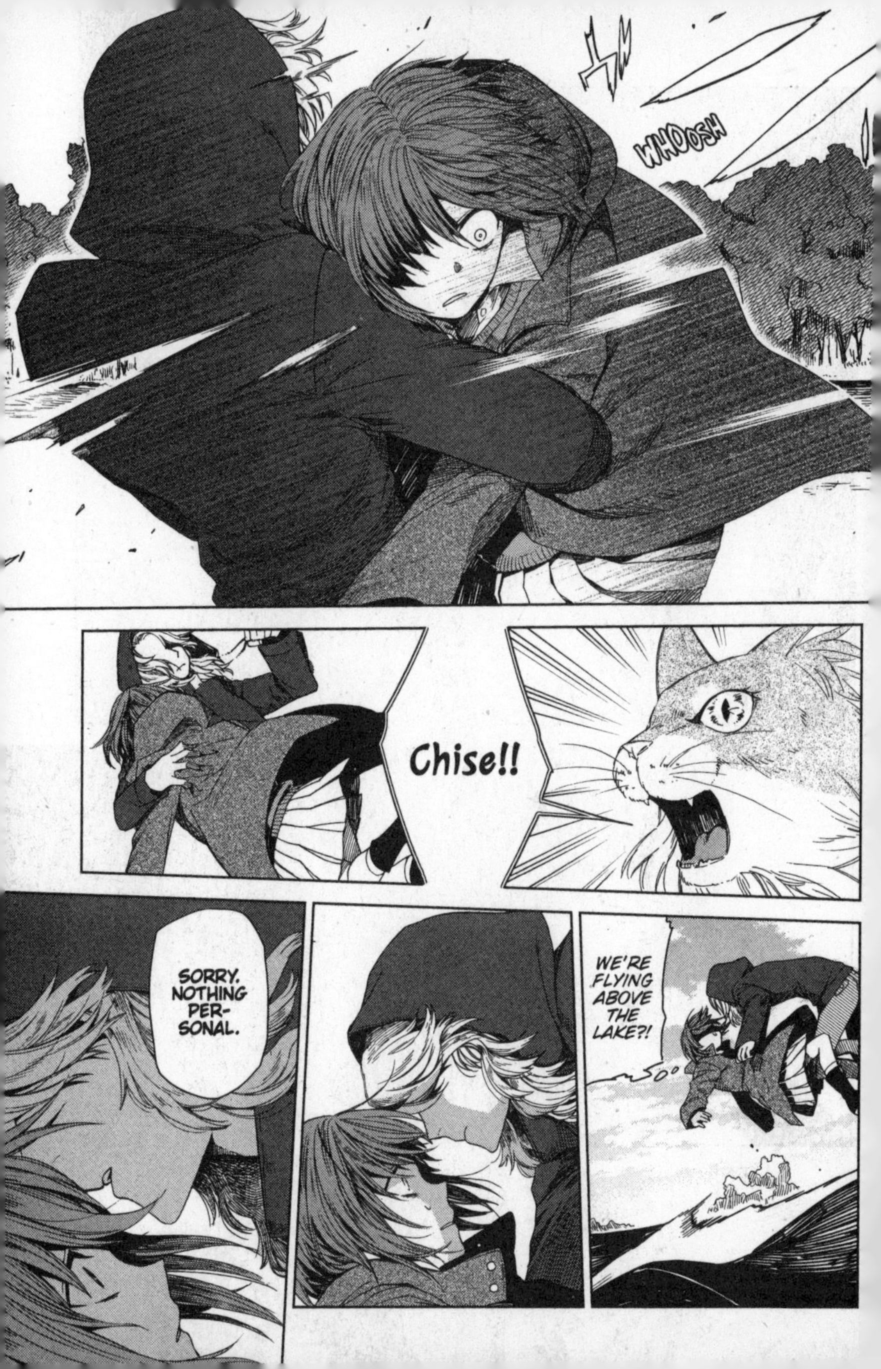
WHOOSH
Chise!!
WE'RE FLYING ABOVE THE LAKE?!
SOO
SORRY. NOTHING PER-SONAL.

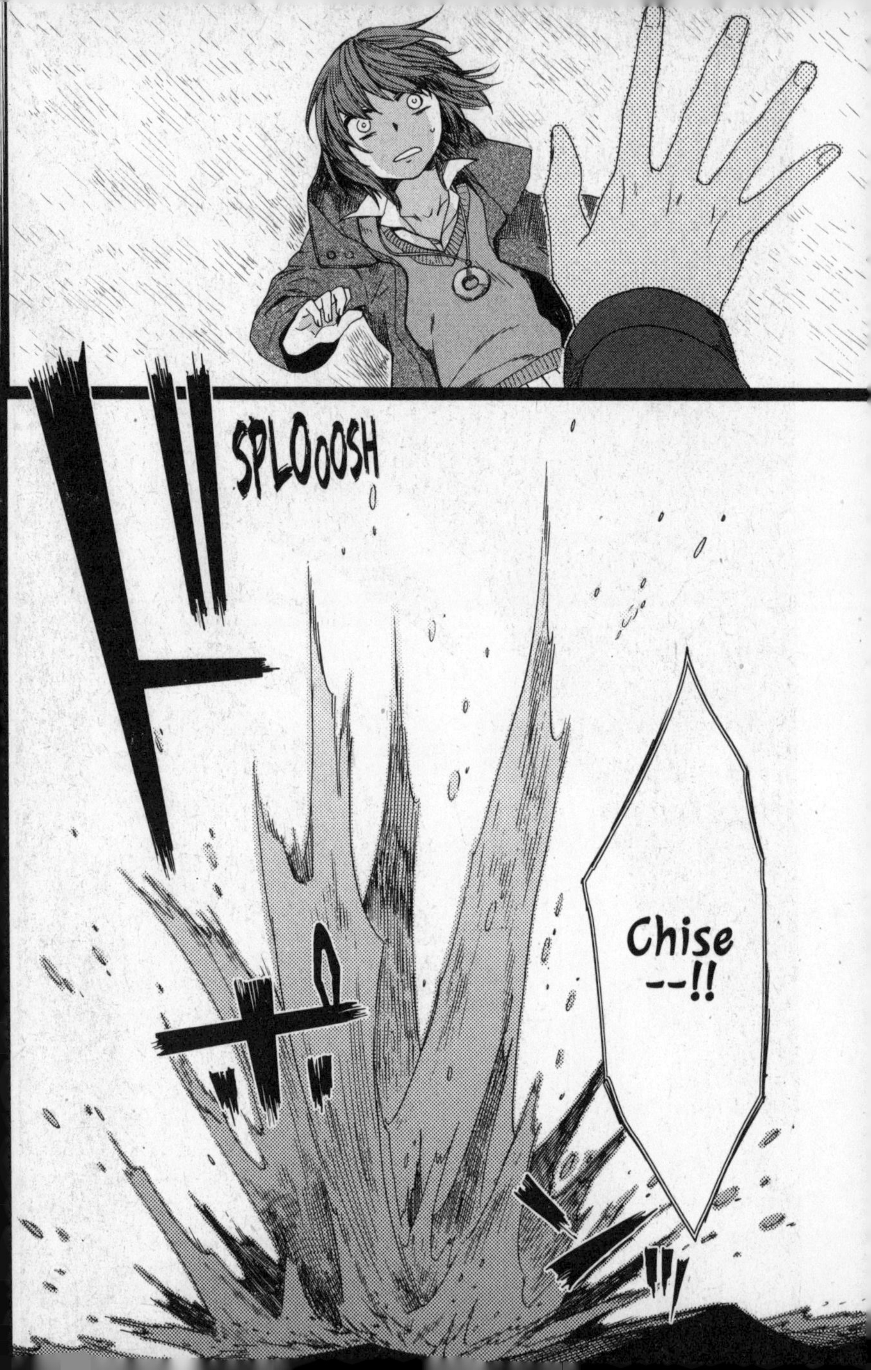
SPLOOOSH
Chise --!!

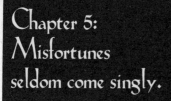

Chapter 5:
Misfortunes
seldom come singly.

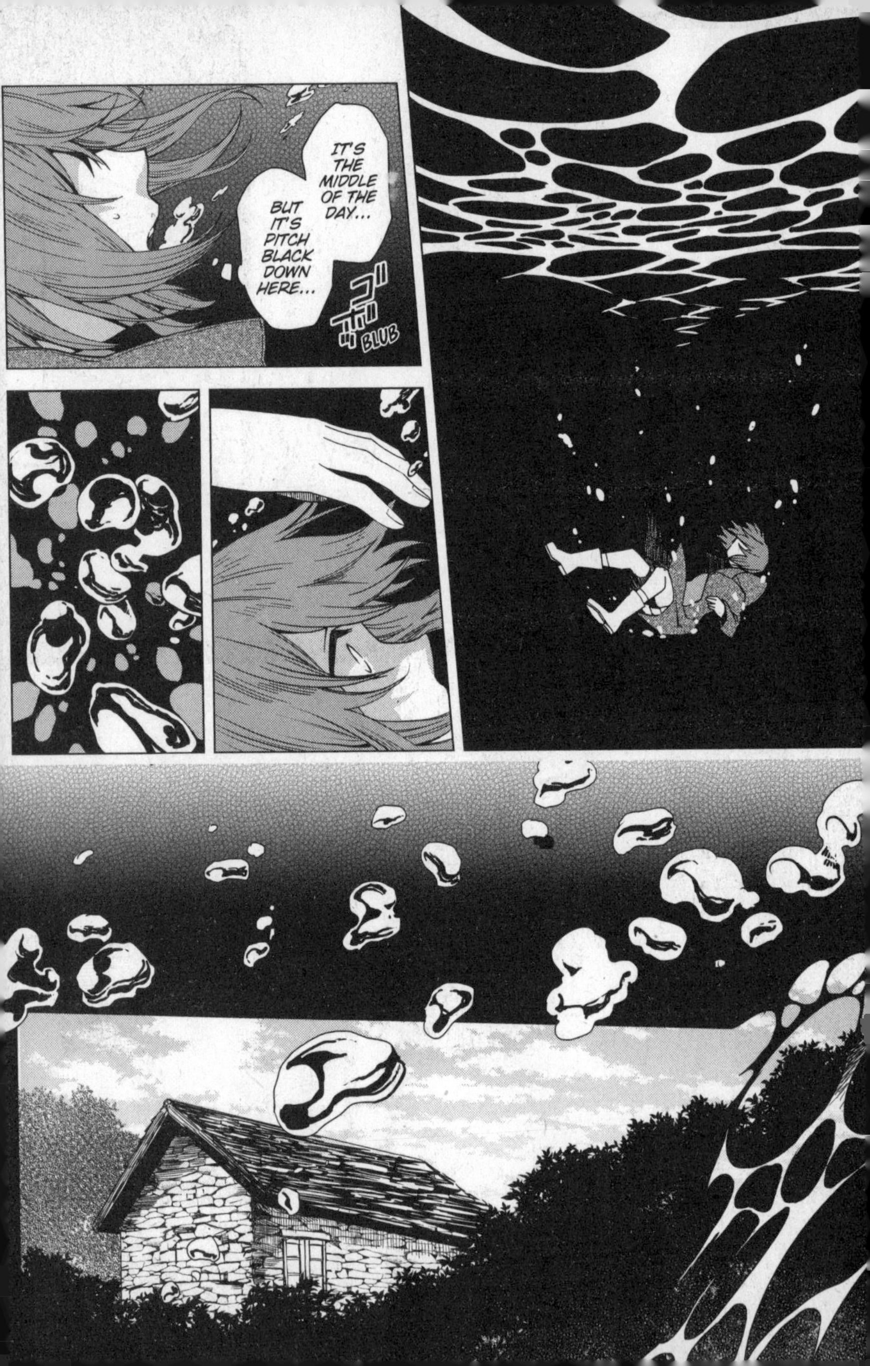
IT'S THE MIDDLE OF THE DAY...
BUT IT'S PITCH BLACK DOWN HERE...
ゴボ
BLUB

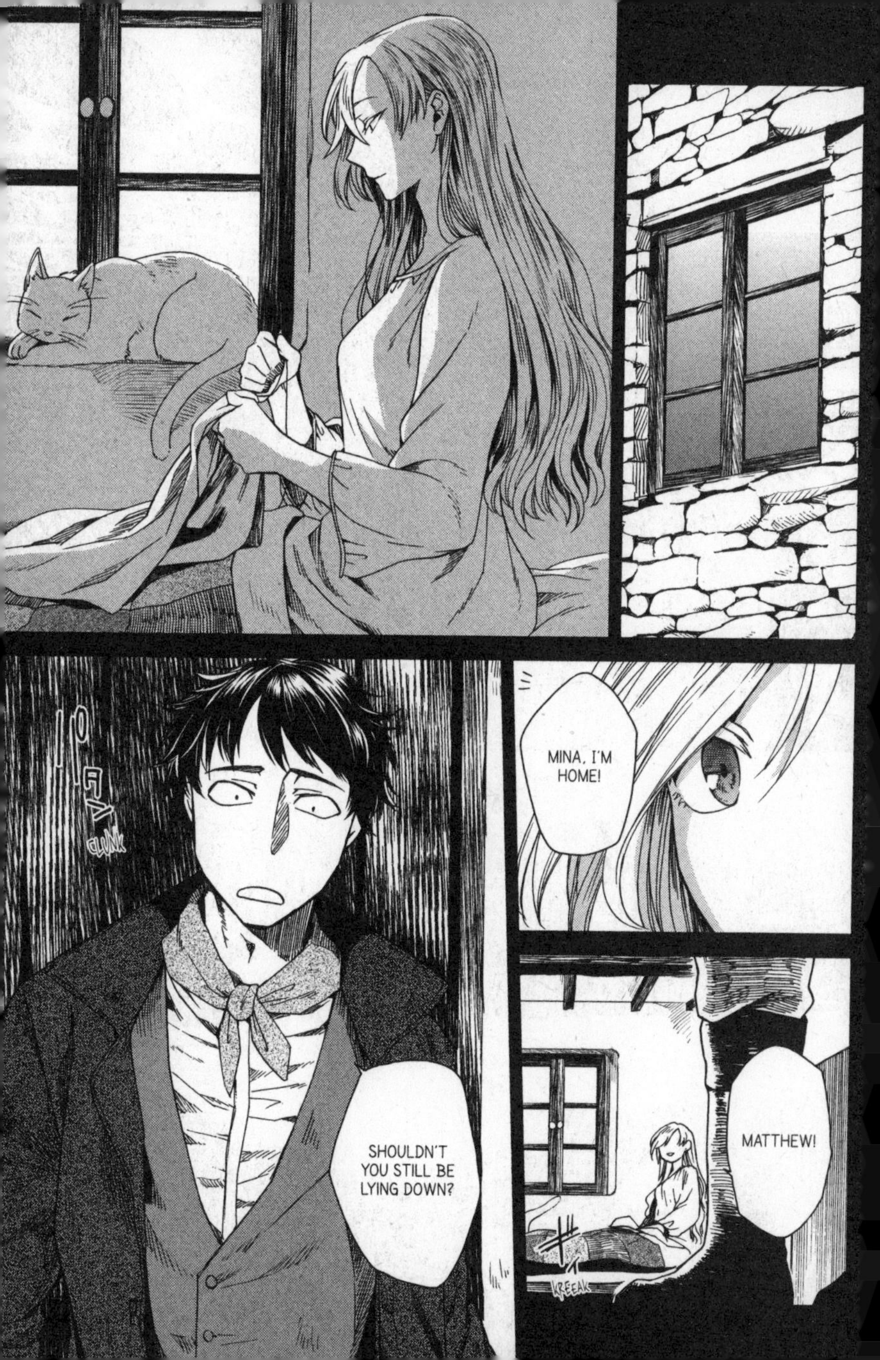
MINA, I'M HOME!
MATTHEW!
KREEAK
CLUNK
SHOULDN'T YOU STILL BE LYING DOWN?

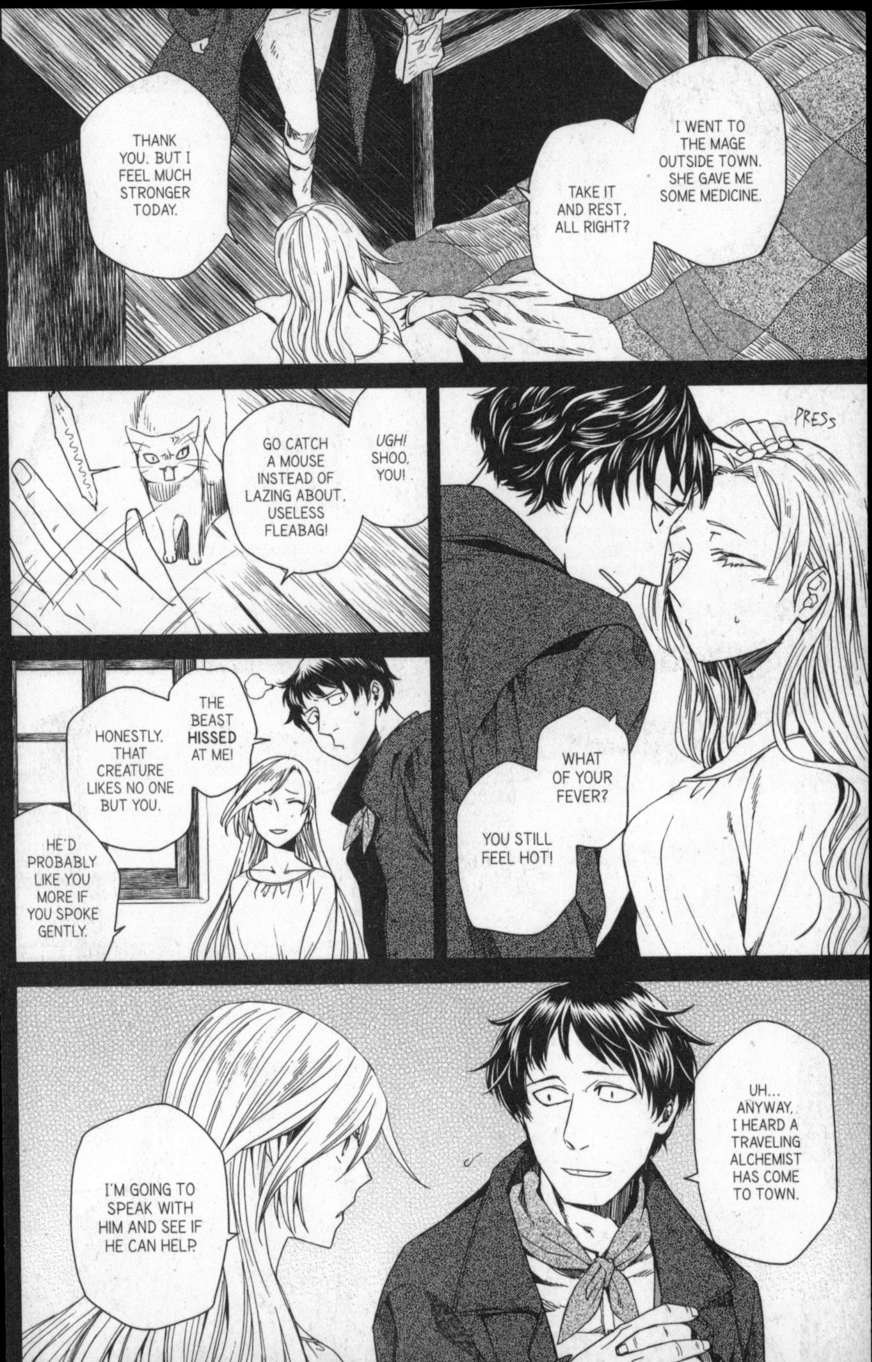
I WENT TO THE MAGE OUTSIDE TOWN. SHE GAVE ME SOME MEDICINE.
TAKE IT AND REST, ALL RIGHT?
THANK YOU. BUT I FEEL MUCH STRONGER TODAY.
PRESS
WHAT OF YOUR FEVER?
YOU STILL FEEL HOT!
UGH! SHOO, YOU!
GO CATCH A MOUSE INSTEAD OF LAZING ABOUT, USELESS FLEABAG!
HISSSSS!
THE BEAST **HISSED** AT ME!
HONESTLY, THAT CREATURE LIKES NO ONE BUT YOU.
HE'D PROBABLY LIKE YOU MORE IF YOU SPOKE GENTLY.
UH... ANYWAY, I HEARD A TRAVELING ALCHEMIST HAS COME TO TOWN.
I'M GOING TO SPEAK WITH HIM AND SEE IF HE CAN HELP.

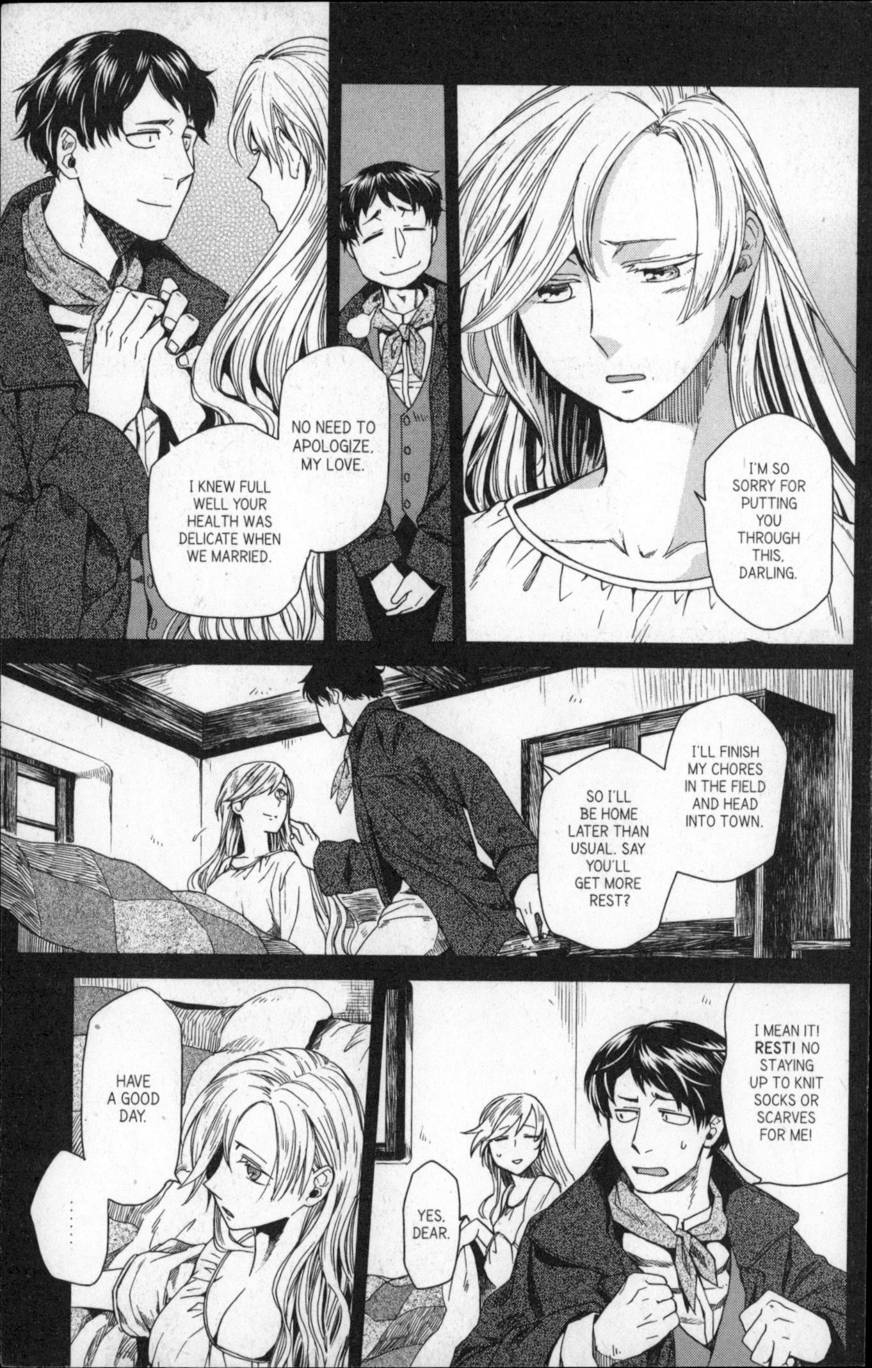
I'M SO SORRY FOR PUTTING YOU THROUGH THIS, DARLING.
NO NEED TO APOLOGIZE, MY LOVE.
I KNEW FULL WELL YOUR HEALTH WAS DELICATE WHEN WE MARRIED.
I'LL FINISH MY CHORES IN THE FIELD AND HEAD INTO TOWN.
SO I'LL BE HOME LATER THAN USUAL. SAY YOU'LL GET MORE REST?
I MEAN IT! **REST!** NO STAYING UP TO KNIT SOCKS OR SCARVES FOR ME!
YES, DEAR.
HAVE A GOOD DAY.
......

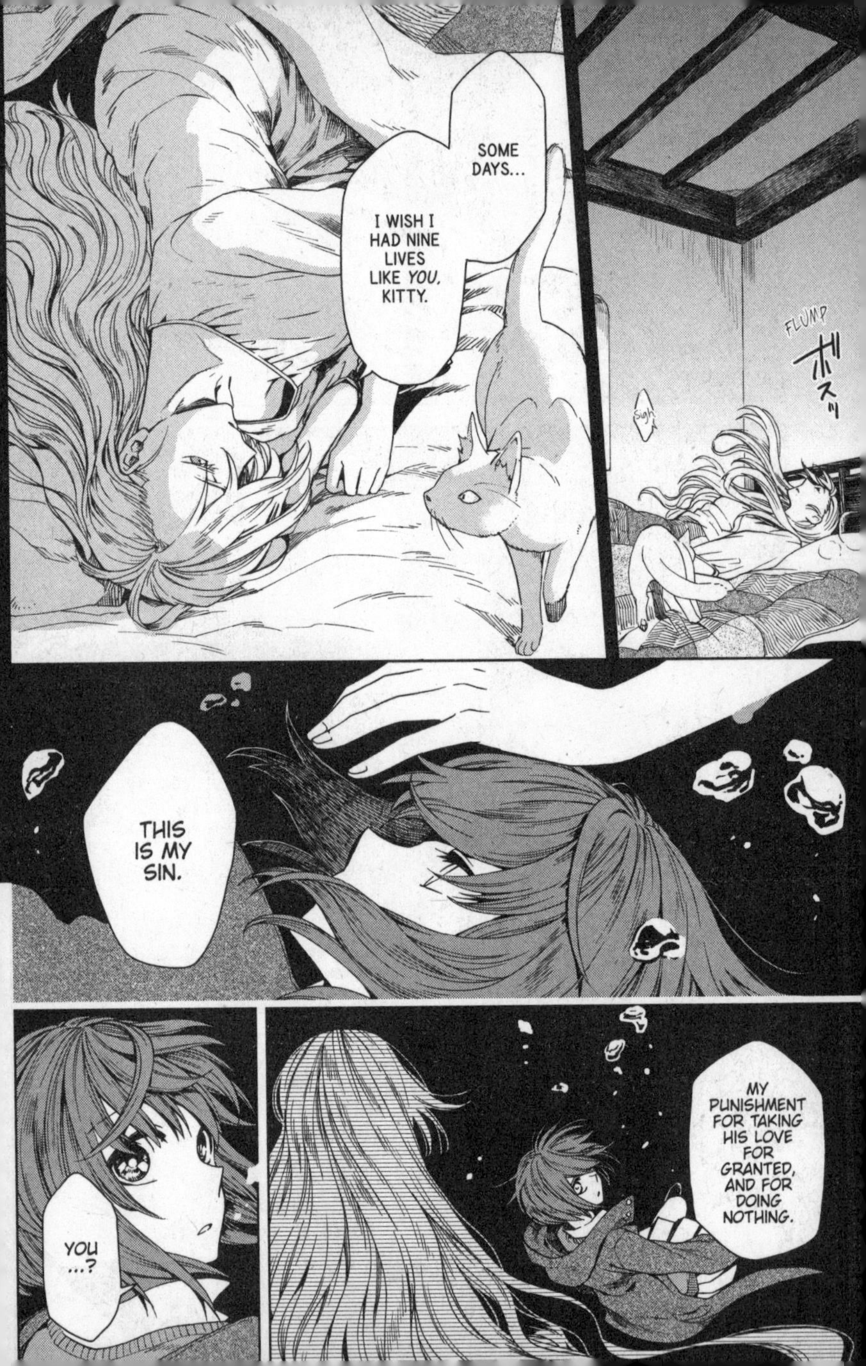
Sigh
FLUMP
ボスッ
SOME DAYS...
I WISH I HAD NINE LIVES LIKE *YOU*, KITTY.
THIS IS MY SIN.
MY PUNISHMENT FOR TAKING HIS LOVE FOR GRANTED, AND FOR DOING NOTHING.
YOU ...?

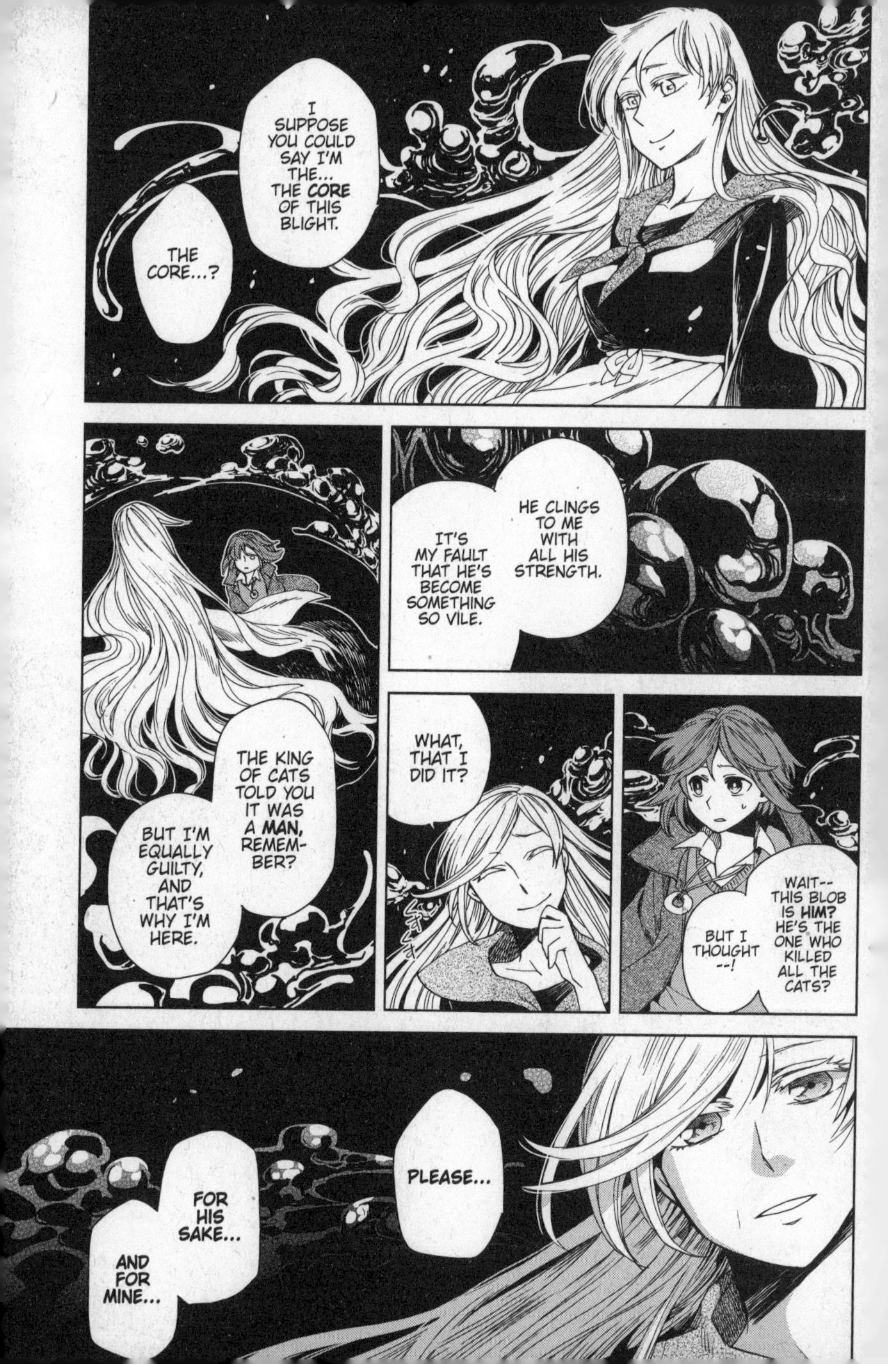
I SUPPOSE YOU COULD SAY I'M THE... THE **CORE** OF THIS BLIGHT.
THE CORE...?
HE CLINGS TO ME WITH ALL HIS STRENGTH.
IT'S MY FAULT THAT HE'S BECOME SOMETHING SO VILE.
WAIT-- THIS BLOB IS **HIM**? HE'S THE ONE WHO KILLED ALL THE CATS?
BUT I THOUGHT --!
WHAT, THAT I DID IT?
THE KING OF CATS TOLD YOU IT WAS A **MAN**, REMEMBER?
BUT I'M EQUALLY GUILTY, AND THAT'S WHY I'M HERE.
PLEASE...
FOR HIS SAKE...
AND FOR MINE...

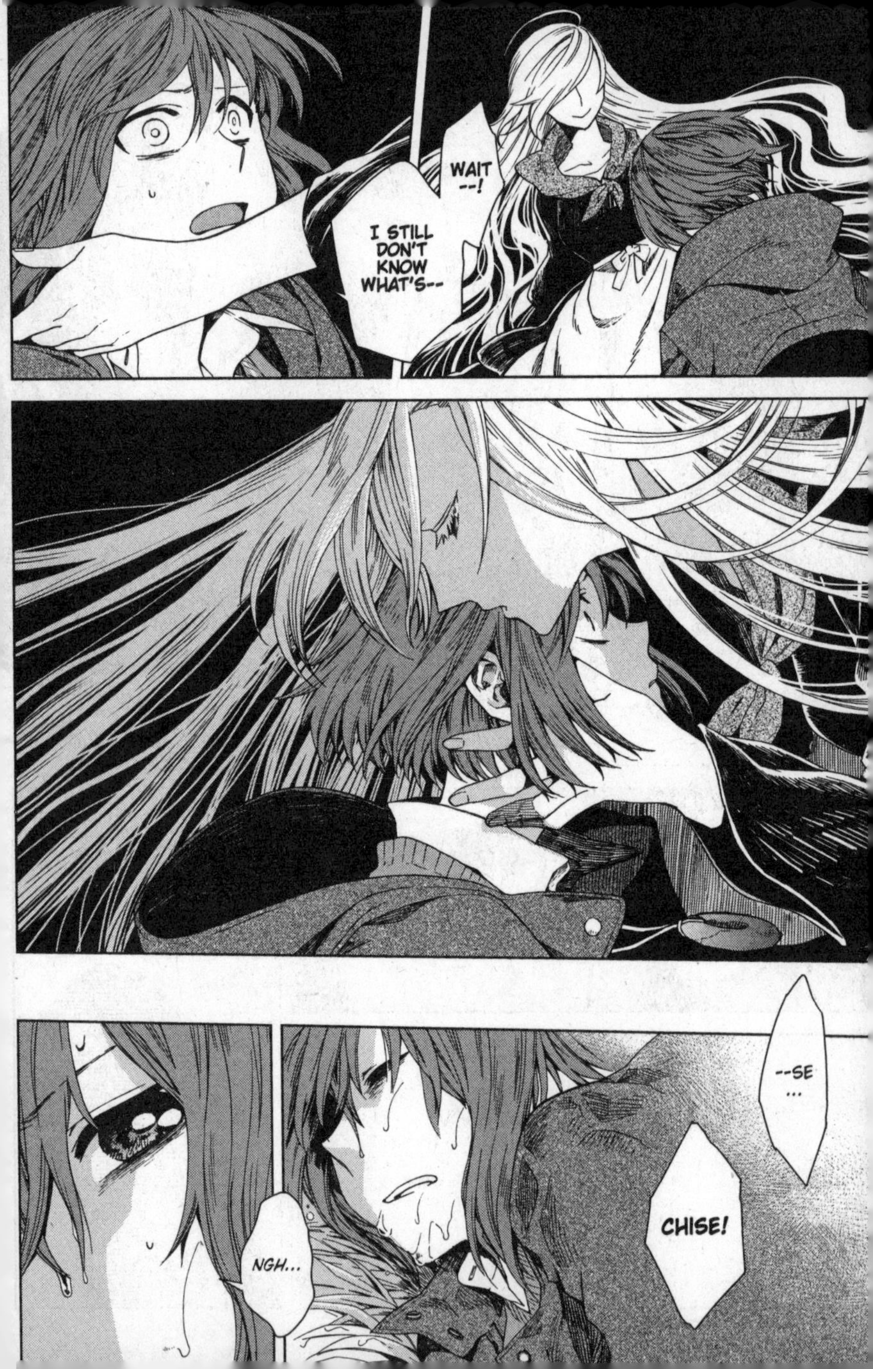
WAIT --!
I STILL DON'T KNOW WHAT'S--
--SE ...
CHISE!
NGH...

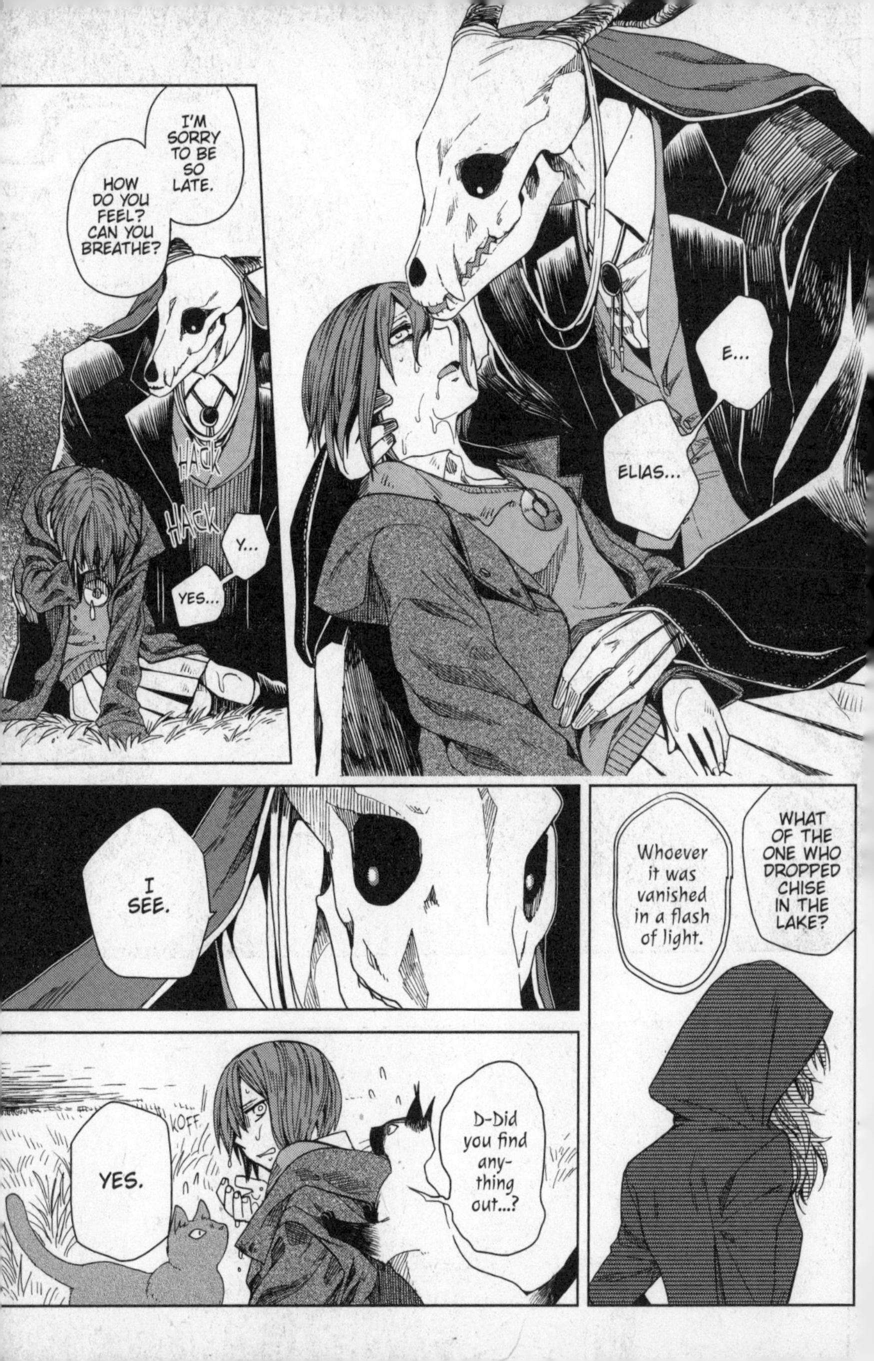
E...
ELIAS...
I'M SORRY TO BE SO LATE.
HOW DO YOU FEEL? CAN YOU BREATHE?
HACK
HACK
Y...
YES...
WHAT OF THE ONE WHO DROPPED CHISE IN THE LAKE?
Whoever it was vanished in a flash of light.
I SEE.
D-Did you find any-thing out...?
KOFF
YES.

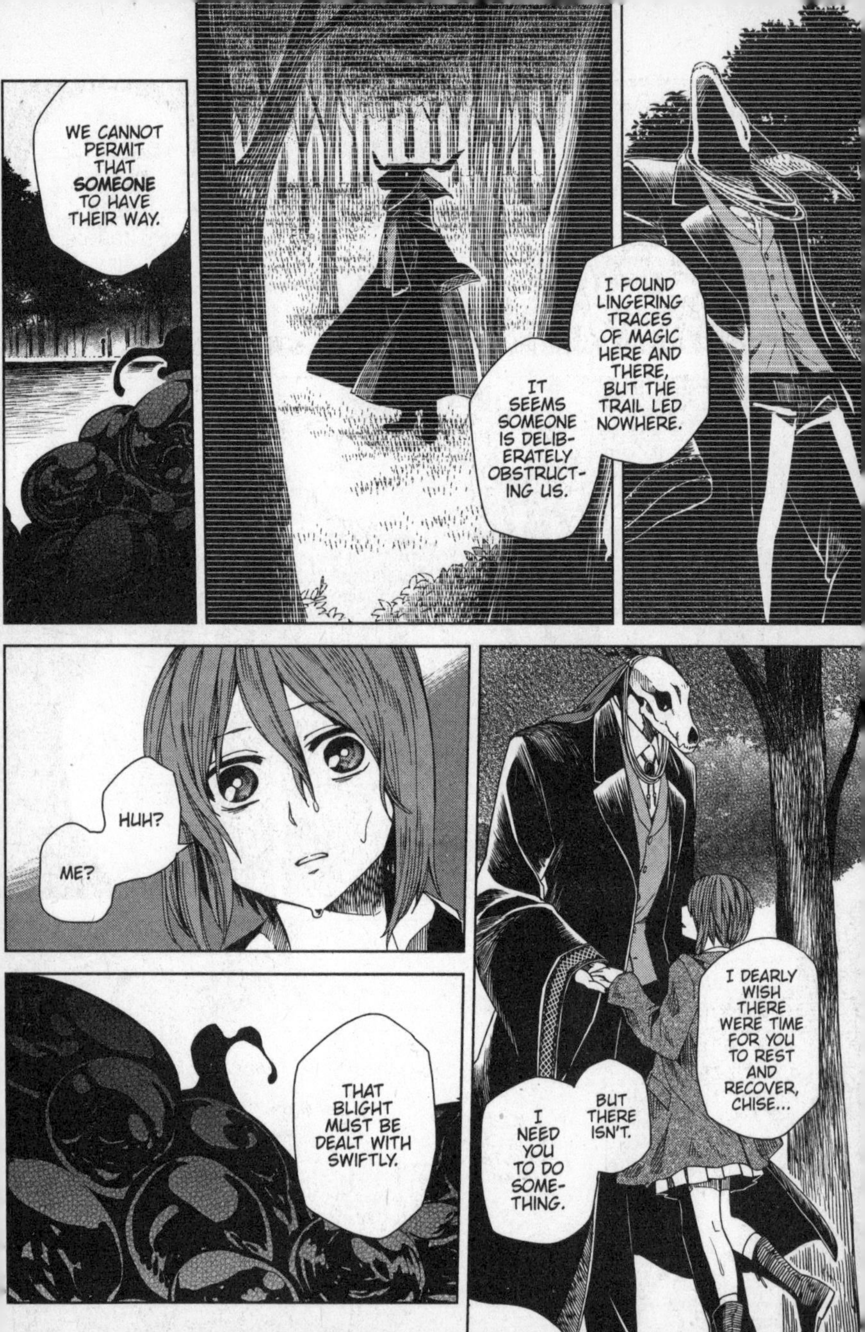
I FOUND LINGERING TRACES OF MAGIC HERE AND THERE, BUT THE TRAIL LED NOWHERE.
IT SEEMS SOMEONE IS DELIBERATELY OBSTRUCTING US.
WE CANNOT PERMIT THAT SOMEONE TO HAVE THEIR WAY.
I DEARLY WISH THERE WERE TIME FOR YOU TO REST AND RECOVER, CHISE...
BUT THERE ISN'T.
I NEED YOU TO DO SOMETHING.
HUH?
ME?
THAT BLIGHT MUST BE DEALT WITH SWIFTLY.

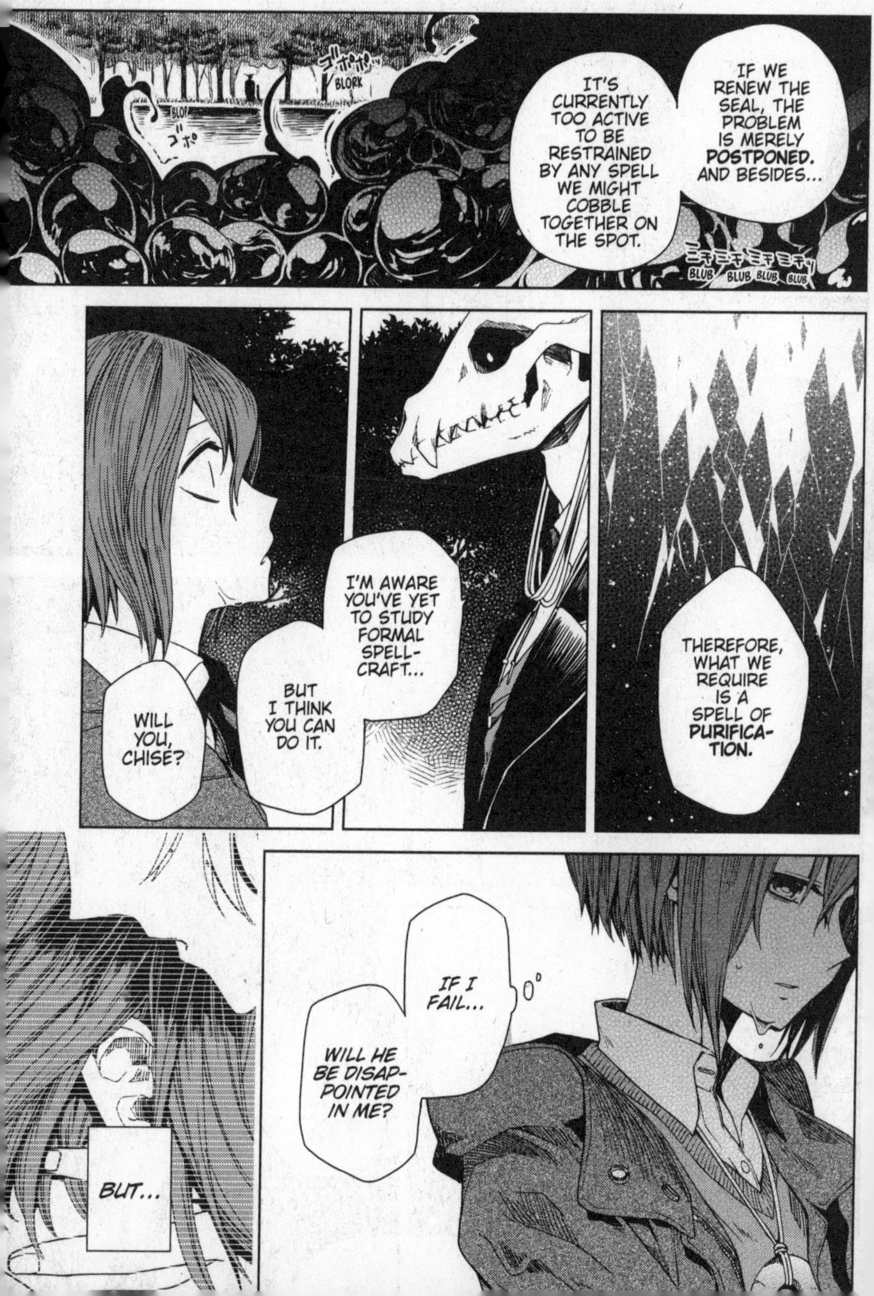

IF WE RENEW THE SEAL, THE PROBLEM IS MERELY POSTPONED. AND BESIDES...
IT'S CURRENTLY TOO ACTIVE TO BE RESTRAINED BY ANY SPELL WE MIGHT COBBLE TOGETHER ON THE SPOT.
BLUB BLUB BLUB BLUB
BLORK
BLOP
THEREFORE, WHAT WE REQUIRE IS A SPELL OF PURIFICATION.
I'M AWARE YOU'VE YET TO STUDY FORMAL SPELLCRAFT...
BUT I THINK YOU CAN DO IT.
WILL YOU, CHISE?
IF I FAIL...
WILL HE BE DISAPPOINTED IN ME?
BUT...

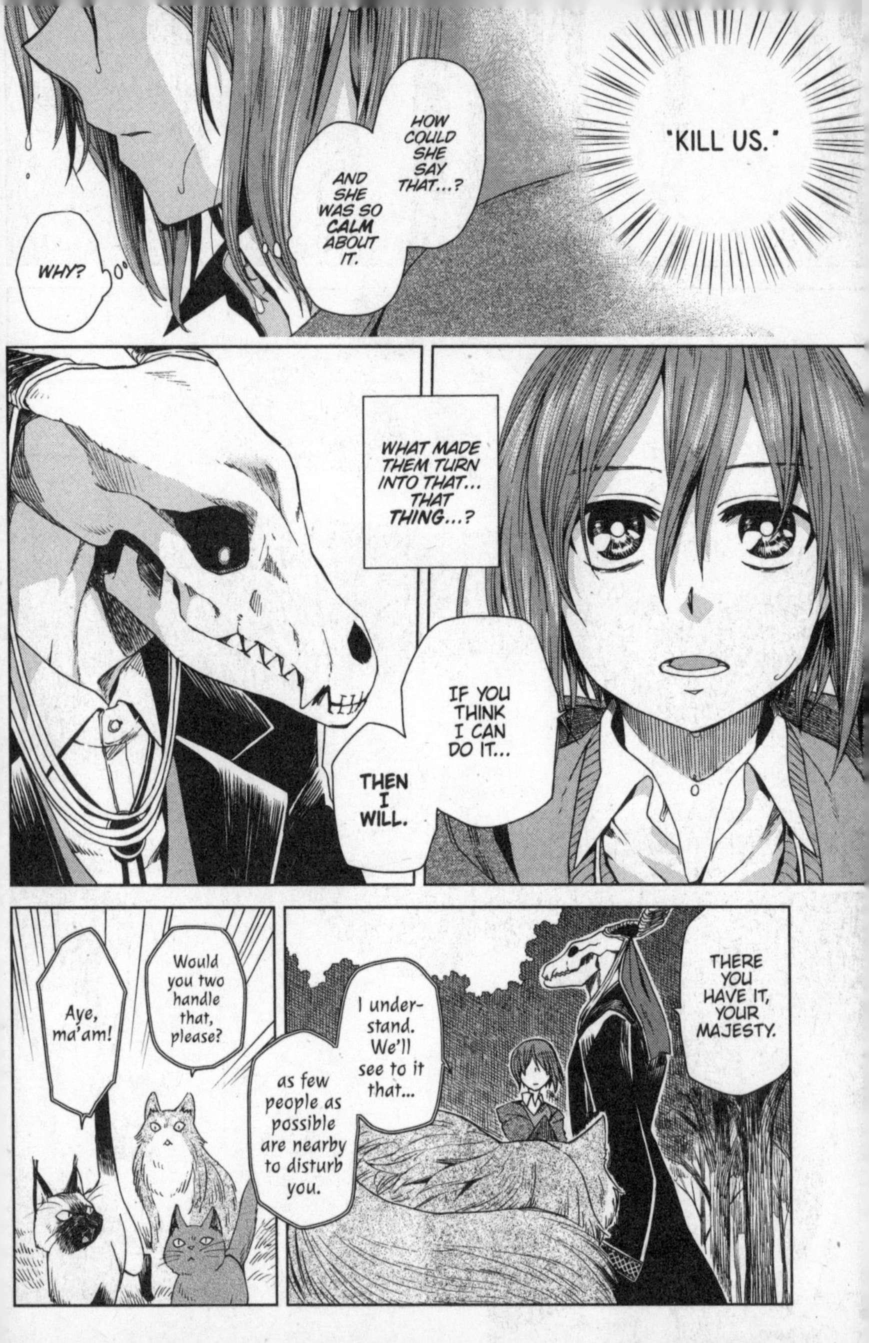
"KILL US."
HOW COULD SHE SAY THAT...?
AND SHE WAS SO CALM ABOUT IT.
WHY?
WHAT MADE THEM TURN INTO THAT... THAT THING...?
IF YOU THINK I CAN DO IT...
THEN I WILL.
THERE YOU HAVE IT, YOUR MAJESTY.
I under-stand. We'll see to it that...
as few people as possible are nearby to disturb you.
Would you two handle that, please?
Aye, ma'am!

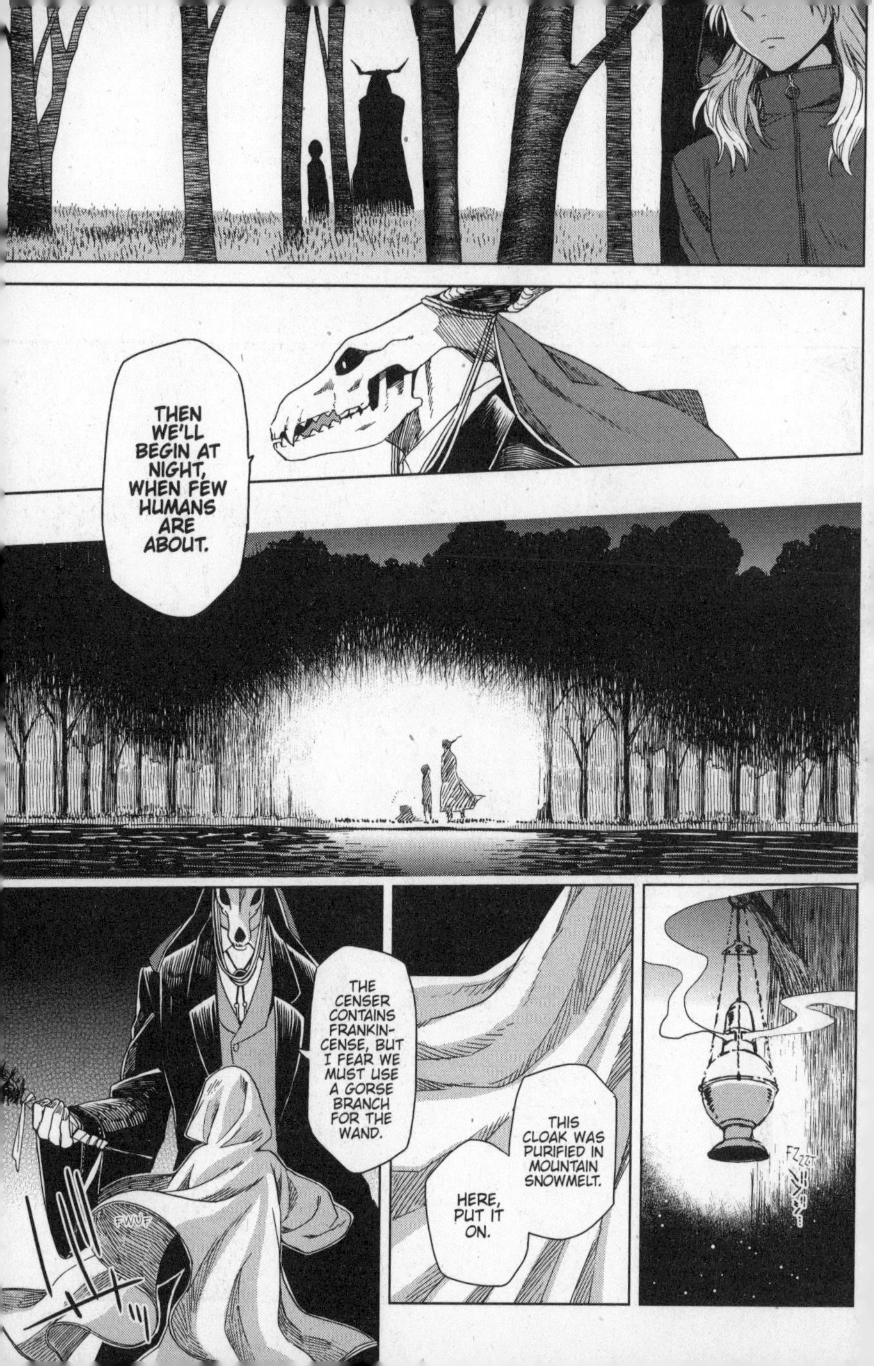
THEN WE'LL BEGIN AT NIGHT, WHEN FEW HUMANS ARE ABOUT.
FZZZT
THIS CLOAK WAS PURIFIED IN MOUNTAIN SNOWMELT.
HERE, PUT IT ON.
THE CENSER CONTAINS FRANKIN-CENSE, BUT I FEAR WE MUST USE A GORSE BRANCH FOR THE WAND.
FWUF

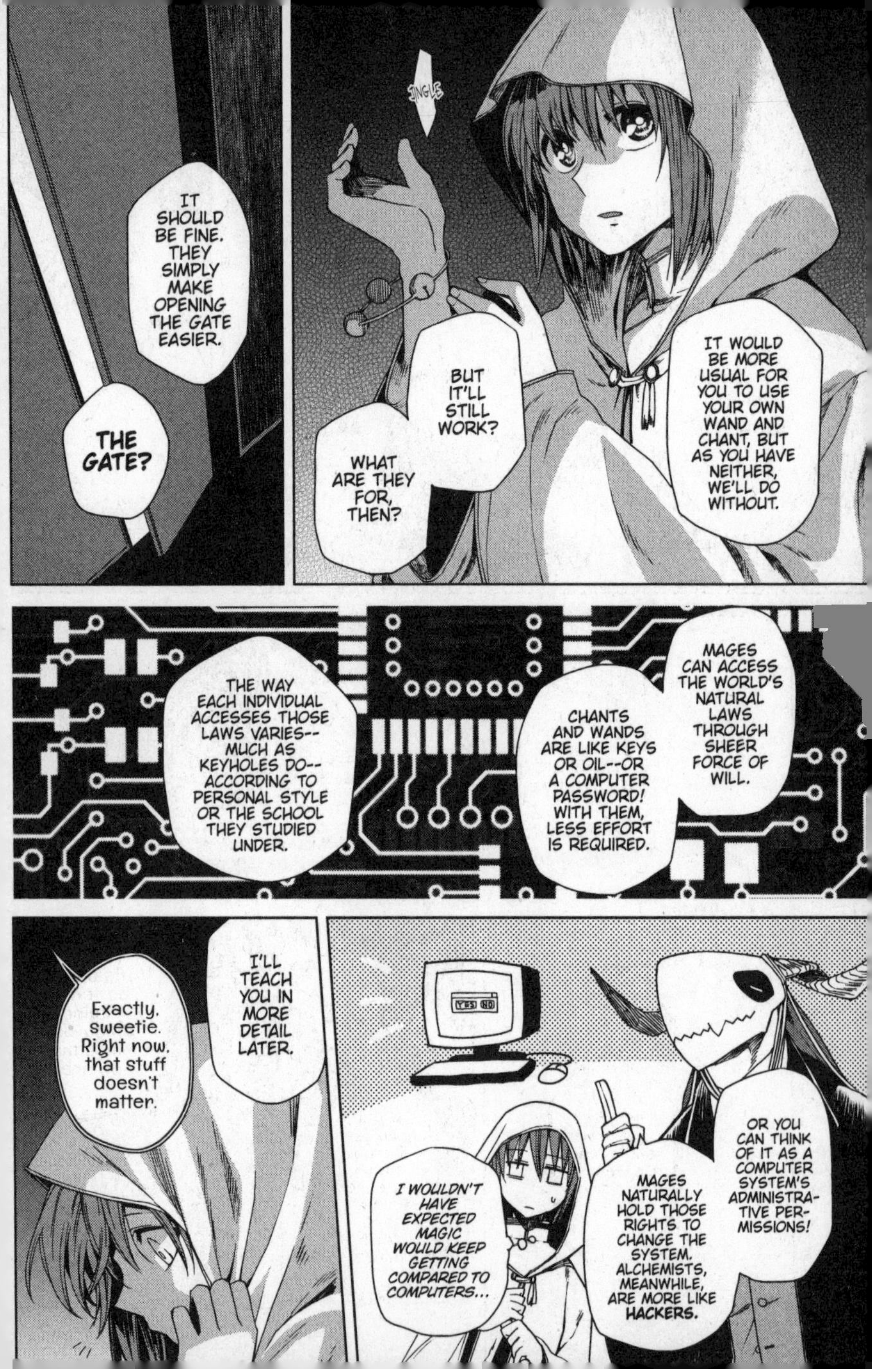
JINGLE
IT WOULD BE MORE USUAL FOR YOU TO USE YOUR OWN WAND AND CHANT, BUT AS YOU HAVE NEITHER, WE'LL DO WITHOUT.
BUT IT'LL STILL WORK?
WHAT ARE THEY FOR, THEN?
IT SHOULD BE FINE. THEY SIMPLY MAKE OPENING THE GATE EASIER.
THE GATE?
MAGES CAN ACCESS THE WORLD'S NATURAL LAWS THROUGH SHEER FORCE OF WILL.
CHANTS AND WANDS ARE LIKE KEYS OR OIL--OR A COMPUTER PASSWORD! WITH THEM, LESS EFFORT IS REQUIRED.
THE WAY EACH INDIVIDUAL ACCESSES THOSE LAWS VARIES--MUCH AS KEYHOLES DO--ACCORDING TO PERSONAL STYLE OR THE SCHOOL THEY STUDIED UNDER.
YES NO
OR YOU CAN THINK OF IT AS A COMPUTER SYSTEM'S ADMINISTRATIVE PERMISSIONS!
MAGES NATURALLY HOLD THOSE RIGHTS TO CHANGE THE SYSTEM. ALCHEMISTS, MEANWHILE, ARE MORE LIKE HACKERS.
I WOULDN'T HAVE EXPECTED MAGIC WOULD KEEP GETTING COMPARED TO COMPUTERS...
I'LL TEACH YOU IN MORE DETAIL LATER.
Exactly, sweetie. Right now, that stuff doesn't matter.

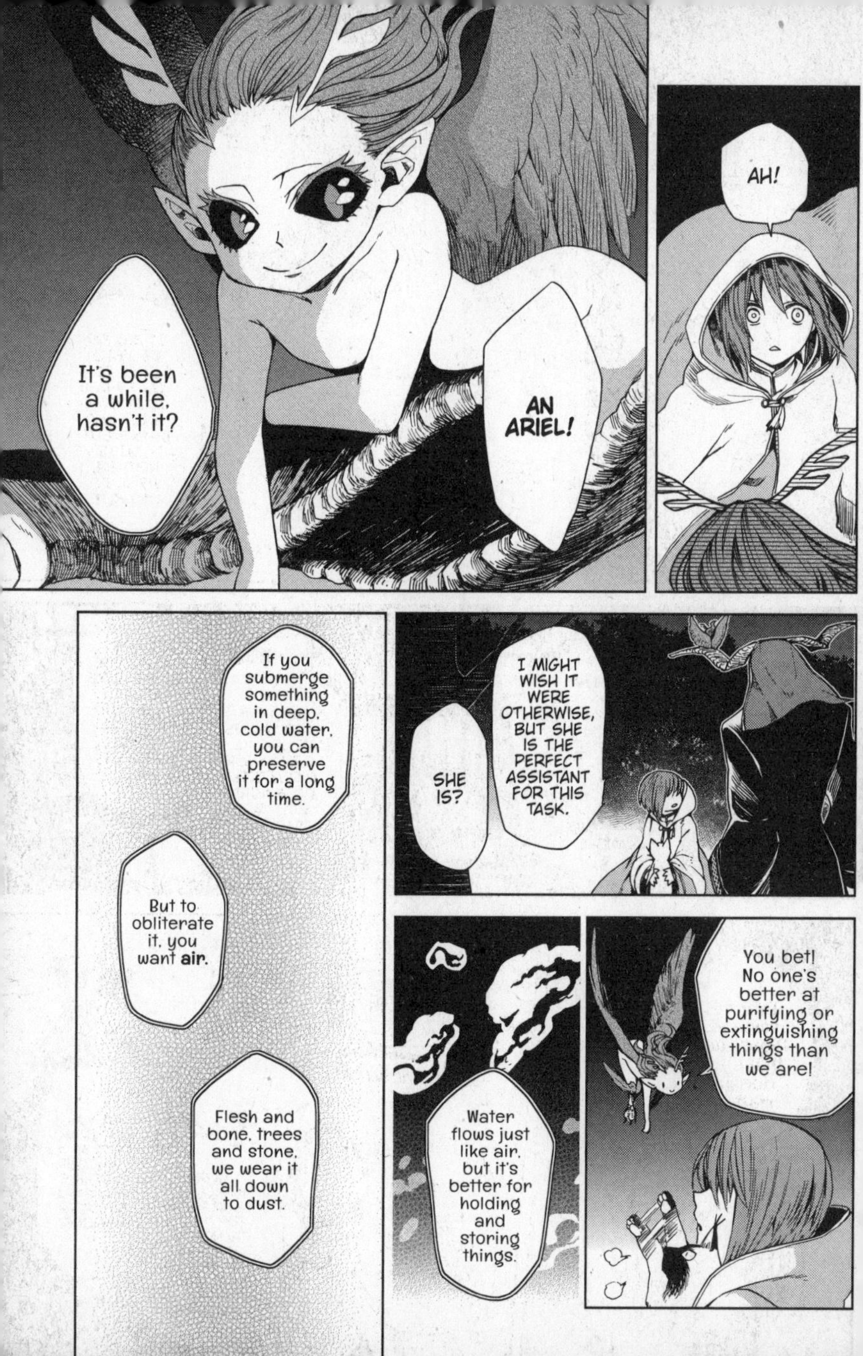
AH!
AN ARIEL!
It's been a while, hasn't it?
I MIGHT WISH IT WERE OTHERWISE, BUT SHE IS THE PERFECT ASSISTANT FOR THIS TASK.
SHE IS?
You bet! No one's better at purifying or extinguishing things than we are!
Water flows just like air, but it's better for holding and storing things.
If you submerge something in deep, cold water, you can preserve it for a long time.
But to obliterate it, you want **air**.
Flesh and bone, trees and stone, we wear it all down to dust.

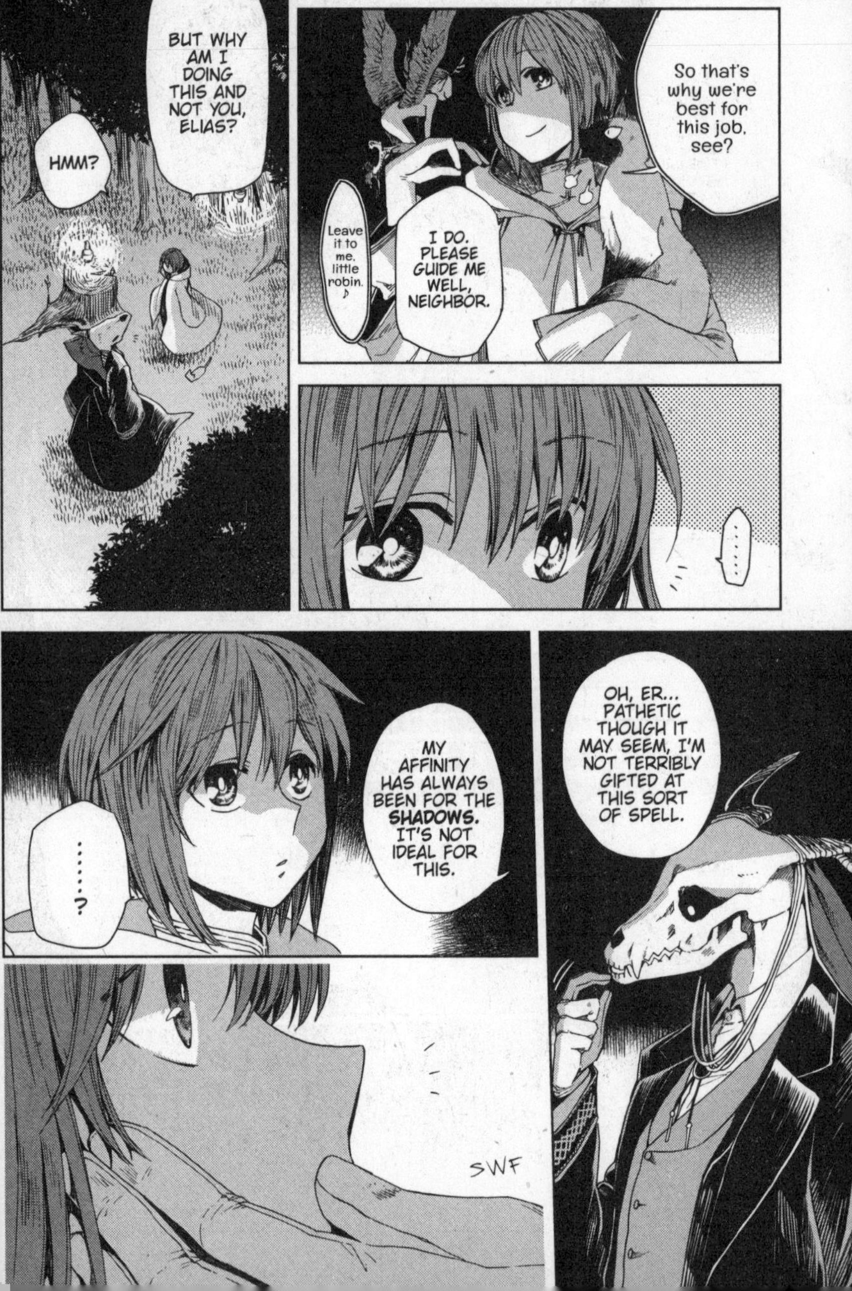
So that's why we're best for this job, see?
I DO. PLEASE GUIDE ME WELL, NEIGHBOR.
Leave it to me, little robin. ♪
......
BUT WHY AM I DOING THIS AND NOT YOU, ELIAS?
HMM?
OH, ER... PATHETIC THOUGH IT MAY SEEM, I'M NOT TERRIBLY GIFTED AT THIS SORT OF SPELL.
MY AFFINITY HAS ALWAYS BEEN FOR THE SHADOWS. IT'S NOT IDEAL FOR THIS.
......?
SWF

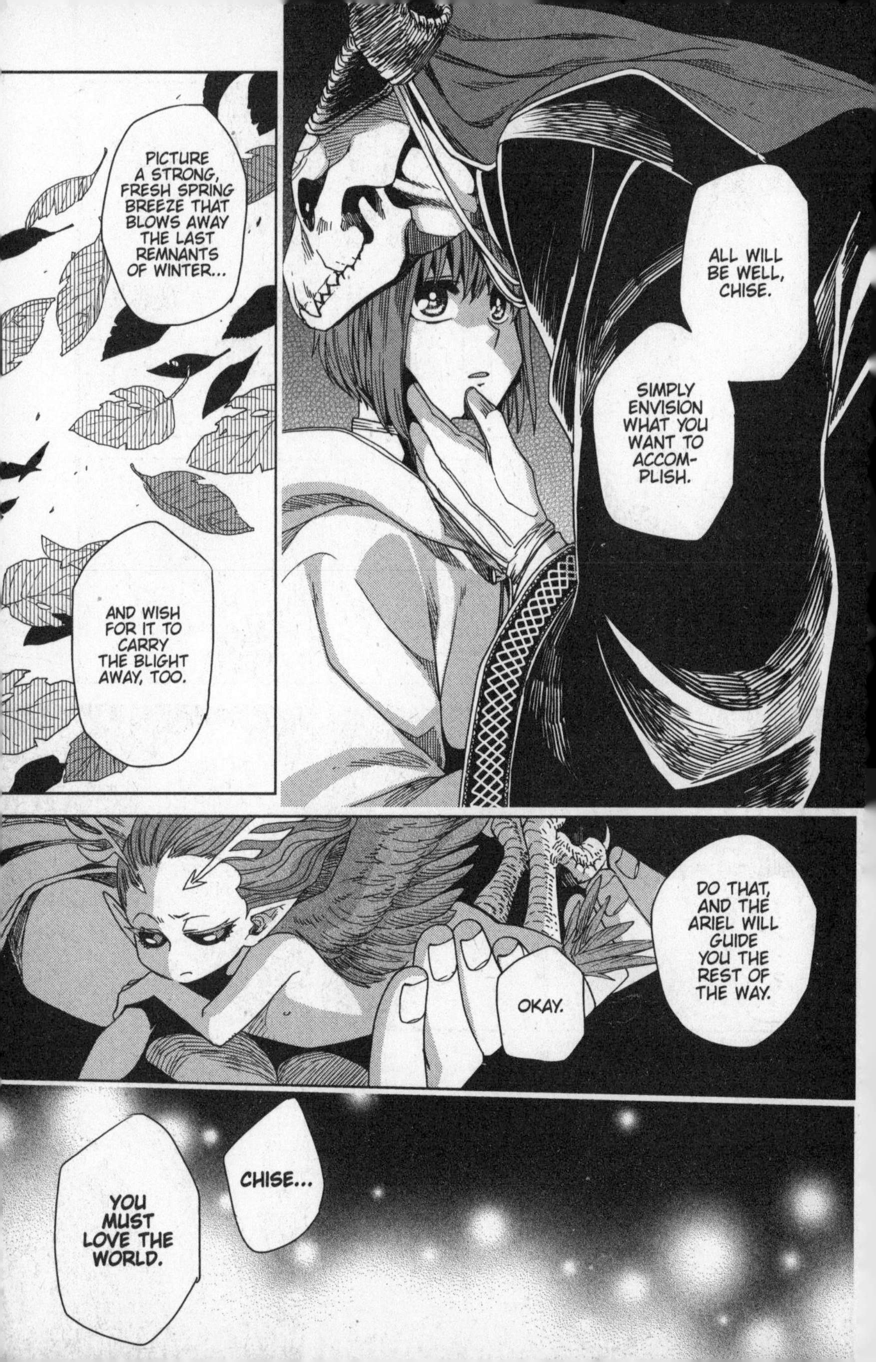
ALL WILL BE WELL, CHISE.
SIMPLY ENVISION WHAT YOU WANT TO ACCOMPLISH.
PICTURE A STRONG, FRESH SPRING BREEZE THAT BLOWS AWAY THE LAST REMNANTS OF WINTER...
AND WISH FOR IT TO CARRY THE BLIGHT AWAY, TOO.
DO THAT, AND THE ARIEL WILL GUIDE YOU THE REST OF THE WAY.
OKAY.
CHISE...
YOU MUST LOVE THE WORLD.

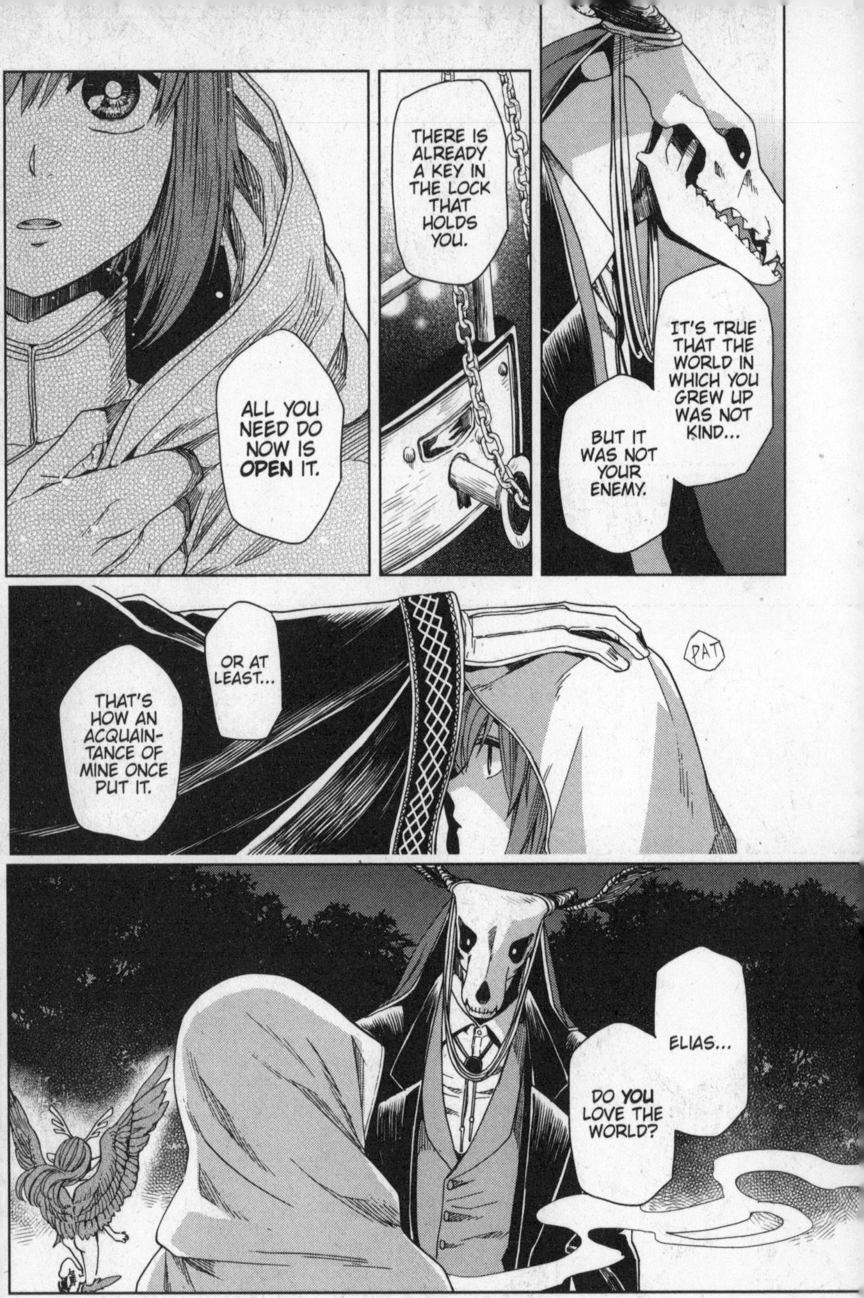
IT'S TRUE THAT THE WORLD IN WHICH YOU GREW UP WAS NOT KIND...
BUT IT WAS NOT YOUR ENEMY.
THERE IS ALREADY A KEY IN THE LOCK THAT HOLDS YOU.
ALL YOU NEED DO NOW IS **OPEN** IT.
PAT
OR AT LEAST...
THAT'S HOW AN ACQUAINTANCE OF MINE ONCE PUT IT.
ELIAS...
DO **YOU** LOVE THE WORLD?

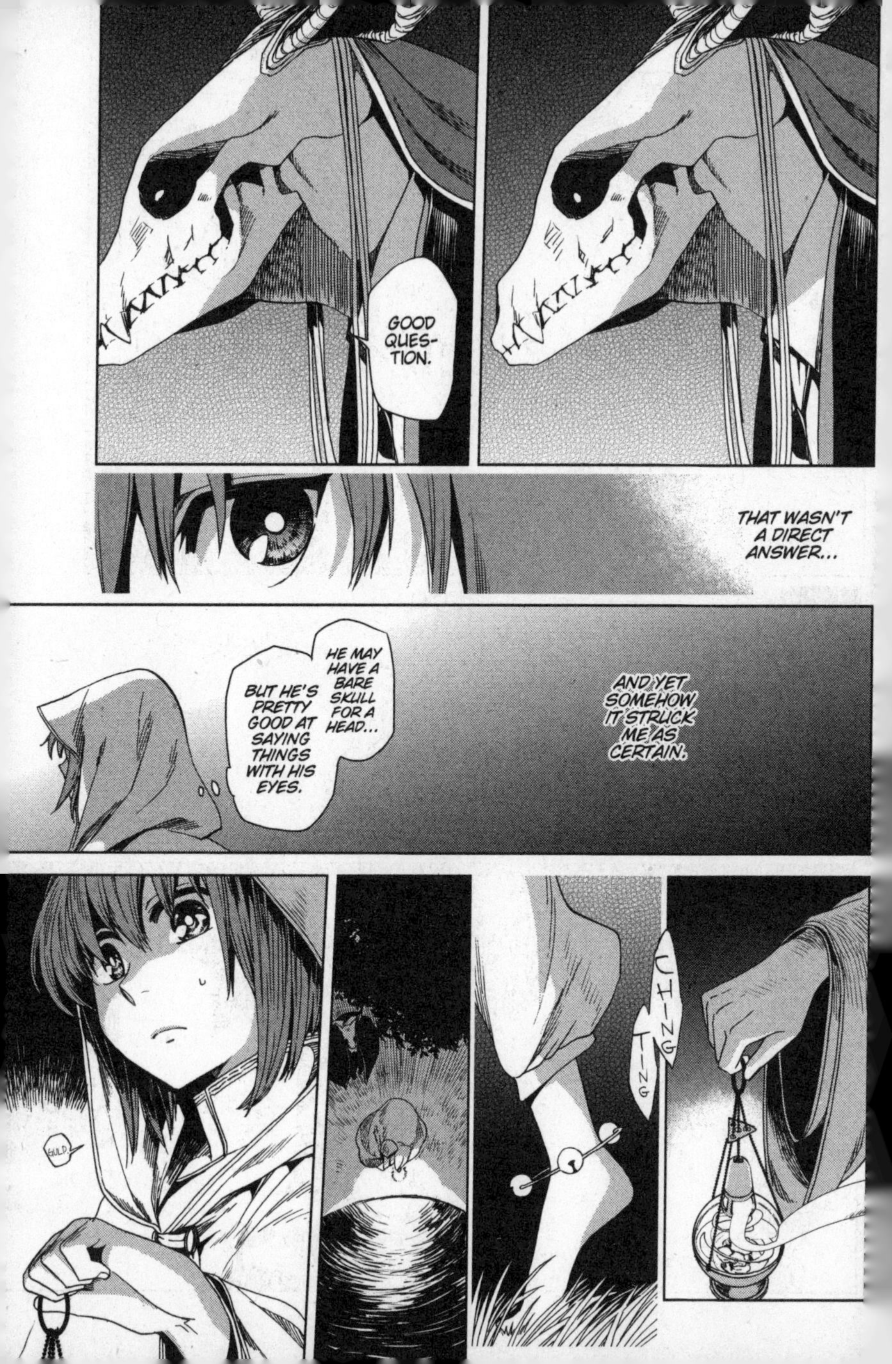
GOOD QUES-TION.
THAT WASN'T A DIRECT ANSWER...
AND YET SOMEHOW IT STRUCK ME AS CERTAIN.
HE MAY HAVE A BARE SKULL FOR A HEAD...
BUT HE'S PRETTY GOOD AT SAYING THINGS WITH HIS EYES.
CHING
TING
GULP

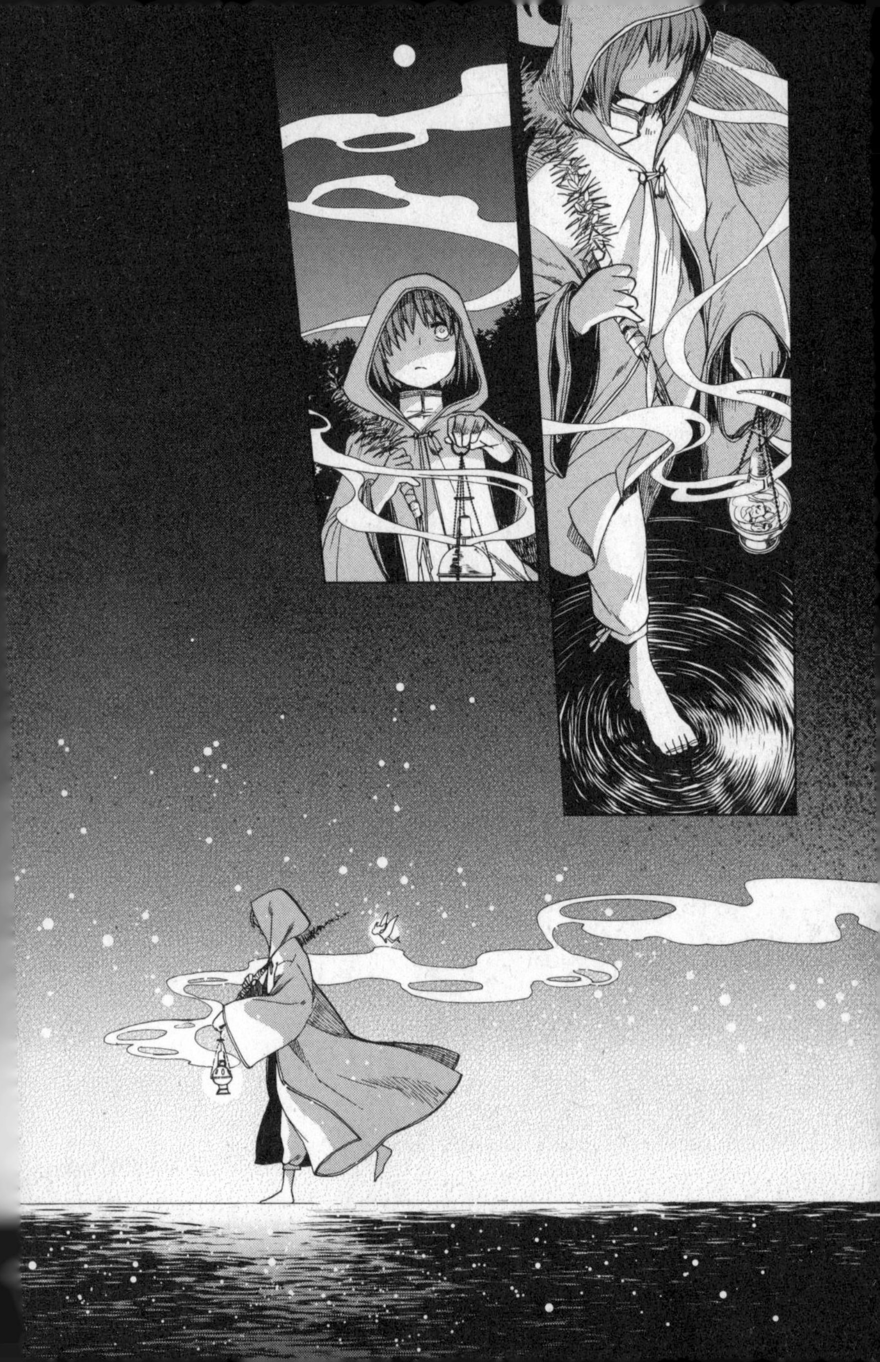

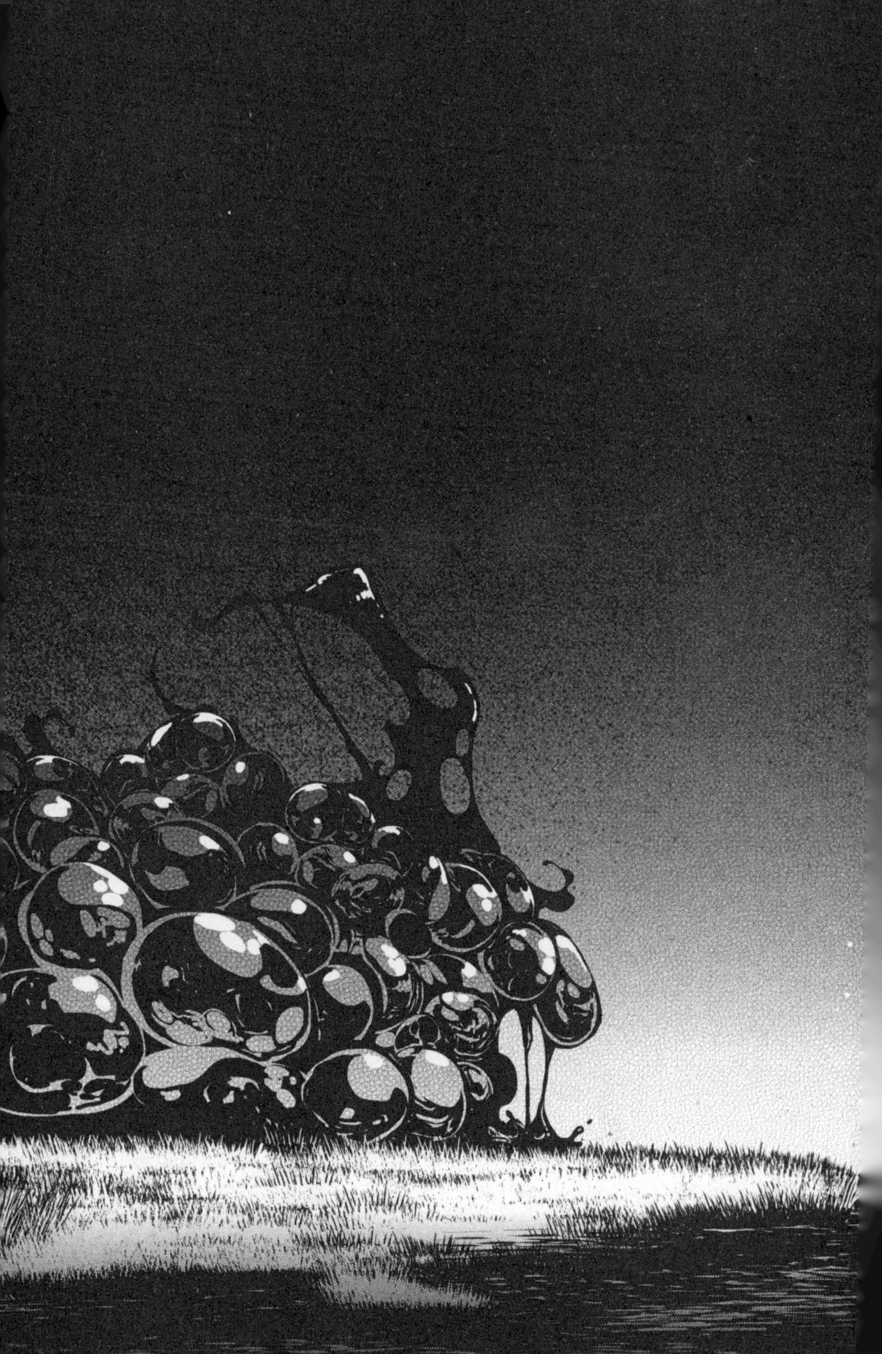

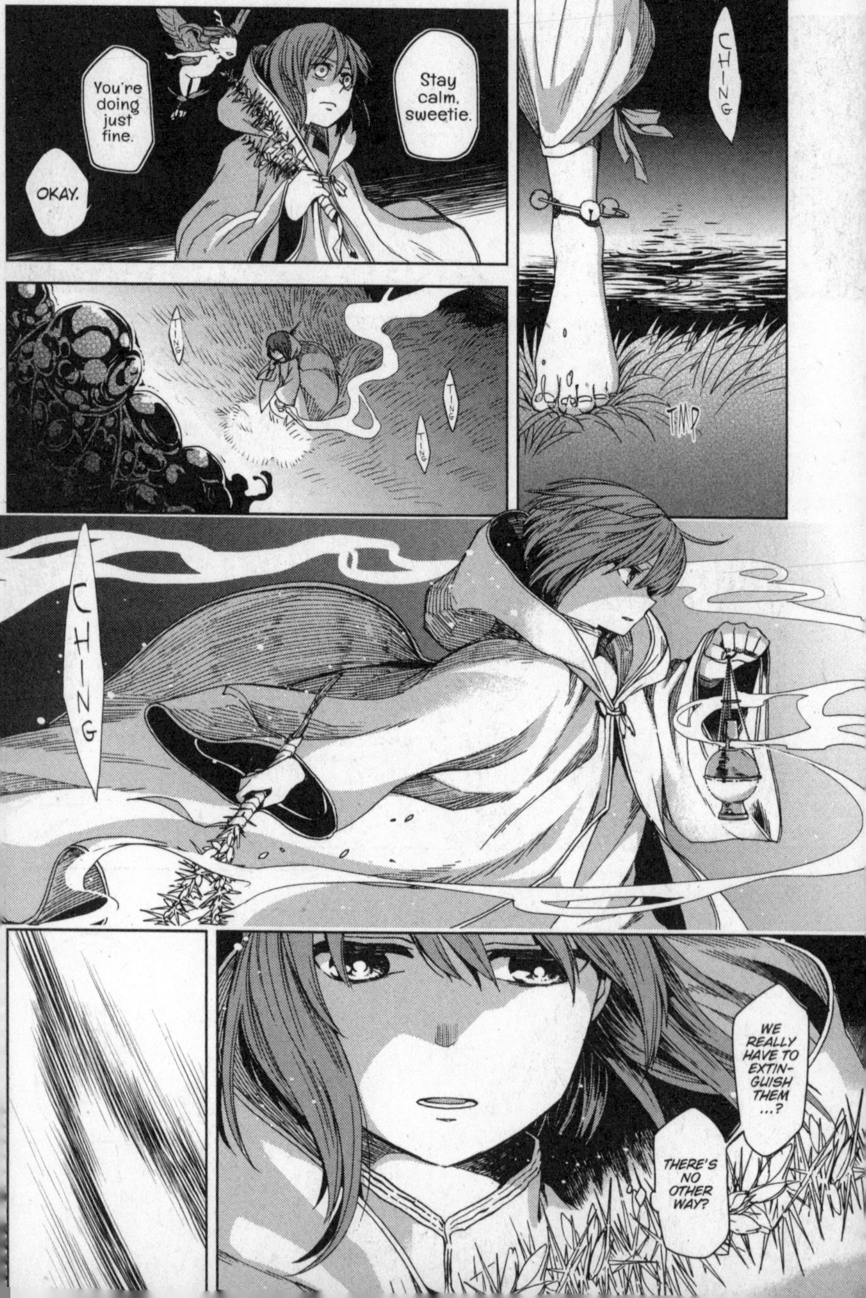
CHING
TMP
Stay calm, sweetie.
You're doing just fine.
OKAY.
TING
TING
TING
CHING
WE REALLY HAVE TO EXTIN-GUISH THEM ...?
THERE'S NO OTHER WAY?

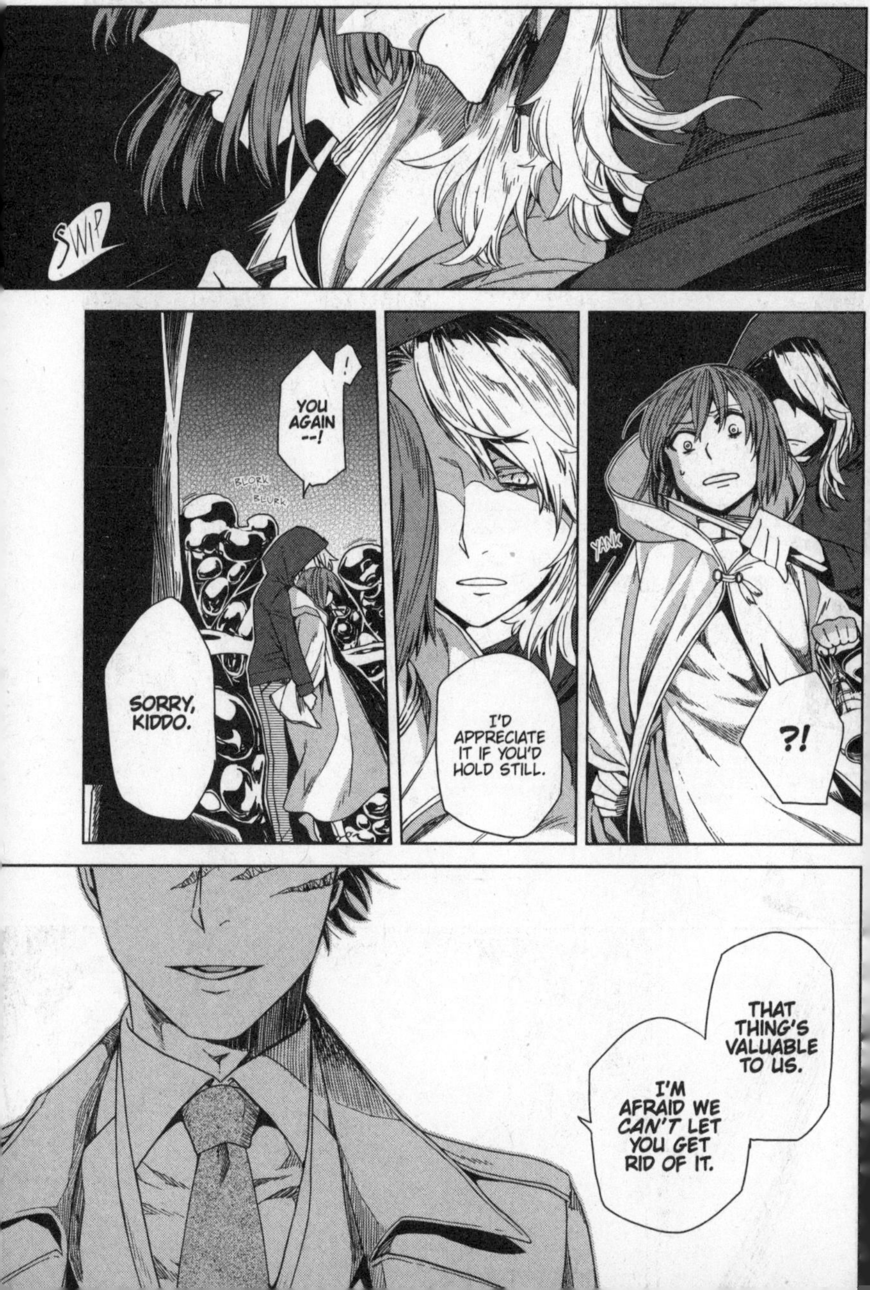
SWIP
YANK
?!
I'D APPRECIATE IT IF YOU'D HOLD STILL.
!
YOU AGAIN --!
BLORK BLURK
SORRY, KIDDO.
THAT THING'S VALUABLE TO US.
I'M AFRAID WE *CAN'T* LET YOU GET RID OF IT.

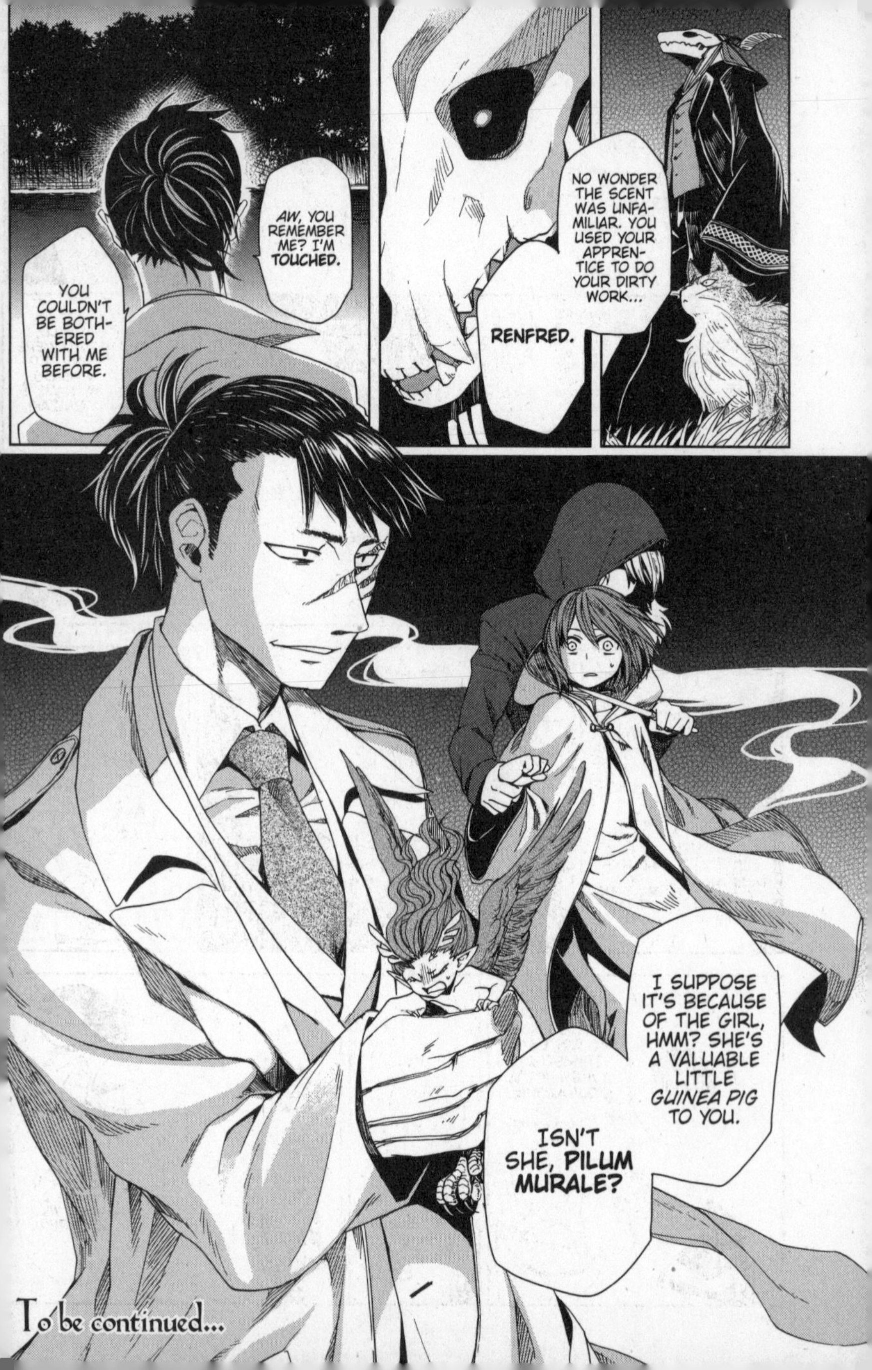
NO WONDER THE SCENT WAS UNFAMILIAR. YOU USED YOUR APPRENTICE TO DO YOUR DIRTY WORK...
RENFRED.
AW, YOU REMEMBER ME? I'M TOUCHED.
YOU COULDN'T BE BOTHERED WITH ME BEFORE.
I SUPPOSE IT'S BECAUSE OF THE GIRL, HMM? SHE'S A VALUABLE LITTLE GUINEA PIG TO YOU.
ISN'T SHE, PILUM MURALE?
To be continued...

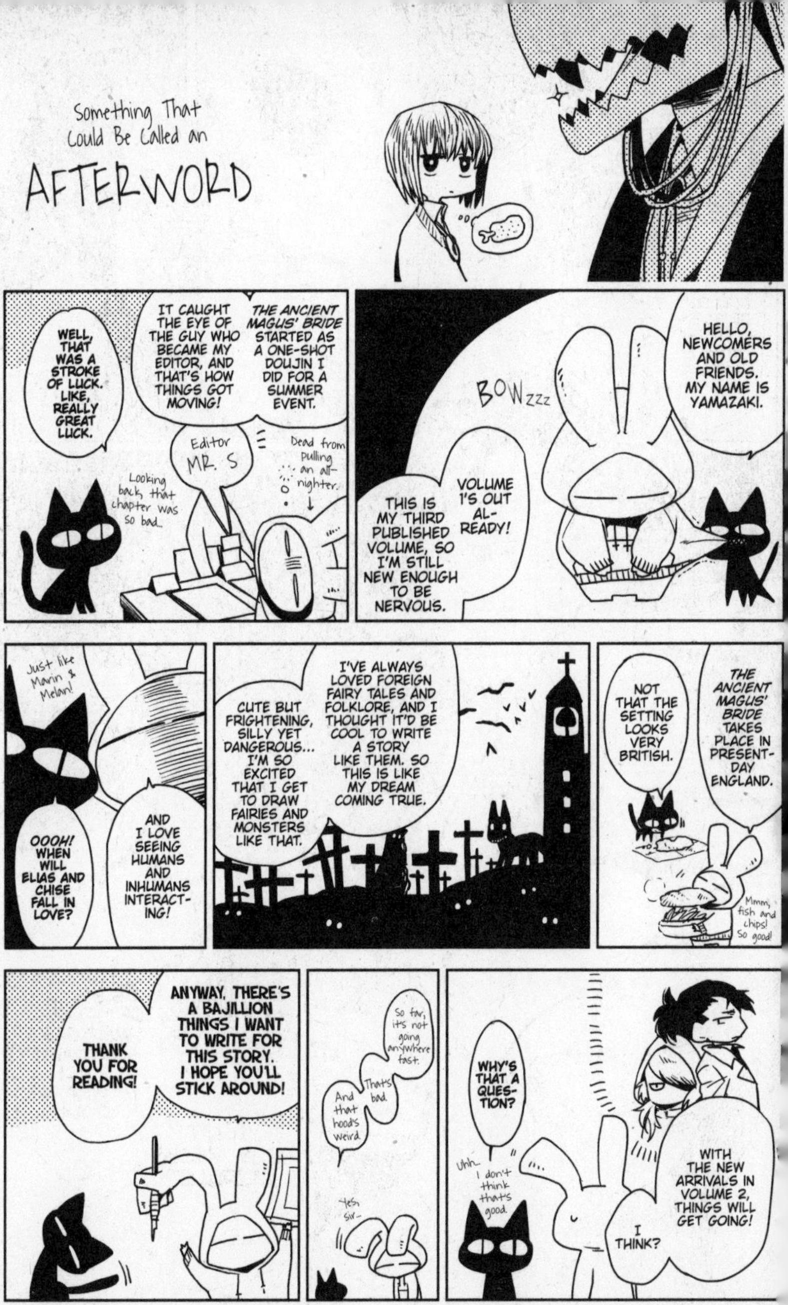
Something That Could Be Called an
AFTERWORD
HELLO, NEWCOMERS AND OLD FRIENDS. MY NAME IS YAMAZAKI.
BOWzzz
VOLUME 1'S OUT AL-READY!
THIS IS MY THIRD PUBLISHED VOLUME, SO I'M STILL NEW ENOUGH TO BE NERVOUS.
THE ANCIENT MAGUS' BRIDE STARTED AS A ONE-SHOT DOUJIN I DID FOR A SUMMER EVENT.
IT CAUGHT THE EYE OF THE GUY WHO BECAME MY EDITOR, AND THAT'S HOW THINGS GOT MOVING!
WELL, THAT WAS A STROKE OF LUCK. LIKE, REALLY GREAT LUCK.
Dead from pulling an all-nighter.
Editor MR. S
Looking back, that chapter was so bad...
THE ANCIENT MAGUS' BRIDE TAKES PLACE IN PRESENT-DAY ENGLAND.
NOT THAT THE SETTING LOOKS VERY BRITISH.
Mmm, fish and chips! So good!
I'VE ALWAYS LOVED FOREIGN FAIRY TALES AND FOLKLORE, AND I THOUGHT IT'D BE COOL TO WRITE A STORY LIKE THEM. SO THIS IS LIKE MY DREAM COMING TRUE.
CUTE BUT FRIGHTENING, SILLY YET DANGEROUS... I'M SO EXCITED THAT I GET TO DRAW FAIRIES AND MONSTERS LIKE THAT.
AND I LOVE SEEING HUMANS AND INHUMANS INTERACT-ING!
Just like Marin & Melan!
OOOH! WHEN WILL ELIAS AND CHISE FALL IN LOVE?
WITH THE NEW ARRIVALS IN VOLUME 2, THINGS WILL GET GOING!
I THINK?
WHY'S THAT A QUES-TION?
Uhh... I don't think that's good.
So far, it's not going anywhere fast.
That's bad.
And that hood's weird.
Yes sir...
ANYWAY, THERE'S A BAJILLION THINGS I WANT TO WRITE FOR THIS STORY. I HOPE YOU'LL STICK AROUND!
THANK YOU FOR READING!

When Our Tale Resumes...

While working on the three tasks given to them by the church, Elias and Chise are unexpectedly attacked. What are their assailants after? And what is the true nature of the powers Chise possesses as a Sleigh Beggy?! The fairy tale continues...

The Ancient Magus' Bride
Volume 2
Coming Soon!